THE
RAF 100
COOKBOOK

100 YEARS
100 COUNTRIES
100 RECIPES

WWW.RAF100COOKBOOK.CO.UK

This book is dedicated to all those
who have worn Air Force Blue

IT IS MY great pleasure to introduce *The RAF100 Cookbook*, produced by Squadron Leader Jon Pullen, Flight Lieutenant Crispin Chapple and their team to commemorate the essential part that food has played in the history of the Royal Air Force. On 1 April 2018, the RAF celebrates the completion of its first century since my grandfather was appointed Chief of Air Staff of the new service, formed from the merger of the Royal Flying Corps and the Royal Naval Air Service.

The authors have volunteered their time to compile this excellent book in order to raise money to support the exceptional work that the RAF charities undertake to help those members of the wider RAF family, both serving and retired, and their families, who are in need of some assistance. It is a way to repay "the debt we owe", in the famous words of Sir Winston Churchill.

My grandfather believed that by selecting the very best people for the force, regardless of their background, the RAF would develop a strong professional identity and an outstanding esprit de corps. It is this powerful spirit that has motivated the authors in their impressive endeavour to produce this book.

It is a widely accepted axiom that "an army marches on its stomach". One has only to be present in the mess tent at the end of an operation to understand the value food has to the armed forces! I am sure that my grandfather would have approved of the way the team have pulled together to produce this book. While the challenges facing the current and future generations may seem a world apart from those that confronted the air force that he helped to build, there are some things that will always remain constant – the spirit, the humour, the ingenuity and, of course, the appetite of the airmen and airwomen who serve.

Hugh Trenchard, 3rd Viscount Trenchard DL

CONTENTS

THE POST-WAR ERA
1946–1963

THE COLD WAR
1964–1989

THE MODERN AGE
1990–2018

INTRODUCTION

Words by
SQUADRON LEADER JON PULLEN

LOOKING BACK TO the start of our journey in November 2013, it was neither a love of food nor an interest in the amazing history of the Royal Air Force that served as the catalyst for this book. Instead, it was the unfailing determination of Flight Lieutenant Crispin Chapple to rid me of my spare change with his constant raising of money for the RAF Benevolent Fund.

Crispin and I were both working in different parts of the Air Mobility Force Headquarters at RAF Brize Norton, and it was his passion for supporting the charity that first drew him to my attention. Back in 2009, I had led a hugely committed team of RAF personnel in producing a book for the charity Help For Heroes, imaginatively titled *Food For Heroes*, and, while I am immensely proud of that book – which sold an unbelievable 25,000 copies and raised an amazing amount of money for the charity – I knew I could improve on it and was looking for an excuse to give it another go. It took all of five minutes to persuade Crispin that what was missing in his life was the excitement, stress and pressure of a publisher's deadline!

We were aware that 1 April 2018 would mark the RAF's centenary and, after a brief search online, it became apparent that in that time, the RAF had operated around the globe from some 100 countries. Having coloured them in on a map of the world, we were struck, not only by the extraordinary history of the service, but also by how amazing it would be to create a cookery book that combined this history with a recipe from every country. Now all we had to do was write the thing ...

I should confess that, while I am an aero-systems engineer, frustrated musician and ageing footballer with 33 years of RAF service, and Crispin is a new dad, amateur veg-grower and an RAF pilot of some 20 years, neither of us are chefs, historians or publishers. However, thankfully we also appear to lack the wisdom to recognise our own limitations.

After a little consideration, we decided that it would be easy to coerce 100 of our colleagues to research and write up the country histories, which just left us with the challenge of the food. How to find someone to research and write the recipes, pay for the food, find a kitchen, cook the dishes, present them and photograph them ... 100 times ... for free? Our search repeatedly turned up the same response: "You need Stu Harmer".

An ex-Flight Sergeant and RAF chef, combined services champ and British Meat Military Chef of the Year – yes, that's a thing – Stu was now working as the Senior Executive Chef of ISS, the international facility services company that works closely with the RAF. The route to me and Crispin gaining his help was a 10-minute, *Dragons' Den*-style showdown with ISS executives Allan Vaughan and Craig Smith; a meeting that went from strikingly low expectations, to the acceptance that we may be onto something, to a level of support that still astonishes us to this day.

COOKBOOK CO-CREATORS FLIGHT LIEUTENANT CRISPIN CHAPPLE (LEFT) AND SQUADRON LEADER JON PULLEN

Stu became a de facto partner in the project, with his employers allowing him to give up two days a month for three years, provide all the food and recipes, and effectively become our artistic director. For our part, we set him a few basic rules. First, each recipe had to be representative of one of the 100 countries. Second, an RAF airman might plausibly have eaten that food had they served in that country. Third, all recipes had to be cookable in a normal home kitchen, with the ingredients available in a UK supermarket. Fourth: some 20 per cent had to be puddings, and a decent number had to be vegetarian-friendly. And fifth: all of them had to appeal to UK palates – and be tested on us! As a result, Crispin and I have spent a day a month for the past two years being fed the most incredible four-course meals under the veiled excuse of completely unnecessary quality control. Tough job.

It was around this time that we approached the RAF Joint Venture in the hope that our project would be embraced as an official RAF100 product. In addition to their praise, they challenged us to "broaden the appeal". After much deliberation, our way ahead was, as ever, simplistic: "We'll just get 10 of the country's most celebrated chefs with a link to both the RAF and the countries we are writing about to give us a recipe!" Well, we've done exactly that and the results are amazing. We have old friends such as Cyrus Todiwala, Paul Gayler, and Chris and James Tanner, who helped us with the first book, new friends Vivek Singh, Sophie Wright and Paul Ainsworth, who are taking the country by storm, national treasures Tom Kerridge and James Martin, and, most excitingly for us, former RAF chefs Rachel Humphries and Graham Howarth, who have both shown civvy chefs how it's done in the military. Our thanks to them knows no bounds (especially if we can persuade them to cook for us).

The final piece of the creative culinary puzzle was finding a photographer who would be available whenever the food needed photographing and could do each dish justice. The solution came in the form of the Joint Aerial Delivery Test and Evaluation Unit (JADTEU). This is the trials unit responsible for the testing, approving and, more importantly, photographing of any equipment requiring transportation or dispatch by all RAF air assets. Led by Sergeant Nige Green, the eight RAF photographers from the unit who have provided their expert services for the past three years were the perfect addition to our team, and all too willing to swap a Hercules load for a dinner plate!

That wasn't the end of our challenge, however. If we had thought that persuading our colleagues to "knock out" a few hundred words on each country's RAF history would be a simple matter, a research trip to the library of the Defence Academy at Shrivenham soon taught us otherwise. We learned that nobody writes military books about countries; they write them about campaigns, or units, or battles, or people. In the end, it took 30 friends and colleagues, giving up hundreds of hours of their free time, to research and write the 100 country histories. Crispin orchestrated and coerced the team for three years before we were happy with what we had produced – a unique view of the service's extraordinary century celebrating the achievements of the RAF family through the lives and work of our colleagues past and present.

We learned many things: that "Goolie chits" were exactly that – promissory notes to save a downed airman's testicles from being

> # "How to find someone to research and write the recipes, cook the dishes and photograph them … 100 times … for free?"

removed during the North East Indian conflict in 1918; that Nissen huts could actually fly when given the correct wind conditions; and, more poignantly and perhaps unexpectedly, that German officers in the Channel Islands buried RAF airmen with full military honours during the Second World War.

We had decided that the book should be a historical chronology, rather than a traditional cookbook, from early on. For this idea to work we needed to break it up into separate chapters to make it more easily digestible (pun intended). As a linking device, what we needed was some sort of commentary in the form of chapter introductions that told the story of Britain's international influence through the evolution of the RAF. That's where friend and historian Nick Fellows came in, having made the school-boy error of asking how the book was coming along one evening in the local pub, and finding himself committed to writing the introductions and attending a raft of boozy editorial meetings as a result.

From the outset, we were clear that we wanted this book to be an official RAF Centenary product. This called for another *Dragons' Den*-style pitch, this time to Zerrin Lovett and Squadron Leader Jo Roe of the RAF100 Programme Team Organisation, who gave it their enthusiastic support. As an authorised launch product for the Centenary Celebrations, we benefitted from an unexpected windfall: the RAF Centenary leadership was bringing the principal RAF charities together for the occasion under the RAF Joint Venture Appeal. This meant that, as well as the RAF Benevolent Fund, we would be supporting all of the other principle RAF charities. In a single act, we were representing the whole of the RAF family and raising money for everything from support for veterans in need, to the upkeep of RAF national monuments.

This amazing and unique book has been pulled together through the joint efforts of RAF serving men and women, their families, friends and industry colleagues, who have all given their time and talent for free. We've had accounts from veterans, the Air Training Corps contributing the history section for England and pretty much the entire RAF family writing, cooking, tasting, photographing, proof reading, marketing and doing every other job needed in the production of the book you hold before you.

We can take great pride, not only in this book, but in the support and belief we have received from all those who have made it happen. All of the royalties and profits from the sales of this book through our own channels will go directly to RAF causes. Indeed, through our partnership with publisher St James's House and our projected sales, our original target of raising over £100,000 is already assured. As the RAF motto goes: "Per Ardua Ad Astra" – through adversity to the stars!

THE BIRTH OF THE RAF

Words by
NICK FELLOWS

THE ROYAL AIR FORCE came into existence on 1 April 1918, six months before the end of the First World War. It followed an act of Parliament of November 1917 that had established an Air Force and Air Council. This was quite a remarkable achievement – it was only nine years previously that Samuel Cody had made the first recognised flight in Britain and 15 years since the Wright brothers first controlled, powered and sustained heavier-than-air human flight in the United States.

There were developments in air power prior to the outbreak of the First World War. An Air Battalion had been established in 1911 and the Royal Flying Corps and Royal Naval Air Service were set up in 1912 but, when war broke out, there was little equipment (just 63 aircraft supported the British Expeditionary Force) and few trained aircrew.

The war itself would play a crucial role in the development of air power, despite the statement that is usually attributed to General Douglas Haig at the start of the war. "I hope none of you gentlemen is so foolish as to think that aeroplanes will be usefully employed for reconnaissance purposes in war," he told officers in July 1914. "There is only one way for commanders to get information by reconnaissance, and that is by cavalry."

The cavalry was one of the first victims of the Great War. Horses were shot to pieces in bloody battles on the Western Front, despite attempts to camouflage the animals by painting them (something that quickly became problematic when the horses sweated or were rained on). Horses were also a logistical nightmare, consuming vast amounts of fodder, which had to be transported along already congested roads. In contrast, the reconnaissance value of the aeroplane became clear at a very early stage. "I wish particularly to bring to your Lordships' notice the admirable work done by the Royal Flying Corps," said the Commander of the BEF, Sir John French, on 7 September 1914. "They have furnished me with the most complete and accurate information, which has been of incalculable value in the conduct of operations. Fired at constantly by both friend and foe, and not hesitating to fly in every kind of weather, they have remained undaunted throughout." It was soon realised that preventing the enemy from obtaining information was just as important as obtaining it. As a result, fighters were developed to destroy reconnaissance aircraft rather than to attack other fighters.

The fighter aces soon caught the public imagination as the importance of gaining air superiority over the Western Front became ever more crucial. This was encouraged by the appointment of Major General Hugh Trenchard as commander of the RFC in August 1915. He fought battles with the War Office to ensure that the RFC was supplied with new types of aircraft so he was not fighting next year's battles with last year's planes. Even General Haig now saw the advantage of air power and, by 1916, he was requesting 20 more squadrons for the Western Front.

However, these developments created further problems, most notably how to supply and train pilots and observers? To this end, a training squadron was established near Toronto in Canada in May 1917. Later that year, to avoid the Canadian winter, the RFC started to use a facility in Fort Worth, Texas, in return training American squadrons for the US Air Service.

DAMAGE TO THE BUTTER MARKET IN BURY ST. EDMUNDS, CAUSED BY ZEPPELIN LZ 38 ON THE NIGHT OF 29-30 APRIL 1915. GERMAN AIR ATTACKS ON ENGLAND EVENTUALLY LED TO THE FORMATION OF THE ROYAL AIR FORCE

At the same time, the German Zeppelin threat was creating panic and fear in Britain and it was decided that attacks on German airship sheds were the best means of preventing this. However, these raids were to be carried out by the Royal Naval Air Service, as the RFC was fully occupied in France. The immediate consequence was the development of the first strategic bomber but, more importantly in the long term, the Zeppelin raids made it clear that there needed to be a unified air service. This became more apparent with the daylight bombing raids on England in 1917, which killed 219 in London and 183 in other parts of the country. The *Daily Mail* suggested that the Zeppelin raids were the greatest humiliation for Britain since the Dutch sailed up the Thames in 1667.

No historian would claim that the part played by either the RFC or the RNAS was the decisive factors in the ultimate victory during the First World War. However, their roles were significant and the RAF's part in blunting the final German offensive and in the subsequent Allied counter-attack of 1918 was, perhaps, a foretaste of air power's dominance in future campaigns. It was not just on the Western Front, however, that the service was involved in air operations.

The RAF's long history of activity across the world started in 1914 with an RFC detachment in Egypt and continued with a vital role in the defeat of Turkish forces, particularly in Mesopotamia. The RNAS were involved in the Gallipoli campaign and in Macedonia against the Bulgarians, while its contributions to anti-submarine warfare in the Atlantic were also crucial. Aid was also given to the Italians with attacks on the coasts of Austria, Italy, Montenegro and Albania. On a smaller scale, action was also seen in East Africa, Russia, India, Aden and the Red Sea, Gibraltar and Malta. Such involvement only added to the pressures and demands on the forces and furthered calls for reform.

Competition between the RFC and RNAS for engines and aircraft also encouraged the call for unification of the two services and this was furthered by a variety of bureaucratic initiatives designed to solve the problem of supply. To address these issues, Prime Minister David Lloyd George turned to the South African-born General Jan Christian Smuts, the soldier and statesman who had led the South African army in East Africa. Smuts put together a committee whose recommendations were accepted by the British government and so began the process of amalgamating the two forces. Concerns were expressed whether unification could be completed during wartime, but it was not long before the term "the Royal Air Force" was heard for the first time.

But challenges still existed in the establishment of an air force. Lord Rothermere, who was to be the first Secretary of State for the RAF, and Hugh Trenchard of the RFC had opposing views on future policy. Trenchard actually submitted his resignation as Chief of Air Staff two weeks before the RAF came into existence. However, an announcement was delayed until mid April, so that when the RAF came into being on 1 April 1918, Trenchard was appointed as the first Chief of Air Staff of the newly created force.

THE EARLY YEARS
1918–1938

BLUE SKY THINKING

Words by
NICK FELLOWS

BY 1918, THE future of the newly formed Royal Air Force looked uncertain. The Great War was supposed to have been "the war to end all wars", which raised the question as to whether a third armed force was needed. The conflict had cost Britain considerable sums of money and left the country with huge economic problems. The RAF's founder, Lord Hugh Trenchard, successfully convinced the Secretary of State for War, Winston Churchill, that a separate air force was necessary to develop airmanship and engender the "air spirit". But, with many regarding the RAF as a luxury, much of its

early history would be a fight to survive the swathe of government cuts and to establish a peacetime role.

The RAF's first roles were far from peaceful, though. The First World War had started with Russia fighting on the side of Britain, but in 1917 two revolutions had seen the beginnings of a Communist government, one that was soon involved in a Civil War against former supporters of the Russian Tsar. Most western governments were not only frightened by the prospect of communism, but also stood to lose their Russian investments if the Bolsheviks won.

As a consequence, one of the first acts of the RAF was to go to Russia in 1918 to train anti-Bolshevik fighters, as well as to carry out operational sorties against the Bolsheviks. This gave rise to one particularly notable incident when an attack on a Bolshevik gunboat at Tcherni-Yar by William Elliot resulted in him being shot down. The event was seen by Captain Anderson, who managed to land and rescue Elliot and his crew, despite receiving damage that required his gunner, Lieutenant Mitchell, to climb onto the wing and block a leaking fuel tank with his thumb. Anderson and Mitchell were awarded a Distinguished Service Order (DSO) as a result.

Churchill explained the future of the RAF to Parliament in December 1919. "The first duty of the RAF," he said, "is to garrison the British Empire." The RAF offered a number of advantages over the other armed forces in taking on this role.

It could cover large and often inhospitable and undeveloped areas at a far quicker rate than the other services. It could also undertake the task of policing at an acceptable cost to governments that were financially conscious.

The first two operations, in Somaliland and Iraq, allowed the RAF to develop and put into practice an operational theory that became known as "Air Control". Its first test was in Somaliland where a Muslim cleric – the "Mad Mullah" – had frustrated attempts to bring law and order to the area. The army had estimated that it would need many divisions and several million pounds to subdue the unrest. The RAF offered to do the job using one squadron of 12 de Havilland DH9s, along with the local gendarmerie, the Somali camel corps and a battalion of rifles. Within weeks the force had successfully bombed the opposition and driven them from their positions. The operation cost less than £80,000, making it probably the cheapest war in history.

This showed that the RAF could undertake effective policing action in conjunction with a small number of ground troops at a low cost. The operation's success encouraged a similar approach in Iraq, although the challenge there was much larger. The issue was one of unrest among the Kurds of the north of the country, along with the attitude of their former rulers, Turkey. At a meeting in Egypt in 1921, the problem of resolving the dispute was given to the RAF, but soon escalated into a crisis as the Kurds revolted in September 1922. The RAF carried out the world's first air evacuation, lifting out some 70 British forces and civilians – and one dog!

The following year, it was the area around Mosul that was the problem. This time another airlift was launched, but in reverse, as some 480 troops were taken to Kirkuk, completing the first military troop lift in history. The enemy did not think the British could reinforce their positions because heavy rain had made the roads impassable, and they were so shocked that they fled into the mountains. Victory against the Turks was completed when the RAF attacked a cavalry incursion into Iraq and forced their withdrawal. Although Iraq would continue to present a problem, the Turkish element had been removed – and once again at a reasonable cost. "I cannot emphasise too much," said Lord Trenchard to the commander, "the value your successful command in Iraq has been to us."

With Somalia and Iraq began the policy of air control as a method of policing isolated and inhospitable areas, while also providing an effective means of projecting military power in areas such as the Middle East. Another similar area was the North-West Frontier Province of India, where air power provided Britain with speed, strength and mobility. Instead of ground forces moving in columns, which provided easy targets for the warriors who inhabited these areas, aircraft were a much more difficult target and made unrest a much less attractive option. Bombing, following warnings, encouraged compliance and was used to separate the warring tribesmen from food and shelter.

In Kabul in 1928–29, the RAF played a very different role, carrying out the first major civilian airlift in history. A large-scale rebellion meant that the capital was cut off from the rest of the country. The RAF was able to fly some 28,000 miles, during the winter, and evacuate 586 people with the loss of just one plane.

Throughout the decade that followed the First World War, the RAF successfully carried out the role Churchill had ascribed to it – of garrisoning the Empire – at a far cheaper cost than traditional forces. Although policing the Empire continued through the 1930s, the role of the RAF widened as it sought to establish an international reputation for long-distance, high-altitude and high-speed flying. The RAF was also heavily involved in the development of new air routes designed to serve the Empire, initially to Egypt, but then on to India, Singapore and Australia. This meant that a letter from London could reach a soldier in Iraq in five days. Flights were also made across Africa, crossing more than 8,000 miles of desert and jungle as the RAF pioneered journeys between Egypt, Sudan, Kenya and the Cape, which would be later followed by civilian airlines.

Long-distance flights and the prizes won by RAF pilots brought the force prestige both nationally and internationally. This culminated in 1938 with a Vickers Wellesley flying non-stop from Upper Heyford in Oxfordshire to Darwin, Australia, a journey of some 7,000 miles. It was not just distance but also altitude that was conquered, with the Bristol monoplane climbing to over 53,000 feet in 1937.

Publicly, however, it was displays at venues such as Hendon and competitions such as the Schneider Trophy that brought the RAF real prestige and renown. Victories

> # *"The period from 1934 was one of expansion to ensure that the RAF was in a position to defend the skies over Britain"*

in the latter – a speed competition for sea-planes – by the Supermarine would be crucial in its future development as the evolution of the Spitfire and the Merlin engine can be clearly linked to this international contest. Such events captured the public's imagination, despite the financial constraints that the depression of the 1930s imposed on the development of the force. However, as war clouds gathered in the later 1930s, there were still many aircraft in service that reflected the RAF's past rather than its future.

A number of developments in the 1930s would prove vital, not just to the RAF, but to the future safety of the country. The Spitfire and Hurricane, which would play such a crucial role in the Second World War, had made their way from the drawing board to operational squadron, with the first orders made in 1934 and prototypes being flown in 1935 and 1936. In addition, the appointment of the little-known lawyer Sir Thomas Inskip as Minister for Co-ordination of Defence changed strategic thinking. Instead of using air power as an offensive weapon, focusing on bombing, he changed the emphasis to fighters. This was a crucial change: fighters were quicker and cheaper to produce, and would prove their worth in 1940 in the Battle of Britain.

The period from 1934 was one of expansion to ensure that the RAF was in a position to defend the skies over Britain from the Luftwaffe. Ultimately, this led to the re-equipping of the RAF, not only with new fighters, but also heavy bombers. Despite this increase, however, it was clear that, if attempts to prevent war at Munich in 1938 had failed, the RAF would have been less than 40 per cent prepared. The space that the agreement provided was critical for preparations, largely because Britain made better use of it than Germany. Nevertheless, when war did come in 1939, the strength of the RAF was about half that of the Luftwaffe – a fact that only makes its subsequent achievements all the more remarkable.

FRANCE

Words by
FLIGHT LIEUTENANT JAMES WILYMAN

THE ROYAL AIR FORCE can link many of its roots to Britain's ally across the Channel. As the Great War raged across Europe, the skies above France brought about the first effective use of air power as we understand it today. The Royal Flying Corps (RFC) achieved many battle honours over the trenches embedded in muddy fields across France, but our story starts where the RFC's ends.

Travelling frequently between London and France, the symbolic founder of the RAF, Lord Trenchard, developed much of his doctrine from his experiences with Colonel Paul de Peuty, then serving under the Service Aéronautique, an arm of the French Army. Entrenched

and fatigued by ongoing German attacks, it was Lord Trenchard's conversations, arguments and discussions with his French comrade that sowed the seed of how an independent air force could deliver effect. These eventually led to the birth of the RAF on 1 April 1918; the Service Aéronautique gained its independent status in 1934, becoming the Armée de l'Air.

Every story in this book can probably be traced back to the planning rooms and messes of the headquarters of the British Expeditionary Force, located in St Omer,

France. We even owe the iconic "roundel" of the RAF to the Service Aéronautique, taking the French concentric circle identification insignia as inspiration to differentiate from the harsh cross of the Germans – a symbol that, at distance, looked confusingly similar to the red cross of the Union Flag.

It seems only fitting, then, to mention the links that St Omer has with gastronomy. Although officially commissioned in London, the RAF defined itself in France. It is even possible that the inaugural messing of the RAF's first airmen took place from the field kitchens of St Omer, and the first operational concepts of the RAF may well have been discussed around a dinner table there. Such was St Omer's critical role in the feeding of our service men and women's fighting spirit during the First World War that, until 2006, the British Army's catering college was located at the appropriately named St Omer Barracks, Aldershot.

Since those early days, the close relationship between the RAF and France's Armée de l'Air has only grown stronger. During the Second World War our service men and women, from both fighter and bomber command, launched and conducted seemingly endless missions across the skies of France. It was the brave men and women of the French Resistance who often secured safe passage of our downed aircrew across Europe back to safety to fight again.

It was not just bombing missions and dogfights that defined the pace of the air war over France, however. The Allies also understood the importance of maintaining the morale of those under German occupation. After receiving intelligence that the Nazis paraded down the Champs-Élysées in Paris every day, the British Special Operations Executive devised Operation Squabble; a daring, low-level mission to fly directly down the boulevard of the Champs-Élysées and drop a giant French tricolore flag onto the Arc de Triomphe.

After numerous practice runs on a shipwreck in the Channel, Wing Commander Gatward of 404 Squadron Royal Canadian Air Force took his Bristol Beaufighter across to Paris. Flying dangerously, low his navigator Sergeant Fern successfully draped the flag across the monument and strafed the ministry building before dropping a second flag. This "bombing" raid was different in nature to those the people of Paris and Wing Commander Gatward were used to, but the image of the French tricolore – dropped from a British bomber and hanging, centre stage, as a symbol of defiance in occupied France – was a huge boost to morale.

The RAF still enjoys a close relationship with its French allies. Launching joint exercises, planning and maintaining relationships with France's Armée de l'Air remain strategically important and honour both nations' shared history. The very foundations of the RAF were, without a doubt, moulded by and born of great minds planning war over French soil.

1 SQUADRON PERSONNEL AT RAF CLAIRMARAIS, NEAR YPRES, 3 JULY 1918

Navarin d'Agneau Printanier
Spring Lamb Stew

by RACHEL HUMPHREY
EX-SENIOR AIRCRAFTWOMAN AND EXECUTIVE CHEF AT LE GAVROCHE

There are two schools of thought as to why this stew is called "navarin". Some say it's named after the battle of Navarino where French, British and Russian warships defeated the Ottoman armada in 1827. The more likely theory is that it's simply named after the turnips, or "navets", in the dish. The "printanier" refers to spring, when this lamb stew is made with fresh young spring vegetables. If you're using more mature carrots, turnips and onions, then cut them into large chunks or wedges.

INGREDIENTS

Serves 4

For the navarin

500g boned shoulder of lamb

700g middle neck of lamb

olive oil

1 large carrot, diced

1 large onion, diced

1 stick of celery, diced

30g brown flour (flour toasted
  until golden brown and sieved)

200ml white wine

3 tomatoes, peeled, deseeded
  and chopped

2 cloves of garlic

1 bouquet garni

1⅓ litres chicken stock

salt and pepper

To finish

12 baby carrots

12 baby turnips

12 button onions

12 small new potatoes

300g fresh peas in the pod

15g unsalted butter

METHOD

To make the navarin

- Preheat the oven to 165°C.
- Dice the lamb into large pieces removing any excess fat from the shoulder.
- Place a sauté pan on a high heat, add a little olive oil, season the meat and add to the pan colouring on all sides. Once caramelised drain off any excess fat from the meat.
- Return the pan to the heat with a little more oil and, on a medium heat, add the diced vegetables and sweat until soft. Add the flour and cook for a couple of minutes stirring with a spatula.
- Add the white wine and bring to a rapid boil before adding the tomatoes, garlic and bouquet garni along with the chicken stock.
- Return the pieces of meat to the pan and bring everything to a simmer. Cover with a lid or cartouche (a round piece of parchment or greaseproof paper cut to fit the pan) and place in the oven for around 1¼ hours.
- Once cooked the meat should be tender. Remove the pan from the oven and set aside to cool and rest at room temperature then, ideally, chill overnight in the fridge.

To finish

- Peel, wash and blanch the new potatoes and baby vegetables until just cooked through. Refresh the baby vegetables, and shell and blanch the peas.
- If using, remove the cartouche from the lamb and skim off any fat from the surface. Remove the pieces of meat and set aside.
- Return the sauce to the boil and reduce until it thickens, then pass it through a conical sieve, adjust the seasoning if necessary and add the butter to make the sauce glossy.
- Return the meat to the sauce and reheat gently until the lamb is piping hot, adding the vegetables to reheat at the last moment.
- Place in a large serving dish with any extra sauce on the side.

ENGLAND

Contributed by
290 SQUADRON (WESTON-SUPER-MARE), AIR TRAINING CORPS

THE ROYAL AIR FORCE has operated in England since its formation on 1 April 1918 with its first headquarters established in the Hotel Cecil in London. Throughout its existence, the RAF has operated numerous roles across the breadth of the country and, at the height of the Second World War, Fighter and Bomber Command had approximately 140 operational airfields between them in England, ranging from Durham in the north to St Eval in Cornwall.

The RAF won many battle honours throughout the century. The most famous of these is undoubtedly the Battle of Britain, fought over England between May and October 1940, in which "the few" – as Churchill famously described the RAF's pilots – faced almost insurmountable odds to claim victory over Germany's Luftwaffe. It was during the Battle of Britain that 23-year-old Flight Lieutenant James Nicolson won the only Fighter Command VC of the Second World War, on 16 August 1940. During engagement with the enemy, his aircraft was hit by four cannon shells with two wounding him and a third setting fire to a fuel tank. As Nicholson set to abandon the aircraft, he spotted an enemy fighter and chose to engage. He shot the aircraft down, but his delay in leaving the aircraft resulted in him suffering serious burns to his face, neck, hands and legs.

The Battle of Britain clearly demonstrated the importance of air power and the growing need for air-minded young men to be trained in various aviation-related roles. So was born the Air Training Corps (ATC) to help meet this need. The ATC's predecessor, the Air Defence Cadet Corps (ADCC) was formed in 1938, due to the foresight of Air Commodore Chamier, to prepare boys for service in the RAF. When war was declared, those units closest to RAF airfields provided invaluable assistance undertaking many simple but onerous tasks, thus freeing the airmen to concentrate on the more technical work.

During the Battle of Britain cadets filled sandbags, pushed bomb trolleys, helped to manhandle aircraft and loaded miles of ammunition belts after a full day at work or school. The need for a pre-service training regime was clear and recognition of the huge contribution made by the ADCC came in the form a Royal Warrant issued by King George VI. This created the ATC just three months after the end of the Battle of Britain, in February 1941.

Many boys had left school aged 14, so the syllabus to prepare them for service in RAF ground and air trades included maths and English alongside PT (physical training) and technical subjects. 1(F) City of Leicester Squadron was the first to form and in six months, more than 100,000 cadets had joined their local squadron. In the towns and cities they acted as fire and police messengers during the air raids, while those near airfields continued the work undertaken by the ADCC.

Some even helped the Air Transport Auxiliary in delivering aircraft from

maintenance units to the front line as pilots' assistants. Cadet Eric Viles (later Wing Commander RAF) flew from RAF Aston Down in Anson planes, taking ferry pilots to various units. He also flew into Europe on several occasions, going as far as Berlin before hostilities officially ceased.

Today, the ATC is one of the largest uniformed youth organisations in the UK, comprising around 32,000 boys and girls between the ages of 12 and 20, and around 12,000 uniformed and civilian volunteer staff. Cadets follow a formal training syllabus covering a wide range of subjects including the history and principles of flight, radio, radar and satellite communications, which can lead to the award of a BTEC in aviation studies. They learn many new skills including radio procedures, map reading and shooting, and get the opportunity to go flying, gliding and to earn a Duke of Edinburgh's Award. While the RAF is celebrating its centenary in 2018, the ATC will also be celebrating the fact that, for 77 years, it has been producing self-confident, resilient young men and women equipped with skills to benefit them in whatever walk of life they choose.

MEMBERS OF THE AIR DEFENCE CADET CORPS AT DUNSTABLE, 1939

Bread & Butter Pudding

by PAUL AINSWORTH
CHEF-PATRON AT PAUL AINSWORTH AT NUMBER 6

English bread and butter pudding is the epitome of simplicity, but there are a few pointers to make it perfect. The bread should be stale, not fresh. White bread can be substituted with brioche, fruit loaf or left-over panettone at Christmas. Fruit can be soaked in rum, brandy or a liqueur, such as Cointreau, and should be layered in the pudding and not sprinkled over the top. Before baking, the buttered bread should soak up the vanilla-flavoured custard prior to topping up with a final layer of custard. It can be baked as it is, but cooking in a bain-marie allows it to cook and set evenly.

INGREDIENTS
Serves 6–8
For the bread and butter pudding
12 slices of white bread
125g butter
30g sultanas
450ml double cream
150ml milk
2 vanilla pods, split lengthways
 and seeds scraped
7 large egg yolks
175g caster sugar

To serve
good quality vanilla ice cream,
fresh egg custard or a bit of both

METHOD
- Butter the bread, remove the crusts and cut into triangles. Butter a 5 litre ovenproof dish to stop the bread baking to it.
- Build up the bread in the dish like a jigsaw, sprinkling sultanas over each layer except for the top one – otherwise, you'll think of rabbits straight away when it comes out of the oven!
- Now make your custard: bring the milk, cream and vanilla (pods and seeds) to the boil. Meanwhile, whisk your egg yolks and sugar together until they become very pale, almost beige. Pour the cream mixture over the egg mixture and stir with a wooden spoon, then place the bowl over some boiling water and stir the custard until it coats the back of the spoon.
- Pass the custard through a sieve – not a fine one, you just want to get rid of the vanilla pod – then pour it over the bread leaving a bit behind to top up later.
- Leave the pudding at room temperature for around 6 hours to soak up the custard, then top up with the excess custard and put the dish in a bath of water, or bain-marie, and place in the oven at 130°C. Cook for around 25 minutes until it has just a slight wobble.
- Leave to cool slightly.
- Sprinkle caster sugar on top and glaze using a blowtorch or under a hot grill to create a crispy top, then dish up.

IRELAND

Words by
PETER DEVITT

ON 1 SEPTEMBER 1913, four biplanes of 2 Squadron, Royal Flying Corps, flew from Stranraer in Scotland to Limerick to participate in the British Army's Irish manoeuvres. This was the RFC's first deployment overseas and heralded the birth of military aviation in Ireland. Eleven months later, the United Kingdom of Great Britain and Ireland declared war on Germany. Between 1914 and 1918, 240,000 Irish volunteers joined the British forces, 40,000 of whom lost their lives. Some 6,000 Irish personnel served with the RFC, Royal Naval Air Service and Royal Air Force, and suffered 500 deaths.

A remarkable 495 aerial victories were credited to only 39 Irish aces. One was Major Joseph Creuss Callaghan from County Dublin, last seen attacking 25 German fighters single-handedly. Another was Captain George McElroy who, as an infantry officer, served in his home city of Dublin during the Easter Rising of April 1916. Unwilling to fire on the rebels, McElroy was posted away, but later destroyed 46 enemy aircraft while serving with the RFC/RAF. The most successful pilots were Victoria Cross winners Major James McCudden and Major Edward Mannock; two working-class heroes from the Irish diaspora in England credited with 57 and 61 victories respectively. Sadly, all four were killed in July 1918.

In 1917, Major William Sholto Douglas, a young Scot with bright prospects, travelled Ireland selecting sites for training airfields. "Whenever I made any journeys by road the 'corner boys' lounging at the street corners in the villages almost invariably scowled at me, and a few even threw stones," he wrote in his 1963 autobiography. "But, when I flew anywhere and landed in a field near some village or other, the young men would come running out onto the field cheering and shouting wild Irish cries and throwing their hats in the air, all because most of them had never seen an aeroplane before."

By the end of the war, flying training schools were operating at Gormanston, County Meath, and at Baldonnel, Collinstown and Tallaght in County Dublin. Students were taught to fly using the revolutionary methods pioneered by Lieutenant-Colonel Robert Smith Barry, another gifted airman of Irish heritage. Bases were also established around the Irish coast from which British and US aircraft mounted anti-submarine patrols.

After the Armistice, Sinn Fein won a landslide victory in a general election and, in January 1919, the Anglo–Irish War began. The RAF never used bombs or machine-guns against the Irish Republican Army, but its squadrons supported the security forces by maintaining communications and spotting rebel activity from the air. On the ground, RAF personnel escorted vehicle convoys.

On a happier note, on 15 June 1919, RAF veterans Captain John Alcock and Lieutenant Arthur Whitten Brown crashlanded their Vickers Vimy near Clifden, Connemara, having completed the first direct Atlantic crossing by air. At a dinner in their honour, the menu included "Poached Eggs Alcock", "Sole à la Brown", "Spring Chicken à la Vickers Vimy" and "Gâteau Grand Succès".

In July 1921, a truce was agreed and talks began in London, leading to the creation of a 26-county Irish Free State, leaving six Ulster counties under British rule. Former RAF pilots Jack McSweeney and Charles Russell kept a Martinsyde aircraft on standby to spirit away Irish leader Michael Collins if the talks failed. Fortunately, the Martinsyde was not needed and "The Big Fella", as it was nicknamed, became the first aircraft of the Irish Republic's new National Army Air Service.

Boiled Bacon, Kale & Parsley Sauce

Historically, many rural Irish families grew their own vegetables and reared pigs, so the ingredients for this dish would have been readily available. This recipe for the quintessential Saint Patrick's Day dinner is served with colcannon cakes, which are made in advance, chilled, formed into patties, dusted with a little flour and shallow fried until browned and crispy on the outside. The boiled bacon can, of course, be simply served with a generous spoonful of creamy mash or boiled potatoes.

INGREDIENTS

Serves 4

For the parsley sauce

1 medium onion, peeled and
  left whole
1 bay leaf
4 cloves
25g parsley, leaves coarsely
  chopped and stalks retained
500ml milk
40g butter
40g plain flour
freshly grated nutmeg
salt and white pepper

**For the colcannon cakes
(optional)**

50g kale, stalks removed and
  coarsely chopped
600g Charlotte (or other waxy
  variety) potatoes, peeled and
  cut into even-sized pieces
25g butter
3 tbsp double cream (optional)
salt and pepper
flour, for dusting
3 tbsp bacon fat or vegetable oil,
  for frying
15g butter, for frying

METHOD

To make the parsley sauce

• Attach the bay leaf to the onion by pinning it on with the cloves (an onion studded like this is known as a piqué – French for "pricked")
• Pour the milk into a saucepan, add the studded onion and the parsley stalks and bring to a simmer. Take off the heat and set to one side for 30 minutes to infuse.
• Remove the studded onion (discard the bay leaf and cloves, reserve the onion for use in the colcannon) and parsley stalks, return the infused milk to a low heat and bring to a simmer.
• Melt the butter in a separate saucepan over a moderate heat and, once frothing, stir in the flour. Turn the heat to low and continue to cook, stirring constantly, for around 2 minutes.
• Gradually add the hot milk, a ladleful at a time, ensuring each addition is thoroughly incorporated before adding the next until it is a smooth sauce. Simmer for 10 minutes, stirring frequently, then set aside.
• When ready to serve, bring the sauce back to a simmer, seasoning with a pinch of nutmeg, salt and ground white pepper. Simmer very gently, stirring occasionally to prevent the sauce from catching, for around 5 minutes, then pass through a fine sieve and stir in the chopped parsley.

To prepare the colcannon cakes

• Place the chopped kale into a saucepan, season lightly with salt and pour in just enough boiling water to cover about a quarter of the kale. Place over a high heat, bring to a boil, cover with a lid, turn the heat to medium and steam for around 5 minutes until soft. Drain the kale and set to one side.
• Cut the cooked onion (reserved from infusing the milk for the parsley sauce) into small dice.

For the bacon and kale

1.5kg bacon joint (cured pork loin)

1 large bunch of kale (or savoy cabbage), shredded

50g butter

pepper

- Boil the potatoes in lightly salted boiling water for 15 to 20 minutes until soft. Drain and crush with a fork to form a coarse mash.
- Mix in the butter and cream (if using), season to taste, mix in the cooked kale and diced cooked onion, then set aside to cool.
- Once cool, divide the potato mix into four or six equal-sized portions and, with floured hands, form into neat disc shapes. Place on a tray lined with a piece of greaseproof paper or baking parchment and chill in the fridge until ready to cook.

To cook the bacon
- Place the bacon in a large saucepan, cover with cold water and bring to a boil over a moderate heat. Remove the bacon and discard the water (this first boiling gets rid of the excess saltiness, as well as any white solids that may rise to the surface).
- Return the bacon to the saucepan, cover with boiling water and bring to a simmer over a moderate heat. Cover with a lid and simmer for 1¼ hours (skimming occasionally).
- Transfer the bacon to a plate (the bacon stock can be kept and is ideal for making soups, such as tomato or lentil), cover with foil and set aside to rest for 15 minutes.
- While the bacon is resting finish the parsley sauce, fry the colcannon cakes and cook the kale.

To cook the kale and colcannon cakes
- Place the shredded kale into a saucepan, add a ladleful of the bacon cooking liquor and the butter, then bring to a simmer, cover with a lid and cook for 5 minutes or until just tender. Remove the lid and continue to cook until the liquid has evaporated. Season with plenty of freshly ground black pepper (only add salt if required, the kale should be quite salty after cooking in the bacon liquor and butter).
- Dust the chilled colcannon cakes with flour and tap off the excess.
- Heat the bacon fat or oil and the butter in a frying pan over a moderate heat and, when the butter is foaming, add the potato cakes and fry on both sides until golden brown and heated through to the middle.

To serve
- Carve the bacon and serve with the sauce, kale and colcannon cakes.

JORDAN

Words by
SQUADRON LEADER JONATHAN ROOKE

JORDAN (KNOWN AS Transjordan until 1946) was, first and foremost, a strategic air-power outpost of the British Empire, with its development being important in the dynamics of the Middle East. At the start of the 1916 Arab Revolt, the Hashemite army was facing Bedouin encampments being bombed by unopposed Turkish aircraft. Assistance was sought from the British Royal Flying Corps (RFC) and the first military air activities in the skies of Jordan took place on 28 August 1917 when four aircraft successfully raided in and around the railway station in the town of Ma'an.

In January 1918, six RFC aircraft were stationed in Aqaba and were used for both reconnaissance and bombing raids on Turkish positions. From then on the RFC, the newly created Royal Air Force and the Australian Flying Corps supported the forces of the Arab Revolt and the Allies until they reached Damascus, establishing complete air superiority over the Turks. T E Lawrence – later known as Lawrence of Arabia – recognised the effectiveness of air power and used aircraft to cut enemy rail lines and logistic routes. The RAF operated in support of the Arab Legion and the Transjordan Frontier Force and, during the 1920s and 1930s, the RAF assisted with reconnaissance missions and support with tribal problems.

In September 1918, RAF aircraft, operating in support of General Allenby's campaign in Palestine, attacked and destroyed the retreating Turkish Army at Wadi el Far'a. "It was the RAF which had converted the Turkish retreat into a rout," wrote T E Lawrence, "which had abolished their telephone and telegraph connections, had blocked their lorry columns, scattered their infantry units."

During this time, the Victoria Cross was awarded to Lieutenant F H McNamara, the only Australian airman to be so decorated, for his rescue of a downed fellow pilot, Captain D W Rutherford, following a bombing raid on a railway across Wadi Hesse at Tel el Hesi in Palestine.

RAF activity in Transjordan was initially controlled from Palestine, but moved to Amman with No. 14 Squadron being formed to assist the new Emirate of Transjordan in April 1921. The air bases of RAF Amman and RAF Mafraq were established in 1931, but Amman airfield was too small for large aircraft so Mafraq – surrounded by a large, flat desert – became the major international base.

The roots of the modern RAF Regiment go back to the 1920s with the introduction of the RAF Armoured Car Companies in the Middle East. No. 1 Armoured Car Company (AAC) was formed at Heliopolis, Egypt in December 1921, for service in Iraq. No. 2 AAC was also formed at Heliopolis, on 7 April 1922, for service in Transjordan, and remained at Amman, equipped with Rolls-Royce Armoured Car and Morris tenders. The unit was engaged in active operations against a Wahhabi tribe that was causing unrest in Transjordan. In 1946, the AACs were incorporated into the RAF Regiment.

These early aviation ties inspired Emir Abdullah to form an air force in Jordan along RAF lines, and have continued to this day. Most recently, Operation Telic, the UK's military effort in Iraq between 2003 and 2011, saw two Canberra PR9s of 39 Squadron (a photo-reconnaissance unit) based at Azraq Air Base, Jordan.

Tabbouleh & Baba Ganoush

Communal, mezze-style eating is the most popular type of dining in Jordan, especially on festive occasions, when small plates of a variety of different dishes are laid out for diners to help themselves. The dishes in this recipe are Jordanian mezze staples; tabbouleh is essentially a lightly spiced herb and tomato salad with fine or medium bulgur wheat, and baba ganoush is a smoked aubergine dip.

INGREDIENTS

Serves 4

For the tabbouleh

75g bulgur wheat

200g flat leaf parsley, washed in cold water and shaken dry

50g mint

400g ripe tomatoes

4 spring onions

2 lemons, juiced

100ml extra virgin olive oil

1 tsp mixed spice (optional)

salt and black pepper

½ pomegranate, seeded

METHOD

To make the tabbouleh

- Place the bulgur wheat in a saucepan, cover with cold water, bring to a boil, reduce the heat, cover with a lid and simmer for 8 minutes until just tender.
- Tip into a sieve, drain, refresh under cold running water and leave for half hour to drain off the excess water.
- For an optional added texture, spread a couple of tablespoons of the cooked and drained bulgur wheat in a single layer on a metal tray and toast for a few minutes under a hot grill until it is lightly browned and popping under the heat. Remove from the heat and allow the toasted bulgur wheat to cool on the tray. Once cool, transfer to an airtight container and store at room temperature until required.
- Gather the parsley bunches together and, starting from the top, finely

For the baba ganoush

6 cloves of garlic, whole and
  unpeeled

1 tsp olive oil

2 medium aubergines

50g tahini

2 lemons, juiced

¼ tsp ground cumin

1 tsp smoked paprika

2 tbsp extra virgin olive oil

salt and pepper

1 tbsp flat leaf parsley, coarsely
  chopped

To serve

grilled flatbread or pittas

little gem lettuce leaves

mixed olives

lemon wedges

shred the leaves down to the stalks. Pick the mint leaves, finely shred
and place all of the herbs in a large mixing bowl.

• Finely dice the tomatoes and add to the herbs along with any juice.

• Finely slice the spring onions and add to the mixing bowl with the
drained bulgur wheat, most of the lemon juice, three quarters of the
olive oil and the mixed spice (if using). Mix well and season with salt
and freshly ground black pepper, taste and add more lemon juice,
mixed spice or seasoning as required.

• Transfer the tabbouleh to a serving bowl, scatter over the pomegranate
seeds, drizzle with the remaining extra virgin olive oil and sprinkle over
the toasted bulgur wheat.

To make the baba ganoush

• Preheat the oven to 200°C.

• Toss the garlic cloves with the olive oil and a pinch of salt, place in
a small ovenproof dish, cover with foil and roast in the oven for 15
to 20 minutes until golden brown and very soft.

• When cool enough to handle, squeeze the garlic flesh out of the
skins onto a chopping board and mash with a fork, then set aside
until required.

• Prick the aubergines all over with a fork, place under a hot grill on
a metal tray and char the skin all over — for around 10 to 15 minutes on
each side — until the flesh is very soft through to the middle.

• Set the aubergines aside to cool on the tray.

• When the aubergines are cool enough to handle, cut each in half, place
cut side down on a chopping board and peel off the skin. Coarsely
chop the aubergine flesh then mash with a fork.

• Transfer the mashed aubergine to a mixing bowl, mix in the roast garlic,
tahini, three quarters of the lemon juice, the ground cumin, smoked
paprika, half of the extra virgin olive oil and season with salt and freshly
ground black pepper. Taste and add more lemon juice, cumin and
seasoning as required.

• Transfer the baba ganoush to a serving bowl, make a depression in the
centre, fill it with the remaining extra virgin olive oil and scatter over
the chopped parsley.

To serve

• Serve the bowls of tabbouleh and baba ganoush with grilled flatbreads,
little gem lettuce leaves, a bowl of olives and lemon wedges.

UNITED STATES OF AMERICA

Words by
**FLIGHT LIEUTENANT SIMON STAFFORD
& ALISON STAFFORD**

THE RELATIONSHIP BETWEEN the United Kingdom and the United States, of course, dates back many years, One of the earliest collaborations between the two nations' air forces was realised during the First World War. The need to supply large numbers of pilots and observers for the frontline squadrons had reached critical shortages on mainland Britain. A training base that had been set up in Canada at Lake Ontario in 1915 was dispatched to Texas by September 1917 given the sunnier training climate.

The three airfields in Fort Worth, Texas would be used for Royal Flying Corps and observer training as a result of a deal with the US government that would see cross-nation training and flying tactics shared. One of these sites is currently still in use and is now home to more than 30 Royal Air Force personnel receiving Lightning II (Joint Strike Fighter) technical training.

In a similar reciprocal arrangement in 1941, the UK government made another agreement with US Congress to allow the USAF to lease a number of bases; the Lend-Lease scheme. This gave the US a foothold in Europe and brought benefits to the UK in the form of aid to address an equipment shortage. The bases included RAF Alconbury, one of many built by the RAF for use in the event of a raid or attack by enemy forces. Such bases were accessible by the main RAF bases but at a safe distance. They were kept purposefully basic and camouflaged, leading the German Luftwaffe to believe that they were abandoned and concentrate their efforts on the larger bases during the Second World War. This allowed the RAF to "hide" aircraft in a relatively safe environment. It was fairly successful, with losses on these sites remarkably low. RAF Alconbury was handed over to the US in 1942.

Additionally, RAF Croughton, RAF Mildenhall and RAF Lakenheath were also leased and, by 1950, RAF Lakenheath had become one of the most important bases in the Cold War, home to some of the most advanced aircraft of the day. Unfortunately, it also became the site of a tragic incident in 1956 when a bomber crashed, killing everyone on board. The nuclear bombs that the bomber was carrying were, amazingly, undetonated, to the relief of all in the surrounding area.

During the conflicts in Iraq and Afghanistan, the RAF has also had pilots embedded at Creech Air Force Base, Nevada operating the unmanned Reaper aircraft. Although operating since 2004, the first Reaper squadron (39) was stood up on 23 January 2008. The squadron's mission is to provide persistent intelligence, surveillance, target acquisition and reconnaissance, as well as offensive support to operational theatres. Operations are now co-located between Nevada and RAF Waddington in Lincolnshire.

The relationship between the US and the UK is set to continue well into the future with RAF personnel still present in multiple locations across the States to this day.

> *"Three airfields in Fort Worth, Texas would see cross-nation training and flying tactics shared. One is still used today"*

Green Chilli Con Carne

by **TOM KERRIDGE**

CHEF-PATRON AT THE HAND AND FLOWERS

I've always been drawn to the raw flavour and heat that you get from green chillies and green peppers. They're really great in this dish, and mixing them with loads of fresh mint and lime makes for a lively and tasty combination. Unlike a regular chilli con carne, this one is dry in style and is quite quick to make. Said to have originated from San Antonio, chilli con carne is the state dish of Texas.

INGREDIENTS

Serves 4–8

For the chilli

1kg minced pork

1 tbsp cumin seeds

1 tsp dried thyme

2 medium onions, diced

4 cloves of garlic, finely grated

2 green peppers, cored,
 deseeded and diced

8 green chillies, chopped
 (seeds and all)

6 ripe tomatoes

150ml water

½ bunch of spring onions,
 trimmed and chopped

1 bunch of mint, stalks removed
 and leaves shredded

2 unwaxed limes, finely grated
 zest and juice

salt and pepper

To serve

whole milk yoghurt

tortillas

METHOD

To make the chilli

• Heat a large, non-stick frying pan over a medium-high heat. When it's hot, add the minced pork, cumin seeds and thyme and dry-fry for 10 to 15 minutes, breaking up the meat and stirring frequently, until it's dry, browned and crispy.

• Using a slotted spoon, transfer the browned spicy meat to a bowl. Drain off any excess fat, keeping a little in the pan to cook the vegetables.

• Return the pan to a medium-low heat. Add the onions and garlic and cook for around 10 minutes, stirring from time to time, until softened. Stir in the green peppers and chillies, cook for a further few minutes, then return the browned meat to the pan. Give everything a good stir and cook for another 5 minutes.

• Deseed and roughly chop the tomatoes.

• Pour the water into the pan, add the tomatoes and bring to the boil. Turn the heat to its lowest setting and let the chilli bubble away, uncovered, for around 15 to 25 minutes, until a lot of the liquid has evaporated. You want the mixture to be juicy but not too liquid and saucy.

• Stir in the spring onions, salt and pepper. Finally, stir through the mint, lime zest and juice. Allow to bubble for a couple of minutes longer, take off the heat and leave to stand for 10 minutes to let the flavours develop before serving.

To serve

• Spoon the chilli into warmed bowls and serve with plenty of yoghurt and tortillas, with a crisp green salad on the side if you like.

RUSSIA

Words by
SQUADRON LEADER (RETIRED) ROB SWINNEY

OFTEN OVERLOOKED AS less significant than both the Great War and the larger Russian revolutions of 1917, British intervention in the subsequent Russian Civil War (1917-22) was part of the joint action among western allies attempting to keep Russia in the Great War against Germany. For the first part of this war, the British assisted in trying to defeat the revolutionary Bolshevik Red Army, and supporting the remaining loyal Imperial forces, or "White Army".

Major Roderick Carr, whose remarkable exploits in Lithuania are also explored on page 44, commanded the Slavo–British No. 2 Squadron at Bereznik as part of the British North Russian Expeditionary Force. In 1919, he won a Distinguished Flying Cross (DFC) for action against the enemy. "On 17 June, 1919, this officer flew a scout machine over the enemy aerodrome at Puchega at an average height of only 50 feet, for 30 minutes," reads a citation in the *London Gazette*. "During this time he succeeded in setting fire to a Nieuport enemy machine, to a hangar which contained three aeroplanes (all of which were destroyed), drove all the personnel off the aerodrome, and killed some of the mechanics."

The actions of western forces soon escalated to a somewhat chaotic offensive against the Bolsheviks. Some suggested the plan included an undercover Royal Air Force squadron steaming through the heart of Russia with its aircraft strapped to railway cars on a mission to bomb Moscow! However, this was allegedly stopped by Churchill, who saw no advantage, and is discussed in the book *The Day They Almost Bombed Moscow: The Allied War in Russia 1918-1920* by Geoffrey Dobson and John Miller. It is suggested that one can trace the origins of much of today's East–West antagonism back to that vaguely remembered clash on the contested soil of Revolutionary Russia.

Although much of the equipment sent to Russia was essential in enabling the Imperial "Whites" to mount such campaigns as they did in 1919, only a few thousand allied troops ever set foot in Russia, and even fewer actually saw action. After the Armistice, most official allied efforts were directed towards managing a graceful retreat from Russia, rather than intervening more forcefully. However, this often meant demobbed allied veterans leaving under their own devices, rather than any official strategy.

In the Second World War, the RAF really did see action in Russia, flying Hurricanes in support of the Soviet forces during late 1941, this time enforcing Allies in the fight against Nazi Germany. Despite having agreed a peace treaty, Germany invaded Russia, having also signed a pact with Finland. In response to Operation Barbarosa, the invasion of Russia, a British expedition to the northern Russian port of Murmansk, close to the borders of

Norway and Finland, showed the Finns that offensive action against the Soviet Union would result in a confrontation with western Allies.

The RAF provided air support and quickly trained the Soviet pilots. After several months, and hundreds of operational sorties, they handed over the aircraft and returned to Britain along with four Order of Lenin medals and an Order of the Red Star. 81 Squadron received the battle honour "Russia, 1941".

A recent press article, written following the discovery of the forgotten Order of Lenin medal won by Wing Commander Ramsbottom-Isherwood, the leader of the British Expedition, colourfully describes life at that time. "On the very first day, the Russian hosts produced a welcoming breakfast that included champagne and brandy – delights that were not, however, to be repeated," he wrote. "The only complaints came from younger officers who found the daily menu of smoked salmon, caviar and cold ham a poor substitute for the bacon and eggs and sausages they were used to. The youngest occasionally complained: 'Oh, hell, here's that smoked salmon again'."

In 1944, the RAF carried out Operation Paravane – a bombing mission against the German battleship *Tirpitz* in a Norwegian fjord. The *Tirpitz*, the sister ship of the *Bismark*, was out of range from the UK, so Lancasters were staged from an airfield in Yagodnik, Russia before carrying out the attack. From the two squadrons, a single Tallboy bomb hit the ship and disabled her. She would be sunk a few weeks later.

221 SQUADRON IN PETROVSK, RUSSIA WITH DH9 BOMBERS, 1919

Beef Stroganoff

There are many variations of stroganoff around the world, some of which include chicken, white wine, tomato purée or even soy sauce. The original dates back to mid-19th century Russia (reputed to be named after a member of the influential Stroganov family) and consisted of sautéed diced beef in a sauce of mustard, stock and sour cream or "smetana". Stroganoff is traditionally served with fried potatoes although nowadays it is generally served with either rice or pasta. Here it is accompanied with lemon wedges and cornichons for a piquant note, and extra sour cream for added richness.

INGREDIENTS

Serves 4

For the stroganoff

600g beef fillet, cut into thin strips

2 tsp smoked paprika

2 tbsp olive oil

50g butter

200g shallots (or onions),
 finely diced

2 cloves of garlic, finely chopped

300g chestnut mushrooms,
 thickly sliced

4 tbsp brandy

150ml chicken stock

2 tsp dijon mustard

150ml double cream

150ml sour cream

½ lemon, juiced

2 tbsp parsley, chopped

salt and pepper

To serve

sauté potatoes, rice or pasta

8 small cornichons, sliced

75ml sour cream

½ lemon, cut into wedges

METHOD

To make the stroganoff

• Place the beef strips in a bowl, add the paprika, season well with salt and black pepper and mix to coat completely.

• Place a pan over a high heat, add half of the oil and half of the butter then, when foaming, add the beef and fry for 2 to 3 minutes until browned.

• Remove the beef from the pan, add the remaining butter and oil, and return the pan to a medium heat. Add the shallots and cook, stirring frequently, until soft and translucent.

• Add the garlic and mushrooms. Continue to cook for another 4 to 5 minutes.

• Turn the heat to high, deglaze the pan with the brandy, reduce by half, add the chicken stock and bring to a boil.

• Stir in the dijon mustard, the double cream and the seared beef and simmer gently for 5 minutes until thickened to a coating sauce consistency (add a little hot water if the sauce becomes too thick).

• Stir in the sour cream, lemon juice and half of the chopped parsley, season with salt and black pepper and gently heat through without boiling.

To serve

• Transfer the stroganoff to warmed plates or shallow bowls, garnish with the remaining chopped parsley and serve with sauté potatoes, rice or pasta, with the sliced cornichons, sour cream and lemon wedges on the side.

NORTH-WEST FRONTIER PROVINCE

Words by
FLIGHT LIEUTENANT CRISPIN CHAPPLE

LORD CURZON, VICEROY of India, established Waziristan in 1901 in a region that now overlaps present-day Pakistan and Afghanistan. His aim was to focus attention on the area after tribal uprisings resulting from the Durand Line, the common border between India and Afghanistan created in 1896. It was known as the North-West Frontier Province and, between 1916 and 1947, the Royal Flying Corps and subsequently the Royal Air Force established themselves there in order to help the British and Indian armies curtail tribal insurgency. It was during this period that many RAF doctrinal concepts we know today were first considered.

"Air power" as we know it became a recognised concept from 1919. Ground operations were often planned for good-weather periods so that air support would be possible. It quickly became the inexpensive and effective means by which to punish tribal outbursts with an almost instantaneous response. Intelligence was key and, along with wireless and telephone, the carrier pigeon came into its own, carried by army scouts. Using a combination of these means, and given their "Quick Reaction Alert", or QRA, status (armed and fuelled with a duty pilot at the highest readiness), aircraft could be airborne within 30 minutes of the first pigeon or message relay.

Typical missions involved reconnaissance, offensive action, resupplies, pamphlet drops to warn locals of impending attack and "reassurance" missions to isolated scouting posts. However, the extreme weather played a major part: mists, heavy cloud, sandstorms and strong convective currents all meant that the mountains were not to be taken lightly. Narrow valleys were negotiated with extreme skill, lest a catastrophic wing-tip strike occur. The requirement to be at low level also brought added danger, with tribesmen taking pot shots at passing planes. It became normal for returning aircraft to be filled with bullet holes: on occasion these became fatal, if not for the crews, certainly for the aircraft. Any straight pieces of road or flat areas of ground were frantically sought, not always successfully, for crash landings.

Even if a crew survived, its members often had to deal with angered tribesmen, and crews were often captured and killed. The government therefore started issuing personnel with "blood" or "goolie" chits (the latter so called as testicles were often brutally removed by hostile locals). These chits were promises of a reward to any captor should the bearer be returned alive.

It wasn't just operational issues that dogged the RAF. The government was averse to allocating resource and capital, which often left routine maintenance impossible and serviceability states low. Deployed aircraft often had outdated instructions that meant an aircraft's capability would never be fully understood or exploited. This left the British Army questioning the validity of what was still a rather new RAF. They saw the offensive nature of missions as brutal and indiscriminate and yearned for a return to planned ground movements.

Sir John Slessor, Marshall of the RAF, successfully countered this, ensuring that the RAF undertook carefully controlled missions. He saw the future and set the scene for the RAF to continue, not just until partition drove the British out in 1947, but to this day, making air power a key enabler in today's modern warfare.

Lamb Sajji
Peshawari Spiced Roast Lamb

Peshawar is the capital of the Pakistani province of Khyber Pakhtunkhwa (formerly the North-West Frontier Province). Lamb (or traditionally mutton) sajji is relatively simple to prepare but time must be taken to marinate the lamb to ensure it is succulent and tasty. It is eaten in Peshawar on special occasions with rice or naan breads, and is often served with pickles and chutneys. As the lamb needs time to marinate, it is best prepared the day before and left in the fridge overnight.

INGREDIENTS

Serves 4

To prepare the lamb

800g leg of lamb, boned

2 tsp salt

1 lemon

For the sajji masala

1 tbsp coriander seeds

1 tbsp cumin seeds

½ tsp green cardamom seeds
  (from around 12 pods)

1 tsp black peppercorns

1 tsp salt

¼ tsp ground nutmeg

For the marinade

3 cloves of garlic, finely chopped
  or crushed

150g plain yoghurt

sajji masala (see above)

**For the red onion and
tomato chutney**

½ medium red onion, finely
  diced

75g cherry tomatoes, quartered

1 tsp ground cumin

1 tbsp fresh coriander,
  coarsely chopped

METHOD

To prepare the lamb

- Open up and flatten out the lamb leg and prick all over with the point of a small sharp knife, rub the salt well into the lamb on both sides, squeeze the lemon juice all over the meat, rub in and place in a container. Cover and allow to marinate in the fridge for 1 hour.

To prepare the sajji masala

- Place a frying pan over a moderate heat. Add the coriander, cumin and cardamom seeds and the peppercorns, and dry fry until lightly toasted and aromatic.
- Place the toasted spices, salt and nutmeg in a mortar and grind to a coarse powder with a pestle. Alternatively use a spice grinder.

To marinate the lamb

- Mix the garlic, yoghurt and sajji masala in a bowl. Coat the lamb thoroughly with the marinade then roll it up and tie with string.
- Place the lamb in a container, cover, place in the fridge and leave to marinate for around 8 hours or overnight.

To make the red onion and tomato chutney

- Mix the diced onions, cherry tomatoes, ground cumin and chopped coriander together and season with salt and pepper.

To make the garlic dressing

- Mix the yoghurt with the garlic and lemon juice, and season with a little salt to taste.

To cook the lamb

- Preheat the oven to 200°C, place the sliced onions, carrots and potato

For the garlic dressing

100g natural yoghurt

2 cloves of garlic, finely chopped
  or crushed

½ lemon, juiced

To cook the lamb

2 onions, peeled and halved
  crossways

2 carrots, peeled and halved
  lengthways

1 baking potato, peeled and
  cut into 2.5cm slices

To serve

1 lemon, cut into wedges

rice and/or Peshawari naan

in a roasting tray and position the lamb on top of the vegetable trivet. Roast in the preheated oven for 20 minutes until the marinade has formed a golden crust and the vegetables have started to caramelise.

• Reduce the oven temperature to 160°C, pour around 2.5cm of boiling water into the roasting tray, cover the lamb with a piece of baking parchment and cover the roasting tray with foil. Return the lamb to the oven and continue to cook, basting regularly, for a further 45 minutes.

• Transfer the lamb to a plate with the onions and carrots, cover, and leave to rest for 15 minutes. Meanwhile, pour off the excess fat from the roasting tray and pass the cooking liquid and potatoes through a sieve (the potatoes with give the sauce a little body and added flavour).

• Pour any collected juices from the rested lamb into the sauce and bring to a simmer.

To serve

• Carve the lamb into slices, place on the roasted onions and carrots, pour over the roasting juices and serve with the lemon wedges, red onion and tomato chutney, garlic dressing, rice and/or naan bread.

LITHUANIA

Words by
SQUADRON LEADER (RETIRED) ROB SWINNEY

WHEN THE BALTIC states of Lithuania, Latvia and Estonia joined NATO in March 2004, the task of policing that airspace fell to NATO states. This was conducted on three- and later four-month rotation from Lithuania's First Air Force Base in Zokniai/Šiauliai International Airport, near the northern city of Šiauliai, and from 2014, from the Ämari Air Base in Harju County, Estonia. Usual deployments consisted of four fighter aircraft with around 100 support personnel, formed from 11 and 25 Squadrons from RAF Leeming, in support of four Tornado F3 fighters.

However, this was not the RAF's first time in Lithuania. Alongside Russia and

Estonia, it was embroiled in the chaotic mess that was the Baltic in the wake of the First World War. Previously, the area had been part of the Imperial Russian Empire but both Poland and Germany considered it part of their expanded territory. Indeed, the various populations were so mixed at the time that it's hard to imagine the cultural situation let alone the culinary aspects. For example, Vilna (now Vilnius) – the natural capital of the region – housed only a small percentage of indigenous Lithuanians.

When the Russian Revolution and the ensuing civil war broke out in 1917, Lithuania declared independence and tried to defend its borders. On one side they fought against the Poles, on another they fought alongside them against the Bolshevik Red Army at Dvinsk, with the Russian White Army. Elsewhere they fought with Slavo-Germans against other German factions, such as the German Iron Division, to name but a few of the minor conflicts.

Then, enter the British. Much of the official history is far from clear, but in 1919, a German Junkers F13 low-wing passenger monoplane – on a secret flight from Germany to Russia – came down in Lithuania and was subsequently confiscated. This caused a diplomatic row, as flying the Junkers outside Germany was breaking the Treaty of Versailles. As a result, German pilots were withdrawn from the region, and four RAF pilots were hired in their place.

One of these was a Major Roderick Carr, who became Commander of the

Lithuanian Air Unit for his short spell in the country. Carr was born in Feilding, New Zealand in 1891 and seems to have lived a life straight out of a Boy's Own adventure. He served as an airman in the British Royal Navy and the Royal Air Force during the Great War but then also participated in the Russian civil war, first in the RAF, but then as a member of the Lithuanian army.

Later, in 1921, Major Carr was a part of Sir Ernest Shackleton's final Antarctic expedition. He returned to the RAF in 1922 and, in 1927, he and a colleague, Flight Lieutenant L E M Gillmann, attempted to fly non-stop from RAF Cranwell to India. Unsuccessful in this endeavour, they were forced to ditch near Bandar Abbas, Iran, after running out of fuel. This flight gained them a very brief world record for flight distance, but Charles Lindbergh would beat this new record by over 125 miles within hours. Carr served throughout Second World War before retiring from service in 1947 having attained the rank of Air Marshal.

Major Carr and his colleagues in Lithuania were effectively seen as mercenaries, neither formally encouraged nor discouraged from the British military missions or the Foreign Office. However, it was soon decided that whatever the British had initially hoped to achieve in Lithuania was quickly deemed unsuccessful, or unnecessary, and the pilots eventually gracefully withdrew.

MEMBERS OF THE LITHUANIAN
AIR SERVICE IN KAUNAS,
LITHUANIA, CIRCA 1919

Balandėliai
Lithuanian Cabbage Rolls

Variations of savoury stuffed cabbage rolls are common across the Balkan countries, as well as Central, Northern and Eastern Europe. Balandėliai (which literally translates as "little doves") are the Lithuanian version of this dish in which the cabbage rolls, stuffed with seasoned pork and rice, are braised in a slightly piquant tomato sauce. Here they are topped with a spoonful of sour cream but this can be mixed into the tomato sauce instead, once the cabbage rolls have been cooked, for a creamier texture.

INGREDIENTS

Serves 4

For the cabbage rolls

1 savoy cabbage

50g long grain rice

1 tbsp vegetable oil

½ medium onion, finely diced

1 stick of celery, finely diced

2 cloves of garlic, finely chopped
 or crushed

400g pork mince

METHOD

To prepare the cabbage rolls

• Bring a large saucepan of salted water to a rolling boil.

• Cut away the stalk and core from the cabbage and remove the tough outer leaves. Pick eight of the largest leaves and blanch for 1 minute in the boiling water (take care not to overcook the cabbage leaves as they will tear when rolling around the filling). Refresh in iced water then pat dry on a tea towel or absorbent kitchen paper. Using a small sharp knife cut away the thickest part of the stalks in a "V" shape.

• Cook the rice in lightly salted boiling water for around 10 minutes until tender. Place in a colander and set aside to cool and drain. Do not

1½ tsp dried marjoram
1 tbsp parsley, coarsely chopped
salt and pepper

For the tomato sauce
1 tbsp vegetable oil
1 medium onion, finely diced
1 tbsp white wine vinegar
1 tsp tomato purée
1 tin (400g) of chopped tomatoes
1 tsp caster sugar
150ml water

To serve
4 tbsp sour cream
potatoes, boiled

refresh the rice under cold water as the starch helps to bind the filling.
- Heat the oil in a large frying pan over a moderate heat, add the onions and celery and cook, stirring frequently, for 5 minutes until softened and translucent. Add the garlic and cook for another couple of minutes. Drain off any excess oil, transfer to a clean container and set aside to cool.
- Thoroughly mix the pork mince with the cooked rice, marjoram, parsley and cooked onion, celery and garlic mix. Season with salt and pepper and shallow fry a small patty of the mixture in a little vegetable oil to test the seasoning. Add more salt and pepper as required.
- Divide the mixture into eight even portions and form each into a cylinder shape around 8cm long.
- Lay the cabbage leaves on the worktop with the stalk ends facing you, place a cylinder of the filling on the bottom edge of each cabbage leaf and, one by one, roll up each halfway, fold over the ends then continue to roll up the leaves.

To make the sauce
- Heat the oil in a saucepan over a moderate heat, add the onions and cook, stirring frequently, for 5 minutes until softened and translucent. Add the vinegar and allow to boil until most of the liquid has evaporated.
- Stir in the tomato purée, chopped tomatoes, caster sugar and water. Bring to a boil, reduce the heat, simmer for 5 minutes and season lightly with salt and freshly ground black pepper.
- Pass the sauce through a sieve (if preferred, leave the sauce as it is for a chunkier texture), discard the solids and transfer the sauce to a baking dish just large enough to contain the balandėliai in a single layer.

To cook the balandėliai
- Preheat the oven to 180°C
- Place the cabbage rolls on top of the sauce, seam side down, in a single layer, cover with a lid or aluminium foil and cook in the oven for 45 minutes until thoroughly cooked through.

To finish and serve
- Remove the cabbage rolls from the sauce and set to one side.
- Serve 2 balandėliai per portion on individual plates, ladle over the sauce, spoon over a little sour cream and serve with boiled potatoes.

ESTONIA

Words by
SQUADRON LEADER (RETIRED) ROB SWINNEY

WITH ESTONIA AND other Baltic states joining NATO after gaining independence following the collapse of the Soviet Union, there was soon a need to give practical support in the areas that these nations were lacking. In 2004, the UK took a leading role in policing the skies over the Baltic states as a part of the NATO Baltic Air Policing Mission, designed to deter threats and aggression from Russia.

Since 2014, RAF Typhoons have been on the Baltic Air Policing Mission at Amari Air Base, Estonia, in rotation with other nations. But this is not the first time that the RAF had operated from Estonia – its history their dates back to the Great War.

The situation in the Baltic after the war was chaotic. British campaigns stretched across the region and North Russia from 1917, and continued beyond Armistice Day. The Estonians, among others, were fighting for independence, while the Germans and pro-German nations were fighting for more influence and an increased realm in the east. In addition, following the collapse of the imperial Russian Empire, the Bolshevik Red Army was fighting just about everybody, including remnants of the Imperial Russian "White Army". Both, of course, wanted to take over the Baltic states, which were long considered Russian territory.

Initially, the British had been using their campaign to keep the Russians in the Great War, and to keep the Germans occupied on the Eastern Front. Later this expanded to supporting the Russian White Army against the Red Army and, not too overtly, to having influence on the independence of the Baltic States. At the time, it even seemed likely that the Communist Red Army might be defeated.

Into this sailed the aircraft carrier HMS *Vindictive* in July 1919, dispatched to the Baltic in support of the White Army and the newly independent Baltic states. Besides carrying out naval attacks on the Bolshevik-held port at Kronstadt, the *Vindictive* delivered aircraft and equipment that would remain in Estonia.

Thanks to Ray Sturtivant's *The Camel File*, which collects and records serial numbers and operational details, we know that "2F.1 Camel N6616 from HMS *Vindictive* arrived at Biorko (Estonia) on 20 July 1919 (believed given number "4"). It was flown only by RAF Captain Claude Emery, who was posted to the Aviation Company as Chief Instructor and served in Estonia until 31 December 1926."

In September 1919, eight DH9 aircraft arrived in Estonia for use as observation aircraft, bought from ex-RAF stocks by the provisional Estonian government. However, they were rarely used operationally and most reconnaissance missions were carried out by a DFW CV aircraft. In addition to the Camel and the DH9s, Avro 504s and Short 184s were British aircraft used by the Estonians. These new aircraft had only a minor effect on the war, flying some 25 operational sorties by just two pilots. At the time any formal support from the RAF in Estonia was very much a grey area, as it was with the other Baltic states.

From these Baltic campaigns, 107 Royal Navy personnel and five RAF personnel from HMS *Vindictive* lost their lives. They are commemorated by a memorial plaque unveiled in 2005 at Portsmouth Cathedral, with similar memorials in the Church of the Holy Ghost, Tallinn and in St Saviour's Church, Riga, now in Latvia.

Mulgikapsad
Pork Casserole with Sauerkraut & Barley

Mulgikapsad is a traditional all-in-one casserole or stew from southern Estonia. It is often eaten with a regional blood sausage called verivorst and accompanied with black sourdough rye bread or potatoes and sour cream or sometimes lingonberry preserve. This recipe is slow-cooked in a low oven but it can also be cooked, covered with a lid, on the stove over a very low heat.

INGREDIENTS

Serves 4

For the mulgikapsad

25g butter

1 medium onion, finely diced

2 cloves of garlic, finely chopped
  or crushed

800g sauerkraut

1 Granny Smith apple, peeled,
  cored and coarsely diced

1 tbsp soft brown sugar

200g thick-cut smoked bacon,
  cut into 2.5cm cubes

150g pearl barley, rinsed under
  cold water and drained

600g pork shoulder, rolled
  and tied

1 bay leaf

500ml chicken stock

salt and pepper

To serve

flat leaf parsley, finely chopped

potatoes, boiled

sour cream

METHOD

To make the mulgikapsad

• Preheat the oven to 150°C.

• Heat the butter in a casserole over a medium heat, add the onion and cook, stirring frequently, for 5 minutes until softened and translucent. Add the chopped garlic, continue to cook for a further 2 minutes then stir in the sauerkraut.

• Scatter the apples over the top of the sauerkraut and sprinkle over the brown sugar, diced bacon and pearl barley.

• Lightly season the pork with salt and plenty of black pepper, make a well in the sauerkraut and place the rolled pork joint in the well. Add the bay leaf and pour over the hot chicken stock. If the ingredients aren't immersed in the stock add enough boiling water to cover.

• Cover the casserole with a lid, place in the oven and cook for 3 hours until the pork is very tender and the pearl barley has swollen with absorbed liquid. Check occasionally and top up with a little boiling water if necessary.

To serve

• Remove the pork and give the casserole a good stir.

• Carve the pork shoulder into thick slices and ladle the casserole onto plates or into bowls.

• Arrange the sliced pork on top of the casserole and serve with boiled potatoes tossed in chopped parsley and garnish with a spoonful of sour cream and chopped parsley.

SOMALIA

Words by
FLIGHT LIEUTENANT VICTORIA SISSON

THE INTER-WAR YEARS were a time when the Royal Air Force was fighting to justify its existence. This led Chief of Air Staff Hugh Trenchard, known as the "father of the RAF", to accept many challenges and opportunities to illustrate that his newly created service deserved to remain independent. He wanted to prove that air power could be applied successfully in situations that would have historically seen the use of conventional land forces and that deploying the RAF was a more cost efficient and effective choice. One such example was the deployment of the RAF to British Somaliland in 1920.

Mohammed bin Abdullah Hassan, more commonly known as the "Mad Mullah", had achieved prominence in 1895 when he led a rebellion against British forces. The UK had taken on protectorate responsibility

> ## *"Trenchard wanted to prove that air power could be applied in situations that would have historically seen the use of land forces"*

of British Somaliland in 1898, with overall responsibility being transferred to the Colonial Office in 1905.

For years, the British Army had struggled to contain the Mad Mullah's forces and failed to come to a decisive victory. Between 1914 and 1918, the Mad Mullah strengthened his grip on British Somaliland, building fortresses that dominated the roadways and training armed gangs. By 1919, Prime Minister Lloyd George had a tough decision to make: abandon British Somaliland to the rule of the Mullah, or mount a large and costly expedition that was sure to see hundreds of soldiers' lives lost.

Trenchard had the answer. "Why not leave the whole thing to the RAF?" He insisted that this would negate the need for any ground troops further than those already deployed. He called his special RAF force the Z Force and he trained them to be completely self-sufficient. It comprised 12 De Havilland bombers, 36 officers and 183 airmen. They left Britain in October and November 1919 and, upon arrival in Egypt in December, embarked on their journey to Berbera harbour where they arrived on 30 December.

By mid January eight of the aircraft were ready and were flown to Eil Dur Elan, the advanced base. The first raid was flown on "Zero Day", 21 January 1920, and resulted in direct bombing hits – one of which killed the Mullah's uncle and chief councillor, who was stood beside him, and singed the Mullah's clothes.

The following days saw a campaign of reconnaissance flights followed up by bombing raids. By 18 February, the raids were completed, the Mullah defeated and his influence quashed. The RAF suffered no fatalities, although eight men had to be evacuated by air to hospital facilities in Berbara, which took mere hours, in contrast to the usual road trip, which took days. The mission had been completed with months to spare before the re-embarkation for home, which came in April.

The entire campaign cost £77,000 and was hailed at the time as the cheapest war in history; a resounding success for Trenchard in his fight to secure the future of his Royal Air Force. The theory that Trenchard applied to cement this success went on to become the basis for "Air Control" and would be applied in many conflicts to come.

Kaluun iyo Bariis
Fried Fish & Rice

Somalia has developed a cuisine that is a fusion of many influences including its neighbouring countries as well as India, Arabia and Italy (a legacy of the Italian occupation that lasted until the early 1940s). This recipe is a refined version of a traditional fried fish stew made with tomatoes and tamarind, with the latter providing a pleasant sour note to the overall flavour of the dish. In Somalia either red snapper or king fish would be used, but sea bream works wonderfully with the spicy flavours and tamarind.

INGREDIENTS

Serves 4

For the seasoned flour

75g plain flour

2 tsp ground cumin

1 tsp ground cardamom seeds

1 tsp salt

½ tsp ground cloves

½ tsp black pepper

For the sauce

2 tbsp sunflower or vegetable oil

1 medium onion, finely diced

2 garlic cloves, finely chopped

1 red chilli, finely sliced

1 tbsp tomato purée

1 tbsp tamarind paste

2 ripe medium tomatoes, finely diced

50g fresh coriander, chopped

½ lemon, juiced

For the fish and aubergine

125ml sunflower or vegetable oil

8 sea bream fillets or 4 whole fish with the fins removed

1 aubergine, cut into 1cm-thick slices

To serve

½ lemon, cut into wedges

basmati rice

METHOD

To make the sauce

- Heat the oil in a saucepan over a moderate heat, add the onions and cook for around 5 minutes, stirring frequently, until they start to soften.
- Add the garlic and chilli and continue to cook for another couple of minutes. Stir in the tomato purée, tamarind paste and chopped tomatoes, add 200ml boiling water and simmer for 5 minutes.
- Season with salt and pepper, stir in half of the chopped coriander, continue to simmer for another minute then finish with the lemon juice just before serving.

To cook the fish and aubergine

- While the sauce is cooking, heat half of the oil in a frying pan over a moderate heat.
- Coat the fish fillets (or whole fish) with the seasoned flour (keep the remaining seasoned flour for the aubergine), tap off the excess and shallow fry, skin side down for 4 to 5 minutes. Turn the fish over and continue to cook for a further minute. If using whole fish, once well coloured on both sides, transfer to a baking sheet and finish cooking in a hot oven for 5 minutes.
- Remove the fish from the pan and keep warm.
- While the fish is cooking, heat the rest of the oil over a moderate heat in a frying pan, dust the aubergine slices with the seasoned flour and cook until golden brown on both sides.

To serve

- Place the aubergine slices on warmed plates, top with two fish fillets per person, ladle over the sauce, garnish with the remaining chopped coriander and serve with basmati rice.

IRAQ

Words by
**AIR COMMODORE MARK GILLIGAN
& FLIGHT LIEUTENANT CHLOE BRIDGE**

A VICKERS VERNON AND A ROLLS-ROYCE ARMOURED CAR IN IRAQ, CIRCA 1923

FOLLOWING THE FIRST World War, the tutelage of territories formerly governed by defeated nations was entrusted to Allied powers, under the League of Nations' mandate. The defence and administration of the resulting new parts of the British Empire – including Palestine, Transjordan and Mesopotamia – presented a challenge to a UK government in a period of post-war retrenchment. However, the Royal Air Force's success in quelling unrest in Somaliland and in suppressing an Iraqi revolt in 1920 offered politicians a cost-effective alternative to the use of large numbers of troops and the casualties associated therewith. So, in October 1922, the government gave the RAF full command of British Forces in Mesopotamia (Iraq).

Unrest continued in the early 1920s, with the fledgling third service performing close air support, reconnaissance, leaflet dropping and attack roles in a campaign to dispel Kurdish separatism and threats from Turkish territorial ambitions. The campaign saw the first troop lift, with Vickers Vernons carrying reinforcements for an under-seige Kirkuk. At a time when the RAF was striving to retain and develop its identity, it cemented its utility in counter insurgency and border protection through speed, reach and ubiquity, at minimal cost.

From 1921, to overcome communication challenges, the RAF began delivering air mail between Cairo and Baghdad. The route covered vast tracts of desert, with navigation especially difficult between Amman and Baghdad. To assist, road convoys were dispatched from each location, escorted by 47 and 30 Squadrons, to define a path. Shortly after, the first aircraft made the long crossing from Iraq to Egypt. The Desert Air Mail service had begun, and though it would carry only 700 lbs of mail in its first year, correspondence was to reach troops in Iraq within five days of being sent from London. The RAF improved the service throughout the 1920s, eventually handing over to the British air transport company Imperial Airways in 1927.

Klecha
Iraqi Spiced Date & Walnut Cookies

These sticky date and nut cookies are traditionally served at holiday celebrations, especially during Eid al-Fitr, which marks the end of Ramadan. There are many variations to the fillings and they are often served with Iraqi tea (Assam or Ceylon black tea, flavoured with a cinnamon stick or a few cardamom pods, sweetened and diluted to taste) or coffee.

INGREDIENTS

Makes 20

For the dough

325g plain flour

I sachet (7g) fast-acting yeast

1 tbsp caster sugar

½ tsp ground cinnamon

¼ tsp ground allspice

1 tsp salt

100g butter, melted

175ml warm milk

For the filling

100g walnuts, chopped

250g pitted dates, coarsely
  chopped

25g butter

125ml water

½ tsp ground cinnamon

¼ tsp ground cardamom

¼ tsp ground nutmeg

1 tsp fennel seeds

To glaze

1 egg, beaten

2 tbsp sesame seeds (optional)

METHOD

To make the dough

- Sift the flour into a mixing bowl, add the yeast, sugar, ground spices and salt. Mix well.
- Add the melted butter and warm milk, mix well, turn out onto a floured work surface and knead, adding a little more flour or warm water as necessary, to form a smooth dough.
- Transfer the dough to a lightly oiled bowl and leave to prove for 2 hours at room temperature.

To make the filling

- Put the walnuts into a food processor and blend until they resemble coarse breadcrumbs.
- Place the dates, butter, water, ground spices and fennel seeds in a saucepan. Place over a low heat, simmer for 15 minutes, stirring frequently, until sticky and the water has evaporated. Mix in the chopped walnuts and set aside to cool.

To make the klecha

- Line the work surface with cling film, form the date mixture into a sausage shape, place on top of the cling film and, with damp hands, gently flatten the mixture into a rectangular shape. Place another piece of cling film on top and, using a rolling pin, roll the date filling to a thin rectangular sheet around 38cm long by 24cm wide.
- Gently knock back the dough, lightly dust the work surface with flour and roll out slightly wider (around 4cm wider) than the filling, but the same length. It should be no thicker than 5mm.
- Remove the top piece of cling film from the filling. Lift up the bottom piece of cling film and carefully place, filling side down, in the middle of the dough and peel off the cling film. Cut down the centre, through the filling and dough to form two long thin rectangles.
- Roll up each rectangle of dough starting at the cut edge (so the

filling forms a spiral) into a cylinder and neaten each with lightly floured hands. Each roll should be around 3cm in diameter. Flatten each cylinder slightly with the palm of your hand and cut into lengths around 4cm thick – you should get around 10 from each flattened cylinder.
• Lightly butter a baking sheet (or line with a sheet of baking parchment) and place the klecha around 2.5cm apart, brush with the beaten egg and sprinkle over the sesame seeds (if using).
• Leave at room temperature for 30 minutes to start the proving process (the klecha will continue to rise during the first 10 minutes in the oven).

To cook the klecha
• Preheat the oven to 180°C.
• Place in the oven and bake for 15 to 20 minutes until slightly risen and golden brown on top.
• Transfer to a wire rack to cool, then store in an airtight container.

NIGERIA

Words by
FLIGHT LIEUTENANT VICTORIA SISSON

BY 1925 THERE was growing interest in opening up the African continent for aviation. This was already being explored by both the French and the Belgians in their territories, and Britain needed to follow suit. It was decided that 47 Squadron, stationed at Helwan, near Cairo, would fly three DeHavilland DH9s to Kano, Nigeria. The objectives of this were twofold: to gain experience of flying in tropical countries, which were generally ill equipped to support aircraft on the ground; but more importantly to showcase the Royal Air Force's capabilities to the Nigerians.

The expedition was led by Squadron Leader Arthur Coningham, later to become Air Marshall Coningham. There were considerable obstacles to overcome, not least of which was navigation. Although wireless telegraphy stations were sparsely spread out along the route, the DH9s did not have any transmitting or receiving equipment. This meant that the expedition had to rely on maps of questionable accuracy and hand-held compasses. Coningham also had to overcome the poor reliability of the reconditioned American "Liberty" engines, choosing to run them at 400hp and reducing the aircraft's cruising speed from 90mph to only 80mph as a result.

The expedition began on 27 October 1925, but the trip was fraught with mishaps. The aircraft were initially tail heavy so, due to the heavier forces on the control column, the pilots soon got very sore in their arms and chests, particularly after the first (and longest) leg to Wadi Halfa in Sudan. En route to Al Fashar, confusion caused by an unmapped mountain range meant that the aircraft landed with only moments to spare before running out of fuel. The aircraft were refuelled by the soldiers of the garrison, assisted by officers who cancelled their polo match to help. Fires lit along the route to smoke out game caused poor visibility and worries of aircraft fires, and some stretches were only navigable due to a camel track used by pilgrims to Mecca.

When the aircraft finally reached Nigeria on 1 November there were crowds lining the main road from Maidugari to Kano, which had been gathered since dawn, watching the sky in anticipation. As they landed, the crews wanting to apologise for having kept people waiting, all three aircraft got stuck in the soft earth of the landing strip and had to be towed by engine and man-power onto the harder ground of a polo pitch. This alone caused more damage to the engines than would be done by flying the entire route. The final stretch was flown to get the aircraft to Kano that afternoon, and they landed on a polo pitch there at 5pm, having covered over 3,000 miles. More than 20,000 people gathered to see them.

From there onwards they visited Kaduna, where the welcoming party wore full ceremonial dress. They took the Sergeant Major of the police for a flight. "Once in the air, he sang at the top of his voice until we landed," said Coningham. Flying next back to Maifugari, they were presented to the Emir of Bornu, who presented Coningham with two enormous white rams. Coningham could barely disguise his excitement, which was enhanced by his knowledge that the resident staff would have to hide them for a long time after his departure. The trip achieved the first east–west crossing of Africa by air and was the first aircraft to land in Nigeria.

Jollof Rice with Chicken
Nigerian Rice with Tomato Stew

Jollof rice are common across West Africa. This Nigerian version is made by cooking the rice with a tomato stew and a lightly spiced stock in which the chicken has first been poached. Generally, the chicken, once poached, is simply grilled or roasted and served with the rice.

INGREDIENTS

Serves 4

For the chicken

1 litre chicken stock

1 medium onion, roughly chopped

2 tsp curry powder

1 tsp ground ginger

1 tsp smoked paprika

½ tsp ground nutmeg

4 chicken legs, divided into thighs
  and drumsticks

For the tomato stew

1 tbsp sunflower or vegetable oil

2 small red onions, finely diced

1 red pepper, de-seeded and
  finely diced

2 cloves of garlic, finely chopped

½ or 1 scotch bonnet (or red chilli),
  finely chopped

3 tbsp tomato purée

1 tin (400g) of chopped plum
  tomatoes

salt and pepper

For the rice

3 tbsp sunflower or vegetable oil

500g easy cook long grain rice

2 large sprigs of thyme

2 bay leaves

To serve (optional)

1 fennel, halved and very thinly sliced

mixed green leaves (e.g. rocket,
  watercress, baby spinach)

½ lemon

1 tbsp olive oil

METHOD

To prepare the chicken

- Pour the chicken stock into a saucepan. Add the chopped onion, stir in the curry powder, ginger, paprika and nutmeg and bring to a boil.
- Add the chicken pieces, reduce the heat and simmer for 10 minutes.
- Remove the chicken pieces and strain the stock into a clean container.
- Place the chicken onto a baking sheet and air dry at room temperature.

To make the tomato stew

- Heat the oil in a frying pan over a moderate heat. Add the red onions and cook, stirring frequently, until soft and translucent.
- Add the red pepper, garlic and chillies. Cook for a further 2 minutes.
- Stir in the tomato purée and chopped tomatoes, season with salt and freshly ground black pepper, bring to a boil, turn the heat to low and simmer gently for around 10 minutes, reducing until the sauce is thick.

To prepare the rice

- Preheat the oven to 200°C.
- Measure the reserved stock, make up to 1 litre with water, place in a saucepan and bring to a simmer.
- Heat the oil in a casserole on a medium heat and, when hot, add the rice. Fry for a couple of minutes, stirring continuously, until the rice is coated in oil and has a slightly nutty smell (it shouldn't take on any colour).
- Add the simmering stock, thyme and bay leaves. Stir in the tomato stew, bring to a boil, season with salt and pepper and remove from the heat.

To cook the rice and chicken

- Cover the surface of the rice with a lightly oiled piece of baking parchment or greaseproof paper then cover the casserole with a lid and place in the preheated oven.
- Drizzle a little vegetable oil over the chicken pieces. Season with salt and pepper. Once the rice has been in the oven for 10 minutes place the chicken pieces on the top shelf of the oven to finish cooking for 15 minutes (finish under a hot grill to crisp up the skin if necessary).
- When the rice has been in the oven for 25 minutes (it should be cooked through with a slight bite) take it out and allow it to rest for 5 minutes at room temperature before stirring with a fork to separate the grains. Check the seasoning and remove the thyme stalks and bay leaves.

To serve

- Toss the fennel with the mixed green leaves, lemon juice and olive oil.
- Serve the jollof rice with the baked chicken and the fennel salad.

AFGHANISTAN

Words by
SQUADRON LEADER MAL CRAIG

THINK OF CONFLICT in Afghanistan and you'll inevitably think of recent battles against the Taliban and Al Qaeda. However, look further back through history and you will find that the Royal Air Force has a long and distinguished history of action in that distant and mountainous country.

In 1927, King Amanullah Khan and his Syrian-born wife Queen Soraya Tarzi returned from an extended tour of European capitals. Impressed with what he had seen, the king was keen to impose religious and electoral reform upon Afghanistan, as well as introduce a western-style democracy. However, his reforms were not met with great enthusiasm by the rebellious hill tribesmen who, under the leadership of Habibullah Kalakani, rose up against him. They ultimately laid siege to the capital, Kabul, including the British Legation, located just to the west of city.

Besieged and under pressure, the British Envoy, Sir Francis Humphreys – himself a veteran RAF pilot, made a final wireless transmission to British India on 16 December 1927 requesting the evacuation of women and children to safety. What followed became the first aerial evacuation of non-combatants from danger and the first of many that the RAF would conduct throughout its history.

Within days, the first 27 Squadron aircraft, a DH.9A piloted by Flying Officer Claude Trusk, overflew the Legation and attempted to re-establish communications. With his aircraft damaged by ground fire, he was forced to land at a nearby airfield and complete his mission on foot. Trusk would later be awarded the Air Force Cross for his actions.

With communications re-established, though intermittent, the first of a long stream of aircraft arrived on 26 December 1927 to begin the evacuation of over 300 non-combatant women and children. These aircraft conducted the evacuation until finally, with the Legation under fire, the last aircraft left Kabul to the rebels on 25 February 1928. Sir Humphreys stepped aboard and evacuated to Peshawar, his Union Flag tucked neatly under his arm and wife Gertie by his side. He gave a final glance over his shoulder at Kabul, which was engulfed in flames.

In total, 586 people were lifted to safety by the RAF without loss of life and only the loss of a single aircraft. With the air temperature dropping to -19°C, a Vickers Victoria aircraft, piloted by Flight Lieutenant Ronald Ivelaw-Chapman (Later Air Vice Marshall Sir Ronald Ivelaw-Chapman), lost all power when its air, water and petrol filters all froze. After force landing his aircraft the young Ivelaw-Chapman and his crew were immediately surrounded by wildly excitable and heavily armed Afghans. It was only the intervention of a royalist officer and the unlikely provision of a Chevrolet car to whisk them to the safety of the British Consulate near Charbagh that left Ivelaw-Chapman with a tale to tell and an Air Force Cross for his efforts.

The RAF's ability to conduct non-combatant evacuations such as this first one in Afghanistan would go on to be repeated in every decade that followed, throughout the world. Almost 80 years later, 27 Squadron would again see action in the region when it deployed its Chinook helicopters in the medical evacuation role, echoing that first mission. It demonstrated that air power is not always destructive but can provide a vital safety net to non-combatants in danger and times of crisis.

Qabili Palau
Braised Rice with Chicken

Afghan cuisine is a blend of Asian and Middle Eastern influences and relies heavily on its main crops (including maize, rice, wheat, tomatoes, potatoes, onions and garlic) along with nuts and fresh and dried fruits. The national dish of Afghanistan, Qabili palau, is a mixture of rice, onions and meat (usually lamb or chicken), garnished with carrots, raisins and nuts. It is often the centrepiece of the Dastarkhan, the traditional Afghan floor spread.

INGREDIENTS

Serves 4

For the braised rice

400g basmati or long grain rice

4 tbsp ghee (or olive oil)

1 medium onion, halved and
  finely diced

8 chicken thighs, boned, skinned
  and halved

½ tsp ground cumin

½ tsp garam masala

¼ tsp ground cinnamon

8 cloves

6 cardamom pods (or ¼ tsp
  ground cardamom)

500ml chicken stock

1 pinch saffron strands (optional)

salt and pepper

For the garnish

100g raisins

1 pinch saffron strands (optional)

2 tbsp olive oil

50g blanched almonds

50g pistachio kernels

½ tsp cumin seeds

2 medium carrots, cut into long
  strips with a vegetable peeler

1 tsp caster sugar

To serve

2 tbsp coriander, coarsely chopped

1 tsp garam masala

4 naan breads

METHOD

To prepare the braised rice

- Wash the rice in running cold water until the water runs clear.
- Place the rice in a saucepan, cover with boiling water and simmer for 5 minutes. To blanch, rinse under cold water and drain.
- Heat the ghee or oil in a casserole over a medium heat, add the onions and cook, stirring frequently, for around 10 minutes until the onions have started to caramelise.
- Add the chicken thighs, season with salt and pepper. Cook, stirring frequently, until coloured all over. Transfer the chicken thighs to a plate and set to one side.
- Add the ground cumin, garam masala, ground cinnamon, whole cloves and cardamom pods to the casserole and continue to cook for a further couple of minutes until fragrant.
- Add the chicken stock and saffron, season lightly, bring to a boil, reduce the heat and simmer for 5 minutes. Meanwhile, preheat the oven to 180°C.
- Return the stock to a boil, add the blanched rice, season if required and stir well.
- Layer the seared chicken on top of the rice, cover with a lid or aluminium foil and cook in the oven for around 20 minutes until the rice is tender and the chicken is thoroughly cooked through.

To prepare the garnish

- Place the raisins in a saucepan with the saffron strands, add enough boiling water to barely cover the raisins and simmer for 5 minutes until the raisins have swelled up. Drain, reserve the liquid and keep warm.
- Heat the olive oil in a large frying pan over a moderate heat, add the almonds, pistachios and cumin seeds. Sauté for a couple of minutes until lightly browned, taking care not to burn the nuts.
- Add the carrots, sugar and drained raisins and continue to sauté for a further minute. Drain off the excess oil and keep the garnish warm.

To serve

- Place the cooked chicken pieces on the bottom of a serving dish, stir the braised rice to mix well and spoon over the chicken. Pour over the reserved hot raisin liquor, garnish with the carrots, nuts and raisins and sprinkle over a little garam masala.
- Scatter the chopped coriander on top and serve with the warmed naan breads.

OMAN

Words by
FLIGHT LIEUTENANT (RETIRED) ART LESTER

BRITAIN AND OMAN first shared formal relations with a Treaty of Friendship in 1798. The country, then known as the Sultanate of Oman and Muscat, was a British Protectorate for six decades, from 1891 until its independence in 1951.

From the 1930s, the Royal Air Force had a presence at five bases in Oman, supporting the Sultan with air-control operations. One of these bases, Masirah Island, was originally a refuelling stop for flying boats. In the 1950s, the fuel was delivered by tramp steamer: barrels – each weighing more than 300lb – were pushed over the side, lashed together, pushed to the shore and lifted onto a train for further transport. This "mandraulic" effort required the assistance of local labourers, who were brought across from the mainland for the purpose.

Masirah Island and an operating base at Salalah were used to support the SAS during the 14-year "Dhofar Rebellion", between 1962 and 1976. On 19 July 1972, a team of nine SAS men were surrounded by 250 insurgents at an outpost near Mirbat and attacked in the early morning. Though the SAS men fought skilfully and bravely, they were at serious risk of being overwhelmed. Two RAF Strikemaster jets were sent to their aid, and using instructions radioed from the ground, they made multiple strafing attacks and dropped 500lb bombs as close as 60 yards away from friendly forces. This action saved the day, although the battle and the wider conflict were rarely reported at the time.

Like many RAF bases in the Middle East, the operating conditions in Oman were often austere, remote and lacked communications. Long periods of steady activity were interrupted by the urgent need to respond to uprisings and raids by communist-inspired rebels and dissident tribal groups.

More recently, the RAF has operated out of Mussaneh, Muscat, Thumrait, Seeb and Salalah air bases, supporting operations in Iraq and Afghanistan and in the wider Gulf region, and assisting the security patrols around the highly contested Straits of Hormuz. RAF personnel and equipment formed the nucleus of the Sultan of Muscat and Oman's Air Force when it was formed in 1959. Renamed the Royal Air Force of Oman in 1990, it has grown into one of the most capable air forces in the region.

The RAF Museum at Hendon opened an exhibition in 2014 to mark the continued friendship and partnership between the two air forces. Like so many other countries, Oman helped Britain during the Second World War in many ways, not least through the purchase of Spitfires that were flown by the RAF. The two countries have continued to develop strong links based on mutual respect and friendship. The two air forces continue to share a common bond and still regularly train together in the "Magic Carpet" series of annual exercises.

VICKERS VINCENTS OF 84 SQUADRON AT KHORGHARIM, OMAN, CIRCA 1935

Thareed
Braised Beef with Flatbread

Thareed is a popular dish often eaten at Iftar, the evening meal taken during Ramadan when Muslims break their fast once the sun has set. Thareed is a hearty meal in itself, frequently eaten communally, comprising meat, vegetables, potatoes and bread that softens to a pulpy consistency as it absorbs the sauce. This recipe includes courgette, but diced butternut squash or pumpkin can be used as a substitute.

INGREDIENTS

Serves 4

For the bizar a'shuwa (Omani spice blend)

2 tsp ground coriander

1½ tsp ground cumin

½ tsp turmeric

METHOD

To make the bizar a'shuwa

• Mix all of the spices and store in an airtight container until required.

To make the braised beef

• Place the diced beef in a saucepan, completely cover with the beef stock and bring to a boil over a high heat.

¼ tsp ground cinnamon

¼ tsp ground ginger

¼ tsp ground black pepper

⅛ tsp ground cloves

For the beef

500g beef, cut into large chunks

1 litre beef stock

2 tbsp olive oil

1 medium onion, finely diced

3 cloves of garlic, finely chopped
  or crushed

2.5cm piece of ginger, finely
  chopped or grated

1 large green chilli, finely chopped

¼ tsp cayenne pepper (more or
  less according to taste)

6 cardamom pods, crushed with
  the flat of a knife

1 tbsp tomato purée

2 medium tomatoes, coarsely
  chopped

1 large (200g) waxy potato,
  coarsely chopped

1 medium carrot, coarsely chopped

1 courgette, cut into large dice

2 tbsp coriander, coarsely chopped

1 tbsp mint, shredded

salt

To serve

4 thin flatbreads (e.g. chapati or
  pittas), torn or cut into pieces

1 lemon, cut into wedges

- Reduce the heat to low and simmer for 1½ hours, skimming
  regularly and topping up with boiling water to cover as required.
- Strain and reserve the stock from the beef and set the beef to
  one side.
- Heat the olive oil in a casserole or large saucepan over a medium heat,
  add the onion and cook, stirring frequently, for 10 minutes until soft
  and lightly browned.
- Add the garlic, ginger and chopped chilli, continue to cook for 1 minute
  then add the bizar a'shuwa spice mix, cayenne pepper and cardamom
  pods. Continue to cook for a further 2 minutes, stirring continuously to
  prevent the spices from sticking to the bottom of the pan.
- Add the tomato purée and diced tomatoes and continue to cook until
  the tomatoes have released their juices, then add the diced potatoes,
  carrot and cooked beef. Stir well until thoroughly mixed.
- Stir in the reserved stock, season with a little salt as required, bring
  to a boil then simmer for around 20 to 30 minutes, topping up with
  boiling water if required to keep the beef and potatoes covered with
  the sauce, until the potatoes are just tender.
- Stir in the courgette and continue to simmer for around 5 minutes
  until the courgette is soft but still retains its shape and has a
  slight bite.
- Stir in the chopped coriander and mint, reserving a little for
  the garnish.

To serve
- Line the bottom of the serving dishes with the torn bread.
- Ladle over the thareed and garnish with the remaining chopped
  herbs and wedges of lemon.

TANZANIA

Words by
FLIGHT LIEUTENANT VICTORIA SISSON

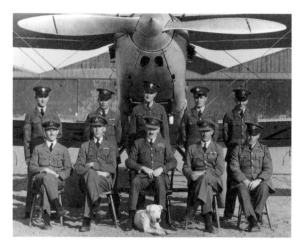

THE EAST AFRICAN FLIGHT CREW VISITED TANGANYIKA IN 1932

IN THE INTER-WAR years, several campaigns were carried out by the RAF in order to display the significant amount of defensive potential offered by air power. One such campaign, led by Arthur "Bomber" Harris himself, took place in Tanzania in March 1932. The country, known then as Tanganyika, was under the imperial defence of the King's African Rifles. The proposal of the RAF's founder, Lord Trenchard, was that a mobile air defence system should be set up, which would link the air routes between Tanganyika, Uganda, Kenya and Nyasaland (now part of Malawi). These would not only allow for the disbanding of the King's Royal Rifles, a total of six battalions, but would also offer a plethora of other benefits including air ambulance cover and cartographic reconnaissance.

In order to convince the native administration that utilising air power was the way forward, and impress them with the great potential air power could offer in a defensive role, a number of aircraft visited countries including Tanganyika. In each of these countries, a five-minute air display of "air drill" was completed; designed to awe the local administrations. Great care had to be taken to ensure that the aircraft arrived for these displays on time, as previous poor time-keeping by Imperial Airways had left a very bad impression, and Bomber Harris was keen to overcome this.

The Governor of Tanganyika, Sir George Symes, was no stranger to the potential of this air policing, having seen the benefits for himself while previously serving as the Resident of Aden. The Civil Secretary of Tanganyika, Douglas Jardine, however, was not so easily convinced. He was an unusual man and Bomber Harris described him as: "Very anti-air. The author of an anti-air book about the Mad Mullah show." One complaint that had not been anticipated by Harris was made by the Society for the Preservation of the Fauna of the Empire. They complained that the low-flying aircraft were causing game to stampede.

Fortunately for the Air Ministry, the scales were tipped in its favour by the Officer Commanding of the Kenyan Defence Force, Brigadier-General A C Lewin. He was a pilot himself and told Harris that he looked forward to "the day when the RAF take over the whole bag of tricks".

Two years after the RAF visited Tanganyika, in March 1934, the Norman-Newell proposal was released, recommending that two battalions of the Kings Royal Rifles be disbanded and replaced by an RAF squadron. In December of that year, Italy began its invasion of Abyssinia, transforming the situation in East Africa forever. The premise of the scheme for air control had been a stable international environment. With the collapse of this environment, the British will to save money in the East African territories suddenly fell to a lower priority, and the threat of war with Italy became a greater concern. The Norman-Newell proposals were indefinitely shelved and the Air Ministry did not gain control over East Africa.

Nyama Choma with Kachumbari
Barbecued Meat with Tomato & Onion Salad

In essence, nyama choma, literally "grilled meat" in Swahili, is any meat (originally goat) cooked over an open flame, a method that's hugely popular across East and Central Africa. The simple spiced marinade gives the meat a wonderful flavour when cooked on a barbecue (or a searing hot griddle pan) and the fresh salad (with lime and fresh coriander) is a perfect accompaniment. The meat needs time to marinate, so ideally start the preparation a day in advance.

INGREDIENTS

Serves 8

For the nyama choma

2kg meat or fish (e.g. steaks, jointed chicken, goat, whole fish, kebabs or whole joints such as butterflied shoulder of lamb)

4 tbsp vegetable oil

4 cloves of garlic, finely chopped

2.5cm piece of ginger, grated

2 lemons, juiced

4 tbsp ground coriander

2 tbsp ground cumin

2 tbsp paprika

1 tbsp turmeric

1 tbsp salt

2 tsp freshly ground black pepper

For the kachumbari

400g tomatoes

1 medium red onion, halved and thinly sliced

½ cucumber, halved lengthways, seeds removed and thinly sliced

1 carrot, grated or pared into strips with a vegetable peeler

1 tsp salt

2 tbsp olive oil

1 lime, half juiced and half cut into 4 wedges

2 tbsp coriander, coarsely chopped

METHOD

To make the nyama choma

- If using whole joints prick the meat all over with the point of a small sharp knife (this will allow the marinade to penetrate into the flesh).
- Mix the vegetable oil with the garlic, ginger, lemon juice, ground spices, salt and pepper to a thick paste.
- Rub the marinade into the meat, cover and allow to marinate in the fridge for 6 to 8 hours or overnight.
- Scrape off and reserve the excess marinade and sear the meat quickly over very hot barbecue coals until almost blackened then either move to a cooler part of the barbecue (basting the meat with the reserved marinade during cooking) or wrap in foil to finish cooking through. Alternatively, for large joints slow cook, covered with aluminium foil, in a low oven at 150°C until very tender then finish off on the barbecue to char the outside of the meat before resting and carving.

To make the kachumbari

- Cut the tomatoes in half, remove the seeds and cut into thin wedges.
- Put the tomatoes into a bowl with the onions, cucumber, carrot, salt, olive oil and lime juice. Mix well, cover and set aside for 20 minutes before mixing in the coriander.

To serve

- Serve the barbecued meat with the kachumbari salad.

ALGERIA

Words by
FLIGHT LIEUTENANT VICTORIA SISSON

IN 1937, TENSIONS were high in the Mediterranean. With the Spanish Civil War raging, submarine attacks were a constant problem and British ships were being sunk without warning. Britain and France were becoming increasingly concerned as the summer progressed, which led to a conference led by the two nations at Nyon, Switzerland. The end result was the signing of the Nyon Agreement, whereby both the British and French would carry out anti-piracy patrols in the Mediterranean to protect shipping from attack.

In order to support this agreement, on 13 September 1937, Britain called up two squadrons: 209 Squadron based at Felixstowe and 210 Squadron based at Pembroke Dock. Both flew RAF Short Singapore Mk III flying-boats, which were ideally suited to the task. Preparations for the deployment were hastily made by both squadrons, whose aircraft flew out across the Mediterranean to the small French-Algerian port of Arzeu, near Oran. The flight took 17 hours, spread over three days, finally arriving on 22 September.

The ground crew took a much more leisurely trip to reach Arzeu. As luck had it, a Canadian Pacific cruise liner was departing for a Mediterranean cruise. This meant that the ground crew made the first leg of their journey to Gibraltar in luxurious style aboard the SS *Montclare*. Once they had arrived at Gibraltar, the ground crew were transferred onto HMS *Cyclops*. She was a Royal Navy submarine depot ship, which, alongside at the port of Arzeu, would effectively be the home base for the three-month detachment.

The first Nyon anti-piracy patrol was flown on 27 September and there was a short period of excitement and panic when the wireless operator, Wyndham Bowen, thought he saw a submarine. "Thought we spotted a 'sub' but no luck, saw German destroyers in the distance," his diary entry read. Bowen would go on to complete 15 missions under the agreement, flying for anything up to seven hours at a time over the Med. These patrols fulfilled the all-important early-warning role. They communicated to any endangered British merchant ships who were supplying the legitimate Spanish government with food, but they were also trying to warn off any submarines they saw.

The detachment returned home in December 1937 to what felt like a rather cold British winter after its time in the Med, but just in time to enjoy Christmas with friends and family.

A SHORT SINGAPORE MK III OF 210 SQUADRON IS
HOISTED BY FLOATING CRANE IN ARZEU, ALGERIA, 1937

Chakhchoukha
Lamb & Chickpea Stew with Flatbread

This one-pot dish is eaten all over Algeria where it was originally a peasant dish cooked for shepherds after a long working day. It is now commonly eaten at festive celebrations. The marqa (stew) is ladled over the torn pieces of a thin flatbread made from semolina flour, known as rougag. Rougag is quite tricky and time-consuming to make, but can be substituted with chapatis or thin pancakes. Traditionally cooked with lamb, this recipe also works with other meats such as chicken or beef and is substantial enough to make as a vegetarian main course.

INGREDIENTS
Serves 4

For the rougag

500g tipo '00' pasta flour
 (a mix of wheat and durum
 wheat semolina flours)
½ tsp salt
450ml cold water
sunflower oil, for hands, tray
 and work surface

For the marqa (stew)

8 thin-cut lamb chops
 (or 600g diced lamb)
2 tbsp sunflower oil
1 medium onion, finely diced
2 cloves of garlic, finely chopped
 or crushed
1 tsp ras el hanout
¼ tsp cumin seeds
¼ tsp caraway seeds
¼ tsp cayenne (optional)
1 medium carrot, peeled and
 cut into large pieces
1 medium courgette,
 cut into large pieces
1 large potato, peeled and
 cut into large pieces
1 tin (400g) of chopped plum
 tomatoes

METHOD
To make the rougag

- Mix the flour and salt together in a bowl. Gradually add enough cold water to form a soft, smooth dough, knead for 10 minutes, cover and set aside to rest for 5 minutes.
- Continue to knead the dough, adding a small amount of cold water as required, for 5 minutes until it has a smooth and elastic consistency.
- Lightly oil your hands and divide the dough into pieces the shape and size of a golf ball. Place on a lightly oiled tray, cover with a tea towel and leave to rest for 10 minutes.
- Lightly oil the work surface and, with lightly oiled hands, flatten and press out with your fingertips to a round and very thin sheet.
- Heat a large frying pan over a medium heat, brush with a little oil and cook each rougag for about 30 seconds on each side until it is cooked but still soft and pliable.
- Fold each rougag in half three times to form thin triangles. Place on a plate and cover with a tea towel until required.

To make the marqa (stew)

- Lightly season the lamb chops (or diced lamb) with salt and pepper.
- Heat the oil in a casserole dish or large saucepan over a medium to high heat, add the lamb chops and sear on both sides (or all over if using diced lamb) until well coloured.
- Remove the lamb from the casserole dish and set aside on a plate.
- Reduce the heat to medium, add the onions, cook for 5 minutes until starting to soften, add the garlic, ras el hanout, cumin seeds, caraway seeds and cayenne; cook, stirring frequently, for a further 5 minutes.
- Add the chopped carrot, courgette and potatoes to the casserole along with the chopped tomatoes and stock. Bring to a simmer, season lightly with salt and pepper and return the lamb to the pan.

500ml chicken stock

1 tin (400g) of chickpeas, drained

2 tbsp fresh mint, shredded

salt and black pepper

For the vegetarian alternative

2 tbsp sunflower oil

1 medium onion, finely diced

2 cloves of garlic, finely chopped
 or crushed

1 tsp ras el Hanout

¼ tsp cumin seeds

¼ tsp caraway seeds

¼ tsp cayenne (optional)

1 medium carrot, peeled and cut
 into large pieces

1 medium parsnip, peeled and
 cut into large pieces

1 medium courgette, cut into
 large pieces

1 small aubergine, cut into large
 pieces

1 red or green pepper, deseeded
 and cut into large dice

2 large potato, peeled and cut
 into large pieces

200g swede, peeled and cut
 into large pieces

1 tin (400g) of chopped plum
 tomatoes

500ml vegetable stock

1 tin (400g) of chickpeas, drained

2 tbsp fresh mint, shredded

salt and pepper

- Turn the heat to low, cover with a lid and simmer very gently for 1 hour.
- Stir in the drained chickpeas and continue to cook uncovered for a further 25 minutes or until the lamb is tender, the potatoes are soft and the sauce has thickened enough to coat the back of a spoon.
- Stir in two thirds of the mint and simmer for 5 minutes before serving.

To serve

- Tear the rougag into small pieces and arrange on the base of a large serving plate (or on individual plates).
- Arrange the lamb chops on the torn rougag and ladle over the rest of the vegetables and sauce.
- Garnish with the remaining mint and a sprinkling of ras el hanout.

VEGETARIAN ALTERNATIVE

VEGETABLE CHAKHCHOUKHA

- Make the rougag as above.
- Heat the oil in a casserole dish or large saucepan over a medium heat, add the onions, cook for 5 minutes until starting to soften, add the garlic, ras el hanout, cumin seeds, caraway seeds and cayenne (omit the cayenne for a milder sauce); cook, stirring frequently, for a further 5 minutes.
- Add the chopped carrot, parsnip, courgette, aubergine, pepper, potato and swede to the casserole along with the chopped tomatoes and stock.
- Bring to a simmer, season lightly with salt and pepper, turn the heat to low, cover with a lid and simmer very gently for 45 minutes.
- Stir in the drained chickpeas and continue to cook uncovered for a further 25 minutes until the vegetables are soft and the sauce has thickened enough to coat the back of a spoon.
- Stir in two thirds of the chopped mint and simmer for 5 minutes before serving.

To serve

- Tear the rougag into small pieces and arrange on the base of a large serving plate (or on individual plates).
- Ladle over the marqa and garnish with the remaining chopped mint and a sprinkling of ras el hanout.

THE SECOND
WORLD WAR
1939–1945

A FORCE TO BE RECKONED WITH

Words by
NICK FELLOWS

IF AIR POWER was in its infancy for the First World War, it had truly come of age by the start of the Second World War. In the early stages of the war – particularly in the Battle of Britain – the RAF played a crucial role in preventing Nazi Germany from invading. In the later stages of the war, the RAF was pivotal in destroying Germany's means of waging war through bombing campaigns, either alone or in conjunction with the US Army Air Forces (USAAF).

However, this basic summary does not do justice to the scale of its work. In the years after Dunkirk, when there were no other means to attack the enemy, it was the RAF that boosted morale through the bombing of German coastal towns. In North Africa it played a vital role in supporting the British army, leading to the first major ground victory at El Alamein in 1942. This strategy was later repeated in Italy, North West Europe and the Far East. The RAF was also instrumental in attacking targets in Northern France in preparation for D-Day. At the same time, it had a day-to-day role protecting Britain's coastline, as well as over the North Atlantic, the Mediterranean and the Indian Ocean.

Planning during the 1930s had focused on the RAF playing an offensive role through the bomber, but there were simply not the aircraft or bombs to execute such plans. Despite rapid rearmament in the period after the Munich Conference in 1938, it took time for planes to roll off the production lines. When the war began, new Spitfires and Hurricanes were only gradually replacing bi-planes that were more reminiscent of the First World War.

With both wars, one of the primary tasks of the RAF was to support forces on the ground, firstly through reconnaissance, then through the bombing and strafing of supply lines and front-line trenches. However, despite the bravery of the pilots, the aircraft were no match for the Luftwaffe, which was able to launch devastating attacks on British ground forces with its Stukas and ME 109s. By the time of the Battle of France, in May 1940, the RAF had suffered enormous losses with some 1,000 aircraft destroyed, more than 300 pilots killed or missing, and another 100 taken prisoner. With defeat in France and the evacuation from the beaches of Dunkirk, the RAF played a crucial role in trying to protect the troops on the beaches, despite heavy losses. The RAF's position was made worse by heavy losses sustained trying to defend Norway in April and May of 1940.

However, the greatest test for the RAF came in the late summer of 1940 with Hitler's decision to launch Operation Sea Lion, the invasion of Britain. The RAF's heroism is clear when you consider how outnumbered it was. Germany possessed some 3,500 aircraft, of which two thirds would be usable each day. Britain had just

SPITFIRES OF 548 SQUADRON, ONE OF THE THREE RAF SQUADRONS TASKED WITH THE DEFENCE OF DARWIN, AUSTRALIA BETWEEN 1943–45

700, of which around 600 were Hurricanes and Spitfires, the rest being obsolete Blenheims, Defiants and Gladiators. Pilots could not be replaced quickly enough: those that were left were going into action several times a day. The crucial period came in the last week of August and first week of September, with Fighter Command exhausted, and 295 Hurricanes and Spitfires lost in this period, 171 severely damaged and 231 pilots killed or wounded.

Hitler did not realise how close he was to success. He abandoned the attacks on Fighter Command and turned his attention instead to attacking London: the Blitz. It gave Fighter Command the chance to recover and, by mid September, Spitfires were taking on the German fighters that were accompanying the bombers, while Hurricanes attacked the bombers. Such was their

success that Germany lost a quarter of its bomber force and lost control of the skies, forcing Operation Sea Lion to be abandoned.

The victory was crucial. Not only had invasion been prevented, but also it meant that the Allies had a base for the later air offensive against Germany. From here, the Allied invasion of Europe could be launched in 1944. It is why the pilots of the Battle of Britain, with an average age of 20 , have been enshrined in history. "Never in the field of human conflict was so much owed by so many to so few," said Churchill in a speech to Parliament in August 1940. "The gratitude of every home in our island, in our Empire and

"The war would have gone on for longer and victory would have been at a higher cost if it had not been for the bomber offensive"

indeed throughout the world, except in the abodes of the guilty, goes out to the British airmen, who, undaunted by odds, unwearied in their constant challenge and mortal danger, are turning the tide of the world war by their prowess and devotion."

With the loss of mainland Europe, the only way damage could be inflicted on the enemy was through bombing raids. The initial plans for bombing by the RAF were to attack key points in the German war machine, but the bombers – Wellingtons and Hampdens – could not survive German air defences and so night-time bombing was adopted. Although the accuracy of such attacks was poor, it not only boosted morale at home but also showed the US and USSR that Britain was capable of fighting back.

Moreover, lessons were learned from these costly campaigns and would result in the "Bomber Command" offensives of 1942–45 under Air Chief Marshall Sir Arthur "Bomber" Harris, who had taken over as Commander in Chief of Bomber Command in 1942. He believed that Germany could be brought to its knees by the destruction of its industrial cities and demoralising of the civilian population: that Berlin should be bombed "until the heart of Nazi Germany ceases to beat".

As the war progressed Bomber Command developed the ability to launch more accurate raids, culminating in the major offensives of 1944. However, it is the "Dams Raid" of May 1943 that is most remembered. Many commentators now argue that it failed to achieve its objectives, but it did disrupt the German war economy and forced resources to be diverted from the Atlantic Wall to repair the breaches. It also boosted morale within both the Royal Air Force and among the population.

The impact of these ever-increasing bombing raids on Germany has been heavily debated given how few aircraft, at least initially, reached their target and how even fewer bombs were dropped on their targets. However, these raids did much to disrupt the German war effort, preventing Germany from increasing its arms production, as well as causing industrial destruction and breaking down communications. It forced Germany to divert resources to the construction of anti-aircraft installations, employing around 750,000 men in manning air defences.

It therefore appears that the war would have gone on for longer and victory would have been at a higher cost if it had not been for the bomber offensive. This was admitted by the German armaments minister, Albert

Speer. "The air war opened a second front long before the invasion of Europe," wrote Speer in 1959. "That front was the skies over Germany, every square metre of the territory that we controlled was a kind of front line. Defence against air attacks required the production of thousands of anti-aircraft guns, the stockpiling of tremendous quantities of ammunition all over the country, and holding in readiness hundreds of thousands of soldiers, who in addition had to stay in position by their guns, often totally inactive, for months at a time."

Air superiority was also vital for D-Day, as the invading forces could land in Normandy without significant air threat. "You needn't worry about the air," said General Eisenhower to troops before the invasion of Europe. "If you see a plane it will be ours." Airborne forces were able to secure the flanks of the invading force and hold vital bridges, most notably Pegasus Bridge, across the Caen canal.

This would continue to be of significance as Allied forces advanced towards Germany. Not only were the Germans unable to interfere with the invasion, but they could do little from the air to prevent the breakout from the beaches, the advance across France or the crossing of the Rhine. Raids were launched against railway centres in the "Transportation Plan" to disrupt the mobility of German land forces.

The RAF had less success in securing vital bridges over the Dutch rivers, resulting in the failure of Operation Market Garden at Arnhem in September 1944. But in March 1945, the story was reversed as the last major airborne operation of the war, the crossing of the Rhine, was a complete success. Lessons from Arnhem had been learnt as airborne divisions were taken in one lift and supplies were dropped the same evening. It was this operation that enabled Allied armies to sweep into Germany and to victory in May 1945.

The role of the RAF in the Second World War was not confined to North-West Europe. One of its most significant contributions was in the Battle of the Atlantic. During the

First World War, Britain had come close to being starved into defeat because of the unrestricted German U-boat campaign. The Germans' submarine warfare was even more of an issue by the start of the Second World War. At first, there was insufficient cover for merchant shipping and their losses were very high, with 800,000 tons sunk in November 1942. The subsequent use of bases in the Azores and Iceland enabled the mid-Atlantic gap to be covered.

However, it was the development of Air-to-Surface Vessel radar (ASV) and the Leigh Searchlight (LS) that were crucial. Both made possible the detection of U-boats on the surface at night, denying them shelter. With the closing of the mid-Atlantic gap, German U-boats were withdrawn to the Bay of Biscay, while the development of the ASV and LS forced German U-boats to the surface during the day, with many being destroyed. British shipping losses dropped dramatically – the average merchant shipping tonnage sunk for every U-boat loss fell from 40,000 tons to 6,000 tons during 1943. The RAF's success in the Battle of the Atlantic prevented German ships from beating the blockade established by the Royal Navy in the Channel and the North Sea. It also meant that the build-up of forces for D-Day could take place without the threat of U-boats.

Following the evacuation of British forces from Dunkirk in 1940, the army only faced German forces in North Africa and the Middle East. Campaigns in Greece, Crete and

Syria meant that air forces were thinly spread in the North African desert. Even though the army was pushed back to Egypt by 1942 the RAF was able to achieve a degree of air superiority with attacks against enemy airfields. Then, as German forces were driven back, the RAF attacked the stores and supplies of the Germans and Italians. It was these attacks that did much to halt the Axis forces.

The final battles in Tunisia saw Allied air forces destroy attempts by Germany to reinforce its ground troops by air from Sicily and then prevent the evacuation of its forces, which could have been used elsewhere. By May 1943, victory had been achieved and, as the Commander of Allied Air Forces, Air Chief Marshall Tedder commented to the air and ground crews, "You have shown the world the unity and strength of air power." What made the campaign so crucial was not just the victory, which was achieved at a high cost, but the experience of the Desert Air Force, which became the model for future Allied tactical air forces.

In the Mediterranean, the RAF initially suffered defeats with the invasion of Greece in April 1941 and then Crete. It withdrew to Egypt to regroup and became crucial in the defence of Malta. Initially, planes were flown from aircraft carriers, but once the island was secured it served as a base for attacks on German and Italian supply lines across the whole of the Mediterranean, playing a significant role in the defeat of the German army in North Africa.

Once North Africa was secured, the next role for the RAF was the invasion of Italy. The RAF played an important part in securing air superiority so that an airborne and amphibious assault could be launched against Sicily in July 1943. The invasion of Italy in September was preceded by a bombing campaign and, following the Italian surrender on 8 September, the RAF was gradually able to occupy enemy airfields, using them as a base for attacks on Yugoslavia, Bulgaria, Albania and Greece. Once again, the RAF

had played a crucial role in bringing victory in the Mediterranean.

The final area of conflict was the Far East. Once again, at the start of the war, the RAF lacked the resources, and within a few weeks, its units in Malaya and Singapore were defeated. Those that survived withdrew to India and Burma. Once it had recovered, the RAF was able to launch attacks against the Japanese on all sides, alongside its American Allies.

However, perhaps the most important role the RAF played in the Far East was the resupply of some 300,000 men, who would go on to reconquer Burma. Even when armies were surrounded by Japanese forces they were supplied by air, and the RAF also moved large numbers of troops to vital areas. Crucially, its role did not cease with the end of the war, as supplies were dropped for former prisoners of war in camps, while others who needed urgent medical treatment were evacuated.

The RAF, and the establishment of air superiority, played a decisive role in the ultimate victory. The technological changes it had undergone were immense: at the start of the conflict, the RAF was still using biplanes, by 1944 it was using its first jet, the Meteor. The Battle of Britain and the Dambusters may be the most celebrated of the RAF's contributions to the Second World War, but its role and impact was far greater, playing an indispensable part in the victory over Germany, Japan and Italy.

GIBRALTAR

Words by
FLIGHT LIEUTENANT EMMA STRINGER

GIBRALTAR IS A small peninsular attached to one of the most southern parts of Spain. These 6sq km serve as the western access point into the Mediterranean, which has made it a highly contested territory. However, it has remained under British sovereignty since 1704, when the British Navy captured it from Spain.

The RAF first sent military aircraft to Gibraltar in 1935 with 210 Squadron who, at the time, flew a three-engined biplane flying boat called the Rangoon. Flying boats were essential, as the "runway" (a grass strip on the grounds of a racecourse) was still under construction. Construction of a solid runway didn't commence until late 1939, following the declaration of war with Germany.

It wasn't long before Gibraltar's strategic location for aircraft use was considered essential and the runway extended further through reclamation of the land into the bay area. The famous Gibraltar rock provided the building materials from the blasting and excavation of its limestone. Not only did this provide the foundations for the runway extension, but it also helped with the removal of rock to build an underground city from which to operate; one that was impervious to enemy bombs.

One of Gibraltar's many uses was that of an intermediate stopover for aircraft flying from Britain onwards to North Africa, the islands of the Mediterranean and as far as the Middle East. In 1942, as Malta was being targeted by the German and Italians, the British needed to bolster the number of fighter aircraft based there to help defend the island. As the shipping routes to Malta were vulnerable, it was decided to send the aircraft reinforcements by ship as far as Gibraltar, where they would then be built and flown on to Malta.

To this end, a "Special Erection Party" of 136 airmen were sent out to build the aircraft. It took the team just 11 days to assemble, test fly and disperse a total of 70 Spitfires, 22 Hurricanes and six "Hurri-bombers". With the large numbers of personnel being deployed to Gibraltar at this time, accommodation was at a premium, so much so that the empty crates delivering the aircraft were converted into airman's living quarters!

The newly extended runway also played a major part in Operation Torch, the highly successful joint Anglo–American operation that saw the invasion of French North Africa, leading to the defeat of the Axis powers in the area. The operation provided the Allies with vital naval control of the Mediterranean. As well as housing the headquarters for the operation, Gibraltar provided an essential base for 600 Allied fighters. The operation was kept top secret until the day of execution. As it had done previously for the Malta campaign, the island began to receive a further supply of fighter aircraft in crates.

The Special Erection Party, now bolstered by some 150 soldiers, began to build the aircraft. In just over a week, working 15-hour days in all weathers, the party had managed to build 13 Hurricanes and 108 Spitfires. By the early hours of 8 November 1942, the first day of the operation, some 650 aircraft were crammed wing-to-wing around the runway. Churchill wrote in his memoirs that the development of the new airfield and its use during Operation Torch was "Gibraltar's greatest contribution to the war".

Rosto
Beef & Pasta Casserole

Gibraltarian food and culture is a reflection of the diverse origins of the territory and its people. British and Spanish are the dominant cultures, but Gibraltar's cuisine also has ethnic influences from Portugal, Morocco, Italy and Malta. Rosto has Genoese origins and is a popular warming winter dish. Traditionally the meat (usually beef or pork) is slowly cooked separately then served together with the pasta (generally penne or macaroni), coated with the cooking sauce and grated cheese.

INGREDIENTS

Serves 4

For the casserole

1kg beef joint (topside or top
rump/thick flank), tied

30g beef dripping or lard,
 or 2 tbsp vegetable oil

1 medium onion, halved and cut
 into 1.5cm-thick wedges

2 medium carrots, halved
 lengthways and cut into
 1.5cm-thick slices

2 sticks celery, cut into
 1.5cm-thick slices

1 clove of garlic, finely
 chopped or crushed

300g ripe tomatoes, coarsely diced

3 tbsp tomato purée

2 whole cloves

1 bay leaf

125ml white wine (optional)

1 tbsp sugar

2 tsp dried oregano

30g butter

250g chestnut mushrooms,
 quartered

2 tbsp parsley, coarsely
 chopped or shredded

For the pasta

500g penne or macaroni pasta

200g grated edam cheese
 (or parmesan)

40g (1 slice) fresh breadcrumbs

paprika to dust

METHOD

To prepare the casserole

• Season the beef all over with salt.

• Heat the dripping, lard or oil in a casserole over a high heat and
 sear the beef until well browned all over. Remove the beef from
 the casserole and set aside on a plate.

• Reduce the heat to medium, add the onion, carrot and celery to
 the casserole and cook, stirring frequently, for 10 minutes until
 they start to soften and caramelise slightly.

• Add the garlic and continue to cook for a further minute.

• Add the chopped tomatoes, tomato purée, cloves, bay leaf, white
 wine, sugar, oregano and 275ml of boiling water (400ml if omitting
 the white wine). Bring to a simmer and season lightly with salt
 and pepper.

• Return the beef to the casserole (with any juices that have
 accumulated on the plate), turn the heat to its lowest setting, cover
 with a lid and cook for 2½ hours until the beef is very tender. Stir
 occasionally adding a little more water if the sauce starts to become
 too thick (alternatively the beef can be pot roasted at 160°C).

• Remove the beef from the casserole, cover, set aside and keep
 warm to rest.

• Heat the butter in a frying pan until foaming, add the mushrooms
 with a little salt and pepper. Sauté until soft and lightly browned.

• Add the mushrooms and chopped parsley to the sauce and simmer
 for 5 minutes; the sauce should have a rich coating consistency so
 it might need a little hot water stirring in. Check the seasoning.

To prepare the pasta

• Preheat the grill.

• Meanwhile bring a pan of salted water to a rolling boil, add the pasta,
 cook until al dente and drain.

• Place half of the pasta in a warmed serving dish, ladle over a quarter
 of the sauce then scatter over half of the cheese. Repeat with the
 remaining pasta, a further quarter of the sauce and remaining cheese.

• Scatter the breadcrumbs evenly over the top of the cheese, dust with
 paprika and a grind of black pepper. Place under the hot grill until the
 cheese is bubbling and has browned slightly.

To serve

• Carve the beef into thick slices and serve with the pasta and
 remaining sauce.

MALTA

Words by
SQUADRON LEADER JON PULLEN

BRITAIN HAS HAD a long relationship with Malta that dates back to 1800, when its people petitioned the British government to blockade the island and remove Napoleon's French forces. In 1814, Malta became a British Crown Colony and this status was still the case on 10 June 1940, when Mussolini declared war on Britain and France.

Due to Malta's strategically critical location in the centre of the Mediterranean, it was inevitable that the island would be drawn into the war. Malta was ill-prepared for the immediate Italian bombing campaign, even though there had been a small RAF Station at Hal Far since 1929. By 1940, it was operating a flight of just three obsolete Gloster Gladiators that had been left crated by the Royal Navy in storage for its Mediterranean Fleet.

Although they were only in operation for a short time, these three Gloster Gladiators became a symbol of the Maltese people's spirit of defiance. They were affectionately known as Faith, Hope and Charity, and their age and inferior performance didn't stop them from being credited with the first kills of the campaign. By the end of June 1940, the RAF had started reinforcing the island with Hurricanes but, due to the island's isolation and with continual attacks from Italian and German air forces, high attrition rates were not matched due to the challenges of the resupply routes.

TWO OF MALTA'S ICONIC GLOSTER SEA GLADIATORS, CIRCA 1940

A turning point in the Malta campaign was the introduction of Spitfires. By spring 1942, they had wrested air superiority away from Axis forces, providing much needed relief for an island that had become the most bombed place on earth.

This immense pressure bred an environment of ingenuity. On one occasion in April 1942, with all the fighters grounded, the Axis powers launched a large raid. There were several pilots in the operations room and, in an attempt to fool the enemy, one was given dummy orders over the radio and he replied as if he were flying his fighter. A cry of "Achtung Schpitfeuer" was heard on the German's own radio and two ME109s shot each other down without any RAF aircraft being airborne.

After the war, the RAF maintained its presence in Malta until 1979, when the British government made the decision to not renew its lease on RAF Luqa. During these years, Malta had played important roles in the Cold War, including maritime and photo reconnaissance, as well as a strike role during the Suez Crisis.

The Gloster Gladiator known as Faith was salvaged from a quarry in Kalafrana in 1943 and presented to the people of Malta in a ceremony that same year. But it wasn't until 1974 that volunteers from the engineering wing at RAF Luqa refurbished her. In 1975, the aircraft was handed to the War Museum in Valetta, where it can still be seen today as a permanent reminder of the indomitable spirit of the Maltese people.

Pudina tal-Hobż
Maltese Chocolate & Fruit Bread Pudding

The Maltese have adapted the classic English bread pudding and made it their own with the addition of dried fruit and chocolate. Nuts such as almonds, walnuts or hazelnuts can also be added for extra flavour and texture. This dessert is an ideal alternative to Christmas pudding, especially with the addition of some chopped crystallised ginger.

INGREDIENTS

Serves 8–12

For the pudding

1 large loaf (800g) white bread,
  1 or 2 days old

500ml milk

125ml double cream

150g soft brown sugar

150g caster sugar

2 tbsp rum, sherry, triple-sec
  or brandy (optional)

2 tsp vanilla paste or extract

3 large eggs, beaten

50g butter, melted

75g plain flour

1 tsp baking powder

50g cocoa powder

1 tsp ground cinnamon

1 tsp mixed spice

1 orange, finely grated zest only

1 lemon, finely grated zest only

100g dark chocolate (70%),
  finely chopped

200g sultanas or raisins

75g glacé cherries, quartered

50g candied mixed peel

50g desiccated coconut flakes

To serve

vanilla ice cream or custard

METHOD

To make the pudding

- Preheat the oven to 180°C.
- Cut the crusts from the loaf and either cut or tear the bread into large pieces.
- Whisk together the milk, cream, sugars, rum (or preferred liquor, if using), vanilla paste or extract, beaten eggs and melted butter.
- Mix the bread into the wet mix and leave to soak for about 15 minutes.
- Sift over the flour, baking powder, cocoa and spices. Mix well to thoroughly incorporate.
- Fold in the orange and lemon zest with the chopped chocolate, sultanas, glacé cherries, mixed peel and desiccated coconut flakes.
- Butter an ovenproof dish (23cm by 28cm) and pour into the bread mixture.
- Place in the preheated oven and bake for about 40 minutes until well browned on top and a skewer comes out clean when inserted into the centre.

To serve

- Let the pudding rest in the baking dish at room temperature for 10 minutes before cutting into even-sized squares or rectangles and serve warm with a scoop of good quality vanilla ice cream or custard, alternatively the pudding can be served cold with a cup of tea or coffee.

SOUTH AFRICA

Words by
VICTORIA EDWARDS

WITH THE BATTLE of Britain raging over Britain's skies during the summer and autumn of 1940, the need for alternative training facilities to ensure minimal loss of life and equipment for the Allied aircrews was growing. The open skies of South Africa, Canada, and the USA were eminently more suitable locations for training than the cloudy, unsavoury climate and crowded skies of Britain. From this need, the British Commonwealth Air Training Plan (BCATP), or "The Plan" grew.

In 1940, as part of The Plan, the Allied forces set up a parallel agreement with the slowly growing South African Air Force (SAAF). A new training scheme, imaginatively titled the Joint Air Training Scheme (JATS), would aim to deliver both practical and theoretical training to Allied forces pilots, navigators, bomb aimers, wireless operators, flight engineers and air gunners from 36 South Africa-based air schools in and around Pretoria, Cape Town, Germiston, Bloemfontein and Baragwanath. Aircraft and other equipment for the training of Allied aircrews across the South African savannahs were provided free of charge by the United Kingdom.

In an effort to confuse the enemy, personnel making the long sea journey to both Canada and South Africa for their training were provided with alternate kit. Those who were Canada-bound were issued with tropical clothing, while those destined for the searing heat of South Africa were given full cold-weather rig. This certainly made for an interesting arrival for the troops who, in most cases, were unaware of where they were bound anyway. At the port of Durban, cadets were met with great pomp and ceremony at the quayside, then housed in ex-pigsties and fed a welcome meal of Koo jam and bread, a disastrous combination for the shrunken stomachs accustomed to six months' ships rations.

Although the influx of aircrew trainees and their subsequent spending power in local stores and hostelries was undoubtedly a positive action for the local economy, local farmers may not have been so keen, judging by the surviving records of letters. Some of these letters expressed concern about the loud aircraft flying overhead and, in some cases, making "unscheduled landings" on their land, and many worried what effect this would have on their livestock!

Two years of intensive training followed for the young cadets, encompassing an average of 320 hours flying experience, mainly in Tiger Moths, Hinds and Hart type aircraft among others, compared to the 200 to 250 hours average flight training time of the rest of the BCATPs training initiatives in other allied countries. RAF and Allied pilot training schemes at this time were more extended and thorough than those of the Luftwaffe and Russian Air Forces. During its five years of operation, the JATS scheme successfully trained a total of 33,347 air crew. This meant that, thanks to the training initiatives in South Africa and other Allied air schools, the RAF was still left with a strong, well-trained fighting force in the air by the close of the Second World War,.

However, life as a trainee in South Africa was not all study and practice. Outside of training duties, the cadets enjoyed a lively social life with local residents, and many chose to remain and settle in South Africa as instructors upon completion of their training, or to return to sweethearts and wives there at the close of the war.

Bobotie
Spicy Minced Meat with Egg Topping

Bobotie (pronounced baboortie) might be South Africa's national dish. Dutch colonists first encountered Indonesian "bobotok" in the Dutch East Indies, took it back to Holland and later introduced it to the Cape of Good Hope, where it was adopted by the Cape-Malay community. The dish can be made with beef or lamb, although pork tends to retain more moisture. The meat filling should be quite dry, but with a creamy texture imparted by the soaked bread. It is baked with a savoury egg custard poured on top and is often served with rice, chutneys and pickles.

INGREDIENTS

Serves 6

For the spice mix

2 tsp ground coriander

1½ tsp medium curry powder

1 tsp ground cumin

1 tsp turmeric

1 tsp paprika

½ tsp ground allspice

¼ tsp ground cloves

METHOD

To make the spice mix

• Mix the ingredients for the spice mix together and store in an airtight container until required.

To cook the spiced mince filling

• Place the sultanas in a small bowl and pour over enough boiling water to cover. Set aside for 15 minutes to steep.

• Heat the butter and oil in a casserole or saucepan over a moderate heat and, when the butter is starting to foam, add the onions; cook,

For the spiced mince filling

75g sultanas

25g butter

1 tbsp vegetable oil

2 medium onions, finely diced

500g lamb or beef mince

500g pork mince

2 cloves of garlic, finely chopped
or crushed

2.5cm piece of ginger, finely
chopped or grated

2 large chillies (medium hot),
halved lengthways, deseeded
and shredded

1 Granny Smith apple, peeled,
cored and coarsely chopped

2 tbsp mango chutney

1 bay leaf

1 lemon, juice and finely grated zest

salt and pepper

2 thick slices of bread, crusts
removed and torn into roughly
2–3cm pieces

250ml milk

For the topping

2 large eggs

4 fresh bay leaves (optional)

To serve (optional)

boiled rice (can be boiled with
1 tsp turmeric)

1 small banana, sliced

mango chutney

chopped almonds or walnuts

toasted flaked coconut

lime or lemon wedges

stirring frequently, for about 5 minutes until the onions start to soften.
• Add the spice mix, cook for a couple of minutes, increase the heat,
add the minced meat and fry until well browned, stirring frequently
to ensure the spices don't catch and burn.
• Stir in the garlic, ginger and chillies; continue to cook, stirring
continuously for a couple of minutes.
• Stir in the sultanas (including the soaking water), diced apple, mango
chutney, bay leaf, lemon juice and zest; mix well and season with salt
and pepper. Turn the heat to low, cover with a lid and simmer very
gently for 1 hour. Stir occasionally and only add a little boiling water
if the mix becomes very dry.
• While the mince is cooking, place the torn bread pieces in a bowl, pour
over the milk, mix well and set aside to soak.
• Once the mince has been simmering for 1 hour, remove from the heat
and preheat the oven to 180°C.
• Press the excess milk from the bread through a sieve (reserve the milk),
stir the bread into the mince mixture until thoroughly combined and
check the seasoning.
• Transfer the mince mixture to an ovenproof baking dish and smooth
over the top until it is flat. This can be done a day in advance, cooled
and kept, covered in the fridge.

To top and cook
• If the mix has been prepared in advance and is chilled, cover with
a layer of aluminium foil and warm through in the oven for about
20 to 25 minutes before removing the foil and continuing as below.
• Beat the eggs in a bowl with the reserved milk (from soaking the
bread), mix well, season with a little salt, pour over the mince and
arrange the whole bay leaves on top. For a deeper custard layer,
use 4 eggs and an extra 250ml of milk.
• Place in the preheated oven for about 20 minutes until the mince
has reheated through to the middle and the custard has set and is
lightly browned on top.

To serve
• Serve with boiled rice and a selection of accompaniments.

NORWAY

Words by
SQUADRON LEADER JONATHAN ROOKE

THE RAF's INVOLVEMENT in Norway started in earnest in May 1940. Some Hawker Hurricanes and Gloster Gladiators were deployed to the north of the country, supporting ground troops in the Narvik and Bardufoss areas from an improvised airfield on Lesjaskogsvatnet lake. Neither aircraft type was suited to the harsh conditions. Several were lost through crashes and all withdrew as part of Operation Alphabet on 7 June. Tragically, the carrier HMS *Glorious* was sunk the following day with a death toll of 1,519, more than any other British naval disaster of the war.

Although officially neutral, Norway acted as a staging post for Allied aircraft transiting to Finland in early 1940. A single-engined crossing of the

GLOSTER GLADIATOR OF 263 SQUADRON, WRECKED ON LAKE LESJASKOG IN NORWAY, 1940

"The fjords became the arena for a game of hide-and-seek between German shipping and RAF aircraft"

North Sea to make landfall at Sola Airfield near Stavanger to refuel was still perilous. On one of these flights, four Westland Lysanders became lost in the fog and, running low on fuel, tried to find the airfield. One attempted to land on the island of Hundvåg, crashing in the process and writing off the aircraft.

Throughout the war, the sheltered inlets and fjords of the Norwegian coastline served as havens for Axis vessels. One example was the Altmark Incident of 16 February 1940, when a German supply ship, the *Altmark*, carrying British prisoners, sought refuge in the Jøssingfjord. The German ship was boarded by sailors from HMS *Cossack*, ultimately bringing Norway fully into the war.

The fjords became the arena for a continuous game of hide-and-seek between German shipping and the RAF aircraft of Coastal and Bomber Commands. The RAF's manoeuvrable twin-engined Beaufighters and Mosquitos from the Strike Wing airfields in northern Scotland were ideally suited to operating in the close confines of the steep-sided fjords. Later in the war, the German battleship *Tirpitz* took refuge in the Fættenfjord, and later near Tromsø. The RAF carried out a number of unsuccessful raids against the ship, with Lancaster bombers finally succeeding in sinking her on 12 November 1944.

The frozen lakes of Norway assisted Allied aircraft returning from raids, serving as emergency landing grounds for damaged aircraft and enabling crews to escape before the aircraft settled through the ice. Many aircraft were later recovered from Norwegian lakes where the ice-cold water kept the metal in excellent condition.

In addition to flying operations over Norway, two RAF squadrons – 331 and 332 – were formed entirely of Norwegian personnel, operating Hawker Hurricanes and Supermarine Spitfires respectively throughout the war. After the German surrender they relocated to Norway, where they were disbanded as RAF squadrons and reformed as part of the new Royal Norwegian Air Force.

Lapskaus
Norwegian Beef & Root Vegetable Stew

A traditional Norwegian dish, lapskaus, in its simplest form, is a stew of beef, pork or mutton/lamb with root vegetables. Although it is great eaten with crusty bread, it is traditionally served with crisp, unleavened Norwegian flatbreads (flatbrød).

INGREDIENTS
Serves 4
For the lapskaus

3 tbsp sunflower or vegetable oil

600g braising beef e.g. chuck or shin, cut into large chunks

2 medium onions, coarsely chopped

3 medium carrots, coarsely chopped

2 sticks celery, coarsely chopped

½ medium swede, coarsely diced

1 litre chicken stock

2 bay leaves

500g floury potatoes (e.g. Maris Piper), coarsely diced

2 large parsnips, coarsely chopped

50g parsley, coarsely chopped

salt and pepper

For the flatbrød

(makes 8)

175g wholemeal flour

150g plain flour

½ tsp bicarbonate of soda

¼ tsp salt

3 tbsp vegetable oil

200ml buttermilk

METHOD
To make the lapskaus

- Heat 2 tbsp of the oil in a casserole dish or saucepan over a high heat. Season the beef and sear all over in a couple of batches; transfer to bowl with a slotted spoon.
- Return the casserole to a medium heat with the remaining oil and add the onion, carrots and celery. Stir frequently for 10 minutes until the vegetables have started to soften and the onions are translucent.
- Stir in the diced swede and seared beef (including any juices that have accumulated in the bowl), add the chicken stock and bay leaves, stir well, partially cover with a lid and simmer over a low heat, stirring occasionally, for 1½ hours.
- Stir in the potatoes and parsnips and continue to simmer for a further hour until the potatoes are soft and have partially dissolved and thickened the stew.
- Stir in the chopped parsley and season with salt and pepper.

To make the flatbrød

- Sift the flours with the bicarbonate of soda and the salt.
- Mix in the oil, add the buttermilk, knead to a stiff dough, cover and leave to rest for 5 minutes.
- Divide the dough into 8 equal sized pieces (about 70g each) and roll each piece out on a well-floured surface to a very thin disc to around 22cm diameter (these can be trimmed around a plate or pasta bowl for a neat finish), transfer to a baking sheet and score four shallow lines through the centre to create eight even-sized wedges.
- Preheat the oven to 180°C cook each flatbrød for 10 minutes until dry and lightly coloured.
- Transfer to a wire rack to cool completely before breaking into pieces along the score lines.

To serve

- Ladle the lapskaus into bowls and serve with crusty bread or flatbrød.

ZIMBABWE

Words by
SQUADRON LEADER CHRIS POWELL

WITH THE OUTBREAK of the Second World War, the Royal Air Force's requirement to train large numbers of aircrew could not be accommodated in the UK. Southern Rhodesia – the predecessor to modern-day Zimbabwe – was an ideal alternative location. The climate provided excellent flying weather throughout the year and it was located far enough away to not be concerned with enemy interference. In May 1940, the Rhodesian Air Training Group was established to train pilots, navigators, observers and air gunners on a range of aircraft including Tiger Moths, Havards and Fairchild Cornells.

A prime concern when selecting locations for aerodromes was the threat of malaria, so sites were chosen away from mosquito breeding grounds. Higher altitude locations with cooler climates were found to reduce the risk. A total of 15 airfields were built, with some being established from raw veldt to fully operational in just 11 weeks.

Trainees were transported to Africa by troop ships, which were escorted in convoys by the Royal Navy. On arrival in Durban, South Africa, the cadets were pleasantly surprised; food was not rationed and there was little of the austerity they were used to at home. A further two-day rail journey then followed to South Rhodesia.

Training flights commenced early in the morning, just after dawn, as the mid-afternoon turbulence proved challenging and hazardous for trainee pilots in lightweight Tiger Moths. Southern Rhodesia was wild frontier country and there were few landmarks, which necessitated excellent dead-reckoning navigation. Crews did get lost, sometimes fatally, so it came as no surprise that survival training was taken very seriously.

Night flying was considerably easier than in the UK as there were no blackouts. However, dust devils – small whirlwinds – would frequently sweep across various airfields at the hottest times of the day during the summer months. These were treated with respect, as they could have potentially disastrous consequences for taxying aircraft or if flown through at low-level.

Southern Rhodesia proved a popular and enjoyable location for personnel. Huge herds of game wandered the veldts, providing a breathtaking site for aircraft on low-level flights. Victoria Falls was a favourite location for personnel on leave, while others spent their down time accommodated on the local farms, passing their days relaxing or roaming the vast estates.

During the Second World War, over 10,000 airmen were trained in Southern Rhodesia, including the late Labour MP Tony Benn, who underwent his pilot training in 1944. The Southern Rhodesia Air Force deployed to Kenya prior to the start of the conflict, before being amalgamated into the RAF. It was not re-established as an independent force until 1947, making the RAF the only military force to fly in the Southern Rhodesian skies during the war.

The end of the war saw a reduced training requirement as fewer pilots were needed. Rhodesian airfields entered a phase of care and maintenance, with very limited flying training occurring. The escalation of the Cold War and the start of the Korean War resulted in increased training activity, although on a much smaller scale than in the Second World War. For financial reasons, the RAF returned all flying training to the UK in the early 1950s, leading to the disbandment of the Rhodesian Air Training Group on 12 March 1954.

Nhopi
Zimbabwean Squash & Peanut Mash

Nhopi is a traditional Zimbabwean dish that can be served on its own as a snack, or as an accompaniment to a meal. It can also be chilled and served as a dip for crudités or spread onto flour tortillas or flatbreads before filling with salad leaves and roasted vegetables, chicken, lamb or pork.

INGREDIENTS
Serves 4–6

For the nhopi
2 butternut squash
25g butter
150g smooth peanut butter
75ml single cream (or milk)
1 tbsp soft brown sugar (optional)
salt

To serve (optional)
2 tbsp natural yoghurt
1 tbsp runny honey
50g roast peanuts, chopped
ground cinnamon

METHOD
To make the nhopi
• Preheat the oven to 180°C.
• Peel the butternut squash, halve, scoop out the seeds and roughly chop. Place in a baking dish, melt half of the butter and toss with the squash. Cover tightly with aluminium foil and bake for around 30 to 40 minutes until very soft.
• Mash the squash until smooth and mix in the remaining butter with the peanut butter.
• Heat the cream (or milk) in a saucepan until simmering and mix into the squash mash with the sugar (if using) and season with a little salt.

To serve
• Serve the nhopi in a bowl, spoon over the yoghurt, drizzle the honey and garnish with the chopped roast peanuts and a dust of cinnamon.

BERMUDA

Words by
**FLIGHT LIEUTENANT SIMON STAFFORD
& ALISON STAFFORD**

THINK OF BERMUDA and you may think of palm trees, sunshine and beaches, but not, perhaps, the Royal Air Force.

As it did with many of the RAF's more distant outposts, Britain established a base at Darrell's Island just before the outbreak of the Second World War. One of the small islands of the archipelago that forms Bermuda, Darrell's Island sits in the Great Sound – a large ocean inlet – and was to become a valuable stopping point for cross-Atlantic journeys. Subsequently, it also became the ideal rendezvous for wartime convoys.

One interesting and lesser-known aspect of the island was that it became the centre of a huge censorship operation that was pivotal to the war effort. Under the cover of the Princess Hotel in Hamilton, the few local postmen who formed the mail censorship unit found their department expanded to become Bermuda's version of Bletchley Park. Up to 700 UK personnel were stationed there, and, located in the basement rooms, intelligence staff inspected and censored all mail that passed through the colony, much to the frustration of any pro-German Americans whose ships and aircraft passed through Bermuda. It was to become an intelligence hub; the filter for all mail in the Northern hemisphere.

In 1940, the Bermuda Flying School, which trained volunteers from local territorial units for the RAF and Royal Navy, was established on Darrell's island

The school trained 80 pilots before it closed in 1942.

As a UK invasion by Germany looked increasingly imminent, the US used Canada as an intermediary to try to persuade the British Royal Family to relocate to Bermuda for the duration of the war. It was believed that, once France fell, Britain would not be able to keep up the fight against Nazi domination for long and may agree a settlement with Hitler to turn over the whole of the empire. Of course, this was not to happen and the Royal Family famously remained in London alongside the people of Britain.

A public appeal in Bermuda in 1941 resulted in the acquisition of a Spitfire, named Bermuda, for the RAF. The plane shot down five German aircraft before its final sortie when it sadly failed to return.

In 1946, the RAF gave over its runways to the US Air Force, a process that was overseen by the senior RAF Officer in Bermuda, Wing Commander E M "Mo" Ware. Buildings were relocated from Darrell's Island to form the first terminal of the new Civil Air Terminal.

In April 1968, there was growing unrest in Bermuda and when the Governor, Lord Martonmere, declared a state of emergency, the UK was quick to respond. Fresh from a ladies guest night in the mess, the Royal Irish Rangers (B Company) boarded two RAF VC10 aircraft at Brize Norton headed for Bermuda, seen off by officers still in their mess dress!

They landed at Kindley Air Force Base in the North of Bermuda at the same time as HMS *Leopard* arrived to the south and, seeing that Britain was serious about restoring order, the rioting and disorder were quick to cease. Britain's assistance in this incident has helped to ensure that the relationship between Bermuda and the UK remains strong to this day.

Although Britain no longer maintain a detachment in Bermuda, the RAF continues to use the island for transatlantic staging, employing the former RAF end of the airfield. Large detachments of tactical aircraft, accompanied by larger refuelling, transport, and maritime patrol aircraft, regularly visit Bermuda on transits between the UK and the US. It is not uncommon for crews to find themselves stranded there when they suffer technical problems en route, but this definitely counts as one of the more enjoyable locations to end up!

THE FLYING-BOAT BASE AT DARRELL ISLAND, BERMUDA

West Indies Curry
with Rice & Peas

Although generally associated with Jamaica, curry is popular throughout the West Indies. After the emancipation of the British West Indies in 1834, thousands of Indians were hired to work on the plantations, bringing their culture with them. West Indies curry powder is a blend of aromatic spices that doesn't contain any chilli; all of the chilli flavour and heat comes from the fiery scotch bonnet chillies. Traditionally made with goat, this curry can also be made with lamb or mutton. For the best flavour, the meat should be marinated overnight, cooked on the bone and served with rice and peas.

INGREDIENTS
Serves 4

For the curry powder

3 tsp coriander seeds

1½ tsp cumin seeds

1½ tsp mustard seeds

1 star anise, crumbled

4 tsp ground turmeric

2 tsp ground ginger

1 tsp ground fenugreek

¾ tsp ground allspice

For the curry

4 tbsp vegetable or sunflower oil

1.2kg goat, lamb or mutton meat, bone in, or 600g, bone off, cut into large dice

500g onion, coarsely chopped

2 green peppers, coarsely chopped

2 cloves of garlic, finely chopped

1 scotch bonnet chilli (or more according to taste), deseeded and finely chopped

75g yellow split peas

1 litre lamb or beef stock

2 bay leaves

2 sprigs of thyme

salt and pepper

METHOD
To make the curry powder

• Dry toast the coriander seeds, cumin seeds, mustard seeds and star anise pieces in a frying pan over a moderate heat until aromatic and lightly browned.

• Remove from the heat and transfer to a heatproof plate to cool. Once cool, grind to a powder in a spice grinder or pestle and mortar; mix with the ground spices and store in an airtight container until required.

To cook the curry

• Season the meat well with salt and freshly ground black pepper; add half of the curry powder, toss to evenly coat, place in a bowl or container, cover and marinate in the fridge for at least a couple of hours or overnight.

• Heat 3 tbsp of the oil in a large casserole dish or saucepan over a high heat. Sear the meat all over until well browned in two or three batches, transferring each batch to a bowl with a slotted spoon.

• Add the remaining oil to the casserole, reduce the heat to medium and add the chopped onions and peppers. Cook, stirring frequently, for about 5 minutes until the vegetables start to soften.

• Add the garlic, chilli and remaining curry powder; continue to cook, stirring constantly for a further 2 minutes.

• Return the meat to the casserole, mix well, stir in the split peas, stock, bay leaves and thyme. Bring to the boil reduce the heat and simmer very gently for 2 hours, stirring occasionally, and occasionally topping up with boiling water ensuring that the meat stays submerged in the liquid.

• Once the meat is very tender, increase the heat and reduce the sauce to a thick coating consistency.

For the rice and peas

3 tbsp vegetable or sunflower oil

1 medium onion, finely diced

2 cloves of garlic, finely chopped
  or crushed

300g long grain rice

400ml coconut milk

1 tin (400g) of kidney beans,
  drained and rinsed

¼ tsp ground allspice

1 sprig of thyme

1 scotch bonnet chilli, whole

salt and pepper

2 tbsp flat leaf parsley, coarsely
  chopped

To serve

400g ripe tomatoes, thinly sliced

½ cucumber, thinly sliced

• Remove the bay leaves and thyme stalks; check the seasoning, adding a little more salt and black pepper as required.

To make the rice and peas

• Heat the oil in a saucepan over a moderate heat, add the onion and cook, stirring frequently, for 5 minutes until they start to soften and turn translucent; stir in the chopped garlic.

• Add the rice. Stir well and fry for a couple of minutes, stirring continuously, until the rice is well coated in the oil and has a slightly nutty smell (it shouldn't take on any colour).

• Stir in 300ml of boiling water and the coconut milk. Bring to a simmer, add the beans, ground allspice, thyme and whole chilli, season with salt and black pepper, cover with a lid, turn the heat to low and cook for 30 minutes.

• Once cooked, leave to stand with the lid on for 5 minutes before removing the thyme and scotch bonnet, checking the seasoning and stirring in the chopped parsley.

To serve

• Arrange the sliced tomatoes and cucumber neatly on a plate and season well with salt and pepper.

• Serve the curry in bowls with the rice and beans. Serve the tomato and cucumber salad on the side.

FAROE ISLANDS

Words by
SQUADRON LEADER MAL CRAIG

IF ANY ARMED occupation can be "friendly", then surely the British occupation of the Faroe Islands between 1940 and 1945 was the friendliest of them all. Strategically located in the North Atlantic, midway between Iceland and Norway, this wind-battered collection of 18 major islands would play a significant part in the Battle of the Atlantic.

When Germany invaded Denmark and Norway on 9 April 1940, Hitler secured both air and sea bases right up to Cape North. This posed a threat to Allied shipping using the high-latitude routes across the North Atlantic and placed the Royal Navy's home base of Scapa Flow in the Orkney Islands within easy reach of German long-range bombers.

As a result, the extension of RAF radar coverage northward and north-eastward of Scotland became an increasing priority. On 11 April 1940, 250 commandos, in company with RAF radar technicians and engineers, began the occupation of the islands under the codename Operation Valentine. Winston Churchill, then First Lord of the Admiralty, speaking a month before he became Prime Minister, made the following announcement in Parliament: "We are also at this moment occupying the Faroe Islands, which belong to Denmark and which are a strategic point of high importance, and whose people showed every disposition to receive us with warm regard. We shall shield the Faroe Islands from all the severities of war and establish ourselves there conveniently by sea and air until the moment comes when they will be handed back to Denmark liberated from the foul thraldom into which they have been plunged by German aggression."

The islands had, until that time, held the status of an "amt" or county of Denmark. They were notionally taken under the control of Frederick Mason, the new British Consul, though Britain resolved not to interfere in the islands' internal affairs. Immediately, the RAF began establishing six radars stations, an airfield and a relief sea-plane base on the islands. The radar sites were designed to provide early warning of both aircraft attacking Scotland and German maritime craft attempting to enter the North Atlantic. Though it was intended to operate fighter aircraft from the new airfield at Viggar, the regularity of high winds made this virtually impossible. However, Viggar airfield enjoyed a new lease of life after the war, when it became the Faroe Islands' only runway, and remains in operation today.

The sea-plane base would see occasional use throughout and after the war, including the tragic loss of a Catalina aircraft in 1942 and a Sunderland aircraft in the 1950s. In total, there are 37 Allied graves in the Faroes, maintained to this day by the Commonwealth Graves Commission.

With a garrison strength that would peak at 6,000, relations with the local population became inevitable. It is believed that some 170 marriages resulted, including that of Frederick Mason himself, who married a local woman, Karen Rorholm.

Although occasionally bombed by the Luftwaffe, the islands would never be the target of a concerted attack from the Germans. Following the invasion of Europe in 1944, the British presence on the Faroe Islands was greatly reduced until the last British personnel retired from the islands in September 1945. The experience of wartime self-government did, however, mean that a return to its pre-war status of an amt was unrealistic. A referendum on independence was held in 1946 and formal autonomy was established in 1948 – albeit within the Danish realm.

Hazelnut Oatcake

Traditional Faroe Islands cuisine is quite distinctive: its main commodities are lamb or mutton, fish, puffin meat, whale meat and blubber, with the emphasis on fermentation. This recipe, however, contains none of these ingredients. Instead it is a tasty cake that can be served with afternoon tea or as a dessert with a scoop of vanilla ice cream, whipped cream or crème fraiche.

INGREDIENTS

Serves 8

For the cake

150g rolled oats

300ml water

175g plain flour

1 tsp baking powder

1 tsp ground cinnamon

¾ tsp caraway seeds

½ tsp salt

225g unsalted butter

300g light soft brown sugar
 (plus extra for the top)

2 medium eggs, beaten

100g hazelnuts, finely chopped

For the vanilla pastry cream

500ml milk

4 large egg yolks

100g light soft brown sugar

2 tsp vanilla paste or extract

75g plain flour

2 tsp cornflour

pinch of ground cinnamon
 (optional)

To finish and serve

50g hazelnuts, toasted and finely
 chopped

whipped cream or crème fraiche

METHOD

To make the oatcake

- Preheat the oven to 180°C.
- Lightly butter a 19cm by 26cm baking dish and line the base with baking parchment.
- Place the oats in a heatproof bowl, boil the water, pour over the oats and allow to soak for 15 minutes.
- Sift the flour and baking powder into a bowl and mix in the ground cinnamon, caraway seeds and salt.
- Melt the butter, pour into a clean bowl and whisk in the brown sugar and eggs.
- Beat the wet mix into the dry mix then stir in the soaked oats and chopped hazelnuts until thoroughly combined.
- Pour into the prepared tin, level the top, sprinkle over a thin layer of brown sugar and bake in the preheated oven for about 45 minutes until a skewer comes out clean when inserted into the middle of the cake.
- Once cooked allow the cake to sit in the tin for 15 minutes before transferring to a wire rack to cool.

To make the vanilla cream

- Bring the milk to a simmer.
- Whisk the egg yolks, brown sugar and vanilla paste or extract together in a bowl until well blended.
- Sift the plain flour, cornflour and cinnamon (if using) together and stir into the egg yolks and sugar.
- Gradually whisk the hot milk into the egg, sugar and flour mix.
- Strain the mixture through a sieve into a clean pan and bring to a simmer and cook gently for 2 to 3 minutes stirring constantly to ensure the mix doesn't catch on the bottom of the pan.
- Remove from the heat and pour the mixture into a bowl to cool.
- Cover the top of the pastry cream with cling film or alternatively sprinkle the top with a little caster sugar to prevent a skin forming.

To finish and serve

- Once the cake is cool, spread over the vanilla cream, sprinkle over the chopped toasted hazelnuts and chill in the fridge to set.
- Once set, cut into even-sized portions and serve with a spoonful of whipped cream or crème fraiche.

AN RAF DAKOTA AT JERSEY AIRPORT, MAY 1945

CHANNEL ISLANDS

Words by
FLIGHT LIEUTENANT CRISPIN CHAPPLE

AIRCRAFT OPERATIONS IN and around the Channel Islands were mainly concentrated at the beginning of the Second World War, before German forces occupied them from the end of June 1940 up to May 1945.

Not long before the bombing and subsequent German occupation of the islands and, in fact, as a direct result of the attack and invasion of France, 17 Squadron was forced to retreat from the French mainland. The squadron, one of the stalwarts of the British Fighter Defence Force, defended the French airfields being used for the Allied retreat. In early June, the squadron moved from Brittany, retiring to the Channel Islands, where it remained for just two days before returning to the UK. This would be a short but necessary respite from operations before taking up duties over southern England during the Battle of Britain.

In the same month, Italy declared war on the Allies and was met with a swift response. At the time, the RAF was using Jersey Airport as a forward operating base for 102 Squadron Whitley bomber aircraft. On 11 June 1940, these Whitleys were sent to bomb the cities of Turin, Milan and Genoa, in particularly the Fiat works (which built aircraft engines) and the Caproni aircraft works. Thunderstorms and severe icing forced the majority of these bombers back, but, of those that reached their targets, only two were lost in action.

Unfortunately, Churchill did not afford the islands great import and they were not well defended. It was a simple matter for Germany to occupy them and, following this, military tactics were changed to the attacking of the islands. One of the aircraft attacking Jersey – a Wellington X from 431 Squadron, RAF Burn, Yorkshire – was shot down en route to also bomb Frankfurt. It was seen to ditch just south west of the island. The crew suffered varying fates: one remained missing, three were captured on the Jersey shores and sent to concentration camps, and one was washed up dead. At the time, a dead crewman from 1663 Heavy Conversion Unit Halifax, Sergeant Denis Butlin, had also washed up

ashore, following a training accident in the sea north of Brest. In a break from the norm in Nazi-occupied land, the Luftwaffe granted the two dead full military honours. The bodies were laid in state at the military hospital for islanders to visit and pay their respects, before the funeral on 6 June. The coffins were draped with the Union Flag and hundreds lined the routes, but they were forbidden entry to the cemetery for the final internment. The airmen still lie at St Helier War Cemetery, alongside a memorial to Flight Sergeant George Booth, the missing Wellington crew-member.

After the war, RAF presence in the Channel Islands was sparse. The Commander-in-Chief of Guernsey from 1953–58 was Air Marshall Sir Thomas Walker Elmhirst, who had been the very first Commander-in-Chief of the newly independent Indian Air Force and the organiser of Mahatma Gandhi's funeral. Otherwise, RAF involvement in the islands has been by association and short-term exercise.

The most important of these was with 201 Squadron, one of the UK's former Nimrod maritime patrol squadrons and the oldest squadron in the RAF. It continued to have a strong affiliation with Guernsey right up to its disbandment in 2011 and was known as "Guernsey's Own" squadron.

In 1994, it was given the Privilege of Guernsey, the first in the island's history, and "the right to march with colours flying, drums beating and bayonets fixed." Links remain strong to this day.

Guernésiais Gâche
Guernsey Fruit Loaf

In Guernsey French, "gâche" (pronounced "gosh") translates as "cake", but this recipe is more like a bread than a cake. It is leavened with yeast rather than baking powder and includes a mix of plain and wholemeal flour. The first task is to scald the milk, which inactivates the whey protein which otherwise can weaken the gluten in the dough. This recipe contains a lot of butter, and a high fat content means it takes a relatively long time to prove, which is why it should only be added once the initial dough has been formed (much like a traditional brioche loaf). It is a traditional part of afternoon tea in Guernsey and is best eaten slightly warm and spread with salted Guernsey butter.

INGREDIENTS

175ml full fat milk

200g plain flour

100g strong wholemeal flour

pinch of salt

2 sachets (2x7g) instant yeast

50g light soft brown sugar

1 medium egg, beaten

150g butter, dice and leave at room
  temperature for 20–30 minutes

50g mixed candied peel

200g sultanas

1 egg yolk, to glaze (optional)

METHOD

• Lightly butter a 1kg loaf tin and line with baking parchment.
• Scald the milk (bring just to a simmer) and set aside to cool
  until tepid.
• Sift the flours into a mixing bowl, add the salt, yeast and sugar;
  mix well.
• Once the milk has cooled (enough to be comfortable when a finger
  is inserted for a few seconds), mix the beaten egg into the warm milk.
• Mix the milk and egg into the dry mix and knead for about 5 minutes
  to form a smooth, but quite tight, dough.
• Before adding the butter ensure it isn't too soft as it needs to be
  kneaded into the dough; if it's too soft it will melt into the dough
  making it greasy.
• Knead the butter into the dough a little at a time, dusting the bench
  with a little plain flour if the dough becomes too sticky (take care
  not to add too much flour otherwise the dough will become too
  stiff). This process is quite messy when done by hand, you will need
  to frequently scrape the worktop back into the dough, but it can be
  done in a mixer with the kneading hook attachment.
• When all of the butter is thoroughly incorporated, add the mixed peel
  and sultanas and knead into the dough.
• Shape the dough into a neat oblong shape, place in the lined loaf
  tin, cover with a cloth and leave to prove for 2½ to 3 hours at room
  temperature.
• Once the dough has proved preheat the oven to 220°C, place the loaf
  in the oven and bake for 10 minutes, lower the temperature to 200°C
  and continue to cook for 45 minutes until risen and golden brown on
  top.
• Brush with the beaten egg yolk and return to the oven for 5 minutes
  to glaze.
• Let the loaf cool in the tin for 20 minutes then tip out of the loaf tin,
  remove the baking parchment and transfer to a wire rack to cool.

To serve
• Once cool, cut the loaf into thick slices and eat either plain or toasted
  spread with butter.

GHANA

Words by
SQUADRON LEADER MAL CRAIG

RAF TAKORADI MAY not be as immediately recognisable as Biggin Hill or Brize Norton but, between 1940 and 1943, it was one of the Royal Air Force's most important strategic stations. Located in the Gold Coast (modern-day Ghana), Takoradi was known as the "white man's grave" because of the prevalence of malaria, septicaemia, yellow fever and the like. Conditions were regarded as so harsh that servicemen's time there would count double for overseas service.

Close to the coast, RAF Takoradi would become the launch point from which replacement aircraft could be ferried to the battlefields of North Africa and beyond. With most of Europe under Axis control and U-boat wolfpacks decimating convoys in the North Atlantic, it became vital to find a new route for the delivery of aircraft to the Western Desert, where General Montgomery's Desert Rats battled with Germany's Desert Fox, General Rommel. Takoradi was the only viable option: reinforcement by sea was a 14,000-mile, three-month trip around South Africa to the Red Sea or via the Western Mediterranean, neither of which were practical.

> *"It became vital to find a new route for the delivery of aircraft to the Western Desert, where Montgomery battled with Rommel. Takoradi was the only viable option"*

Founded in 1936 by Imperial Airways, Takoradi was an already established airfield, well to the south of the main transatlantic shipping lanes, and was soon identified by Allied planners as a potential strategic air hub. Crated aircraft could be shipped direct from the USA, assembled, test flown and ferried across Africa along the treacherous 3,600-mile, week-long journey to RAF Abu Sueir, near Cairo.

An RAF advanced party of 24 officers and men arrived at Takoradi on 14 July 1940. They were led by Group Captain H K Thorold, who, after his recent experiences as Maintenance Officer-in-Chief to air forces in France, was unfazed by any difficulties in Africa. He set to work on such necessary facilities as roads, gantries, hangars, workshops, storehouses, offices and living accommodation. The crew also started transforming primitive landing-grounds into efficient staging posts and perfecting wireless communication along the whole route, from the jungles of West Africa to the deserts of North Africa. Many strips, such as Kano in Nigeria, would develop into major regional and international postwar airports.

The main RAF party of some 350 men, including 25 ferry-pilots, joined Group Captain Thorold at Takoradi on 24 August.

Small maintenance parties were sent out to the staging posts, with aircraft and navigators from BOAC (British Overseas Airways Corporation) chartered to return the ferry-pilots from Abu Sueir in Egypt. The first consignment of crated aircraft – six Blenheim IVs and six Hurricanes – docked at Takoradi on 5 September.

It was followed the next day by 30 Hurricanes on the carrier *Argus*, each complete except for their main-planes and long-range tanks. The port detachment of Thorold's unit quickly unloaded the aircraft and transported them to the airfield where the aircraft-assembly unit took over. By 19 September, the first convoy – one Blenheim and six Hurricanes – stood ready on the tarmac for the flight to Egypt.

By now, French Equatorial Africa had joined de Gaulle and the Free French Forces, and the pilots had the consolation of knowing that they would be flying over friendly territory. The Blenheim roared down the runway, climbed and circled, to be quickly joined by its six charges. Seven days later, one Blenheim and five Hurricanes reached Abu Sueir. These would be the first aircraft of many to make the journey until the Allied victory in the Western Desert in 1943.

UNCRATING HURRICANE AIRCRAFT AT RAF TAKORADI, WEST AFRICA, 1942

Red-Red
Ghanaian Red Stew with Black Eye Beans

This simple and nutritious vegetarian recipe derives its name from the combination of red palm oil and tomatoes in its preparation. Traditionally served with fried plantains, it can be accompanied with rice or flatbreads (if you can't get hold of plantains, small green bananas work well as a substitute). Red-red can also be served with pan-fried or grilled fish, chicken breast or pork steak. This dish is often made with dried fish or dried shrimp powder, but this recipe includes neither to keep it vegetarian. Red-red can also be made with vegetable oils such as sunflower, rapeseed or corn oils but it's technically not a red-red without the red palm oil.

INGREDIENTS
Serves 4
For the red-red
200ml red palm fruit oil
2 medium onions, finely diced
2 red chillies, finely chopped
4 cloves garlic, finely chopped or crushed
5 medium, ripe tomatoes, coarsely chopped
2 tins (2x400g) black eye beans in water
5cm piece of ginger, finely grated
75g tomato purée
250ml vegetable stock
salt and pepper
cayenne pepper (optional)

For the plantains
75ml vegetable oil
4 plantains, thickly sliced

To serve
rice or flatbreads

METHOD
To make the red-red
- Heat the palm oil in a casserole dish or saucepan over a moderate heat. Add the onions and cook, stirring frequently, for 10 minutes until they are soft and lightly browned.
- Add the chillies and garlic and cook for a further couple of minutes.
- Stir in the chopped tomatoes and continue to cook for a few minutes until the tomatoes have released their juice.
- Add about a third of the black eye beans, bring back to a simmer then mash the contents in the casserole with a potato masher to a coarse textured sauce.
- Stir in the remaining beans (including the water from the tins), ginger, tomato purée and vegetable stock. Season well with salt and pepper and add cayenne pepper to taste.
- Bring to a boil, reduce the heat and simmer, stirring frequently for 20 to 30 minutes until the sauce has a thick, but not dry, consistency.

To make the fried plantains
- Heat the oil in a frying pan over a medium to high heat and fry the plantains until golden brown on both sides. Drain on kitchen paper.

To serve
- Ladle the red-red into bowls and serve with the fried plantains and rice or warmed flatbreads.

DENMARK

Words by
SQUADRON LEADER MAL CRAIG

THROUGHOUT THE SECOND World War, the Royal Air Force conducted extensive operations against the Nazi occupation forces in Denmark, ranging from Special Operations Missions to more conventional bombing. Although Denmark would not suffer from the massed area bombing seen elsewhere in Europe, it did see its share of tactical bombing, with RAF crews subjected to the full spectrum of stresses and strains that they had come to expect from fighting the Nazi-occupied regions of Europe.

This started with the failure of one of the first penetration raids of the war, on 13 August 1940, with the tragic loss of all 12 Bristol Blenheim aircraft of 82 Squadron, from Watton in Norfolk, during an attack on the Luftwaffe base at Aalborg. Conversely, there was the highly successful Mosquito raid on the Gestapo headquarters in the Danish city of Aarhus on 31 October 1944. Twenty-four Mosquitos penetrated the Nazi defences and – using delayed-action blasts and incendiary bombs – managed to "crack" open the headquarters. Only a single aircraft was damaged by anti-aircraft fire, forcing it to divert to neutral Sweden, where its crew were interned.

It was a highly successful mission. Many experienced Gestapo and SS personnel were killed, and most of the Gestapo's files on the Danish Resistance were destroyed. Two Danish Resistance fighters who were under interrogation at the time managed to escape and make their way to the safety of Sweden.

Special-duties squadrons also kept up a steady supply of weapons and essential materials to the Danish resistance forces, ultimately delivering 6,300 containers and 581 packets with about 650 tons of supplies throughout the country as part of Operation Tablejam. One surreptitious method of delivery used by the RAF in Denmark was to drop floating weapons containers into the many canals and rivers that criss-cross the countryside.

These missions were not without loss to the RAF. However, unlike missions over Germany itself, downed crewmen in Denmark would have the advantage of a friendly population should they be forced to parachute from their stricken aircraft.

One such example was Flying Officer Bill Power, a wireless operator/air gunner from Newry, County Down. His Halifax Bomber was shot down over Denmark on 23 April 1944 while on a mine-laying operation with 77 Squadron. Bill found himself alone on a deserted Danish beach, but was quickly scooped up by the Danish Resistance and fed into the well-established escape network. Within two weeks he was on board an RAF Mosquito destined for home.

THE ATTACK ON THE GESTAPO HQ, AARHUS, DENMARK, 1944

Danish Pastries

These pastries are thought to have been introduced to Denmark by Austrian bakers in the mid-19th century and gradually adapted to the Danish taste. The dough base can be filled with any type of jam, nuts, marzipan, dried fruit, chocolate chips, custard, pastry cream or poached fruits such as plums, peaches or apricots. As well as the simple swirl (or snail) method described below, they can be folded into puffs, triangles, envelopes, twists, cushions, bear claws, pin wheels or rolls. For best results, rest the dough overnight before cooking.

INGREDIENTS

Makes 28 pastries

For the dough

500g strong flour

2 tsp salt

75g caster sugar

1 sachet (7g) instant yeast

1 large egg, beaten

75ml water

175ml milk

250g unsalted butter

METHOD

To make the dough

- Sift the flour into a large bowl, add the salt and sugar on one half of the flour and the yeast on the other half.
- Make a well in the centre of the flour; add the beaten egg, water and milk and stir well until it has formed a sticky dough.
- Wrap the dough in cling film and rest in the fridge for an hour.
- Lay out some cling film and place the slightly softened butter on top, lay more cling film over the top and roll out to a rough rectangle about 1cm thick, place on a baking sheet and briefly chill.
- Lightly knock the dough back and roll out on a floured work surface into a rough rectangle again about 1cm thick and twice the width of the butter rectangle.

**For the cinnamon and raisin filling
(Makes enough for one batch
of dough)**

150g sultanas

75g soft brown sugar

150g butter, softened

2 tsp ground cinnamon

100g icing sugar

**For the pecan and maple filling
(Makes enough for one batch
of dough)**

175g pecan nuts

100g soft brown sugar

50g butter, softened

2 tbsp maple syrup

For the glaze

1 egg, beaten

- Remove the butter from the refrigerator and place on one half of the dough and fold over the other half to completely enclose the butter, press the seams to seal the butter in.
- Roll the dough out into a long rectangle, again about 1cm thick.
- Make a light mark in the centre and fold each end of the rectangle over twice so they meet in the middle, then fold one half over the other. Wrap in cling film and chill the dough for 45 minutes.
- Turn the dough so that one of the short ends is facing you and roll out to the same size as before.
- This time fold each end over so they meet in the middle then fold one half over the other, press the edges together to seal. Wrap in cling film and rest the dough in the refrigerator for 45 minutes.
- Repeat the previous two stages.
- Wrap the dough in cling film and refrigerate overnight before using.

To make the cinnamon and sultana filling
- Mix the sultanas, brown sugar, butter and cinnamon together in a bowl. Mix the icing sugar with 1 tbsp of cold water to make a smooth icing and drizzle over the cooled pastries.

To make the pecan and maple syrup filling
- Finely chop the pecans in a food processor and mix with the brown sugar, butter and maple syrup.

To fill and cook the pastries
- Line a couple large baking trays with baking parchment and preheat the oven to 180°C.
- Cut the rested dough in half; keep one half in the fridge until required.
- Roll the first half of dough into a rectangle around 40cm x 22cm.
- Spread the filling along the length leaving a 1cm margin along the top and bottom, tightly roll up the dough along the long edge; repeat with the remaining half of dough, wrap each in cling film and place in the freezer to firm up for 20 minutes.
- Trim off the ends and cut each roll into 2.5cm-thick slices, place on the baking sheets about 2.5cm apart; leave at room temperature to prove for half an hour.
- Brush with a little beaten egg and bake in the oven for 20 minutes until crisp and golden; transfer to a wire rack to cool.

ITALIAN EAST AFRICA

Words by
SQUADRON LEADER MAL CRAIG

THE LITTLE-KNOWN Italian East African Campaign of 1940–41 would see painfully ill-equipped British forces pitched against the vastly larger Italian military of Mussolini's new East African Empire. By this time, the Italians controlled a large area of land that comprised all of present-day Ethiopia along with Eritrea, Djibouti and parts of Somalia.

The British had operated in the region since 1920, when the RAF had dispatched 12 de Havilland DH9A biplanes, including one converted into an airborne ambulance, to suppress a Dervish uprising. Working with a small ground force against an enemy that had probably never seen an aircraft before, the British ended a 20-year rebellion in three weeks. It was called "the cheapest war in history" by Colonial Under Secretary Lord Amery, and showed how air power could have a disproportionate effect on a vastly larger enemy.

Fast forward to 1940 and, anticipating Britain's defeat and an opportunity to expand his empire, Mussolini declared war on Britain on 10 June 1940 and attacked British Somaliland in August – an attack that coincided with the Battle of Britain. It was said at the time that you could tell how far your unit was away from the Home Islands by the type of aircraft with which it was equipped. At this time, the RAF in East Africa had only around a hundred aircraft, including obsolescent Vickers Wellesleys, Gladiator biplanes and Blenheim Mk 1 bombers. With these resources, it was expected to defend the whole of Britain's East African interests and counter Italy's threat to the Red Sea and the Suez Canal, against an Italian force of some 350 aircraft.

Hopelessly outnumbered, British forces were forced to withdraw, operating from improvised landing grounds in the desert, enduring temperatures in excess of 40°C. British forces were evacuated to Aden on 19 August, having suffered 38 dead, 102 wounded and 120 missing.

It would prove to be Mussolini's only victory of the war. Italians settled into a defensive posture in East Africa, and the RAF began its offensive to retake the region in January 1941. With Gladiators and newly arrived Hurricanes from Egypt, the RAF began aggressively patrolling the Italian positions before supporting British forces advancing from Sudan into Eritrea, driving the Italian forces back into Ethiopia. On 16 March, Operation Appearance – utilising Wellesleys operating initially from Aden – supported the first successful Allied landing on an enemy beach of the Second World War.

With ground forces supported by the RAF striking from Sudan through Ethiopia into Italian Somaliland and simultaneously invading British Somaliland from the sea, Italian forces were effectively removed from the region. The Red Sea and the Gulf of Aden were declared as no longer being combat zones, allowing unarmed American shipping to supply British forces in Egypt and the Middle East. This also allowed the movement of air assets to reinforce Allied forces in the Middle East and India.

"British forces were forced to withdraw: it would prove to be Mussolini's only victory of the war"

Doro Wat
Ethiopian Red Chicken Stew

The foundation of an Ethiopian wat is a large amount of onions simmered slowly in their own juices over a low heat. Once the onions are cooked, a clarified butter called niter kibbeh is added; like Indian ghee but simmered with garlic, ginger and fragrant spices. Berbere spice mix is available in many high street supermarkets, but the recipe is included here if you want to make it yourself. Doro wat is traditionally eaten by hand with a spongy, sour, pancake-like flatbread known as injera, made with Ethiopian teff flour, but it can also be served with chapati or flatbread.

INGREDIENTS

Serves 6

For the berbere spice mix

2 tbsp berbere spice mix
  or 5 dried red chillies

4 green cardamoms, crushed

4 whole cloves

1 tsp black peppercorns

½ tsp cumin seeds

½ tsp coriander

½ tsp allspice berries

½ tsp fenugreek seeds

2 tsp salt

½ tsp ground ginger

½ tsp dried thyme leaves

¼ tsp ground nutmeg

For the wat

3 tbsp white distilled or white
  wine vinegar

2 limes, juiced

6 chicken legs, jointed into thighs
  and drumsticks

1.5kg red onions, thinly sliced

3 tbsp ghee, olive oil or niter
  kibbeh (see introduction)

3 cloves of garlic, finely chopped

2.5cm piece of ginger, finely grated

2 tbsp smoked paprika

¼ tsp ground cardamom

½ tsp fennel seeds

500ml chicken stock

6 medium eggs (room
  temperature)

salt and pepper

To serve

injera, chapati or flatbread

METHOD

To prepare the berbere spice mix

• Heat a heavy-based frying pan over a moderate heat. Add all of the spices except the salt, ginger, thyme and nutmeg. Dry fry the spices until they start to pop and release a pungent aroma; set aside to cool.

• Once cool, remove the seeds from the cardamom pods, discard the husks and grind the spices to a powder in a spice grinder or pestle and mortar. Mix in the salt, ginger, dried thyme and nutmeg.

To prepare the wat

• Mix the vinegar and half of the lime juice together, add the chicken pieces, mix to coat and marinate for 20 minutes.

• Place a large heavy-based saucepan over a moderate heat, add the onions (no oil or liquid) and cook, stirring frequently, for around 15 minutes. Turn the heat to low, add half a teaspoon of salt, mix well and continue to cook the onions, stirring occasionally for about 45 to 60 minutes until they are soft, caramelised golden brown, reduced to a sweet sticky mass and all of the liquid has evaporated.

• Increase the heat to medium, add 2 tbsp of the ghee, oil or niter kibbeh; stir in the garlic and ginger. Cook for a couple of minutes.

• Add the berbere, paprika, ground cardamom, fennel seeds and a few grinds of black pepper; cook, stirring constantly, for 5 minutes.

• Pour in the chicken stock, mix well and bring to a boil.

• Meanwhile, drain the chicken legs, season with salt and pepper. Heat the remaining 1 tbsp of ghee, oil or niter kibbeh in a frying pan, add the chicken pieces and sear to colour all over. Add the chicken to the casserole, turn down to a gentle simmer, cover and cook, stirring occasionally, for around 45 minutes until the chicken is very tender.

• Remove the lid and simmer until the liquid has thickened slightly

To finish

• Check the seasoning, adding salt and black pepper to taste and stir in the remaining lime juice.

• Hard boil the eggs (around 8 minutes) and peel off the shells.

To serve

• Quarter the boiled eggs and arrange on a serving dish with the chicken before ladling over the sauce. Serve with injera, chapati or flatbread.

ICELAND

Words by
**SQUADRON LEADER JON PULLEN
& FLIGHT LIEUTENANT CRISPIN CHAPPLE**

MARINE CRAFT SECTION HUTS IN THE SNOW AT RAF REYKJAVIK

THE ROYAL AIR FORCE has been visiting Iceland since 1931, when an RAF Blackburn Iris landed for the Millenary Celebrations of the Icelandic parliament. But it wasn't until early 1941 that the RAF employed a permanent force when Churchill deemed it to be of strategic significance and landed a small invasion force on the previously neutral island. RAF airfields were constructed by Royal Engineers at Reykjavik, Kaldadarnes and Akureyri, predominantly as part of Coastal Command to undertake reconnaissance, patrol and anti submarine roles, as well as to protect Iceland from a possible German invasion. In the first six months of RAF presence, not one Allied ship was torpedoed, while 22 air attacks on U-boats were undertaken.

RAF Reykjavik played another important role as part of RAF Ferry Command, providing a chain from the newly built Prestwick Airport to Montreal in order to deliver aircraft of lease-lend origin to the fight. Prior to the introduction of this route there had been fewer than 100 successful North Atlantic crossings, with around 50 failed attempts resulting in the loss of 16 aircraft and their 40 crew. By the end of the war, this journey had become routine with more than 9,000 successful crossings.

Operating out of Iceland was a constant battle to overcome boredom and the weather; a 269 Squadron aircraft fitter recalls wearing oversize boots so that he could don three extra pairs of socks. It was no easier for the aircrew, who complained of completely unpredictable weather, with icing, blizzards and gales causing the loss of a large number of aircraft.

Personnel lived in Nissen huts, poorly heated by RAF tortoise stoves, to stave off the 120 mph Arctic winds. "The aerodrome logbook records a Nissen hut proceeding in a northerly direction," recalls one nursing orderly, part of the Princess Mary's RAF Nursing Service, "height approximately 60 feet, in spite of being fastened down with steel cable and earthed up halfway." At one point, in March 1943, the aerodrome at Kaldadarnes even flooded when the Olfusa River burst its banks.

While there was never a shortage of food for the servicemen and women in Iceland, vegetables were extremely scarce, with vitamin supplements the norm. Since there was a large American contingent on the island and no rationing, returning airmen were very popular, taking home large quantities of very rare sweets.

By 1943, the tide of the war had turned. With the perceived threat from the Atlantic diminishing, the British Army left Iceland and its inhospitable environment. However, the RAF maintained its presence on the island, patrolling North Atlantic shipping routes until 1947.

Bakaður Þorskuro
Cod Baked with Tomatoes

Icelandic cuisine has a reputation of being unpalatable to outsiders. Hákarl (fermented shark), Svið (sheep's head), Hvalspik (boiled and pickled whale blubber), ram's testicles and puffin boiled in milk might be all regarded as acquired tastes. However, with fresh local ingredients such as seaweed-grazed lamb, reindeer venison, indigenous herbs, vegetables and fresh seafood, there is much to recommend it. This recipe uses cod but any white fish (halibut, haddock, pollock or plaice) can be used.

INGREDIENTS
Serves 4

For the cod

60g butter

200g spinach

A pinch of nutmeg

4 cod fillets (150g each), skinned

For the tomato sauce

1 medium onion, finely diced

1 tin (400g) of chopped tomatoes

1 tbsp tomato purée

2 tsp caster sugar

1 sprig thyme

2 tbsp dill, coarsely chopped

To finish

125ml double cream

75g breadcrumbs

salt and pepper

METHOD
To prepare the cod
• Melt one third of the butter in a saucepan, add the spinach, season with a little salt, pepper and a pinch of nutmeg, toss in the hot butter until wilted and drain off the excess liquid. Place the wilted spinach either in the bottom of a baking dish large enough to take the cod fillets side by side (or in the bottom of four individual ovenproof dishes).
• Melt the remaining butter in a saucepan. Season the cod fillets lightly on both sides with salt and black pepper, place side by side on the wilted spinach and brush with a little of the melted butter.

To prepare the tomato sauce
• Place the saucepan containing the remaining melted butter over a moderate heat and, when starting to foam, add the diced onions; cook, stirring frequently, for about 5 minutes until the onions have started to soften.
• Add the chopped tomatoes, tomato purée, sugar, thyme and 125ml of boiling water to the onions. Bring to a gentle simmer and cook, stirring frequently, for about 10 minutes until the sauce has reduced slightly. Stir in the chopped dill and season with salt and pepper.

To cook and finish
• Preheat the oven to 180°C.
• Pour the tomato sauce over the cod fillets and bake for 15 minutes.
• Remove the baking dish from the oven, carefully pour over the double cream, scatter over the breadcrumbs in an even layer and return to the oven for a further 10 minutes until bubbling around the sides.
• To glaze the top, place under a hot grill until lightly browned. Serve with new, boiled or mashed potatoes and vegetables such as glazed carrots and steamed broccoli.

GAMBIA

Words by
SQUADRON LEADER MAL CRAIG

IN LATE 1940 and early 1941 – with the tide of war turning against the Allies and the U-boat menace beginning to extend to the waters of West Africa – convoy protection became an increasing priority. With few ships to spare, how were the Allies to patrol the vast, empty ocean off the West African coast? It was a question that would find its answer in the long-range Sunderland flying-boats of the Royal Air Force's Coastal Command.

Dispatched from their Scottish base in January 1941, three Sunderlands – together with crews and ground support – would form the nucleus of a new squadron. Designated 95 Squadron, it would settle in Bathurst (now Banjul) in Gambia to establish the Coastal Command main base of operations in West Africa.

Together with 204 Squadron, which would soon join them from Reykjavik in Iceland, the Sunderland's would form

> *"The main danger faced in Gambia would be marauding Vichy-French fighters operating from neighbouring French colonies"*

the backbone of anti-submarine activity off the West Coast of Africa. In 1943, they were joined by a land-based squadron of long-range Liberator bombers in the form of 200 Squadron. Other than the ever-present threat of malaria, the main danger faced by the Gambia-based crews would be marauding Vichy-French fighters operating from neighbouring French colonies. This threat became a reality on 26 September 1941, when a pair of Vichy-French fighters attacked two Sunderlands returning from a patrol, resulting in damage to both aircraft and the death of one of the pilots.

It is perhaps sadly ironic that later in the war, following the fall of Vichy-France, one of the French pilots involved in this attack would in turn become a Sunderland pilot himself, and even fly one of the very same aircraft that he had attacked at Bathurst.

In response, 95 Squadron developed a Hurricane flight that would eventually become 128 Squadron, commanded by Battle of Britain ace Squadron Leader Billy Drake. He would have the rare distinction of being credited with shooting down a Vichy-French bomber in combat.

While contact with enemy U-boats was rare for the squadrons operating from

Gambia, one incident was particularly significant. On 11 August 1943, Flying Officer Lloyd Trigg, a New Zealander by birth, the holder of a Distinguished Flying Cross and a veteran of over 45 missions, was piloting a Liberator Bomber as part of 200 Squadron when he identified a surfaced U-boat off the West African coast. With incredible determination and skill he pressed his attack and sank the U-boat, sadly at the cost of his and his crew's lives. The only survivors and eyewitnesses of this engagement were the captain and a few crew members from the U-boat. Uniquely, it is through the testimony of the captain that Flying Officer Trigg would be posthumously awarded the Victoria Cross for his actions. It is the only known incidence of a statement by an enemy combatant resulting in the award of this most rare and prestigious medal.

RAF personnel who served in Gambia often did so in extremely uncomfortable conditions. While sightings of enemy vessels were rare and actual combat was rarer still, it is testament to the dedication and skills of all those who served that no allied vessels where lost to enemy action off the coast of West Africa.

A SHORT SUNDERLAND III OF 95 SQUADRON TAKING OFF AT RAF BATHURST IN GAMBIA

Domoda
Gambian Peanut Stew

Domoda is the national dish of Gambia and, in its simplest form, is a stew made with peanuts, tomatoes, onions, garlic, chillies and either pumpkin, squash or sweet potato. It is often made with beef, chicken or lamb, but the meat can be omitted and replaced with a few extra vegetables such as carrot, mushroom, aubergine, courgette or chickpeas for a vegetarian version.

INGREDIENTS

Serves 4

For the domoda

2 tbsp sunflower or vegetable oil

400g chicken breast, cut into
  2.5cm pieces

1 medium onion, coarsely chopped

1 red chilli, finely shredded

2 cloves of garlic, finely chopped
  or crushed

1 red pepper, deseeded and cut
  into 2.5cm pieces

75g tomato purée

400g tomatoes, coarsely chopped

150g smooth peanut butter

½ squash (e.g. butternut or
  coquina), peeled and cut into
  2.5cm pieces

750ml chicken stock

1 lime, halved

salt and pepper

For the garnish

50g blanched peanuts

1 punnet mustard cress

To serve

boiled or steamed rice

lime wedges

METHOD

To make the domoda

- Heat 1 tbsp of the oil in a casserole over a high heat, add the chicken pieces, sear all over and transfer the chicken to a plate with a slotted spoon; keep warm.
- Reduce the heat to medium, add the remaining oil, add the onion and cook, stirring frequently, for 5 minutes until soft and translucent.
- Add the chilli, garlic and peppers; continue to cook for a few minutes.
- Stir in the tomato purée, diced tomatoes, peanut butter, diced squash and stock. Mix well and bring to a simmer.
- Turn the heat to low, add the chicken, season lightly with salt and pepper, cover with a lid and simmer very gently for 30 to 40 minutes until the chicken is cooked through and the squash is soft and tender.
- Squeeze in the lime juice and season with a little salt and pepper.
- While the stew is simmering, heat the oven to 180°C, place the peanuts on a metal tray in a single layer and roast in the oven, shaking the pan occasionally, for around 15 minutes until they are golden brown. Season lightly with a little salt and set aside to cool. Once cool, coarsely chop the roasted peanuts.

To serve

- Ladle the domoda into bowls, garnish with the chopped peanuts and mustard cress and serve with boiled rice and lime wedges.

VEGETARIAN ALTERNATIVE

CHICKPEA DOMODA

- Follow the recipe above from step 2, starting by cooking the onion in 1 tbsp of oil and substituting the chicken stock with vegetable stock.
- Add around 400g of drained cooked chickpeas in place of the chicken, simmering until the chickpeas and squash are both soft, and continue to cook, garnish and serve as above.

SENEGAL

Words by
NICK SMART

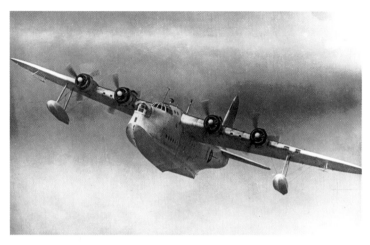

AN RAF SHORT SUNDERLAND FLYING OVER SENEGAL

AFTER THE COLONY of French West Africa – which includes modern-day Senegal – fell to Axis forces in June 1940, the region stayed under the jurisdiction of Vichy France and remained so until Operation Torch signalled the invasion of North Africa by the Allies in November 1942. The region was not the scene of major fighting, with the notable exception of the Battle of Dakar in September 1940 – an unsuccessful attempt to capture the port of Dakar, which Churchill regarded as strategically important.

As the war progressed, Allied coveys making the long trip around South Africa prompted increased U-boat activity in the South Atlantic. This necessitated the use of Sunderland flying boat patrol bombers on the Allied side. These were dispatched in March 1941 and carried out patrols for the next four years. Hurricanes were added and 95 Squadron, became 128 Squadron in October of that year.

Flight Lieutenant George Gregory arrived in this part of Africa in 1942. In his diary he reports being introduced, by a friend, to the native crocodiles at a nearby pool but, on arriving at the pool, being told that the motionless croc was dead. George walked up and gently kicked the beast's tail and, receiving no reaction, repeated the action with greater force. The crocodile whipped round and snapped angrily at the unsuspecting George, who reeled back in astonishment and fear, to peals of laughter from others who had sneaked down to the water to watch the newcomer fall for the traditional prank. George happily inflicted the tradition on other new arrivals.

While families in Britain had little access to exotic foreign fruits during the war, his diary reports that there were plenty of bananas – so many that George never ate another after leaving Africa! There was also no shortage of fish. Much of George's diary revolves around food. On one occasion, he and others came across a "huge bird the size of a turkey". It took four shots to halt the bird's progress and all were looking forward to their turkey dinner, which would provide a welcome change to the usual bush cow. Sadly, the bird turned out to be "the toughest, chewiest thing ever" and was eventually fed to the village dogs.

As the most westerly point in Africa, Dakar is a natural stopping point on the airway across the Atlantic to North Africa and Southern Europe. It retains its strategic importance, particularly for ferry flights of aircraft from the USA, and was used by the RAF during the Sierra Leone conflicts in the 1990s. Sentinels have also been deployed for intelligence gathering and target tracking to support the recent French-led operation to fight the insurgency in Mali.

Thieboudienne
Senegalese Vegetable Rice & Fish

Thieboudienne (also called ceebu jën) is the national dish of Senegal and is essentially a dish of fish, vegetables and rice, cooked in a tomato-based sauce. Recipes vary according to location, availability and cost of ingredients, which means it can be made with a variety of vegetables, squashes, potatoes or starchy tubers such as yams or cassava and any firm fleshed fish. Although, in terms of ethnicity, religion and geographic identity, Senegal has a very diverse culture, thieboudienne is generic to the various cultural identities across the country.

INGREDIENTS

Serves 4

For the fish

4 whole fish (e.g. sea bream, red
mullet, small sea bass or snapper)

25g flat leaf parsley, chopped

4 spring onions, finely chopped

2 red chillies, finely chopped

2 cloves of garlic, finely chopped

1 lime, finely grated zest and juice

salt and pepper

For the vegetables and rice

4 tbsp vegetable or peanut oil

2 medium red onions, cut into
thick wedges

1 red, yellow or green pepper,
deseeded, cut into large pieces

4 cloves of garlic, crushed

2 red chillies, halved lengthways
and finely shredded

1 aubergine, cut into large pieces

2 carrots, cut into large pieces

2 medium sweet potatoes, peeled
and cut into large pieces

75g tomato purée

1 tin (400g) of chopped tomatoes

2 tbsp tamarind paste

2 bay leaves

750ml fish, vegetable or chicken
stock

300g long grain rice

50g plain flour

2 tsp mild chilli powder

2 fillets of hot smoked oily fish

25g parsley, coarsely chopped

1 lime, halved

salt and pepper

To serve

lime, cut into wedges

METHOD

To prepare the fish

• Scale the fish, wash under cold running water and cut three or four
shallow diagonal cuts on both sides of each fish.

• Mix together the chopped parsley, spring onions, chillies, garlic, lime
zest and juice. Season with salt and freshly ground black pepper.

• Use half of the mixture to stuff each fish and rub the remaining half
into the fish skins, cover and place in the fridge until required.

To prepare the vegetables and rice

• Preheat the oven to 180°C.

• Heat 2 tbsp of the oil in a large saucepan over a moderate heat,
add the onion and cook, stirring occasionally, for 5 minutes; add
the peppers and continue to cook for a couple of minutes.

• Add the garlic and chillies and cook for a further couple of minutes.
Stir in the aubergine, carrots, sweet potato and tomato purée, stir
well and cook for 2 minutes.

• Add the chopped tomatoes, tamarind paste, bay leaves and stock.
Bring to a boil, reduce the heat and simmer for 15 minutes until the
carrots and sweet potatoes are tender. Season with salt and pepper.

• Place the rice in a saucepan cover with boiling water and simmer for
5 minutes to blanch, rinse under cold water and drain. Transfer the
blanched rice to a casserole or saucepan.

• Place a colander or sieve over the pan containing the rice and pour
in the cooked vegetables straining off the liquid into the rice pan.
Transfer the cooked vegetables to a container or bowl and set to
one side until required.

• Return the rice pan to the heat, stir well and bring to a boil. Cover
with a lid and cook in the oven for 20 minutes until just cooked.

• Heat the remaining 2 tbsp oil in a frying pan over a moderate heat.

• Mix the flour and chilli powder together in a bowl with a little salt
and pepper. Coat the oily fish in the seasoned flour, tap off the
excess and shallow fry on each side until golden brown.

• Remove the rice from the oven, stir in the flaked smoked fish fillets,
chopped parsley and squeeze in the lime juice. Check the seasoning
and place the cooked vegetables and pan-fried fish on top, cover
with the lid and return to the oven for 5 minutes to finish cooking.

To serve

• Divide the rice and vegetables between four plates, place a whole
fish on top and serve with lime wedges.

GREECE

Words by
FLIGHT LIEUTENANT TOM MARSHALL

GREECE WITNESSED FIRST-hand the formation of the Royal Air Force on 1 April 1918, when 222 Squadron was formed from an existing Royal Naval Air Service unit, based on the island of Thassos. The squadron stayed on the island through until the end of the war, using it as a base from which to bomb the Turks in the Balkans. This greatly ingratiated them to the local islanders, who in turn expressed their thanks through constant gifts of food and potent Thasian wine.

As a nation of islands, Greece lends itself to both air and sea power, and the Second World War saw the return of the RAF to the country, with heavy involvement in the fighting that followed. In April 1941, the Luftwaffe was still looking to restore its collective pride and reputation, having been humiliated by the RAF during the Battle of Britain. With Italy bogged down in a protracted mainland war with the Greek forces on the Albanian border, Hitler ordered his German forces to Greece to quickly defeat the country and take control of the Eastern Mediterranean. It soon became apparent that the RAF had not committed enough people and planes to counter this offensive, as they were first shunted out of the north of the country and were then smashed over Athens.

A young Roald Dahl, a Pilot Officer and Hurricane pilot at the time, wrote of the battle in his 1986 memoir, *Going Solo*: "To some extent I was aware of the military mess I had flown into. I knew that a small British Expeditionary Force, backed up by an equally small air force, had been sent to Greece from Egypt a few months earlier to hold back the Italian invaders, and so long as it was only the Italians they were up against, they had been able to cope. But once the Germans decided to take over, the situation immediately became hopeless."

The RAF retreated to the relative safety of Crete, hoping for some respite before having to re-engage with the Axis powers. The Royal Navy controlled the waters around the island, so it was hoped that reinforcements would arrive before the next big offensive, one that would subsequently bring major lessons and advancements for the RAF and is discussed elsewhere in this book.

The RAF did not return to Greece until September 1944, when it thought that it would be helping to defeat a retreating German army. Instead, it ended up primarily fighting the communist-dominated ELAS, the Greek People's Liberation Army. ELAS was committing atrocities on the locals and fighting the Greek national army in an effort to grab power before the proper Greek government could return from exile. This was counter-insurgency warfare of the nastiest kind, with improvised explosive devices and fighting street by street against an enemy that was hiding in the civilian population, and were conquering through fear of reprisal and butchering of innocents.

The RAF worked hand in hand with the Greek army to win over support for the Allies, and it was the "hearts and minds" approach – as much as the precision bombing runs – that won the battle for them. This time the newly formed RAF Regiment was in place, with 2933 Squadron stopping the enemy from taking over Allied airfields. It proved its value, and the RAF left Greece this time as the victors, having saved many innocent lives and stopped evil in its tracks.

Stifado
Greek Beef Stew

Originally made with rabbit or hare, stifado is generally made nowadays with beef. To give that authentic Greek flavour, stewing beef is marinated overnight, slow-cooked with red wine, tomatoes, nutmeg, cinnamon, fennel seeds (which give an aromatic hint of aniseed) and a touch of acidity from a dash of red wine vinegar. It is then finished with caramelised whole shallot onions, which give a delicate sweetness to the sauce. Stifado is wonderful served with pasta, rice, crusty bread, or any kind of potatoes (boiled, roast, chunky chips or mash).

INGREDIENTS

Serves 4

For the marinade

4 cloves garlic, finely chopped

4 whole cloves

1 cinnamon stick

¼ tsp ground nutmeg

1 tsp fennel seeds

2 bay leaves

4 allspice berries (or ¼ tsp ground
  allspice)

2 strips orange peel (pared with
  a vegetable peeler, cut away any
  white pith)

150ml red wine

4 tbsp red wine vinegar

For the stew

1kg stewing beef (e.g. chuck),
  cut into large chunks

4 tbsp olive oil

1 medium onion, finely diced

2 tbsp tomato purée

1 large ripe beef tomato (or 4 small
  ripe tomatoes), cut into large dice

250ml beef stock

2 large sprigs of rosemary

700g round shallots (or baby/
  pickling onions), peeled and
  left whole

salt and pepper

METHOD

To marinate the beef

• Mix the marinade ingredients together. Place the beef in a non-
  metallic bowl, pour over the marinade, mix to coat, cover and leave
  in the fridge overnight to marinate.

To make the stew

• Drain the beef (strain and reserve the marinade), pat dry on kitchen
  paper and season with salt and pepper.

• Heat 3 tbsp of the olive oil in a casserole dish over a high heat.
  Add the beef and sear all over.

• Turn the heat down to medium, add the diced onions and continue
  to cook for a further 5 minutes until they start to soften.

• Stir in the reserved marinade, tomato purée, chopped tomatoes,
  beef stock and rosemary.

• Bring to a boil, reduce the heat, cover and simmer gently for 2 hours.

To glaze the shallots

• Once the stifado has been simmering gently for about 1½ hours, heat
  the remaining tablespoon of olive oil in a frying pan over a moderate
  heat, add the peeled shallots and fry until lightly browned all over.

• Turn the heat to low, cover with a circle of greaseproof paper, cook
  until tender. Transfer the shallots onto kitchen paper.

• Pour off the excess oil from the pan, return to heat, add 100ml of
  boiling water and simmer, scraping the shallot residue from the pan,
  until the liquid has reduced to 3 tbsp. Strain the liquid into the stifado.

To finish

• Once the stifado has cooked for 2 hours add the glazed shallots
  (adding a little boiling water if the sauce has become too thick),
  remove the lid, continue to simmer until the sauce has reduced
  to a thick and rich consistency and the beef is very tender.

• Season with salt and pepper and pick out the rosemary sprigs,
  cinnamon stick, bay leaves and orange peel if preferred.

To serve

• Ladle the stifado into bowls and serve with potatoes, rice, pasta
  or bread.

CRETE

Words by
FLIGHT LIEUTENANT EMMA STRINGER

BY APRIL 1941 the Allies had been driven from mainland Greece by the German advancement. The British had evacuated their troops, taking whatever could be carried; mainly rifles and other small arms. Some of these evacuees were sent to bolster those forces already in the Greek island of Crete, because the British knew that, if the island was captured, the Luftwaffe could use Crete as an airbase to strike at the Mediterranean sea routes to the Allied strongholds of Egypt and Cyprus.

The Allies had a total of 27,500 troops defending the island. However, its air defence was made up of only 15 aircraft, based at three airports, all on the northern coast: Maleme, Retimo and Heraklion. All were new airports built for the Royal Air Force, however no RAF units were permanently based there until the evacuation of Greece began on 28 April 1941. British intelligence intercepted German communications and discovered that a German air attack was imminent. Food and water supplies were low, and the Allies suffered from a severe lack of heavy machinery and air defence. General Freyberg – who was appointed Allied commander at the time – sent a message to his higher headquarters reporting that he would fight, but had no hope of repelling an invasion without the full support of the Royal Navy and the RAF.

While the Allies were preparing to defend the island, the Germans were positioning themselves for the offensive.

The three airports, along with the naval port of Souda Bay, were to be the main focus for the German attack. With the Allied navy controlling the Mediterranean Sea, an airborne mission would be the only way the Germans could penetrate into Crete. Their aircraft contingent comprised some 280 bombers, 150 dive bombers, 90 twin-engine fighters, 90 single-engine fighters, 40 reconnaissance planes and 650 transport aircraft.

By 1 May 1941, the Germans had commenced detailed aerial mapping of the island, spotting all the new Allied positions. Strafing missions began, as well as the bombing of Allied defence positions, and by 13 May, only seven British planes remained. Under impossible bombardment, the RAF started to withdraw. On 19 May, one day before the invasion, German air superiority was complete. An army without a single plane faced an airborne, air-supported army for the first time in history. The 20 May saw the first wave of German paratroopers descend on Meleme airport. More Germans died in that first half an hour than had been lost during the entire previous 18 months of war, but, with no air support, the Allies were overrun. In just 10 days they were forced to retreat from Crete.

The Battle of Crete, and the defeat thereof, highlighted significant lessons for the Allies. The battle saw German paratroopers deployed en masse with devastating effect. Up until this point,

airborne operations had been used mainly in a tactical context, specifically to seize key objectives. The number of German casualties sustained employing such a tactic made the Germans reluctant to use airborne forces again, however, the Allies were impressed by the potential of a purely air-dispatched fighting capability.

The fall of Crete was considered disastrous for the RAF. It was believed that there were ample Allied troops to hold Crete against German land attack

by airborne troops, and that it was German air superiority, with its unrestricted supply and air support, that inevitably enabled the Germans to win. In the aftermath of the invasion of Crete, Winston Churchill insisted that airmen should be able to defend their airfields and, as a result, the Royal Air Force Regiment was formed, giving RAF commanders control over the defence of their own assets – thereby releasing army units for redeployment.

A SHORT SUNDERLAND AT SOUDA BAY ON THE NORTHWEST COAST OF CRETE, 1940

Dakos
Cretan Rusks with Tomatoes & Feta Cheese

Dakos, also known as koukouvayia, is a traditional Cretan mezze dish similar to Italian bruschetta. It is classically made with Cretan barley rusks (also known as dakos) but either dried and diced slices of rustic country style loaf or Swedish wholemeal crispbread rolls (available in most supermarkets) are a good substitute.

INGREDIENTS
Serves 4

4 Cretan barley rusks or
 150g krispbread rolls
6 medium, ripe, on the vine
 tomatoes, coarsely chopped
1 tbsp red wine vinegar
4 tbsp extra virgin olive oil
 (preferably Greek)
150g feta cheese
50g black olives, pitted
2 tbsp capers, drained
2 tbsp fresh oregano, coarsely
 chopped
salt and pepper

METHOD
• Either leave the rusks whole or break into large pieces, place in a bowl, add about 4 tbsp of cold water and toss to moisten. As an alternative, you can make your own by either cutting thick slices of a rustic country style loaf into large dice or cutting thick slices of wholemeal baguette (about 2.5cm) and baking in a very low oven (about 50°C) until dry and crisp.
• Place the rusk pieces in a single layer on the bottom of a serving bowl.
• Place the chopped tomatoes in a bowl with the red wine vinegar, 3 tbsp of the olive oil and season well with salt and freshly ground black pepper. Mix well and set aside at room temperature for 15 minutes.
• While the tomato mix is marinating, crumble the feta into rough, but even-sized, pieces and halve the olives.

To serve
• Spoon the tomato mixture plus all of the liquid over the bread pieces.
• Scatter over the feta cheese, black olives and capers.
• Drizzle over the remaining olive oil, season with a couple of grinds of black pepper and garnish with the chopped oregano.
• Let the dakos stand for a couple of minutes before serving to allow the rusks to soak up some of the liquid – do not allow to stand for too long or the bread will soak up too much of the liquid and become soggy.

SYRIA

Words by
**AIR COMMODORE MARK GILLIGAN
& FLIGHT LIEUTENANT CHLOE BRIDGE**

WHEN MENTIONING SYRIA, the natural inclination is to think topically of the turmoil that it has faced since the onset of its bitter civil war following the Arab Spring of 2011. The rise of Daesh in the region compounded the conflict, displaced thousands of civilians and prompted British MPs to vote in favour of military air strikes late in 2015, which have endured, with Royal Air Force involvement, since. Less well known is that the RAF had previously seen action in Syria over 70 years ago.

Following the First World War, a League of Nations mandate placed Syria under French control, so British involvement in the country prior to the Second World War was limited. Indeed, France maintained its strong influence over the country even after Syria became an independent republic in 1930. At the outbreak of the Second World War, Syria was a friendly territory under Allied influence. However, the fall of France in 1940 changed the dynamic and triggered the need for Allied military intervention. Syria's proximity to Egypt was important to the Allies, and the Vichy government's potential to exert control over its former colony could be exploited by Nazi Germany to support and possibly extend its military campaign in the western desert. Syria presented a strategic threat, so the decision was made to invade.

The invasion occurred under Operation Exporter, between June and July 1941, and also included the invasion of Lebanon. While Bristol Blenheims strafed targets and provided close air-support for the troops on the ground, there was a notable contribution from one of the RAF's less heralded ground units.

The formation of the RAF Regiment in 1942 was not, however, the first unit tasked with ground operations. In the early 1920s, a number of RAF Armoured Car Companies (ACC) were set up and operated in the Middle East to support aircraft and personnel. Number 2 ACC was formed on 7 April 1922 in Egypt and was the predecessor to Number II Squadron RAF Regiment. Serving across the region in the inter-war years, the unit was tasked to support Operation Exporter in Syria in 1941.

Based in Baghdad, 2 ACC moved toward the Syrian border, and was attacked by both Vichy aircraft and ground units. One particular battle between 21 and 30 June 1941 saw the unit come under significant sniper and machine-gun fire around Palmyra, in the centre of the country. For his actions in the campaign, the Officer Commanding of 2 ACC, Squadron Leader Michael Cassano, was eventually awarded the Military Cross, reflecting the significance of 2 ACC's contribution, along with those of Australian, Czech and Free French allies, to an operation that was concluded in a little over two months, with an Armistice signed on 12 July 1941.

A FORDSON VEHICLE OF 2 ARMOURED CAR COMPANY IN SYRIA, 1941

Kibbeh Raas
Syrian Stuffed Bulgur Croquettes

Popular throughout the Levant, kibbeh are considered the national dish of Syria. Some are baked, fried or raw, they can be shaped as balls, cakes or, as in this recipe, torpedo-shaped croquettes. Baharat spice mix is used throughout the Middle East to flavour lamb, rice and lentil dishes and is widely available, but to make your own, just mix up the ingredients listed opposite.

INGREDIENTS

Makes 24

For the kibbeh shell

300g bulgur wheat

400g minced lamb

1 medium onion, finely diced

2 tsp baharat (see recipe below)

1½ tsp salt

For the filling

3 tbsp olive oil

1 medium onion, finely diced

75g pine nuts

1 tsp ground cumin

1 tsp ground allspice

400g minced lamb

salt and pepper

To cook

vegetable oil for deep frying

To serve

1 lemon, cut into wedges

hummus

To make the baharat (optional)

6 tbsp paprika

4 tbsp ground cumin

4 tbsp ground black pepper

3 tbsp ground cinnamon

3 tbsp ground coriander

2 tbsp ground cloves

1 tbsp ground ginger

1 tbsp ground cardamom

1 tbsp ground nutmeg

1½ tsp ground allspice

METHOD

To make the shells

• Place the bulgur wheat in a bowl and add enough cold water to just cover. Set aside to soak, stirring occasionally, for 30 minutes.

• Once soaked, drain the bulgur wheat and place in a tea towel then squeeze out the excess water.

• Make the baharat by blending all the spices together. Any leftover, store in an airtight container.

• Mix the bulgur wheat with the minced lamb, diced onion, baharat and salt. Place in a food processor and blend to a stiff paste, add a little cold water if the paste is too thick. Place in a bowl, cover and place in the fridge for 1 hour to chill and allow the mix to firm up.

To make the filling

• Heat 1 tbsp of the olive oil in a large frying pan over a medium heat, add the onions and pine nuts and cook, stirring frequently, for 5 minutes. Add the ground spices and continue to cook for a further 2 to 3 minutes. Transfer to a mixing bowl.

• Return the pan to a high heat, add the remaining olive oil and add the minced lamb. Fry until well browned and season with salt and freshly ground black pepper.

• Add the cooked lamb to the onion mix, mix well, cover and chill.

To make the kibbeh

• When making the kibbeh, keep your hands wet to prevent the shell mix sticking to your palms.

• Divide the shell mixture into 24 even-sized pieces and roll them into balls.

• Flatten each ball to a thin disc between the palms of your hands, place a tablespoon of the filling in the centre, seal the seam by pinching the opening together and shape into neat torpedo shapes, tapered at each end. Place on a tray, cover and chill for 30 minutes before cooking.

To cook and serve

• Deep fry at 180°C or shallow fry the kibbeh for around 8 minutes until browned all over and the filling is piping hot.

• Drain the kibbeh on kitchen paper and serve with lemon wedges and hummus.

SARDINIA

Words by
SQUADRON LEADER HELEN TRAIN

SARDINIA IS ITALY'S second-largest island and one of the most geologically ancient bodies of land in Europe. As well as being an increasingly popular tourist hotspot it has seen significant military presence since the Second World War: even now, around 60 per cent of all Italian military installations and NATO military installations in Italy are on Sardinia. This despite its area being less than one-tenth of the entire Italian territory.

Decimomannu Air Base, located on the south of the island, became a military airport on 3 June 1940, and throughout the Second World War it hosted both Axis and Allied forces. Its Axis ownership began with the Italian 32nd Wing from Cagliari Elmas. Then, between 1941 and 1943, the 36th Wing operated there, flying the Savoia-Marchetti SM79 bomber and its replacement the SM84. The base experienced heavy losses when Decimmomanu was one of the airfields attacked by nine RAF Wellington bombers in November 1942 to cover the arrival of Allied forces in Algeria.

In September 1941, the 36th Wing was involved in a bloody battle as a convoy of nine Royal Navy ships were resupplying Malta with supplies and equipment totalling 81,000 tons, part of Operation Halberd. This naval mission was escorted by long-range fighters – Bristol Beaufighters and Bristol Blenheims from 252 Squadron, based in Malta – which had been bombing and strafing Italian airfields on Sardinia. They would provide air cover for the convoy before reaching the Sicilian narrows. UK personnel travelling as part of the convoy described this as "the hardest fought" of any Mediterranean convoys. This route needed extensive protection; the base at Malta was an essential bridging station in the Mediterranean war and every effort was being made by the Germans and Italians to prevent its re-supply.

George Gilroy was manning a four-inch gun on the destroyer on HMS *Nelson*. "The air attacks were a combination of high-altitude bombing, dive bombing and low-level torpedo bombing," he wrote. "There was also the threat of attack from German submarines, E boats and the Italian Navy. The sky was often black with our anti-aircraft fire and the enemy gave us little rest between attacks. They were obviously well coordinated and prepared for us."

The 36th Italian Wing scrambled after the convoy was detected, and carried out a number of air attacks causing damage to several ships. The remainder of the convoy arrived at Malta with its cargo as the 36th Wing turned back having seen the strength of the escorting force.

Having spent a number of years throughout the war bombing Sardinia, the RAF based aircraft there from 7 December 1943 when 23(F) Squadron Mosquitos were posted to RAF Alghero. These were shortly followed by 39 Squadron with the Bristol Beaufighter Mk.X and 272 Squadron with its Bristol Beaufighter Mk.VIc's, Mk.X's and Mk.XI's during February 1944. From Sardinia the Beaufighters could easily strike targets in southern France and Italy.

More importantly, they were used as a decoy to convince Hitler that British and American forces were about to invade Sardinia, and not Sicily, as planned. This was part of Operation Mincemeat, a misinformation campaign that led to the Germans reinforcing the Italian army on Sardinia, leaving Sicily relatively free. The Germans used the replacements meant for the Africa Division, which surrendered in Tunisia. The invasion came, of course – but the Allies invaded Sicily.

Seadas
Sardinian Cheese & Honey Fritters

These moreish dessert fritters combine Sardinia's native salty pecorino ewe's milk cheese and sweet honey. Seadas are traditionally made with young pecorino that is still soft, slightly acidic and less salty than the more mature cheeses. So, if using more mature pecorino, you need to balance the lemon and honey to temper the saltiness of the grated cheese. For an extra touch of sweetness, sprinkle some caster sugar. Pecorino can also be substituted with ricotta for a sweeter variation.

INGREDIENTS

Makes 20

For the seada dough

500g tipo '00' flour (or plain flour)

1 tbsp caster sugar

½ tsp salt

300ml cold water

50g lard, diced

For the filling

200g pecorino cheese, grated

1½ lemons, finely grated zest
  and juice of ½ lemon

2 tbsp honey

1 egg, beaten for brushing

vegetable oil for deep frying

To serve

honey, to drizzle

caster sugar (optional)

METHOD

To make the dough

• Sift the flour and mix with the sugar and salt. Add enough of the cold water to form a smooth and elastic dough.

• Gradually add the diced lard and knead until thoroughly incorporated.

• Wrap the dough in cling film and chill in the fridge for 1 hour.

To make and fill the seadas

• Mix the grated cheese with the finely grated lemon zest, the juice of half a lemon and the honey.

• Lightly dust the worktop with flour, roll out the dough to 1.5mm to 2mm thick and cut out 20 discs with a fluted 8.5cm pastry cutter and 20 slightly larger discs with a fluted 9.5cm cutter.

• Mould the cheese, lemon and honey mix into teaspoon-sized balls, flatten slightly and place in the centre of the smaller circles, brush the edges with a little beaten egg and place the larger discs on top of the filling. Firmly seal the edges with your fingers, thinning out the pastry around the edges as you go and neaten each filled disc with the smaller fluted pastry cutter. Place the seadas on a tray lined with baking parchment, cover with cling film and rest in the fridge to firm up for 20 to 30 minutes before frying.

To cook and serve

• Deep fry the seadas in batches at 180°C until lightly browned on both sides and drain on kitchen paper.

• Serve the seadas drizzled with honey and a sprinkling of caster sugar for an extra bit of sweetness.

PORTUGAL

Words by
FLIGHT LIEUTENANT SIMON STAFFORD

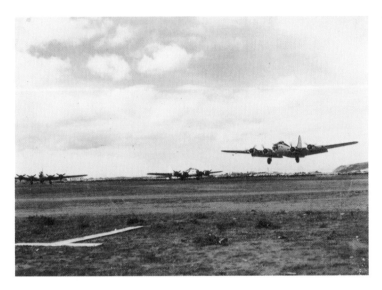

ADRIFT FROM THE rest of Europe, located far into the Atlantic Ocean, around 850 miles west of the Iberian peninsula, the Azores is an autonomous region of Portugal that has long held strategic value for the Royal Air Force. The most utilised area is Lajes Airfield, which dates back to 1928.

Portugal is one of England's oldest allies, with cooperation dating back to 1147. In 1941, Portugal – which, at the time, had no modern fighter planes – invoked the 1373 Anglo–Portuguese Treaty of Military Alliance. This proposed a trade of two bases on the Azores, one at Lajes for the RAF and one at Faial for the Royal Navy, in exchange for sufficient fighters to equip eight fighter squadrons, along with Oxford, Master, Martinet and Magister training aircraft. The first fighters – 11 American Curtiss Mohawks – were sent in October

A BOEING FORTRESS
LANDING IN THE AZORES,
CIRCA 1943

1941, the first 18 Spitfires arrived at the end of 1942 and, during 1943, 65 Hurricanes and more Spitfires were delivered. In total, Britain supplied 116 Hurricanes, over 50 Spitfires, and sundry other aircraft to protect Allied shipping in the Atlantic.

The airfield was designated Air Base No. 4 and the Portuguese government expanded the runway, sending troops and equipment to Terceira, including Gloster Gladiator fighters. On 1 December 1943, British and US military representatives at RAF Lajes Field signed a joint agreement outlining the roles and responsibilities for the United States Army Air Forces (USAAF) and United States Navy (USN) at Lajes Field. By the end of June 1944, more than 1,900 American airplanes had passed through this Azorean base. Using Lajes Field, the flying time compared to the usual transatlantic route between Brazil and West Africa was cut from 70 to 40 hours.

The US and the UK transferred control of Lajes to Portugal in 1946 but there has been a US military presence their ever since, with a tenancy agreement as well as the NATO agreement in 1949. Lajes Field also played a crucial role in Cold War politics, but with the collapse of the Soviet Union, operations were scaled down.

The airfield was also an alternative landing site for the NASA Space Shuttle orbiter, before its retirement. Today, Lajes continues to support transiting aircraft of the RAF for annual exercises in the USA, such as Highrider and Red Flag.

Pastéis de Nata
Portuguese Custard Tarts

Pastéis de nata literally translates as "cream pastries". These wonderful custard tarts are reputed to have been created in the early 19th century by nuns at the monastery of Jerónimos in Belém, a civil parish of Lisbon. It's why the name "pastéis de Belém" has actually been trademarked by the Antiga Confeitaria de Belém, which makes and sells 20,000 of them daily in Lisbon.

INGREDIENTS

Makes 12

For the sugar syrup

150ml cold water

150g caster sugar

1 cinnamon stick, broken into pieces

½ lemon, zest pared into strips with a vegetable peeler

For the custard

225ml milk (full fat)

1 vanilla pod (or 1 tsp vanilla paste)

3 large egg yolks

1 large whole egg

20g plain flour

10g cornflour

ground cinnamon to dust (optional)

For the pastry

3 sheets of ready-rolled all butter puff pastry (215g each)

fine sea salt

METHOD

To make the syrup

• Heat the cold water, caster sugar, cinnamon stick and lemon zest in a saucepan and stir until the sugar has dissolved and it starts to boil.

• Turn the heat to medium, do not stir and simmer for 4 minutes. Remove from the heat, set aside and allow to cool completely.

To make the custard

• Pour the milk into a saucepan, scrape the seeds from the vanilla pod and add to the milk along with the pod. Bring to the boil, remove from the heat and set aside to infuse for a few minutes.

• Whisk the egg yolks and whole egg in a bowl. Sift the plain flour and cornflour together and whisk into the beaten eggs until smooth.

• Gradually strain the hot vanilla-infused milk into the egg and flour mix stirring continually. Strain the lemon and cinnamon-infused sugar syrup into the egg mix and stir well until thoroughly combined.

To prepare the pastry cases

• Preheat the oven 250°C (or to its highest setting).

• Lightly butter a 12-hole, deep, non-stick muffin tray (each mould 7cm across by 3cm deep).

• Place one puff pastry sheet on the worktop with the long edge facing you and evenly sprinkle over a generous pinch of salt.

• Place the second sheet squarely on top of the bottom sheet, sprinkle with a little salt and place the third sheet squarely on top.

• Tightly roll the pastry from the bottom to the top to form a log, trim the ends (it should be around 5cm in diameter and 30cm long) and cut into 12 equal-sized slices around 2.5cm thick.

• Form each slice back into a disc and flatten with the palm of your hand. Place each disc into the moulds and press into the base and shape; prick the base of each tartlet three times.

To cook the pastéis de nata

• Skim off any foam from the surface of the custard and pour the mix into the pastry cases, to about 1cm from the top; dust with ground cinnamon (optional) and bake in the hot oven for 15 to 20 minutes until the pastry is flaky and the custard is darkly glazed in places.

• Remove from the oven, brush the tops with a little cold water, cool in the tray for a few minutes then transfer to a wire rack to cool. The tarts are best eaten still slightly warm.

BURMA

Words by
WING COMMANDER MARC HOLLAND

THE FORMER BRITISH colony of Burma (also known as Myanmar) is known as one of the world's most hazardous places to fly because of huge mountain ranges, inhospitable jungles and colossal storms in the monsoon season. When the Japanese attacked Burma in 1942, it was woefully defended by the Royal Air Force, which had allocated fewer than 200 flyable aircraft to defend a country the size of France. Although vastly outnumbered by Japanese aircraft, the RAF had to make a stand in order to buy enough time for refugees and ground troops to escape the rapidly advancing Japanese army.

With only a few Hurricanes, antiquated Buffalo fighters and a few Lysanders (usually used for training only), makeshift airstrips were built in paddy fields to cover the retreat. These were testament to the ingenuity of the RAF aircrew and engineers, who kept the aircraft flying from these remote fields without any spare parts. Things became so dire that, for more than a month, Lysander pilots flew without any airspeed indicators and many of the airframes were held together with bits of wire, while the Hurricane tailwheels (lost when landing on the uneven fields) were replaced with improvised skids made of bamboo.

In a country with very few roads, the offensive to recapture Burma was wholly reliant on resupply from the air. The planners identified the airfield of Meiktila, 82 miles to the south of Mandalay, as the key to retaking the country, as it would act as a resupply base and provide a lifeline to the Allied army. In February 1945, this site played host to one of the fiercest ground battles that the newly formed RAF Regiment would encounter during the war.

"My squadron were sent as reinforcements during the battle of Meiktila," says LAC Cyril Paskin of 2968 Field Squadron RAF Regiment. "While we were waiting for aircraft, miles from anywhere, surrounded by Japanese, the RAF sent a padre in to give us the last communion! They did not expect us to survive this operation."

Outnumbered by a determined enemy, the RAF Regiment devised an ingenious system to even the odds. Each night they would retreat to their dug outs, then, at the crack of dawn, would sweep the airfield clear of enemy soldiers before the day's flying activity. With next to no sleep, scorching temperatures during the day and relentless nightly attacks from Japanese mortars and snipers, it must have been extremely demoralising.

After three weeks of constant attacks, the Japanese abandoned their attempts to recapture Meiktila, earning the RAF Regiment battle honours. But, with a casualty rate of one in three, the price was great. The holding of this airfield enabled the resupply of the army, which swept through Burma shortly before the Japanese surrendered. After the war, Burma gained its independence from Britain, but the RAF remained in the country for many years to assist in the creation of the first Myanmar Air Force, which fittingly built its headquarters at Meiktila Airfield.

"With mountain ranges, jungles and storms, Burma is one of the most hazardous places to fly"

Masala Pork Balls
with Burmese Tomato Salad

Burmese cuisine is heavily influenced by its neighbours, Thailand, China and Bangladesh, but has its own distinctive character with fish sauce being a characteristic flavour in many dishes. This dish combines highly spiced pork meatballs with a refreshing tomato salad, the salty crunch of chopped roasted peanuts, the tang of rice vinegar and the heat of fresh and fiery dried chillies.

INGREDIENTS
Serves 4
For the tomato salad
6 medium tomatoes, deseeded and finely diced or cut into thin wedges

3 cloves of garlic, finely chopped or crushed

1 red chilli, finely chopped

3 kaffir lime leaves, finely chopped

1 tbsp mint leaves, shredded

1 tbsp basil leaves, shredded

1 tbsp coriander leaves, chopped

1 spring onion, finely chopped

1 tbsp caster sugar

2 limes (or 1 lemon), juiced

30g roasted salted peanuts, coarsely chopped

For the pork balls
1 tbsp vegetable or sunflower oil

1 medium onion, finely diced

2 tsp turmeric

2 tsp ground coriander

1 tsp ground cumin

1 tsp mild chilli powder

1 tsp garam masala

½ tsp powdered lemongrass (optional)

600g pork mince

2 tbsp fish sauce

salt and pepper

METHOD
To make the Burmese tomato salad
- Mix all of the salad ingredients, except the peanuts, together and season with salt and freshly ground black pepper.

To make the pork balls
- Heat the oil in a saucepan over a moderate heat, add the diced onion and cook until softened and translucent.
- Add the spices and continue to cook for a couple of minutes. Remove from the heat and allow to cool.
- Once cooled, mix the onions and spice mix with the minced pork and fish sauce. Season well with salt and black pepper.
- Roll the mixture into small balls (5 or 6 per portion), place on a tray, cover with cling film and chill in the fridge for half an hour.
- While the meatballs are chilling, preheat the oven to 200°C.
- Cook the meatballs in the oven for 15 minutes until well browned and cooked through.

To make the hot, sweet and sour sauce
- Heat the oil in a saucepan over a medium heat, add the diced onion and pepper; cook for 5 minutes, stirring frequently. Add the red chillies, dried chillies, garlic and ginger; cook for a further couple of minutes stirring frequently.
- Stir in the vinegar, sugar, fish sauce and tomato purée with 125ml of boiling water. Bring to a boil, reduce the heat, season with a little salt and simmer for 5 minutes.

To serve
- Arrange the pork balls on plates with the rice, spoon over the sauce and serve with the tomato salad garnished with the chopped peanuts.

For the hot, sweet and sour sauce

2 tbsp sunflower oil

1 medium red onion, finely diced

1 medium red pepper, diced

2 red chillies, halved lengthways
  and finely sliced

1 tsp dried chilli flakes

2 cloves of garlic, finely chopped
  or crushed

2.5cm piece of ginger, finely
  chopped or grated

4 tbsp rice vinegar

50g brown sugar

3 tbsp fish sauce

2 tbsp tomato purée

To serve

boiled or steamed rice

JAVA

Words by
WING COMMANDER MARC HOLLAND

THE MOST POPULOUS island in Indonesia, Java is the world's 13th largest island and was one of the last Allied outposts in the Far East – one that prevented the Japanese from attacking Australia. In 1942, the rapid Japanese advance had resulted in Allied forces from all over the Far East retreating to Java. Almost immediately, the order was given to evacuate all Allied personnel as they were hopelessly outnumbered by the advancing Japanese force. When the final evacuation ship had sailed from Java, over 10,000 people were still left behind, many of them were Royal Air Force personnel, untrained in combat, carrying very few weapons and little ammunition.

It was clear that any resistance to the superior Japanese forces would only delay the inevitable. However, to buy Australia more time to bolster its defences, the decision was taken to split the remaining force into two, with one half being a fighting force armed with the limited weapons they had and the other (made up of mainly RAF personnel) to remain in the jungle and await capture. One group of officers awaiting capture decided to hide the £1,000 (£30,000 in today's money) that they had been issued for their escape by wrapping the money in canvas and concealing it in the roof of a local school to prevent it falling into enemy hands. Many years later, they returned to find the package exactly where they'd left it, but the notes had been turned to confetti by ravenous white ants.

The resistance lasted only a few days before the enemy seized control of the island and its airfields, leaving the Allied POWs in Java to suffer three years of brutality from their Japanese captors. Death and loss of sight from malnutrition were commonplace. "The food supplied was appalling: dirty unwashed rice with millet or sweet potato and cabbage tops," recalls Squadron Leader Aiden McCarthy, an RAF doctor who volunteered to stay behind on the island to care for the sick and wounded. "The complete absence of taste in food made POWs constantly alert for orange skins, chillis and salt." When the Japanese surrender was announced on 2 September 1945, the newly liberated prisoners were overjoyed to find Red Cross parcels, which their captors had kept for themselves, laden with foods the Japanese were not accustomed to, such as butter, cheese and sticky sponge puddings!

Sadly, the jubilation was to be short lived as Javanese rebels, who opposed a return to Dutch rule, immediately seized control of the island. To mount a rescue effort, a permanent RAF detachment was established under 904 Air Wing at Kemajoran airfield. Using Dakota transport aircraft and Thunderbolt ground attack fighters, it took nearly a year to rescue the surviving 5,000 prisoners across the island while combating the Javanese militia.

The commanding officer of the RAF detachment remembers the sight of the first POWs to be rescued. "Almost without exception, they had to be helped down the steps from the Dakota, most of them desperately thin, with swollen bellies." As soon as the last prisoner was rescued in August 1946 the airfield was handed over to the Dutch military, marking the end of 904 Air Wing and the RAF presence in Java. In recent years, 904 Expeditionary Air Wing was re-established in Kandahar, Afghanistan for ground attack and transport aircraft, a role similar to that which it played in Java in 1946.

Sate Ayam Ponogoro
Chicken Satay with Peanut Sauce

Ponogoro is a town in East Java famous for its variant of chicken satay which is a single piece of marinated chicken threaded onto a skewer. The marinating process is known as "bacem", which is a method of prolonging the life of prepared food in a mixture of spices and Indonesian sweet soy sauce known as kecap (or ketjap, the derivation of "ketchup") manis. The satay are ideally cooked on a barbecue but can be grilled or griddled and served with a sweet peanut and chilli sauce alongside rice or lontong rice cakes (pressed cylindrical cakes of sticky rice).

INGREDIENTS

Serves 4

8 bamboo or wooden skewers,
  soaked for 1 hour in cold water

For the marinated chicken

1 tsp coriander seeds

½ tsp cumin seeds

¼ tsp caraway seeds

4 cloves garlic, finely chopped or
  crushed

1 tsp galangal paste (or a 1cm piece
  of galangal, grated)

METHOD

To marinate the chicken

• Heat a small frying pan over a moderate heat, add the coriander, cumin and caraway seeds and toast, shaking the pan constantly, for a couple of minutes until fragrant. Tip onto a plate to cool.

• Once cool, place the toasted spices into a small hand-held blender with the garlic, galangal, kaffir lime leaves, salt, oil, kecap manis and sugar. Blend to a paste – alternatively crush the toasted spices, garlic, galangal and kaffir lime leaves to a stiff paste with a pestle and mortar then mix with the salt, oil, kecap manis and sugar.

• Coat the chicken strips in the marinade, place in a container, cover and refrigerate for 1 hour.

2 dried kaffir lime leaves, crumbled

½ tsp salt

4 tbsp peanut oil or sunflower oil

2 tbsp kecap manis (Indonesian
  sweet soy sauce)

2 tbsp palm or soft brown sugar

500g chicken breast, cut into 5cm
  thick strips

For the peanut sauce

300g blanched peanuts

4 pecan nuts

2 tbsp peanut oil or sunflower oil

2 red chillies, coarsely chopped

2 bird's eye chillies, coarsely
  chopped

30ml kecap manis

1 tsp salt

2 tbsp palm or soft brown sugar

300ml cold water

1 lime, halved

To serve

boiled rice

2 bird's eye chillies, finely sliced
  (optional)

4 lime wedges

To make the peanut sauce

• Heat the oven to 180°C, place the peanuts and pecans on a metal tray in a single layer and roast in the oven, shaking the pan occasionally, for 15 minutes until they are golden brown. Set aside to cool.

• Heat the oil in a small pan over a moderate heat, add the chillies and cook, stirring frequently until softened. Cool slightly then tip into a blender with the peanuts, pecans, kecap manis, salt, sugar and three quarters of the water. Blend to a coarse paste (there should still be small pieces of nut in the sauce), adding more water as required to make a thick sauce consistency.

• Transfer the sauce to a saucepan, place over a low heat and bring to a simmer, squeeze in the lime juice to taste when ready to serve.

To cook

• Thread the chicken strips onto the soaked wooden skewers and cook on a barbecue, under a hot grill or in a griddle pan for 4 to 5 minutes on each side brushing with the remaining marinade as they cook.

To serve

• Serve the satay with the peanut sauce, lime wedges and boiled rice; sprinkle over the sliced bird's eye chillies.

SRI LANKA

Words by
FLIGHT LIEUTENANT CRISPIN CHAPPLE

THE RAF FIRST based personnel in Ceylon (now Sri Lanka) in September 1941 when No. 222 Gp established an outpost to patrol the Indian Ocean. By the start of 1942, the Japanese had made vast inroads into and around the Far East, and were poised to enter the Indian Ocean unopposed. Were they to seize Ceylon, it would give them control of routes to the Far and Middle East.

"The capture of Ceylon, the consequent control of the Indian Ocean, and the possibility of a German conquest of Egypt would have closed the ring," wrote Winston Churchill. "The future would have been black." The RAF therefore had to defend Ceylon. 30, 258 and 261 Hurricane Squadrons were transferred from the Middle East, along with 413 Squadron Catalinas. On 5 April 1942, Japan started its approach on Ceylon, something that Churchill described as "the most dangerous moment of the Second World War".

30 Squadron was based at Ratmalan airfield, Colombo and, on 28 March, intelligence reports stated that the Japanese fleet had left the East Indies bound for Ceylon. The squadron was ready for action and morale was high. Just before dusk on 4 April, a Catalina crew reported sighting the Japanese fleet a mere 400 miles from Ceylon.

A CATALINA FLYING BOAT OVER RAF KOGGALA, CEYLON, CIRCA 1944

Japanese Zero fighters subsequently shot the RAF jets down, but the Japanese now knew they had been rumbled.

The following morning, the Japanese launched some 125 aircraft, bombers and fighters, led by Commander Mitsuo Fuchida, who had led the attack on Pearl Harbour. Their aim was to find and defeat the Eastern Navy Fleet, with some 180 aircraft ready to follow once located. However, with most of this fleet concentrated some 500 miles west of Ceylon, the Japanese were unable to locate it. Instead, they continued towards the island to bomb its harbours.

Due to heavy cloud and the radar being unusually unmanned, the Japanese approached Ratmalana without resistance. 30 Squadron were caught off-guard and, with the Japanese attacking, confusion and a lack of coordination forced the Hurricanes into the air without formulating any tactics.

Unable to locate the Eastern Fleet, the Japanese bombers were swiftly recalled, leaving Zero fighters to engage RAF fighters. Eight aircraft from 30 Squadron and five from 258 Squadron were lost, along with a number of Fleet Air Arm aircraft. But the Japanese lost around 70 aircraft. Historians argue that this affected subsequent battles at Midway and the Coral Sea, tipping the balance in the Pacific war in the Allies' favour.

Ceylon did not fall. By October 1945 this outpost became Air HQ Ceylon, until 1956 when the Royal Ceylon Air Force commenced the official take-over.

Mairaisa Maāḷau Haeādai
Chilli Fish Curry

Sri Lankan cuisine uses a plethora of indigenous produce, particularly spices and coconuts, but also fuses foreign influences introduced by international traders, including South Indian, British, Malaysian, Middle Eastern and European. Sri Lanka's fiery curries are usually served with rice and tend to be hotter than their Indian counterparts. This recipe uses river cobbler, which lends itself perfectly to this hot and sour dish. Other white fish such as sea bass, plaice, sole or coley will also work well.

INGREDIENTS

Serves 4

For the fish

300g thin fish fillets, e.g. river cobbler

200g mixed cooked seafood
  (squid, prawns, mussels. clams)

For the curry paste

1 tbsp paprika

2 tsp chilli powder

2 tsp garam masala

1 tsp cayenne pepper

1 tsp ground coriander

1 tsp ground cumin

½ tsp ground cinnamon

½ tsp ground black pepper

¼ tsp turmeric

1 tsp salt

2 tbsp tamarind paste

3 curry leaves

1 tbsp malt vinegar

For the sauce

2 tbsp sunflower oil

1 medium red onion, finely diced

2 green chillies, halved lengthways
  and finely sliced

2.5cm piece of ginger, grated or
  finely chopped

2 cloves of garlic, finely chopped
  or crushed

2 tbsp tomato purée

½ lime, juiced

To serve

4 tbsp coconut cream

½ lime, cut into wedges

red or green chillies, sliced (optional)

deep fried garlic chips (optional)

basmati rice and/or roti, paratha
  or naan bread

METHOD

To prepare the fish

• Cut the fillets into 2.5cm pieces. Defrost the mixed seafood if
  using frozen.

To make the curry paste

• Mix the spices, salt, tamarind paste and curry leaves together.
  Add the vinegar and 2 tbsp of cold water to make a paste.

To make the sauce

• Heat the oil in a saucepan over a moderate heat, add the onions
  and cook for 5 minutes, stirring frequently, until starting to soften.

• Add the chillies, ginger and garlic. Continue to cook for a further
  2 minutes.

• Add the curry paste and continue to cook, stirring continuously,
  for another couple of minutes.

• Stir in the tomato purée and 500ml of boiling water. Bring to a
  simmer, add the fish pieces and simmer gently for around 5 minutes.
  Add the mixed seafood and continue to simmer for 5 minutes until
  the fish is cooked and the mixed seafood is thoroughly heated through.

• Stir in the lime juice and test the seasoning, adding a little more salt
  and lime juice if necessary.

To serve

• Ladle into bowls, spoon over the coconut cream, garnish with chillies
  and garlic chips if using and serve with the lime wedges, basmati rice
  and/or roti, paratha or naan bread as preferred.

ISLE OF MAN

Words by
SQUADRON LEADER MAL CRAIG

AS THE SHADOW of the Second World War spread across Europe in 1939, it was not long before the conflict had reached every corner of the UK, including the sheltered Isle of Man.

When the Royal Air Force first arrived in 1939, few would have believed that it would have a presence on the island for over half a century, centred on the three airfields of RAF Ronaldsay, Jerby and Andreas. The Isle of Man would serve not only as a training base for the instruction of RAF observers and gunners, but also as a strategic fighter base for the protection of Belfast, Glasgow and Liverpool.

At a most basic level, war is not about machines or strategic intent, it's about people and the tragedies that can sometimes occur unexpectedly. So much of war is luck, such as the fortunate escape that Flight Lieutenant B Brooke, the signals officer at RAF Andreas, had on the 23 August 1942. For the 21-year-old Brooke, a single phone call from his annoyed girlfriend Joyce would mean the difference between life and death.

Brooke had been planning to meet with Joyce but had been made Duty Officer and invited to lunch by his Commanding Officer, when a 296 Squadron Armstrong-Whitworth Whitley glider tug, piloted by Pilot Officer Thomas Tennyson, landed short of fuel. Tennyson had been ferrying a Hotspur glider with a dozen army personnel on board to Northern Ireland when the tow broke and the glider crashed into the Irish Sea. He circled the slowly sinking glider for an hour and a half until a Royal Navy Destroyer arrived to rescue the cold and miserable passengers. With the passengers safe, Tennyson, short of fuel, diverted to RAF Andreas.

He was not expecting that the RAF Andreas Station Commander, Wing Commander Edward Knowles DFC, would demand to "borrow" his aircraft for a joyride. Knowles – a decorated former fighter, bomber and SOE Special Duties pilot who was known to make any party swing – had been enjoying a particularly convivial lunch with his "friend" Thelma Kersley, Major Wait MC (OC Airfield Defence), Flying Officer Paton (Duty Pilot) and Brooke when Knowles decided to pull rank on Tennyson and take his aircraft up for a spin, despite Tennyson's objections. Just as the party was boarding the aircraft, Brooke received a phone call from his girlfriend, delaying him sufficiently for them to leave without him.

With the addition of four airmen in the tail of the aircraft acting as ballast – but possibly still not refuelled – the lighter than usual Whitley (stripped of guns and turrets) trundled down the runway into a strong headwind, straining to get airborne. Knowles then appears to have lost control and crashed just outside the camp perimeter. All the passengers in the front of the aircraft were killed, while the airmen in the back were all injured, and one would later die of his injuries. The graves of those immediately killed in the crash are all located in the St Andrew Churchyard at Andreas.

Brooke's girlfriend, who was on duty at the nearby Ramsey Radar Sector Control, had to endure a torturous 30 minutes after hearing of the crash before Brooke walked into the control room to let her know he was safe. Joyce and Brooke would go on to enjoy a long and happy marriage.

Manx Broth
Beef, Barley & Vegetable Soup

This simple, hearty broth is traditionally served at a Manx wedding. It is full of beef flavour (along with the shin, the marrow bone gives both flavour and body to the broth), pearl barley and root vegetables. Diced potatoes are sometimes added for a more robust dish.

INGREDIENTS
Serves 6–8

For the broth

800g beef shin on the bone or
 a 500g piece of brisket

1 beef marrow bone (optional)

100g pearl barley

1 medium carrot, peeled and
 coarsely chopped

75g turnip or swede, peeled
 and coarsely chopped

1 medium parsnip, peeled and
 coarsely chopped

½ small leek, halved lengthways
 and thickly sliced

2 sticks of celery, thickly sliced

1 sprig of thyme

1 sprig of rosemary

1 bay leaf

75g savoy cabbage (¼ of a head),
 coarsely chopped

2 tbsp parsley, coarsely chopped

salt and pepper

To serve

crusty bread

METHOD
To make the broth

• Place the beef shin and marrow bone in a casserole cover with cold water, season with salt, bring to a boil, reduce the heat, skim off the impurities from the top and simmer for 2 to 3 hours, skimming occasionally, until the meat on the shin is tender.

• Remove the shin and marrow bone from the stock (set the shin aside to cool slightly), add the pearl barley and simmer for 20 minutes, again skimming the surface occasionally.

• Add the carrot, turnip (or swede), parsnip, leek, celery, thyme, rosemary and bay leaf; continue to simmer for 20 minutes, add the savoy cabbage and simmer for a further 10 minutes until all of the vegetables and cabbage are tender. Remove the thyme, rosemary and bay leaf.

• Remove the meat from the shin and cut into 1cm pieces.

To finish

• Add the beef to the broth with half of the parsley, bring back to a simmer and season with salt and black pepper.

To serve

• Ladle the broth into bowls, scatter with the remaining chopped parsley, garnish with a small sprig of parsley, thyme or rosemary and serve with crusty bread.

SICILY

Words by
SQUADRON LEADER HELEN TRAIN

SICILY IS THE largest island in the Mediterranean. Despite being a major tourist hot-spot, it has been an area of focus by the Royal Air Force for a considerable period of time. This interest began in 1943, when the RAF first entered Sicily from its bases in Malta as part of a pre-planned invasion. More recently, during the post-war era, Sicily was used extensively in support of Operation Ellamy, the British effort during the Libyan Crisis.

Trapani, one of its main military airfields, was used as a forward-operating base for 2Gp Air Mobility and Air Transport aircraft. These included the VC10s of 10 Squadron and Tristars of 216 Squadron, supporting air-to-air refuelling of coalition aircraft, and the AWACS airborne warning aircraft of 8 Squadron, RAF Waddington.

The wartime invasion of Sicily, known as Operation Husky, was the brainchild of Theodore Roosevelt and Winston Churchill during the Casablanca Conference in January 1943. Despite now being overshadowed by the Normandy Invasion, the Sicilian operation was the largest amphibious invasion in history until D-Day, and in its first day included more divisions and a larger landing area than the first day of D-Day operations.

At the time of Operation Husky, the Allied air forces in the North African and Mediterranean theatres were organised as the Mediterranean Air Command (MAC) under the command of Air Chief Marshal Sir Arthur Tedder.

On 9 July 1943, the RAF began an invasion of Sicily. To ease the invasion, British Naval Intelligence devised Operation Mincemeat – a plan devised to convince German intelligence that the Allies would initially attack elsewhere. The Germans fell for the ploy and improved defence measures on the proposed targets of Greece and Sardinia. Ewen Montagu was responsible for this plan while working at Bletchley Park with a young intelligence officer named Ian Fleming, later distinguished as the author of the James Bond novels.

Until 1870, Sicily was more prosperous than most other northern areas of Italy. However, following increasing poverty, many radical Sicilians desired independence. This may in part explain the reluctance of Sicilians to defend their shores following the invasion of the Allies during 1943. Furthermore, due to this extreme poverty, many locals had already migrated to the USA, and many Sicilians had close relatives in the States who sent money across. As a consequence, most usefully, many islanders did not accept the fascist propaganda that was being proffered by the Italian government, which painted the Americans as barbaric animals.

The airborne assault was not altogether the success that had been expected. 137 gliders were released, carrying the army's 1st Air Landing Brigade. These were towed by United States Dakotas and Albemarles and Halifax aircraft belonging to No. 1575

Flt Wing, RAF. Unfortunately, 69 gliders landed in rough seas, 56 landed on the south eastern-coast and only 12 made the landing zone. It should be noted, however, that all of those successful landings were made by gliders towed by the RAF! Throughout the assault, fighter cover was provided by 73 Squadron Hurricanes.

Operation Husky ended on 17 August 1943. Strategically, it achieved the goals set out for it by Allied planners: the Allies drove Axis air, land and naval forces from the island, and the Mediterranean sea lanes were opened for Allied merchant ships for the first time since 1941.

CURTISS KITTYHAWKS OF
RAF 112 SQUADRON AT
PACHINO, SICILY, JULY 1943

Pasta alla Norma
Sicilian Pasta with Aubergines

This is an iconic Sicilian dish from Catania on the east coast of the island, comprising pasta with fried aubergine, garlic, tomatoes, basil and cheese. It is suggested that this dish derived its name from Bellini's opera *Norma*, as the "guerra, guerra" chorus from the second act was sung in Palermo cathedral to celebrate the liberation of Sicily from Ferdinand II of the House of Bourbon in 1848.

INGREDIENTS

Serves 4

For the sauce and pasta

135ml olive oil

2 medium aubergines, diced

2 tsp dried oregano

4 cloves of garlic, finely sliced

½ tsp dried chilli flakes

1½ tins (600g) chopped tinned tomatoes

250g cherry tomatoes, halved

50g basil leaves, torn

salt and pepper

400g pasta, e.g. fusilli, penne, spaghetti, linguini or rigatoni

To serve

100g salted ricotta (ricotta salata), grated grana padano or pecorino

oregano leaves (optional)

basil leaves

METHOD

To cook the sauce and pasta

- Heat 4 tbsp of the oil in a frying pan or sauteuse over a medium heat, add half of the aubergines and fry, stirring frequently until well browned all over. Transfer the aubergines to a bowl with a slotted spoon and repeat with the remaining aubergine.
- Season the aubergine with salt and freshly ground black pepper; toss with the dried oregano.
- Return the pan to the heat with the remaining 1 tbsp of olive oil, add the sliced garlic and dried chilli flakes; cook, stirring constantly, for a couple of minutes.
- Return the aubergine to the pan, stir in the chopped tomatoes, season lightly and simmer for 5 minutes. Add the halved cherry tomatoes and continue to simmer for a further 5 minutes.
- While the sauce is simmering, bring a large pan of well-salted water to a rapid boil and cook the pasta until just al dente.
- Reserve about 250ml of the pasta cooking water, drain the pasta and toss with the sauce in the pan. Add the basil and enough of the reserved pasta cooking water to loosen the sauce to coat the pasta.
- Check the seasoning and simmer for a couple of minutes.

To serve

- Spoon into pasta bowls, grate over the cheese and garnish with fresh oregano leaves and/or a few torn basil leaves.

LUXEMBOURG

Words by
FLIGHT LIEUTENANT JAMES WILYMAN

THE LANDLOCKED GRAND Duchy of Luxembourg has, throughout history, rarely avoided conflict in Western Europe. In 1914, at the outbreak of the First World War, Imperial Germany violated Luxembourg's neutrality by invading it as part of its war against France. During the Second World War, the Nazis considered Luxembourg to be "Germanic" and, in May 1940, the country was absorbed by Germany.

In 1944, General Patton's infantry arrived in Luxembourg as Nazi Germany retaliated against Allied advances. At the height of the Battle of the Bulge, accounts from foxholes across Luxembourg regaled fond and grateful memories of the familiar hum of bombers attacking German supply lines, eventually punishing the German counterattack.

However, the real story of the Royal Air Force in Luxembourg comes from the debt of thanks that Britain owes to the Luxembourg Resistance for bringing RAF pilots back to their families after being shot down over these contested lands. The resistance helped to smuggle RAF

Aircrew through occupied Luxembourg into France and onward to home. One such story starts in the small town of Redcar in the north-east of England.

The UK government-launched "Wings for Victory" appeal prompted the people of Redcar to raise £210,000, which bought Bomber Command a brand new Halifax II bomber. It was emblazoned with the slogan "JAFBO", an acronym for "Just About Feeling Browned Off", which embodied the disgruntled yet resilient attitude of the British public. On 27 August 1943, the bomber, crewed by seven personnel, took off from RAF Lissett only to be shot down by night fighters over Luxembourg.

The aircraft, piloted by Royal Australian Air Force pilot PO Clarke, is believed to have crashed in Marscherwald near Echternach, Luxembourg. Three of the seven crew members were killed in the crash but four survived. Sergeant Robinson was captured and held as a POW. Sergeant Dix, the second to jump from JAFBO, landed unharmed in a field and, after tearing his insignia from his uniform, headed west. He was smuggled by farmers into the hands of a Luxembourg Resistance group, led by Pierre Maroldt. The group then continued to move Dix across Luxembourg, finding refuge in farms and family rooms. Finally, moving through France, Spain and Gibraltar, Dix returned to England on 17 December 1943. The final crew members of JAFBO – Sergeant Brearley and Sergeant Hirst – joined Dix nine months later in September 1944. These three airman could not have made it safely back to Allied shores was it not for the Luxembourg Resistance taking great risks to smuggle them home.

There are two sides to every story. For the RAF in Luxembourg it was the people of Redcar that put Halifax JAFBO into the skies. But it was those of Marscherwald and Luxembourg that brought some of its crew safely home.

"Britain owes a debt of thanks to the Luxembourg Resistance for bringing RAF pilots home"

Quetschentaart
Damson Tart

Traditionally made in the autumn, after the damsons have ripened in September, this quintessentially Luxembourgish open fruit pie is simplicity itself. The crust is either a yeast-risen dough or, as in this recipe, a sweet, shortcrust pastry.

INGREDIENTS

Serves 6–8

For the sweet short crust pastry

250g plain flour

pinch of salt

125g butter

50g icing sugar

1 egg

2–3 tbsp milk

1 tsp vanilla extract

½ lemon, finely grated zest only

For the filling

600g damsons or plums

30g icing sugar

To serve

100g damson plum conserve
 or jam

icing sugar, to dust

whipped cream or crème fraiche

METHOD

To make the sweet short crust pastry

- Sieve the flour with the salt and rub in the butter to a sandy breadcrumb texture. Sieve the icing sugar and rub into the flour and butter mix.
- Beat the egg with the milk, vanilla extract and lemon zest.
- Make a well in the centre of the dry mix and add the egg mix to make a firm dough.
- Wrap in cling film and allow to rest in the refrigerator for at least 20 minutes before using.
- Lightly butter a 24cm diameter by 2cm deep false bottomed tart case or flan ring with softened butter.
- Dust the work surface and the top of the dough with a little flour then roll out the rested, chilled pastry to around the thickness of a £1 coin. The pastry should be large enough to cover the base and sides of the case or ring as well as about 2.5cm overhang. Drape the pastry loosely over the tart case and carefully ease it into the case ensuring it is tucked well into the corners. Leaving around 1cm overhang trim off any excess dough with a sharp pair of scissors, crimp the pastry edge and place in the refrigerator for 20 to 30 minutes to rest.

To make the filling

- Cut the damsons or plums in half, remove the stones then cut each half into half again or into 3 wedges, depending on size.
- Toss the damson or plum wedges in the icing sugar to coat.
- Line the base of the pastry with the damsons, skin side down, in concentric circles.

To cook and serve

- Preheat the oven to 220°C.
- Cook the quetschentaart in the oven for 10 minutes, reduce the heat to 180°C and continue to cook for about 30 minutes until the damsons are soft and the tips are starting to brown.
- Remove the tart from the oven and allow to stand at room temperature for 15 minutes.
- Meanwhile warm the damson conserve and strain through a sieve.
- Remove the quetschentaart from the flan ring, brush with the conserve, dust with icing sugar and cut into wedges.
- Serve each portion with a spoonful of whipped cream or crème fraiche.

CORSICA

Words by
FLIGHT LIEUTENANT EMMA STRINGER

© A. Bennett Collection

THE CORSICAN RATS IN 1943: FREDERICK BENNETT PICTURED TO THE RIGHT OF FLAG WITH ARMS FOLDED

THE MEDITERRANEAN ISLAND of Corsica has strong cultural and historic links with Italy but has been a region of France for nearly 250 years, and played its part in both world wars.

Like many countries, Corsica was left vulnerable after the Great War. The percentage of dead or wounded Corsicans was almost double that of mainland France. This, coupled with the effect protectionist policies had on the island's export of wine and olive oil, meant that young Corsicans started to emigrate in droves to seek a better future. This turmoil sparked a nationalist movement in the 1920s that sought to break away from France; however, many exponents of the movement became irredentist, seeing Corsica's future as an annex to fascist Italy.

The fragility of communications to mainland France, a weakened economy and divided political allegiances made the island susceptible to occupation. In November 1942, after the Allies landed in North Africa, the Axis forces responded by moving through southern France and making their way into Corsica. With a population of only 220,000, the island was occupied by 80,000 Italian troops, bolstered by some 20,000 German troops in June 1943, making it the most densely occupied area in Europe.

The occupation, however, aroused a renewed loyalty to France among the islanders and a Corsican–French resistance movement grew. In September 1943, following the Italian armistice, the liberation of Corsica began. Operation Vesuvius (8 September to 4 October 1943) saw the Free French forces and parts of the Italian forces push the Germans off the island. Corsica is now considered to be the first French Department to be freed during the war.

While little is written about the role of the Royal Air Force in Corsica during the Second World War, its part was vital. Andrew Bennett, the son of Frederick Arthur Bennett – one of the first RAF personnel to land on Corsica – recalls his father's memories:

"My father was in RAF 500, County of Kent Squadron throughout the war and spent much time in North Africa and Italy. He was known as 'Torso' after a newspaper character of the time because of his great physique.

> "*Despite the odds, and to the relief of all on board, the crew successfully landed, hopping over craters*"

"On one occasion, when the squadron were based in Bilda in North Africa, they touched shoulders with the SOE (Special Operations Executive) who were involved at the time with underwing rockets and radar on the Lockheed Hudson. On 28 September, during the start of the liberation of Corsica and before the Germans had left the island, the SOE requested a 500 Squadron plane and personnel fly a secret mission from Blida to Bone, and then on to Ghisonaccia Gare in the east of Corsica, where they were to 'establish squatters rights' – apparently the actual wording of the orders!

"Despite the odds, and to the relief of all on board, the crew successfully landed, hopping over craters, and the men began the task of restoring the aerodrome to working order. By mid-November, Frederick and his team were nicely established in the bombed up Continental Hotel and quickly became known as 'The Corsican Rats' due to their expert foraging skills. On one occasion, they went fishing using a hand grenade to gather fresh food, and sometimes they rode one of the three-wheeled Italian bikes with a machine gun to catch the odd steer or two for a slap-up meal in the mess for the men."

With the island liberated and now in the hands of the Allies, Corsica became one of the staging posts for operations in Italy as well as the landings in the south of France as part of Operation Dragoon (August 1944). It became a base for the US Army Air Forces and the US Navy, earning it the nickname "USS Corsica".

Fiadone Corse
Corsican Cheesecake

Renowned as the birthplace of Napoleon, Corsica has much in common with its close neighbour Italy. Fiadone is a baseless baked cheesecake usually made with brocciu – a traditional Corsican cheese made from ewe's milk – which can be substituted with ricotta. Once cooked, the fiadone should have quite a dense texture and should only be about an inch thick. Ideally, it should be made a day in advance, chilled overnight and brought to room temperature before serving.

INGREDIENTS
Serves 8

For the fiadone
500g ricotta cheese
200g caster sugar
6 medium eggs
2 lemons, finely grated zest
  and juice
1 tsp vanilla extract
1 tbsp eau de vie, brandy or orange
  blossom water (optional)
pinch of salt
melted butter for greasing

To serve
icing sugar for dusting
crème fraiche
seasonal berries

METHOD
To make the fiadone
• Preheat the oven to 180°C.
• Lightly brush the sides and base of a 25cm spring-form cake tin with melted butter, line the base and sides with baking parchment and lightly brush again with melted butter.
• Place the ricotta in a bowl with the sugar. Separate 4 of the eggs, add the 2 whole eggs and the 4 egg yolks to the ricotta with the lemon zest, 2 tbsp of the lemon juice, the vanilla extract and the eau de vie. Mix well until thoroughly combined.
• Beat the egg whites with a pinch of salt until they form stiff peaks and carefully fold into the ricotta mix.
• Pour the mix into the prepared cake tin and bake in the preheated oven for around 40 to 45 minutes or until a skewer comes out clean when inserted into the centre of the fiadone and the top is an even brown colour.
• Leave the fiadone in the cake tin and allow to sit at room temperature until cool. Remove from the tin, peel off the parchment paper and chill in the fridge overnight (this allows the flavours to develop).

To serve
• Remove the fiadone from the fridge and leave it to sit at room temperature for 20 minutes before dusting with icing sugar.
• Cut into portions and serve with a spoonful of crème fraiche and some fresh seasonal berries and/or a lemon wedge.

INDIA

Words by
FLIGHT LIEUTENANT CRISPIN CHAPPLE

THROUGH COLONIALISM AND the Raj, the British have had a long connection with India, and the military has played a big part in this rich history. From its inception, the Royal Air Force played an integral role in one location or other in British India, including in Waziristan, East India and Bangladesh, to name but a few.

During the Second World War, once Japan had shown her cards, there was more necessity than ever to position here. The country was littered with RAF bases, the most important of which were situated around the city of Calcutta, with bombers placed at the likes of Jessore, Dhubablia, Salboni and Digri. These housed such squadrons as 99, 215 and 159; all flying Wellingtons, initially, followed by Liberators later on.

Digri proved to be one of the most important during the Japanese occupation of Burma, having a much stronger runway surface than the better-situated Dhubablia. 185 Fighter Wing and 3 Fighter Control Section, later subsumed into a Heavy Bombing Wing, were situated here between December 1943 and June 1945, before being moved on into Malaya.

As Sergeant E W Robinson, an airfield controller there at the time remembers, 159 Squadron Liberators had an enviable reputation, regularly flying 12- to 16-hour missions as far as Bangkok, but also to Rangoon and Moulmein in Burma in

support of the re-occupation. One such mission lasted over 19 hours but, due to the weight of the aircraft at take off, necessitated a short hop and refuel at Kharagpur, a longer and better-prepared runway.

The main threat became Japan's insistence on marching to Delhi. Such was the swiftness of its move through Burma, however, that its supply lines became overstretched and the Japanese forces needed to reform and regroup. During this time, the British grouped in the town of Imphal, surrounded by almost impenetrable mountains. Roads were continually washed away by monsoons, so the British built roads and airfields to improve the extremely poor communications and supply lines. The Japanese saw this as a precursor to British moves into Burma and put Imphal under siege.

Fighting was fierce, with more than 150,000 men effectively cut off from the rest of the country, and the role of the RAF became integral to its successful defence. Some 14,000,000lbs of rations, 1,000,000 gallons of petrol, 43,000,000 cigarettes and 1,200 bags of mail were successfully delivered over the period of the 80-day siege. On return flights to bases behind the lines, they were also able to take some 13,000 wounded and 43,000 non-combatants, replacing them with around 12,000 reinforcements.

The trips were made all the more dangerous by the slow speeds and

proximity of the enemy. Fighters supported every mission in and out. To further add to the sheer enormity of the feat, the lack of the RAF Regiment on the ground meant that not only did the fighter crews need to support the mission in and out, but also during the night they were required to defend the airfields against Japanese attack.

The siege was ultimately unsuccessful; Japan did not enter India. The Japanese Foreign Office official at the time, Toshikazu Kase, said: "The disaster at Imphal was perhaps the worst of its kind yet chronicled in the annals of war." General Slim could now concentrate his resources on the retaking of Burma now that the invincibility of the Japanese army had been shattered.

Indian independence followed very swiftly after the war, by which time the RAF had pretty much departed Indian bases. The Indian Air Force, formed as an auxiliary force of the British Empire in 1932, became the Royal Indian Air Force in 1945 – soon dropping the "Royal" prefix once India became a republic in 1950 – and the RAF's role in India ceased.

A CONSOLIDATED LIBERATOR OF 159 SQUADRON OPERATING FROM INDIA

Grilled Aubergine
with Sesame & Peanut Crumble

by VIVEK SINGH

FOUNDING CHEF OF THE CINNAMON COLLECTION

Vivek serves this delicious vegetarian dish, full of soft and crunchy textures on the menu at the Cinnamon Kitchen. If carom seeds (also known as ajwain) are unavailable, substitute an equal amount of dried thyme. To get the best out of this recipe, Vivek recommends using Japanese or Bengali aubergines, although any small, firm aubergines can also be used.

INGREDIENTS

Serves 4

For the aubergines

2 firm Japanese or Bengali
  aubergines, cut into halves
  lengthways

2 tbsp vegetable or corn oil

1 tsp salt

½ tsp red chilli powder

½ tsp turmeric powder

¼ tsp carom seeds

¼ tsp black onion seeds

¼ tsp fennel seeds

For the spice crust

1 tbsp poppy seeds, roasted

1 tbsp white sesame seeds, roasted

1 tsp jaggery (or soft dark brown
  sugar)

2 cloves of garlic, crushed

1 tbsp desiccated coconut, roasted

1 tbsp peanuts with
  skin, deep fried

½ tsp red chilli powder

1 tsp chaat masala

1 tsp tamarind pulp

To garnish

1 tbsp tamarind chutney

METHOD

To prepare the aubergine

- Score and marinate the aubergine with oil, salt, red chilli powder, turmeric, carom seeds, onion seeds, fennel seeds and salt. Keep aside for 3 to 4 minutes.

To make the spice crust

- In the meantime, combine all the ingredients for the spice crust and pound using a pestle and mortar to a coarse powder. Spread the spice crust on a tray and leave to dry.

To cook

- Place the flat side of the aubergine on a hot grill or pan and sear for 2 minutes. Repeat the same on the other side by brushing it with butter or oil and cooking for around 3 minutes. Ensure it is cooked completely through.

To serve

- Place the aubergines on a plate with the flat side facing upwards. Apply a dash of tamarind chutney on the aubergines, sprinkle the spice crust and serve hot with green salad.

BELGIUM

Words by
FLIGHT LIEUTENANT JAMES WILYMAN

LIEUTENANT-COLONEL JOHN McCrae's 1915 poem "In Flanders Fields" – which includes lines such as: "We shall not sleep, though poppies grow" – is a familiar and emotive poem for service personnel and civilians alike that is read annually at Remembrance Day services across the country. The words act as a poignant reminder of those that paid the ultimate sacrifice. Although written in response to heavy ground losses during the Battle of the Somme, the contribution that air power made to the battlefields of the Great War should not be ignored.

In Flanders itself, the British Expeditionary Force (BEF) saw perhaps the most significant test of the Royal Flying Corps' operational performance at the third Battle of Ypres in 1917. A total of 50 squadrons comprising 858 aircraft were deployed to West Flanders in support of ground troops. Although precise figures are varied, the BEF took an estimated 244,897 casualties in the third battle alone.

Once the RAF was formed in 1918, many of the Royal Naval Air Service and Royal Flying Corps squadrons transferred to the new service, with some staying in action in Flanders. Units such as the new No. 204 Squadron found themselves based from Heule carrying out fighter and ground attack missions on the Western Front.

During the Second World War, Ursel in Flanders was home to the Belgium air force, acting as a rear defence to German invasion. When the Belgium army surrendered in May 1940, Ursel airfield was used by the Luftwaffe and even hosted the Italian air force in its support during the Battle of Britain.

In June 1944, as the Allies launched Operation Overlord to liberate Europe, four squadrons of 123 Wing, Second Tactical Air Force RAF arrived at a newly liberated Ursel. With help from the Royal Engineers, the basic concrete airfield was extended using metal strips, designated the codename "B-67" and was to act as a staging point for the heavy Hawker Typhoons.

The Typhoons' role was in part to support Operation Infatuate, the invasion of the Dutch island of Walcheran; a German defensive position blocking the Allies' entrance into the port at Antwerp. Flying through heavy fog as low as 300ft, the Typhoons launched over 600 air-

support sorties until eventually, with bomber support from the UK, a bridgehead was formed allowing safe passage for the convoys into Antwerp.

However, this convoy route would quickly become a target for retaliating German forces, who saw Antwerp as an important strategic asset. It is the work of the lesser-known RAF 85 Group of the 2nd Tactical Air Force, which became essential to its protection. Setting up radar stations along the Flemish coast stretching out to the lighthouse in Walcheran, these specialist units were able to detect and track incoming German attacks.

One veteran remembers how, in 1938, he visited the lighthouse as part of a Scout trip. Seven years later, when deployed to Brussels and serving under 85 Group of the RAF, his unit was tasked with the maintenance of these coastal radar defences and he found himself climbing the familiar stairs under very different circumstances. Critical to the protection of the supply chain to Antwerp, the radar defences highlight the importance of ground support to air operations.

The Typhoon's legacy remains to this day in the shape of the Eurofighter and the modern successors to the Second World War's ground radar installations. Their heritage can be traced back to the liberation of Europe from Nazi Germany. The monuments and battlefields across Belgium remain as scars and reminders of all that was lost both in and over Flanders fields.

AN RAF PILOT WITH HIS HAWKER TYPHOON, CIRCA 1944

Moules Frites
Belgian Mussels & Fries

In most Belgian cities you'll encounter diners, both indigenous and visitors, feasting on huge bowls of the ubiquitous moules frites. When buying mussels look out for clean, bright, shiny and unbroken shells with a fresh and briny – but not fishy – smell. The frites are usually served with mayonnaise.

INGREDIENTS
Serves 4

For the frites

600g floury potatoes, peeled

oil for deep frying

For the moules

2kg mussels

75g butter

75g shallots, finely diced

4 gloves garlic, finely chopped

2 sprigs of thyme

4 tbsp flat leaf parsley, coarsely
  chopped

300ml dry white wine

60g crème fraiche

To serve

1 lemon, halved lengthways
  (1 half cut into 4 wedges)

mayonnaise

METHOD
To prepare the frites
- Trim off the rounded edges of the potatoes and cut into thin slices about 5mm thick then cut into 5mm thick sticks.
- Soak the potato sticks in cold water for half an hour to remove the excess starch. Drain well and dry with a tea towel.
- Heat the oil to 180°C.

To prepare the moules
- Rinse the mussels well in a large bowl of cold water, drain and pull away any beards. Give the mussels a tap and discard any that remain open.

To cook the moules and frites
- Melt the butter over a moderate heat in a large saucepan and, when foaming, add the shallots and sweat for about 5 minutes until softened. Add the chopped garlic and thyme sprigs and cook for a few minutes.
- Tip in the mussels, stir well, cover with a lid and cook for 2 minutes.
- Remove the lid and add the wine. Bring to a boil and cook for a further 1½ to 2 minutes.
- Place a colander over a bowl. Strain and reserve the cooking liquor. Pick out and discard any mussels that haven't opened.
- While the mussels are draining, fry the frites in the oil for 2 to 3 minutes until golden brown and crisp.
- Pour the cooking liquor back into the saucepan, bring to a simmer, stir two thirds of the chopped parsley and the crème fraiche. Bring back to a simmer and season with salt and freshly ground black pepper.
- Tip the mussels back into the saucepan and stir well to coat.
- Drain the frites on kitchen paper and season salt and pepper.

To serve
- Divide the mussels between four bowls, squeeze over a little lemon juice, pour over the remaining sauce, garnish with the remaining parsley and serve with the frites, lemon wedges and mayonnaise.

POLAND

Words by
SQUADRON LEADER MAL CRAIG

THE HISTORIC TIES between the Royal Air Force and the people of Poland run deep. They were forged in the heat of the Battle of Britain, in which 145 Polish pilots (the single largest non-British fighting contingent) helped defeat the Luftwaffe, but also throughout the rest of the Second World War. Regarded as fearless by some, and reckless by others, a total of 19,400 Polish airmen served in both the RAF and what would become the Polish Air Force in Great Britain by the end of the war.

Typical of their bravery and skill is the story of Kazimierz Szrajer who, along with thousands of Poles, escaped from his homeland via France to arrive in the UK in 1940. Anxious to get into the war, Szrajer initially worked as an instrument mechanic with 303 Squadron, one of the first of 16 Polish Fighter Squadrons within the RAF. Once trained as a bomber pilot and assigned to 301 (Polish) Squadron operating Wellington bombers, Szrajer went on to complete 21 operational raids with the squadron. In April 1941, his last month with 301, Szrajer crashlanded with a seized engine, and later crashlanded after being shot up by a JU-88. In May 1942, Szrajer returned with an assignment to 138 Squadron RAF, which was engaged in special ops, including the dropping and collection of agents behind enemy lines and the arming of the Polish Resistance.

Szrajer's most daring flight of the war would occur on 25 July 1944. In a joint operation between the British Special Operations Executive and the Polish Resistance, his task was to act as translator and co-pilot on a mission to collect a virtually intact crashed V2 rocket from a marsh in Poland, for UK personnel to study. When the mission aircraft arrived, it turned out to be a Dakota transport aircraft that he'd never flown before. But – following a five-minute introduction – Szrajer found himself suitably qualified to act as co-pilot.

On what would be his 20th flight to his occupied homeland, Szrajer – along with the Dakota's crew – arrived behind enemy lines at an abandoned airstrip near Tarnow in southern Poland. After disembarking five passengers, the recovered V2 parts were quickly loaded aboard, but the aircraft became bogged down in the mud and its brakes seized. It was more than an hour before Szrajer and his crew, having freed the aircraft from the clawing mud and cut the break lines, were airborne, with an undercarriage that could not be retracted because of the cut hydraulic lines. The crew had to refill the hydraulic system with any available fluids – including some human ones – in order to make a safe landing at Brindisi.

Following the war, Szrajer became a successful civilian commercial pilot, flying 149 trips as part of the Berlin airlift in 1948–49 with the Lancashire Aircraft Corporation. After amassing an incredible 25,000 flying hours Szrajer retired from aviation in 1981, moved to Ontario and died in 2012, aged 92.

Pierogi
Polish Stuffed Dumplings

Pierogi can be boiled or boiled then shallow fried until golden brown, and can be stuffed with any kind of filling. The recipe below uses beef; vegetable variations include potato, sauerkraut, cabbage, mushrooms or cheese. Sweet pierogi can be stuffed with soft fruits or jams and served with cream.

INGREDIENTS

Makes 35–40

For the pierogi dough

500g plain flour

½ tsp salt

175ml hot water (about ⅔ boiling to ⅓ cold)

½ tsp vegetable oil

For the filling

75ml olive oil

1 large onion, finely diced

2 cloves of garlic, finely chopped

2 medium carrots, finely diced

METHOD

To make the dough

• Sift the flour into a mixing bowl, mix in the salt and make a well in the centre. Add the hot water and mix until well combined.

• Cover the bowl with a tea towel and set aside for 20 minutes.

• Turn the dough out onto a floured worktop, make an indentation in the top and work in the oil.

• Knead the dough for about 5 minutes, adding a little more flour if the dough becomes too sticky, until smooth and silky in texture. Return to the bowl, cover with the tea towel and leave to rest for a further 20 minutes.

To make the filling

• Heat 3 tbsp of the olive oil in a casserole over a low heat and add

1½ sticks of celery, finely diced

⅓ medium leek, finely diced

500g minced chuck steak

250ml beef stock

50g fresh bread, crusts removed

1 large egg, beaten

2 tbsp flat leaf parsley, coarsely chopped

salt and pepper

To cook

3 tbsp vegetable oil

50g butter

To serve (optional)

sour cream, crispy fried onions, mustard, chopped parsley or dill, chopped crispy bacon or pork crackling

the onions, garlic, carrot, celery and leek. Sweat gently, stirring occasionally to ensure even cooking, for around 15 minutes until the vegetables have started to soften but without any colour.

• Heat a frying pan or skillet with the remaining 2 tbsp olive oil over a high heat and add the minced beef. Season with salt and pepper and fry until well browned and starting to caramelise (this is best done in a couple of batches to ensure that the meat caramelises over the fierce heat and doesn't boil in its own juices; removing each batch of browned meat with a slotted spoon to drain off the excess fat).

• Add the seared beef to the casserole with the vegetables, pour in the beef stock, place over a moderate heat and simmer, stirring occasionally, for 30 minutes until the meat is tender, the vegetables are cooked through and most of the stock has been absorbed.

• Remove from the heat and set aside at room temperature to cool.

• Tear the bread into rough pieces and soak in a little hot water for a couple of minutes. Squeeze out the excess water from the bread.

• Once the mince mixture has cooled, add the beaten egg, soaked bread and chopped parsley. Mix well until all of the ingredients are thoroughly combined and season with salt and pepper.

To stuff and shape

• Place the dough on a lightly floured worktop and roll out to a thickness of 2mm to 3mm and, using a pastry cutter, cut into 9cm circles. Gather up the scraps, knead together and repeat until you have between 35 to 40 discs of dough (do not roll them too thin or they will be hard to handle and may tear).

• Place a heaped teaspoon of filling onto the dough discs, brush the edges with a little cold water, fold in half and press the edges together with the tips of your fingers or the prongs of a fork to seal in the filling (alternatively the pierogi can be crimped by either pinching or folding the edges to seal).

To cook and serve the pierogi

• Bring a large pan of well-salted water to a rolling boil. Cook the pierogi in batches for around 4 minutes until soft (they should rise to the surface when cooked) and drain.

• Heat the oil and butter over a moderate heat until the butter is foaming, add the pierogi in batches and cook on both sides until browned. Drain on kitchen paper before serving with a selection of toppings.

COCOS ISLAND

Words by
WING COMMANDER MARC HOLLAND

IN THE FINAL stages of the Second World War, as victory over Germany was approaching, the RAF decided to redeploy 1,000 bombers from Europe to the Far East to combat the Japanese. Even long-range Lancaster bombers could not cross the 3,000 miles of ocean between Ceylon and Australia, so a midway airstrip was needed. The only useable location was the Cocos-Keeling islands, a string of coral atolls in the Indian Ocean and now a territory of Australia.

With no airstrip on the islands, an audacious plan was hatched. RAF personnel would set sail in an unprotected cargo ship to sneak across the Japanese-dominated Indian Ocean, clear a couple of square miles of coconut trees and build the most advanced RAF airfield in Asia in a few weeks.

In March 1945, 8,000 people arrived at Cocos with equipment, including Spitfires in crates. Within four weeks, through sheer physical labour, thousands of coconut trees had been chopped down and a steel matting airstrip built allowing the Spitfires to be assembled and RAF pilots to be available at one minute's notice to scramble and defend against air attacks. Over the coming months, the airfield became a main Far East hub, launching heavy bombers, sea planes, photo reconnaissance and air defence aircraft against the Japanese.

After the Japanese surrender, Cocos became a central hub from which to rescue over 100,000 POWs across the Far East. Food and medical supplies were dropped to two thirds of the POW camps in the Far East by aircraft launched from these tiny islands. For the many malnourished and sick POWs, these aerial supplies kept them alive for many weeks until they could be found and rescued by ground forces.

In true RAF tradition, all ranks and trades mucked in with the work, which would often bewilder visiting senior officers. When a DC6 transport aircraft landed, a very senior RAF officer stepped off the plane and asked to speak to the engineering crew chief. The airman called out to one of the nearby men, who was wearing just shorts and sandals. "Hey Dinger, someone wants to talk to you." When the crew chief arrived, the senior officer asked: "Would you arrange for me to meet your CO?" The sergeant pointed at a shirtless man who was busily pouring petrol. "That's the squadron leader, Sir."

In April 1946, after just a year of operation, the ensign over RAF Cocos Islands was lowered for the last time, marking the end to the story of one of the most remarkable RAF airfields of the war.

AN RAF CONSOLIDATED LIBERATOR ON THE COCOS ISLANDS, 1945

Pisang Goreng
Banana Fritters

The Cocos Keeling Islands are a territory of Australia. This is a popular street vendor treat among the Malay communities who make up the majority of the islands' population, and is commonly made with raja bananas, which can be substituted with small, ripe bananas. The corn and rice flours, and lime juice, helps to make a light batter. The fritters can be topped with honey and whipped cream.

INGREDIENTS

Serves 4

For the batter

100g self-raising flour

50g cornflour

1 tbsp rice flour

¼ tsp salt

200ml cold water (fridge cold)

½ lime, juiced

2 tbsp sunflower oil

To cook

8 ripe bananas (small), peeled
and halved lengthways (or cut
into thick slices)

½ tsp baking powder

vegetable oil for deep frying

To serve (optional)

icing sugar to dust

honey, to drizzle

whipped cream or vanilla ice cream

METHOD

To make the batter

• Mix the three flours together in a bowl with the salt.

• Mix the water, lime juice and oil together in a separate bowl
  or jug and gradually whisk into the dry ingredients to make a
  smooth batter.

To cook the fritters

• Heat the oil to 180°C.

• Just before frying, whisk the baking powder into the batter.

• Dip the bananas into the batter to thoroughly coat and deep fry,
  in batches, until lightly browned and crispy. Drain on absorbent
  kitchen paper.

To serve

• Dust with icing sugar, drizzle with honey and serve with a spoonful
  of whipped cream or a scoop of vanilla ice cream.

AUSTRIA

Words by
FLIGHT LIEUTENANT TOM MARSHALL

WHEN TWO ELDERLY neighbours in the south of England met for a cup of tea, the conversation inevitably drifted to where each had served during the Second World War. As the discussion progressed and the tea went cold, George Rhodes, 99 and ex-British Army, discovered that Graham Brown, 93 and ex-Royal Air Force, had taken part in the same bombing mission in Austria.

The pair lived in the same block of flats in Wells, Somerset, but had no idea that they had supported each other during the raid on the Nazi railyard at Graz in 1945. Graham flew his Wellington overhead, allowing George's regiment to attack from the ground. The mission was a complete success and stifled the Axis railway network, stopping oil supplies from Romania from reaching Western Europe.

The RAF's involvement in Austria dates back to the First World War when, shortly after forming in 1918, it bombed the harbour of Cattaro (now part of Montenegro after border changes), destroying a large number of the Austro–Hungarian submarine fleet. It returned in the Second World War, primarily during the Anglo–US bombing raids of 1944–45, as the offensive was taken to this most belligerent of the Axis powers.

But it from the ground that the majority of RAF airmen saw Austria, primarily in prisoner-of-war camps such as Stalag Luft XVII B. The "Luft" camps were run by the Luftwaffe for the imprisonment of captured aircrew.

Conditions varied from camp to camp and were largely dependent upon the nature of the kommandant in charge.

Escape attempts were frequent, though, until 1945, when it became apparent that the chance of liberation was at hand. It was at this point that Hitler ordered the camps to be emptied and their prisoners to be marched huge distances with little or no food, winter clothing or medical supplies.

An example of this was the April 1945 exit from Stalag Luft XVII B, when Allied airmen were forced to march for 18 days and 281 miles to escape the Russian advance. So grateful were the German guards upon reaching the American lines that 200 of them surrendered to a single Jeep containing just six US soldiers!

After the end of the Second World War, deployment in Austria signalled the end for many RAF squadrons, with the majority that were sent there being demobilised and disestablished. The RAF's presence in the country ended in 1955 with the withdrawal of the final squadron and the establishment of the Austrian Air Force, using Yak aircraft that had been abandoned, still in their crates, by retreating Soviet troops.

Its capability has improved considerably since these humble beginnings, and the Chief of Air Staff of the Austrian Armed Forces recently visited RAF Leuchars, along with a flight of their Eurofighter Typhoons. Such visits are likely to continue as ties are strengthened between the Austrian Air Force and the RAF.

Wienerschnitzel
Veal or Pork Escalope

The secret of a good wienerschnitzel is simplicity. The veal (or pork) should be of good quality and flattened out to just the right thickness. The breadcrumbs should be neither too dry or too fresh, while the frying fat should be a mix of oil and butter. It also needs a good squeeze of lemon juice.

INGREDIENTS

Serves 4

For the escalopes

150g white bread, sliced or
  bread rolls
4 veal or pork escalopes,
  flattened out to 6mm thick
salt and pepper
4 medium eggs
75ml double cream
100g plain flour
150ml sunflower oil
50g butter

To serve

1 lemon, cut into quarters
tossed green or mixed salad

METHOD

To make the breadcrumbs
- Heat the oven to 180°C.
- Tear the bread or rolls into pieces and blend in a food processor to coarse breadcrumbs, spread thinly onto a baking tray and place in the oven. Turn the oven off immediately and leave the breadcrumbs in the oven until completely cool.
- Return the breadcrumbs to the food processor and blend again to a dry even crumb.
- Place the breadcrumbs in a shallow dish or plate.

To prepare the schnitzels
- Season the escalopes lightly with salt and pepper.
- Beat the eggs with the cream in a shallow dish.
- Place the flour in a shallow dish or plate and lightly season the flour with salt and pepper.
- Coat the escalopes with the seasoned flour and tap off the excess.
- Place the escalopes, one at a time, into the egg wash and coat evenly before coating with the breadcrumbs ensuring the coating is even and there are no gaps. Place in a single layer on a tray or large plate.

To cook the escalopes
- Heat half of the oil in a frying pan over a medium heat and place two of the schnitzels into the pan and cook for around a minute until lightly browned, turn the schnitzels over and repeat.
- Add half of the butter and cook for a further minute on each side until they are cooked through to the middle – tilt the pan and constantly spoon over the oil and butter as they cook. Place on kitchen paper to drain and keep warm.
- Wipe the pan clean and repeat with the remaining two escalopes.

To serve
- Serve with tossed salad and lemon wedges.

DROPPING FOOD PARCELS OVER YPENBURG IN THE NETHERLANDS DURING OPERATION MANNA, 29 APRIL 1945

NETHERLANDS

Words by
ED SHARMAN

THE ROYAL AIR FORCE has playedimportant roles in the Netherlands since 1940, and the Dutch people have always held them in deep regard. In the early hours of 10 May 1940, reports reached London that German transport aircraft and paratroopers were descending on Dutch airfields. Six RAF Blenheim fighter aircraft were immediately dispatched from 600 Squadron in London to carry out a strike against the key airfield at Waalhaven near Rotterdam; however, only one aircraft returned.

When the Germans finally invaded the Netherlands in the days that followed, several seaplanes of the Royal Netherlands Naval Air Service were evacuated to Britain, their home bases having become unavailable. During the Second World War, a number of Dutch nationals flew with the RAF, forming several different squadrons. These were later disbanded by the RAF with their numbers transferred to the Royal Dutch Navy and Air Force in recognition of their sacrifices.

After nearly five years of occupation by enemy forces and a particularly difficult winter, the population of the Netherlands was starving. The RAF once again took to the Dutch skies under the name Operation Manna, with the people of the Netherlands first hearing of these plans on 24 April 1945 when they were announced by the BBC.

On 29 April 1945, 10 days before the end of the war in Europe, the people of the Netherlands heard the BBC announce: "Bombers of the Royal Air Force have just taken off from their bases in England to drop food supplies to the Dutch population in enemy-occupied territory." Operation Manna was carried out over 10 days, from 29 April to 8 May, 1945, with 3,181 Lancaster sorties and 147 successful Mosquito sorties from 33 RAF squadrons. A total of over 7,000 tonnes of food was dropped, including 1,800 tonnes of flour, 270 tonnes of cheese, 470 tonnes of bacon and 310 tonnes of sausages.

"There are no words to describe the emotions experienced on that Sunday afternoon," wrote Arie de Jong, a 17-year-old student at the time. "More than 300 four-engined Lancasters, flying exceptionally low, suddenly filled the western horizon. One could see the gunners waving in their turrets. A marvellous sight. One Lancaster roared over the town at 70 feet. I saw the aircraft tacking between church steeples and drop its bags in the south. Everywhere we looked, bombers could be seen. No one remained inside and everybody dared to wave cloths and flags. What a feast! Everyone is excited with joy. The war must be over soon now."

Former air gunner Warrant Officer Dave Fellowes served with 460 Squadron in Bomber Command and took part in the mission. "Now we were doing something totally different," he said, "dropping food to the starving people of Holland. We were doing something humanitarian. We flew over, opened our bomb doors, dropped the food, out it tumbled like you had emptied a big shopping basket. Which it was! A big shopping basket full of food."

Every year, the Dutch hold ceremonies of remembrance to commemorate 10 May 1940, the day the country was invaded by Germany, and 5 May 1945, the day the country was liberated by Allied forces. The RAF is proud to have played a key role in that liberation.

Appelvlaai
Dutch Apple Crumble Tart

There are numerous versions of Dutch vlaai. Some have a fruit base and crumble topping, as in this recipe, and some have a cooked cheesecake-like base which is then topped with raw fruit or berries, but all have a sweet pastry case. Limburg, on the border with Germany and Belgium, is renowned for its vlaai. The raisins can be soaked in warm rum or brandy rather than water. With its dried fruit and cinnamon aromas this appelvlaai makes a delicious alternative at Christmas, especially if served warm with crème fraiche, mascarpone or whipped cream flavoured with brandy and mixed spice.

INGREDIENTS
Serves 8

For the pastry
300g flour
100g icing sugar
¼ tsp Salt
185g butter
1 egg
½ lemon, zest only
a few drops of vanilla extract
  (or the seeds from 1 vanilla pod)

For the filling
125g raisins
6 medium eating apples
100g light brown sugar
1 tsp vanilla extract
1 tsp ground cinnamon
30g cornflour

For the crumble topping
175g plain flour
100g butter, chilled and diced
75g demerara sugar

To serve
icing sugar to dust
whipping cream, crème fraiche
  or vanilla ice cream

METHOD
To make the pastry base
- Sieve the flour, icing sugar and salt together into a mixing bowl and lightly rub in the butter to a breadcrumb-like texture.
- Beat the egg and add the lemon zest and vanilla essence (or seeds).
- Make a well in the flour mixture and add the beaten egg mix, gradually incorporate and knead the mix to a smooth paste.
- Form the dough into a ball, wrap in cling film and rest in the fridge for at least 30 minutes before using.
- Lightly grease a 26cm diameter by 3cm deep false bottomed tart case or flan ring with softened butter.
- Dust the work surface and the top of the dough with a little flour then roll out the rested, chilled pastry to around the thickness of a £1 coin. The pastry should be large enough to cover the base and sides of the case or ring as well as around 2.5cm overhang. Drape the pastry loosely over the tart case and carefully ease it into the case ensuring it is tucked well into the corners. Leaving around 2.5cm overhang trim off any excess dough with a sharp pair of scissors and place in the refrigerator for 20 to 30 minutes to rest.

To make the filling
- Place the raisins in a bowl, cover with boiling water and leave for 20 minutes to plump up.
- Peel, core and coarsely dice the apples; drain the raisins.
- Place the raisins, diced apples, sugar, vanilla extract, cinnamon and cornflour into a bowl and mix well to thoroughly combine.

To make the crumble topping
- Sift the flour into a large bowl, rub the butter into the flour until

it becomes like coarse breadcrumbs. Add the sugar, rub in and squeeze the mix together in your hands, form a large ball then crumble back into the bowl. Repeat until the crumble mixture has a coarse crumbly texture.

To assemble and cook the tart
- Preheat the oven to 180°C.
- Fill the pastry case with the apple filling and top with the crumble mixture.
- Bake in the pre-heated oven for 45 to 50 minutes until the apple filling is cooked through and the crumble topping has browned.
- Set the cooked tart aside to cool slightly before trimming off the excess pastry.

To serve
- Dust with icing sugar and remove from the ring
- Cut into portions and serve warm or at room temperature with cream, crème fraiche or vanilla ice cream.

THE POST-WAR ERA
1946–1963

THE WINDS OF CHANGE

Words by
NICK FELLOWS

AN RAF AUSTER DURING
THE ANTARCTIC FLIGHT OF
1949–50, PICTURED WITH
THE SURVIVAL TENT THAT
SERVED AS A MAKESHIFT
FLIGHT OPERATIONS ROOM

ALTHOUGH BRITAIN HAD been victorious in 1945 and the Axis powers defeated, the country was left virtually bankrupt and international relations were far from smooth. A new type of war, the Cold War, soon emerged as relations deteriorated with former wartime ally the Soviet Union. This breakdown would spread beyond Europe to the rest of the world and create challenges for an RAF that was already involved in recovery operations in Europe, the Middle East and the Far East, bringing home troops and transporting essential items of food, clothing and medical care.

Internationally, many countries of the Empire sought independence, and the new challenge of colonial nationalism would make waging the peace as demanding as war. Britain wanted to ensure that the transition from colonial rule to independence was peaceful, but it also wanted to maintain a military presence and bases in many of these states, as well as ensuring that Cold War enemies did not make gains and influence in these areas. As a result, the RAF was drawn into a series of limited and small-scale "brushfire" wars in countries as diverse as Malaya, Kenya and Cyprus.

Initially, the greatest challenge to stability came in Europe. The wartime alliance between the western powers and the Soviet Union could be viewed as a marriage of convenience to defeat Nazi Germany. Even during the war, that alliance had tensions. The Soviet Union had complained about delays in opening a "second front" in Europe, while the western powers had been shocked by revelations about the Katyn massacres (where Stalin's secret police had executed more than 20,000 innocent Polish nationals in 1940). Divisions had arisen during the wartime conferences and these came to a head over the future of Germany. At the end of the war, the Allies had divided both Germany and its capital, Berlin, into four sectors, and it was over Berlin that matters escalated.

Faced with enormous economic problems in its zones of control, the western powers introduced a new currency without Soviet agreement. In response, the Soviets closed road and rail access to the western zones of Berlin in June 1948, claiming "technical difficulties". The west was faced with either surrendering control of Berlin, which would have been a sign of weakness, or supplying its zone and some two million West Berliners by air. This involved the carrying of not just food, but even coal and clothes through the three air-corridors that linked the western zones of Germany to Berlin. This was an incredible achievement, with West Berlin being successfully supplied by USAF and RAF aircraft flying 24 hours a day until the blockade ended in May 1949.

At the start of the operation, the aim was to bring in 200 tons per day, but at the height of the airlift it was averaging some 8,000 tons, with an incredible 12,940 being delivered on Good Friday 1949. It was not just air crews that made such an operation possible, but the engineers (who built a new airfield using rubble from Berlin) and air-traffic controllers (who ensured that aircraft were landing every three minutes in good weather). Even when the blockade was lifted, flights continued so that supplies were stockpiled. It proved to be a remarkable achievement of continuous flying, showing that air power had a considerable role to play in maintaining the peace.

In many instances colonial nationalism was closely linked to the ideological battles of the Cold War. This was certainly the case in the Malayan Emergency. During the Second World War, Malaya had been occupied by the Japanese. The Allies had supplied arms, equipment and even some men to fight a resistance war against the Japanese, which was largely conducted by the Malayan Communist Party. At the end of the war they began to exploit nationalist feeling and refused to hand back their weapons and retreated to the jungle to plan and plot to free Malaya from colonial rule. Attacks against rubber plantations and tin mines began in June 1948, which led to the British declaring a state of emergency. It was to become Britain's longest campaign since the Napoleonic Wars.

The ground forces took on the brunt of the task but the RAF, from its headquarters in Singapore and bases in Malaya, provided vital support to the police, army and civil government across the country. The RAF's reconnaissance operations were vital to the campaign, as was the movement by air of troops and supplies in and out of the jungle. The RAF also dropped leaflets designed to persuade guerrillas to surrender. Air strikes against the insurgents had little effect, due to the difficulty of locating small groups of insurgents under the jungle canopy, but helicopter lifts proved invaluable, evacuating the injured and helping to move troops around. In the end, it was air transport that was to prove crucial in the final defeat of the insurgents and brought peace, and then independence, to Malaya.

Britain's commitments in Malaya meant that it only had a limited involvement in the contemporaneous Cold War confrontation on the Korean peninsula. The United Nations, largely through the offices of the USA, backed South Korea when North Korean forces invaded in June 1950. The RAF provided Sunderland flying-boat patrols against sea-born incursions and helped to move troops between the UK, Japan and Korea. Operations in Kenya, during the Mau-Mau rebellion of 1952–56 were, in many ways, similar to those in Malaya, but on a smaller scale. A shortage of available armed aircraft meant that Harvard trainer aircraft were armed, supplemented by aircraft from the RAF base in Aden. However, as with Malaya, ground attacks were limited.

If providing ground support was the main concern with the Kenyan Crisis, that was certainly not the case with the Suez crisis that broke in 1956. Egypt had already abrogated the treaty by which the RAF had aircraft based within the zone around the Suez Canal in 1954 and withdrawals had been made to other bases in Aden and Cyprus. Egypt then announced its intention to nationalise the canal in retaliation for the withdrawal of UK and US aid.

Britain and France both had considerable commercial interests in the region and – with Egypt being aided by the Soviet Union – the two western nations built up their forces in Cyprus and Malta. Efforts to find a diplomatic solution failed and a British and French assault was launched. The role of the RAF was to attack Egyptian airfields and prevent the Egyptian air force, with its Russian planes, from attacking the British and French forces. This was achieved in two days by precision bombing from high-altitude. The RAF also dropped paratroopers to seize Gamil airfield. In the whole operation there were four deaths. However, despite the military success, diplomatic pressure and US unwillingness to support the attack led to withdrawal.

Not only was Cyprus used as a base for the attacks on Egypt, but it also became a centre of operations following the violent campaign of the late 1950s waged by the Greek Cypriot guerrillas of the EOKA (Ethniki Organosis Kyprion Agoniston),

who aimed to unite Cyprus with Greece. RAF helicopters provided essential air lift for ground forces hunting the EOKA guerrillas in the mountains. They landed troops, dropped food and ammunition, and evacuated casualties. The rebels were defeated and Cyprus joined the Commonwealth.

Cyprus was also at the centre of affairs in 1961 when it was used as a base to fly troops into Kuwait when it was threatened by Iraq. In an impressive display, the RAF deployed a squadron of Hawker Hunters to Kuwait, a parachute battalion was moved from Cyprus to Bahrain and a Marine Commando unit from Aden to Kuwait. This was accomplished within six days and the RAF was also able to continue to supply them by air. This was sufficient to deter Iraq, but also provided a clear example of the flexibility that air power had given to British forces, while also showing the importance of large transport aircraft in the modern world.

The final challenge in this period came in 1963 when Indonesia threatened the newly independent Malaysia. The RAF was able to provide air defence and reconnaissance of the whole peninsula. This, and the threat of ground attack from Hunters, as well as the ability to deploy troops by helicopter, was a sufficient deterrent and the confrontation did not develop. It illustrated that air power was vital in helping forces on the ground and reassuring the local population, helping to win hearts and minds.

By the time the Cold War reached its climax in 1963 with the Cuban Missile Crisis, the RAF had shown that it could play a prominent role in international affairs, helping to preserve peace, end conflicts and ensure a peaceful transition to independence from colonial rule. Despite financial pressures and an evolving role after the Second World War, the RAF had played a vital part in quelling the insurgencies that developed from the moves towards colonial independence, and in the conflicts and squabbles that emanated from the Cold War.

CANADA

Words by
FLIGHT LIEUTENANT SIMON STAFFORD
& ALISON STAFFORD

THE RELATIONSHIP BETWEEN the Royal Air Force and Canada has a long history that dates back to the very start of the RAF. A handful of Canadians – including First World War veterans John Baker, Raymond Collishaw, Harold Kerby and James Rankin – chose to remain in the RAF after the war and flew in colonial campaigns.

In 1920, Canada was among the colonies invited to recommend two candidates per year to train at the new RAF college at Cranwell in Lincolnshire. Cadets were to be "between 17½ and 19 years of age, physically fit, unmarried and of unmixed European descent".

This "colour bar" is certainly shocking by today's standards, but it did demonstrate the commitment of the RAF to maintain close links with certain colonies. Until 1947 there was no distinct Canadian citizenship, so members of the RAF often made the choice to pursue their career in Canada and vice versa, alternating between the RAF and the Royal Canadian Air Force (RCAF).

RAF Goose Bay was established in 1941 at Labrador in the far north of Canada. The site for the base, affectionately known as "The Goose", was chosen by Eric Fry, who was on loan to the RCAF from the Canadian Department of Mines and Resources. By 1942, there were 1,700 service personnel and 700 civilians at the base. By 1943, it was being used as a refuelling and shuttle stop for international flights throughout the war.

Although built by Canada to aid the war effort, the base was shared by Britain and America. The US remained at Goose Bay after the war, building the state-of-the-art Melville radar station in 1950. Perched at the top of a hill six miles north-west of the airfield, it became an invaluable North American Air Defense Command.

Today, a small number of RAF personnel and their families remain at Goose Bay forming one of the five "wings" that make up the modern Goose Bay. The other wings are the RCAF, the German Luftwaffe, the Royal Netherlands Air Force and the Italian Aeronautic Militaire.

The runway remains one of the longest in the world at 11,046 feet. It is one of the few long enough to be able to accommodate a Space Shuttle and has been designated by NASA as one of its emergency landing sites for Space Shuttle flights, showing that, despite its remote location, Goose Bay remains of service from its inception during the Second World War to the modern frontier of space.

A VICTOR BOMBER AT GOOSE BAY, LABRADOR, CANADA

Tourtière
French Canadian Meat Pie

This is a popular recipe from Quebec and is traditionally eaten in winter, especially at Christmas time. The recipe can include a variety of ingredients: some use only pork; some a mix of pork, beef and veal; and some use turkey or chicken. What they all have in common is a buttery double crust with a filling that is quite a dry mix of minced meat, flavoured with ground spices.

INGREDIENTS

Serves 6

For the short crust pastry

400g plain flour

pinch of salt

200g butter

100ml cold water

For the meat filling

4 tbsp olive oil

1½ medium onion, finely diced

3 cloves garlic, finely chopped

2 large carrots, finely diced

2 sticks of celery, finely diced

300g minced chuck steak

400g minced lean pork, e.g. leg

300g potato, peeled and finely
  diced

1 bay leaf

2 tsp dried sage

1 tsp dried thyme

1 tsp celery salt

½ tsp ground cinnamon

¼ tsp ground cloves

¼ tsp grated nutmeg

375ml beef stock

25g parsley, coarsely chopped

3 slices of thick white bread
  processed to coarse crumbs

salt and pepper

To finish

2 egg yolks, beaten with 1 tbsp
cold water

METHOD

To make the pastry

- Sieve the flour with the salt and rub in the butter to a sandy texture.
- Make a well in the centre, add the cold water and mix with a wooden spoon until the dough starts to come together.
- Continue to mix as briefly as possible with your hands to make a firm paste, taking care not to overwork the dough.
- Wrap in cling film and rest in the refrigerator for at least 20 minutes.

To make the filling

- Heat 2 tbsp of the olive oil in a casserole dish over a low heat and add the onions, garlic, carrot and celery. Sweat gently, stirring occasionally to ensure even cooking, for around 15 minutes until the vegetables are soft but without any colour.
- Heat a frying pan over a high heat with the remaining 2 tbsp of the olive oil, add the beef and pork, season lightly with salt and pepper and fry until well browned and starting to caramelise. This is best done in 2 or 3 batches to ensure that the meat caramelises and doesn't boil in its own juices, removing each batch of browned meat with a slotted spoon to drain off the excess fat. Add to the dish with the vegetables.
- Stir in the diced potato, bay leaf, dried herbs, celery salt, ground spices and beef stock. Bring to a boil, reduce the heat and simmer, stirring occasionally, for 15 minutes or until most of the liquid has either evaporated or been absorbed by the minced meat.
- Check the seasoning and stir in the chopped parsley and breadcrumbs; set aside to cool.

To make the pie

- Preheat the oven to 180°C.
- Divide the pastry in two (about two thirds for the base and one third for the top) and roll out two discs to roughly the thickness of a £1 coin.
- Lightly butter a pie dish (about 20cm in diameter by 5cm deep) and line with the larger of the two pastry discs with the edge overhanging, spoon in the cold filling, brush the pastry edge with a little of the beaten egg and top with the remaining pastry disc.
- Press the edges of the pastry together to seal, trim off the overhanging pastry, crimp neatly, brush the top of the pie with beaten egg and make a slit in the top of the pie.
- Place in the oven and cook for 45 minutes, brushing once or twice more with beaten egg during cooking until the top is golden brown.
- Remove the tourtière from the oven and rest at room temperature for 10 to 15 minutes before cutting into wedges.

JAPAN

Words by
SQUADRON LEADER GORDON PARRY

ON 15 AUGUST 1945, just nine days after the United States had dropped the atomic bomb on Hiroshima and six days after the nuclear destruction of Nagasaki, Japan announced its surrender to the Allies. This would become known as V-J Day, and on 2 September, the instrument of surrender was signed in Tokyo Bay, effectively ending the Second World War.

Iwakuni – located just 30 miles from Hiroshima – had been a major Japanese airfield and seaplane base, and was chosen to house the headquarters of the British Commonwealth Occupation Force (BCOF) Air Group. This was a multinational force comprising squadrons and support units from Australia, Great Britain, India and New Zealand, coming under the operational control of the United States' Fifth Air Force. It was responsible for demilitarising the Iwakuni area. In March 1946, the Royal Air Force arrived at the former Japanese

"After a short while, the girls started to bring gifts, arriving with mandarin oranges, bonsai trees and other small items"

training base. Several RAF units were brought in, including No. 91 Air Stores Park (ASP) from Singapore and No. 241 Air-Sea Rescue Unit. Additionally, No. 56 Mobile Field Hospital arrived in Iwakuni from India and became the British Commonwealth Air Hospital, No. 5 Hygiene and Malaria Control Unit.

Upon arrival, the buildings in Iwakuni were found to be in good condition and mostly of wooden construction. However, the aircraft hangars had lost their roofs in a typhoon and any steel had been taken to help reconstruct the devastated cities. Officers were allocated separate rooms in large dormitory blocks and provided with bat-women, known as "room girls", who looked after the cleaning, laundry and "general requirements".

These girls were daughters of Japanese officers or those of equivalent status and were well educated. They were also very apprehensive as to how they would be treated as "enemy nationals". They were obviously taken aback by little acts of kindness, such as gifts of soap or chocolate. Nevertheless, after a short while, they started to bring gifts of their own, arriving in the mornings with *mikans* (mandarin oranges), bonsai trees and other small

A SHORT SUNDERLAND FLYING BOAT AT IWAKUNI, JAPAN DURING THE KOREAN WAR

items. Officers were fascinated to see the girls wearing their colourful kimonos, although their everyday working clothes were dull. At first they spoke no English but they soon started to pick up enough to carry out limited conversations. Furthermore, a Japanese professor gave language classes to the English once a week, although attendances were a bit hit-and-miss.

Life was easy for the Communications Flight, which was also repositioned there, with the occasional flights to airfields on the adjacent Japanese islands using Dakotas and Austers. The only difficulty encountered was the problem of having to refuel and restart an Auster for the return flight from a remote destination. It was often a case of filling up from a drum of petrol and then, having carefully chocked the wheels, swinging the propeller oneself. This was particularly interesting, given that the Lycoming engine was renowned as a difficult starter when warm, and often a cause of embarrassment if a VIP was in the passenger seat awaiting take-off.

The RAF remained in Iwakuni until early 1948 when the detachment wound down, with No. 91 ASP being the last RAF unit to leave there in 1948.

Crispy Breadcrumbed Squid
with Creamy Ponzu Dressing

by **JAMES MARTIN**
CHEF AND TELEVISION PRESENTER

This snack or starter of crispy squid is made by coating and deep frying squid in panko. Panko are Japanese breadcrumbs made from a special crustless bread, which, rather than being baked, is cooked by having an electrical current passed through it. The resulting crumbs are flaky slivers with a coarse, airy texture that makes them very light and crispy when baked, grilled or fried. The creamy dressing that accompanies the crispy squid is similar to mayonnaise and is flavoured with garlic, chilli and yuzu. Yuzu is a citrus fruit that originates from East Asia and is commonly used as a flavouring or seasoning in Japan, in much the same way as lemon juice is used in European cuisine.

INGREDIENTS
Serves 4
For the squid
4 medium squid, cleaned and
  sliced into 5mm-thick rings
75g plain flour
2 eggs, beaten
75g panko (Japanese breadcrumbs)
salt and freshly ground black pepper

For the creamy ponzu dressing
2 egg yolks
½ tsp sea salt
1 pinch of white pepper
2 tsp rice wine vinegar
4 tsp garlic chilli sauce
2 tsp yuzu seasoning
200ml vegetable oil

For the garnish
spring onion, thinly sliced
red chilli, finely sliced
coriander, coarsely chopped
mint leaves, coarsely chopped

METHOD
To prepare and cook the squid
- Heat a deep fat fryer to 190°C.
- Season the flour with salt and black pepper.
- Toss the squid rings with the seasoned flour, coating thoroughly.
- Place into the beaten eggs then straight into the breadcrumbs and toss to coat once more.
- Drop a few at a time into the fat fryer and cook for 2 minutes until golden and crispy.
- Remove and place onto a kitchen-paper-lined plate.

To make the creamy ponzu dressing
- Place all the ingredients, except the vegetable oil, into a small food processor and blitz to a purée.
- Gradually add in the vegetable oil until a thin mayonnaise forms.
- Check the seasoning and add more yuzu seasoning if desired.

To serve
- Pile the squid onto a plate or bowl and drizzle over the creamy ponzu dressing, then garnish with the spring onion, red chilli and chopped herbs.

PALESTINE

Words by
AIR COMMODORE MARK GILLIGAN
& FLIGHT LIEUTENANT KATHERINE CLARKSON

UNWITTINGLY, THE BALFOUR Declaration of November 1917 was to undermine a future British role in Palestine. "The British Government view with favour the establishment of a national home for the Jewish people," it read, "and will use their best endeavours to facilitate the achievement of this object."

In support of a League of Nations mandate, the Royal Air Force undertook colonial policing tasks in Palestine from the early 1920s. By the 1930s, growing tensions between Arabs and Zionists made the mandate unworkable. In declaring Palestine an independent state, a 1939 White Paper allowed for 75,000 Jews to enter Palestine within five years, and by consent of the Palestinian Arabs thereafter.

Ostensibly, this was a reasonable means of ensuring that neither population

"The quota had been filled: faced with the challenge of curbing immigration, the British deployed elements of the RAF to Palestine"

dominated, but could not have envisaged the atrocities of the Holocaust. A resulting post-Second World War migration to Palestine of thousands of displaced European Jews added significant weight to the Zionist's campaign for a Jewish State, at a time when the 75,000 quota had been filled, and immigration was illegal.

Faced with the thorny challenge of curbing immigration flow, the British government deployed elements of the RAF to Palestine to assist. By 1946, 12 RAF squadrons were based there, operating with 80,000 soldiers of the British Army. While many squadrons were de-mobbing, 208 Squadron Spitfires were conducting anti-immigration patrols and providing anti-terrorist reconnaissance, since acts of terror – like the July 1946 killing of more than 90 by a Jewish terrorists' explosion at the King David Hotel in Jerusalem – were commonplace.

By September 1947, unable to implement the UN's plan to partition Palestine, the British government conceded defeat and began to withdraw its forces. On 22 May 1948, 208 Squadron were based at Ramat David airfield to provide support

SPITFIRES OF 208 SQUADRON AT RAF EIN SHEMER IN PALESTINE, CIRCA 1947

for the evacuation. "This morning we received a literally rude awakening," reads the squadron's diary. "At approximately 0600 Hours, when everyone was blissfully asleep and dreaming of leaving Palestine for good, a Spitfire IX (then unidentified) appeared over Ramat David, circled the airfield, and then dived in and dropped two bombs on the lines of Spitfires."

The record then states that seven of 208 Squadron's aircraft were damaged in what was claimed by the Egyptian Air Force as a navigational error, "mistaking" Ramat Airfield for a nearby Israeli Air Force base. The Egyptians blamed the weather, but as the operational record humorously states, "visibility was down to 50 miles and Cloud 0/10".

Anecdotally, squadron officers had enjoyed an exuberant dining-in night in the mess the evening before the raid. Anticipating their repatriation, they had attempted to destroy the facility to prevent the Israelis benefiting from it. So, the RAF needed little help in destroying Ramat David airfield! On 23 May, the final RAF detachments left Palestine for good.

Mansaf
Braised Lamb in Yoghurt

This spicy and slightly sharp-tasting Bedouin dish is the height of simplicity while tasting wonderful with a contrasting crunch of toasted nuts. It is essentially lamb (traditionally on the bone) simmered in a yoghurt called jameed with a Middle Eastern spice blend known as baharat (see recipe on page 133). Jameed can be substituted with low-fat natural yoghurt but it must be stabilised first to prevent it from curdling during cooking. Palestinians serve mansaf on flatbreads, topped with rice and garnished with whole toasted nuts.

INGREDIENTS
Serves 6

For the yoghurt
1 litre low-fat natural yoghurt
1 large egg white
1 tbsp cornflour
1 tsp salt

For the lamb
75ml ghee, clarified butter
  or olive oil
900g lamb, cut into large dice
1½ tbsp baharat (see recipe on
  page 133)
250ml lamb or chicken stock
salt and pepper

For the rice
50g butter
300g long grain rice
1 tsp turmeric

To serve
4 pitta breads, lavash (see recipe
  on page 263) or taboon
1½ tbsp pine nuts
2 tbsp blanched almonds
15ml ghee, clarified butter
  or olive oil
2 tbsp parsley, coarsely chopped

METHOD
To prepare the yoghurt
- Place the yoghurt in a bowl, mix until smooth then thoroughly beat in the egg white, cornflour and salt.
- Transfer the yoghurt mixture to a saucepan, place over a moderate heat and stir until it comes to a simmer. Reduce the heat and continue to simmer gently for about 5 minutes until slightly thickened and smooth.
- Transfer to a clean container, cool then cover and refrigerate until required.

To cook the lamb
- Heat the ghee or vegetable oil over a medium heat, lightly season the lamb with salt and cook for about 15 minutes until well browned all over.
- Drain off the excess fat from the pan, return to the heat, stir in the baharat, lamb or chicken stock and the prepared yoghurt. Season with salt and pepper and bring to a simmer.
- Ladle off 200ml/7 fl oz of the sauce (reserve for the rice), reduce the heat to low, partially cover with a lid and cook, stirring occasionally, for 2½ hours until the lamb is very tender, adding a little boiling water as required when the sauce becomes too dry.

To cook the rice
- Once the lamb has been simmering for 1¾ hours, soak the rice in cold water for 30 minutes, rinse and drain well.
- Heat the butter in a saucepan over a moderate heat and, when foaming, add the rice and cook, stirring continuously for a couple of minutes until the rice is fragrant and thoroughly coated in the butter.

"This spicy and slightly sharp-tasting Bedouin dish is the height of simplicity while tasting wonderful with a contrasting crunch of toasted nuts"

- Stir in the turmeric, cover with 600ml/1 pt of boiling water, season with salt, cover with a lid and simmer very gently over a low heat for 15 to 20 minutes until tender. Stir in the reserved yoghurt sauce (the rice should have a loose, almost risotto-like consistency) and season with salt and pepper as required.

To serve
- Preheat the grill to high.
- Grill the pitta breads (or flatbreads) until lightly toasted and split horizontally to create 8 thin pieces of bread. If using flatbreads tear into large pieces.
- Grill the pine nuts and almonds until lightly browned.
- Arrange the pitta breads overlapping on a serving dish.
- Spread over a little of the yoghurt sauce from the lamb, top with the rice, spoon over the lamb and sauce then garnish with the toasted nuts, a drizzle of ghee, clarified butter or olive oil and chopped parsley.

ISRAEL

Words by
FLIGHT LIEUTENANT TOM MARSHALL

A SUPERMARINE SPITFIRE OF 32 SQUADRON AT RAMAT DAVID IN ISRAEL, 1948, SHOWING BULLET HOLES AFTER EGYPTIAN ATTACK

AFTER THE UN PLAN of Partition formally divided British Palestine in 1947, Britain was given a deadline of May 1948 to remove all its occupying forces. This partition saw a huge increase in Arab–Jew in-fighting, with 208 and 32 Squadrons caught in the middle at their base on Ramat David Airfield. Both squadrons were called on to attack Jewish forces that had attacked British Army units as part of the counter-measures to the Jewish insurrection. Britain was unable to meet the deadline and was therefore required to cover the retreat of its remaining forces. On 14 May 1948, the independent Jewish State of Israel was declared and this immediately led to a very bitter and confusing period of fighting involving that most iconic of aircraft, the Spitfire.

Egyptian air force Spitfires destroyed two RAF Spitfires on 22 May 1948, claiming to have mistaken them for those of the fledgling Israeli Air Force (IAF). A second attack killed four personnel but, by the third attack, the RAF was prepared, downing five Egyptian Spitfires using patrolling RAF Spitfires and ground fire from the RAF Regiment. The following day saw the full withdrawal to the relative safety of Cyprus and the Canal Zone of all RAF ground forces.

The RAF was now patrolling the Sinai Desert while the IAF recruited volunteers to fly their newly purchased Spitfires, bought from Czechoslovakia. There were therefore three separate air forces operating in contested air space, all flying Spitfires!

When Egyptian Spitfires attacked Israeli forces that had crossed their border in the Sinai desert, the RAF had four of their own patrolling the area. They flew in to investigate the wreckages but were shot at by the Israelis, fearful of another Egyptian attack. When one was seriously damaged, the British pilot had to bail out,

and the remaining three tried to provide top-cover. Concentrating on his descent into the Egyptian desert, they did not see the two IAF Spitfires attacking them from above until it was too late. Ironically, these were manned by volunteers and veterans of the Second World War, trained by the RAF, who downed all three.

As a direct consequence of this attack, a further patrol of Spitfires was sent to find the four missing crew members. Due to the suddenness of the initial attack, none of the RAF aircrew had managed to radio the situation back and, while the attack was almost forgiveable in the RAF's eyes due to the confusing situation on the ground, a subsequent attack on this patrol by the IAF was far more calculated. Four IAF Spitfires "bounced" the RAF flight which, up to that point, was simply on a reconnaissance detail and therefore not really expecting an attack from the air. The RAF lost a young inexperienced pilot, but managed to hold off the rest until it returned back over the border.

The aftermath of these incidents left an understandably bitter taste in the mouth of the squadrons who had suffered losses. They demanded retribution and retaliatory strikes but these requests were denied by Air Command.

In recent years, an uneasy alliance has developed between Britain and Israel, largely at the insistence of Britain's NATO ally, the US. This was tested more recently in 2013 when a Chinook was forced to make an emergency landing in Israel en route from Jordan to Cyprus. Open discussion proved fruitful, however, and the helicopter was retrieved without further incident – something that would have been unthinkable in the 1940s.

> *"There were therefore three separate air forces operating in contested air space, all flying Spitfires!"*

Shakshukha
Baked Eggs in Spiced Tomato Sauce

Although a popular breakfast throughout North Africa and the Middle East, shakshukha has become a staple of Israeli cuisine, popularised by Tunisian Jews. It is traditionally cooked and served in a skillet, but can be baked and served in individual dishes. The method below is a basic recipe, but other vegetables, such as courgettes, aubergines, mushrooms or spinach, can be included to make it more substantial. For a meat version, cooked bacon or sausages can be added to the sauce.

INGREDIENTS

Serves 4

For the spice paste

1 tbsp olive oil

3 cloves of garlic, finely chopped
  or crushed

1 red chilli (medium hot), finely
  chopped

1½ tsp smoked paprika

1 tsp chilli powder (mild or hot)

1 tsp ground cumin

1 tsp caraway seeds, ground
  to a coarse powder in a pestle
  and mortar

1 tsp black pepper

For the shakshukha

2 tbsp olive oil

1 medium onion, finely diced

2 red peppers, deseeded and
  coarsely chopped

2 tbsp tomato purée

800g very ripe tomatoes, chopped
  or tinned chopped tomatoes

pinch of saffron (optional)

2 tsp honey

2 tbsp coriander, coarsely chopped

4 large eggs

salt and pepper

To serve

crusty white bread

METHOD

To make the spice paste

• Heat the oil in a frying pan. Add the garlic and chilli and cook, stirring constantly, for a few minutes until starting to soften.

• Add the spices and continue to cook for a further 2 minutes, add a tablespoon of water to form a firm paste and cook for 1 minute; set aside until required.

To make the spiced tomato sauce

• Heat the oil in a skillet or frying pan over a moderate heat, add the onions and cook for 5 minutes until translucent. Add the peppers and continue to cook for a further 5 minutes until soft.

• Stir in the spice paste, tomato purée, chopped tomatoes, saffron (if using) and honey. Bring to a simmer, reduce the heat to low and cook, stirring frequently, for about 10 minutes until the sauce has reduced and thickened slightly. Season with salt and add a little water if the sauce becomes too thick.

• Stir in two thirds of the chopped coriander.

To finish

• If making individual portions divide the tomato sauce into four shallow oven proof dishes and preheat the oven 180°C.

• Make a shallow indentation in the sauce (whether in the skillet or individual dishes) and immediately crack an egg into the depression. Repeat with the remaining eggs and grind some black pepper and rock or sea salt over the top.

• If cooking in the skillet, cover with a lid and simmer over a very low heat for about 10 minutes until the egg whites are set and the yolks are still runny.

• If cooking individually, cover the dishes with aluminium foil and bake in the oven for about 10 minutes until the whites are set and the yolk is still runny.

To serve

• Garnish with the remaining chopped coriander and serve with crusty white bread.

GERMANY

Words by
ED SHARMAN

A YORK TRANSPORT AIRCRAFT UNLOADS DURING THE BERLIN AIRLIFT, 1949

THE ROYAL AIR FORCE's history of service in Germany dates back to the 8th Brigade Royal Flying Corps (later the 8th Brigade Royal Air Force) and the formation of the RAF in 1918. The RAF has since had a long and varied role across Germany, from offensive to defensive to humanitarian.

From 1 January 1959, RAF Germany was a separate command of the RAF, part of its Cold War commitments. RAF Germany was disbanded in 1993 after the end of the Cold War, and RAF forces in Germany became No. 2 Group RAF, part of RAF Strike Command and later No. 1 Group RAF.

One of the RAF's greatest achievements was the Berlin Airlift. Germany was partitioned into Soviet, American, British and French zones. Berlin, located 100km inside the Soviet zone, was also divided into four. In June 1948, the Soviets – who wanted the western powers out of Berlin – blockaded all roads, railways and canals into the city. At the start of the blockade the population in West Berlin had just 35 days' worth of food and 45 days' worth of coal. To assist

them, allied forces began one of the largest humanitarian missions in history, making some 300,000 flights to support Berlin. At the height of the airlift, an aircraft took off or landed every 30 seconds.

Some 2.3 million tons of cargo were landed during the blockade. The daily supplies needed to sustain Berlin's population included 646 tons of flour and wheat, 125 tons of cereal, 64 tons of fat, 109 tons of meat and fish, 180 tons of dehydrated potatoes, 180 tons of sugar, 11 tons of coffee, 19 tons of powdered milk, five tons of whole milk for children, three tons of fresh yeast for baking, 144 tons of dehydrated vegetables, 38 tons of salt and 10 tons of cheese. Additionally, for heat and power, 3,475 tons of coal and gasoline were also required daily.

The Soviets offered free food to those West Berliners who crossed into the east, and harassed aircraft trying to enter the region. The latter included "buzzing" by Soviet planes, obstructive parachute jumps within the corridors, and shining searchlights to dazzle pilots at night.

Former RAF Dakota pilot Dick Arscott described one "buzzing" incident. "Yaks (Soviet fighter aircraft) used to buzz you and go over the top of you at about 20 feet," he says. "One day I was buzzed about three times. The following day it started again and he came across twice and I got a bit fed up with it. So, when he came for the third time, I turned the aircraft into him and it became a game of chicken. Luckily he was the one who chickened out."

Sauerbraten
Pot Roast Pickled Beef

Sauerbraten (literally "pickled roast") can take a couple of days to make and marinate, but it is worth the wait. Classically, it uses tougher cuts of meat (it was originally made with horse meat) and is well suited to slow cooking. Traditional accompaniments include sauerkraut, braised red cabbage (rotkohl), potato dumplings (kartoffelknödel or kartoffelklöße), noodles (spätzle) or mashed potatoes.

INGREDIENTS

Serves 4–6

For the marinade

500ml cold water

500ml red wine vinegar

250ml red wine

2 medium onions, halved and
  cut into 1cm slices

1 large carrot, cut into 1cm slices

1 stick of celery, cut into 1cm slices

1 tbsp granulated white sugar

1 tbsp juniper berries (crushed
  with the flat of a large knife)

1 tsp mustard seeds

1 tsp black peppercorns

2 tsp salt

2 tsp blade mace or 1 tsp
  ground mace

8 cloves

2 bay leaves

2 sprigs of thyme

1kg beef top rump joint, tied

For the beef

2 tbsp vegetable oil

100g streaky bacon (rindless),
  cut into 2cm long lardons

50g butter

2 medium onions, coarsely chopped

1 large carrots, coarsely chopped

1 stick celery, coarsely chopped

2 tbsp plain flour

2 tbsp granulated white sugar

salt and pepper

For the sauce

75g seedless raisins (optional)

500ml beef stock

50g gingersnap biscuits (around 5),
  blended to fine crumbs

½ lemon, juiced

METHOD

To marinate the beef

- Place all of the marinating ingredients (except the beef) in a saucepan. Bring to a boil, remove from the heat and allow to cool for 15 to 20 minutes
- Place the beef in a bowl, just large enough to hold the joint. Pour over the marinade, cover and leave to marinate in the fridge for a minimum of 2 days, or up to 5 days, turning twice each day.

To cook the beef

- Preheat the oven to 160°C.
- Remove the beef from the marinade, pat dry and set to one side. Strain the marinating liquor into a bowl, discarding the solids.
- Heat the oil in a casserole over a high heat, add the beef joint and sear all over. Remove the beef, season and set aside on a plate.
- Return the casserole to a moderate heat, add the bacon and fry until lightly browned. Remove with a slotted spoon and set aside.
- Add the butter and, when foaming, add the onions, carrots and celery; cook stirring for 10 minutes until softened and lightly browned.
- Stir in the flour and cook, stirring continuously, for a few minutes. Add the sugar and cook for 5 minutes until the roux is lightly browned.
- Stir in the marinade until the sauce is smooth. Simmer for a minute.
- Place the beef joint and half of the bacon in the sauce, cover with a lid and cook in the oven for 2½ hours until the beef is very tender.

To make the sauce

- Place the raisins (if using) in a small bowl, pour over enough boiling water to cover and allow to steep and plump up for 10 minutes.
- Transfer the beef to a plate and cover with foil to rest. Strain the sauce into a saucepan (reserving the vegetables and bacon in a separate saucepan if you want a bit of extra texture to the finished sauce). Add the beef stock to the sauce, bring to a boil, reduce the heat and whisk in the gingersnap crumbs and lemon juice. Simmer for 10 minutes until the sauce has reduced slightly and has thickened enough to coat the back of a spoon.
- Strain the sauce over the vegetables and bacon (if using), bring to a simmer, add the raisins (if using), cook for 5 minutes and season.

To serve

- Warm the reserved bacon.
- Carve the beef into thick slices onto a warmed serving plate, ladle over the sauce and garnish with parsley and the bacon.

KOREA

Words by
SQUADRON LEADER GORDON PARRY

PRIOR TO THE Second World War, Japan had occupied the Korean peninsula since 1910, but the Allies made a pledge that, once Japan had been defeated, Korea would be free to become an independent state.

However, in 1945, the Soviet Union occupied the northern part of Korea, while the United States occupied the south: the two sides separated by what was meant to be a temporary line drawn along the 38th parallel. No agreement could be reached on the withdrawal of forces, however, even with the assistance of the United Nations, with the Soviets using their veto, and the 38th parallel became increasingly fortified. After elections, the southern region formed the Republic of Korea (South Korea), while the north followed a month later with the formation of the Democratic People's Republic of Korea (North Korea).

With the US slowly withdrawing, North Korean forces invaded South Korea in 1950. Within days, US President Harry Truman and the British Prime Minister Clement Attlee had committed forces in support of South Korea and a large-scale conflict against North Korea ensued.

The Far East Air Force, engaged in the Malayan Emergency, had few resources to spare. Sunderlands from 88, 205 and 209 Squadrons of the Far East Flying Boat Wing were able to stage through Hong Kong to carry out more than 1,100 reconnaissance and transport tasks for Korean operations. Patrols were often 12 hours in duration and crews were exposed to temperatures of minus -20°C in their draughty, unheated aircraft.

In the fighter domain, things became very interesting. Although an antiquated North Korean fighter aircraft component was quickly defeated, Russian-backed Chinese MIG-15s joined the battle, operating from airfields that were politically secure from attack in Manchuria. Although the RAF's fighter aircraft were committed to the Cold War in Europe, the RAF sent valuable expertise and experienced pilots to fly with the United States Air Force (USAF) and the Royal Australian Air Force (RAAF). 77 Squadron of the RAAF were equipped with the Meteor 8. Unfortunately, the Meteors' maximum speed was well below that of the MIG, and was inferior in almost every respect.

Having taken losses in the high-altitude role, 77 Squadron was switched to providing medium cover to the bombers, but not before one pilot became the RAF's only POW of the conflict. Uninjured, he spent the rest of the war resisting the fearsome brainwashing techniques of his captors, and enduring a great deal of solitary confinement.

In one of the RAF's less well-known roles, No. 1903 Independent Air Operations Post Flight, based in Hong Kong, and No. 1913 Light Liaison Flight, from the UK, were deployed to a small airstrip near the Divisional HQ at Fort George, just south of the Imjin River. Equipped with the Auster, the role of the two units was to perform battlefield reconnaissance and artillery spotting duties. However, the first task was to be photographed by friendly forces from the air and ground to make sure Britain's US allies, with their anti-aircraft guns, even knew what the friendly aircraft looked like.

The natural runway was a mere 600 yards long and 60 feet wide, which was either a dust bowl or a quagmire depending upon the weather. Indeed, if the mud froze overnight around the Auster's wheels, then the aircraft had to be thawed out of its ruts in the morning before it could be flown. Two aircraft were shot down over no-man's land, with the crews being killed, after which the wearing of parachutes became compulsory for the first time.

Overall, the Korean War demonstrated that the advance of communism could be halted. Furthermore, the advent of the MIG-15 sharpened the determination to procure new-generation jet aircraft. Moreover, it was an early test of the resolve of a relatively young United Nations.

AN RAF AUSTER MILITARY OBSERVATION AIRCRAFT IN SOUTH KOREA, CIRCA 1952

Bulgogi
Korean Barbecue Beef

A popular Korean dish, bulgogi (literally "fire meat") is traditionally cooked in a perforated inverted dome over hot coals. It is important to use a good tender cut of beef such as fillet, sirloin or rib-eye. Bulgogi is generally served with whole lettuce leaves so it can be wrapped up with rice to eat.

INGREDIENTS
Serves 4

600g beef (fillet, sirloin or rib-eye)

For the marinade
⅓ medium onion, finely diced
1 ripe pear (or red apple), grated
4 cloves garlic, crushed
1cm ginger, grated
75ml dark soy sauce
1 tbsp sesame oil
1 tbsp mirin (optional)
50g light soft brown sugar
¼ tsp dried chilli flakes
black pepper

To cook
2 tbsp peanut oil or sunflower oil
1 medium onion, thinly sliced
2 spring onions, finely sliced
1 small carrot, peeled and cut into
  thin roundels or thin batons
1 tbsp sesame seeds

To serve
whole cos lettuce leaves
boiled or steamed rice
combination of sliced peppers,
  cucumber, carrots, red onions, garlic,
  spring onions or coriander leaves
Ssamjang (spicy sweet Korean
  sauce) or sweet chilli sauce
  (ideally chojang)

METHOD
To prepare the beef
- Wrap the beef in cling film and place in the freezer for a couple of hours until firm.
- Remove any excess fat and finely shred the beef as thin as possible and place in a non-metallic bowl.

To marinate
- Place the onion, grated pear or apple, garlic and ginger in a food processor and blend to a smooth purée.
- Mix the purée with the rest of the marinade ingredients, add to the beef, mix well, cover and leave to marinate in the fridge for at least two hours or, preferably, overnight.

To cook
- Heat the oil in a wok or large frying pan over a high heat. Add the marinated beef with the sliced onion, spring onions and carrot.
- Stir-fry until the meat has browned, reduce the heat and simmer for a few minutes until the liquid from the marinade has reduced.
- Add the sesame seeds and stir to combine.

To serve
- Transfer the bulgogi to a warmed serving dish.
- Serve with the lettuce leaves, rice, sauce and any other accompaniments on the side so your diners can stuff their own lettuce leaves with their choice of fillings.

VEGETARIAN ALTERNATIVE
MUSHROOM BULGOGI
- Substitute the beef for 500g of sliced chestnut mushrooms (or a mix of mushrooms e.g. button, chestnut, Portobello, shitake, enoki).
- Use the same marinade, vegetables, accompaniments and cooking method as above.

SCOTLAND

Words by
FLIGHT LIEUTENANT SI MOORE

THE RAF MOUNTAIN Rescue Service (MRS) was formed in early 1942 by the Station Medical Officer, Flight Lieutenant George Graham MBE DSO, at RAF Llandwrog. The service was formed after concerns that aircrew might survive an initial crash but not the mountainous conditions afterwards. Up to that point, each station would send its own personnel to search for missing crews, but they were often untrained for the task. By the end of 1943, 33 survivors had been rescued from 22 crashes, but some 571 aircrew had died in 220 crashes in mountainous and moorland areas.

At its height, the RAF MRS had six UK-based teams and overseas teams in Cyprus, Hong Kong and the Middle East. Today, three remain, at RAF Lossiemouth, Leeming and Valley. They provide cover for the whole of the UK and are also available for overseas deployment.

This Scottish team – first based at RAF Kinloss before moving to Lossiemouth in 2011 – has been involved in a number of significant events over the years, several of which have contributed to the shape and training provided by the

MRS. The most notable resulted from the Avro Lancaster crash on the slopes of Beinn Eighe, Torridon, on 13 March 1951. The aircraft was eventually found in "the wildest corrie I have ever seen", reported Joss Gosling, a team member (a "corrie" being a steep valley caused by glacial erosion). The undercarriage and wings where found high up in the corrie, but the fuselage could not initially be located; this was later found higher up the mountain in what is now known as Fuselage Gully.

The team where driven back by severe winter conditions for which they had not been trained and the last body wasn't recovered until 9 May. This led to a reshaping of the MRS and the development of specific mountaineering training courses. Visitors to the area can still see significant parts of the wreckage that remain on the mountain, including a propeller that sits in Fuselage Gully and is used as a belay by climbers today. Another twisted propeller from the crashed Lancaster forms a memorial outside the MRS Section.

With the motto "Whensoever", today's MRS is manned by up to 36 highly trained volunteers, maintaining a one-hour standby readiness to assist in the search and rescue of passengers and crew of downed aircraft, both military and civilian, and missing military personnel in this country and abroad. However, the service is more renowned for assisting police and civilian mountain rescue teams in the search and rescue of civilian walkers and climbers.

A SEA KING HELICOPTER PICKS UP AN RAF MOUNTAIN RESCUE SERVICE TEAM AT RAF LEUCHARS

Cullen Skink
Scottish Smoked Haddock Soup

Named after the fishing village on the Moray Firth, Cullen Skink is regarded as one of the world's finest fish soups: smokier than an American chowder and more robust than a French bouillabaisse. Some recipes use Arbroath smokies (hot smoked haddock), which can be overpowering. This recipe uses cold smoked haddock. Creamy and hearty, it can be eaten as a starter or as a meal with bread.

INGREDIENTS

Serves 4

For the soup

50g butter

1 large onion, finely chopped

2 medium leeks (white part only), quartered lengthways and finely sliced

500g undyed smoked haddock

1 bay leaf

6 peppercorns

800g potatoes, peeled and coarsely diced

600ml whole milk

50ml single cream

salt and pepper

To serve

1 bunch of chives, half finely chopped and half snipped into 1cm lengths

crusty bread

METHOD

To make the soup

- Melt the butter in a saucepan or casserole dish over a moderate heat, and, when starting to foam, add the diced onions and sliced leeks. Cook, stirring frequently, for about 10 minutes until soft and the onions are translucent.
- Meanwhile place the smoked haddock in a large frying or sauté pan, cover with around 300ml of cold water, add the bay leaf and peppercorns, place over a medium heat and bring to a simmer. As soon as the water starts to simmer, remove the pan from the heat. Check to ensure the haddock is just cooked through to the middle; if not leave it in the water (off the heat) for another minute or two. Once cooked, remove the haddock from the pan, reserving the cooking water, and set to one side to cool.
- Add the potatoes to the saucepan with the onions and leek, stir well, strain over the haddock cooking water (add the bay leaf), season lightly with freshly ground pepper, cover with a lid and simmer until the potatoes are cooked through and tender.
- Meanwhile remove the skin from the haddock and break the flesh into flakes (discarding any bones).
- Once the potatoes are cooked, add the milk, bring back to a simmer, and remove about a quarter of the potatoes, onions and leeks with a slotted spoon. Set to one side in a bowl. Discard the bay leaf and stir in half of the flaked smoked haddock.
- Purée the soup in a blender until smooth, return to a clean saucepan, stir in the cream, remaining haddock and the reserved potatoes, onions and leeks. Bring to a simmer, stir in the chopped chives and season with a little salt if required.

To serve

- Ladle the Cullen skink into bowls (add an extra swirl of cream and/or a drizzle of lemon or olive oil if you want), garnish with the snipped chives and serve with warm crusty bread.

GREENLAND

Words by
FLIGHT LIEUTENANT SIMON STAFFORD

A CRASHED HASTINGS TROOP CARRIER IN GREENLAND, 1952

THE NORTH ATLANTIC air ferry route was a series of air routes on which aircraft were ferried from North America to Britain during the Second World War to support combat in Europe. It originated at army air bases in New England and permitted aircraft to cross the Atlantic using intermediate airfields, some of which were in Greenland. It became one of the major transport and supply routes of the war.

In July 1941, the US sent construction crews to Narsarsuaq in Greenland to build the air base that came to be known as Bluie West 1 (BW-1) and was later the headquarters of Greenland Base Command. They followed this up in October of the same year with Bluie West 8, a more northerly base on the western coast of Greenland. A third airfield was built north of Angmagssalik on the east coast of Greenland (Bluie East 2) in 1942, giving Allied troops a firm foothold on the island.

Following the war, the RAF was heavily involved in the British Greenland Expeditions in July 1952, supporting the 25-man expedition team. The team started its journey from Deptford aboard the former Norwegian sealer *Tottan*, while another cargo ship, loaded with four Weasel tracked vehicles, sailed from Hull. After collecting sledge dogs in south-west

Greenland, the two ships sailed to Young Sund on the north-east coast. From there, RAF Short Sunderland flying-boats airlifted the expedition to the glacial lake Britannia Sø and set up a base camp. Commander Simpson then led a party on dog sleds to establish the North Ice station about 230 miles to the west.

More than 86 tons of equipment was air-dropped from two RAF Handley Page Hastings transport aircraft. On 16 September 1952, a Hastings of 47 Squadron was making a series of freefall drops at an altitude of only 50 feet when it was caught in a white-out, and made a forced belly landing. Three members of the crew were injured, and sheltered in the fuselage until rescued by the US Air Force.

Later in 1952, experienced flying-boat pilots were called to provide assistance to the British Greenland Expedition that was exploring a mountain range in north-east Greenland. The expedition continued its glaciological studies through 1953 and 1954, with seismic and gravimetric teams measure the thickness of the ice sheet. In August 1953, the teams was re-supplied by sea and air, and eight team members left to be replaced by five more. The expedition returned to the UK by ship in August 1954.

The entire expedition team was awarded the Polar Medal in November 1954, while Commander Simpson was also presented with the Patron's Medal from the Royal Geographical Society in 1955, and was made a CBE on 2 January 1956.

Suaasat
Meat & Barley Soup

Suaasat, the national dish of Greenland, was originally a very simple affair consisting of seal meat, water, onions and barley. It is still traditionally cooked with seal, whale, reindeer or seabirds, but also works well with beef, lamb or venison. Even though referred to as a soup, it is more like a hearty winter stew, with the dried cherries and cranberries giving it a unique sweet-and-sour flavour. Although some of the ingredients in this recipe aren't native to Greenland, including the aromatic herbs, they are commonly used in contemporary Greenlandic cuisine.

INGREDIENTS
Serves 4

For the suaasat

800g beef, lamb or venison,
   cut into large pieces
2 litres of beef stock
1 sprig of thyme
1 sprig of rosemary
2 bay leaves
100g dried cherries or cranberries
   (or 50g of each)
3 medium onions, coarsely chopped
1 large waxy potato, coarsely
   chopped
200g swede, coarsely chopped
2 medium carrots, coarsely chopped
   or sliced
150g pearl barley
250g mixed wild mushrooms, torn
salt and pepper

To serve
crusty bread

METHOD
To make the suaasat

• Place the meat in a large casserole or saucepan and pour over the stock.
• Tie the thyme, rosemary and bay leaves together with a piece of string to make a bouquet garni and add to the casserole with the dried cherries and/or cranberries.
• Place over a high heat, bring to a boil, turn the heat to low, cover with a lid and simmer for 1½ hours.
• Stir in the onions, potatoes, swede, carrot and pearl barley; top up with enough boiling water to cover if necessary, replace the lid and continue to simmer for 30 minutes until the potatoes and vegetables are tender and the barley is cooked through and soft. The soup should have quite a thin consistency, only slightly thickened by the starch from the barley and potatoes; top up with a little more stock or boiling water if necessary.
• Stir in the mushrooms, continue to simmer until softened and season with salt and freshly ground black pepper.

To serve

• Pick out the bouquet garni, ladle into warmed bowls and serve with crusty bread.

KENYA

Words by
SQUADRON LEADER CHRIS POWELL

THE GOVERNOR OF Kenya declared a state of emergency in October 1952, following the revolt by the Kenyan African Union and its paramilitary wing, the Mau Mau. Britain's diminished post-Second World War military, combined with the ongoing conflict in Malaya, had left the Kenya garrison ill-equipped to counter the uprising. The RAF station at Eastleigh, just outside Nairobi, was the only RAF airfield in East Africa and had just four aircraft of various kinds.

Following the closure of the Rhodesian Air Training Group, eight Harvard training aircraft were sent to Kenya. These were rapidly adapted to provide a basic offensive capability in the form of a machine gun and bomb racks. The high-pitched scream of the Harvard propeller was found to be very successful in dispersing insurgents, averting the requirement for an actual attack.

Soon after, eight heavy RAF Lincoln bombers were deployed to Kenya with their crews experienced in counter-insurgency operations from their time in Malaya. In 1954, two Meteor PR10 reconnaissance aircraft were also deployed, which were responsible for the overwhelming majority of the 250,000 aerial photographs taken during the emergency.

It was important to maintain the support of Kenya's non-Mau Mau majority and ensure that no innocent civilian casualties resulted from air action. In addition to offensive operations against the insurgents, the RAF conducted psychological operations, with Lincoln bombers dropping more than five million leaflets in 1955 alone. Some were dropped to convince the Mau Mau to surrender, others depicted victories over the Mau Mau, to show that the government was winning. Graphic pictures of Mau Mau massacres were dropped to those members of the population who were undecided on which side to take.

Following Lincoln bombing raids on the Mau Mau, Auster and Pembroke aircraft conducted sky-shouting missions broadcasting messages over a loudspeaker to encourage surrender. This strategy saved lives by reducing the numbers of ground engagements the army had to conduct. The very presence of the RAF helped convince Kenyans that the government were defeating the insurgency. By the beginning of 1955, the Mau Mau was a spent force, and by the end of the year, the army's dwindling requirement for air support enabled the Harvards, Meteors and Lincolns to be withdrawn.

General Erskine, Commander-in-Chief, East Africa Command told pilots that the RAF's participation had allowed the army in Kenya to be far smaller in size than it would otherwise need to be. The situation had improved sufficiently that British troops could be withdrawn in 1956, although the state of emergency only ended in 1960. Today, RAF C17s, C130s, A400M and Voyager aircraft fly many tasks deploying, recovering and supporting the army for the large training exercises conducted in Kenya each year.

AN AVRO LINCOLN BOMBER OVER KENYA, 1954

Githeri with Baked Prawns
Kenyan Corn & Beans with Baked Prawns

Githeri is a popular dish of sweetcorn and beans originating from the Kikuyu tribe. On its own, it can be served with any Kenyan dish, but it can also be bulked up with meat and potatoes for a main meal. Any beans can be used – adzuki, borlotti, black-eye, kidney or flageolet. Here it is served with baked spiced prawns, which have been marinated with spices, chillies and tamarind.

INGREDIENTS

Serves 4

For the prawns

400g large raw, shelled king
 prawns (around 40 prawns)

1 tbsp tamarind paste

2 large red chillies, halved
 lengthways and finely shredded

1 or 2 small hot green chillies, halved
 lengthways and finely shredded

2.5cm piece of ginger, grated

2 tsp ground coriander

1 tsp ground cumin

½ tsp ground cardamom seeds

1 tbsp vegetable oil

1 lemon, juice and finely grated zest

salt and pepper

For the githeri

1 tbsp vegetable oil

1 medium onion, finely diced

1 red pepper, finely diced

1 green pepper, finely diced

3 cloves of garlic, finely chopped
 or crushed

1.5cm piece of ginger, finely grated

2 green chillies, halved lengthways,
 deseeded and finely chopped

1 tbsp curry powder

1 tbsp tomato purée

100g baby plum (or cherry)
 tomatoes, halved

4 ears of corn on the cob

250g cooked mixed beans
 (400g tin), drained

2 tbsp flat leaf parsley, coarsely
 chopped

½ lemon, juiced

To serve

flatbreads or chapatis

METHOD

To marinate the prawns

• Place the prawns one by one on their backs cut down the centre about three quarters of the way through from the tail end towards the heads; ease them apart and remove the dark thread-like digestive tract.

• To make the marinade, place the tamarind paste, chillies, ginger, ground spices, vegetable oil, lemon zest and juice in a bowl, season with salt and freshly ground black pepper and mix well.

• Toss the prawns in the marinade, thread onto metal skewers (if using wooden skewers soak them in cold water first to prevent them from burning in the oven), cover and set aside to marinate.

• While the prawns are marinating, preheat the oven to 220°C and start to cook the githeri.

To prepare the githeri

• Heat the oil in a saucepan over a moderate heat, add the onions and diced peppers; cook, stirring frequently, for about 5 minutes until the vegetables have started to soften.

• Add the garlic, ginger and chillies; cook for a further couple of minutes. Add the curry powder and cook, stirring continuously, for another minute before stirring in the tomato purée and tomatoes. Mix well and remove from the heat.

• Cut the kernels away from the corn husk and place in a saucepan with the drained beans.

• Cover with water, season with salt and freshly ground black pepper. Bring to a boil over a high heat, turn the heat to medium and simmer, uncovered, for 15 minutes until the corn is cooked through and the liquid has reduced by half.

• Stir in the pepper and tomato mix and bring back to a simmer. Add the chopped parsley, check the seasoning, squeeze in a little lemon juice to taste and remove from the heat.

• Once the githeri has been cooking for 10 minutes, put the prawns in the oven and cook for 5 to 7 minutes until just cooked through.

To serve

• Serve the prawns either on or removed from the skewers, spoon over the cooking juices from the baking tray and serve with the hot githeri and flatbread.

SAMOA

Words by
MARTIN SIMPSON

SAMOA – KNOWN UNTIL 1997 as Western Samoa, to differentiate it from the US territory to its south east – is a series of islands on the opposite side of the world from Britain. But it has contributed to the history of the Royal Air Force, as well as hosting its aircraft and crews for decades.

During the Second World War, the islanders of Samoa raised funds to buy a Supermarine Spitfire built at the Chattis Hill assembly site. It initially served with 485 Squadron of the Royal New Zealand Air Force (RNZAF) and bore the name "Western Samoa", inscribed on the engine cowling. On 31 July 1942, while serving with 121 Eagle Squadron, it went missing near Berck-sur-Mer, presumed shot down, with the loss of the pilot, Pilot Officer Norman D Young.

The islands themselves were frequently visited by Allied maritime patrol aircraft operating out of Fiji. Sunderlands, from Lauthala Bay, patrolled the surrounding seas, a role performed today by P-3 Orions of the RNZAF.

In 1953, Squadron Leader F J Vickers, an experienced Sunderland QFI (Qualified Flying Instructor) who flew out of Lauthala Bay, was seconded to 5 Squadron RNZAF.

"Dad joined the RAF on the 3 November 1941, aged 18, to become a fighter pilot," recalls Vickers' daughter. "He trained in Cambridge, Detroit and then Pensacola Naval Academy in Florida, and was awarded his wings in 1943, but not as a fighter pilot, having failed the aerobatics requirement. This was in the days before package holidays meant that anyone could travel abroad at will, and this travel must have been a daunting prospect at that age." After qualifying, Vickers joined 201 Squadron flying Sunderlands and flew in Coastal Command. He rarely talked about the war but did once tell his children of taking surrender of U-Boat 825 in 1945, and of visiting Japan and Hong Kong flying the RAF's only "A" Category Sunderland.

In July 1947, Vickers returned from Hong Kong to become an Instrument Rating Examiner. He took part in the Berlin Airlift in 1948 and in November of that year became a certified Flying Instructor at the Central Flying School. His course report stated: "He has shown himself to be an exceptionally able pilot and has a confident and forceful instructional manner. He tends to be rather reserved and unassuming and had he shown a little more forcefulness of character he would have been exceptional."

In 1952, he was one of the experienced flying-boat pilots who assisted the British North Greenland Expedition. The following year, he was seconded into the RNZAF and posted to Fiji to teach Kiwis to fly Sunderlands: the only RAF pilot to have this posting. Sunderlands served in the region until their replacement by P-3 in 1967.

More recently, following the devastation caused by Cyclone Val in December 1991, a VC10 C1 of 10 Squadron, RAF Brize Norton, was launched to deliver aid to Samoa. It set off in early January and ferried Gurkha engineers to support the re-establishment of critical services and essential medical supplies to the population of the islands.

> *"During the Second World War, the islanders of Samoa raised funds to buy a Supermarine Spitfire, built at Chattis Hill"*

Pani Popo
Samoan Coconut Buns

Pani Popo are a popular sweet treat in Samoa. There are a multitude of varying recipes for these buns but this recipe uses a classic bun dough to make the buns themselves, enriched with a little coconut milk and vanilla paste. Once cooked, the pani popo are like buns on top but sticky with coconut syrup underneath.

INGREDIENTS

Makes 20 buns

For the yeast dough

600g strong flour

1 (7g) of instant yeast

75g caster sugar

1 tsp salt

125ml warm water

100ml milk

100ml coconut milk

75g butter, melted

2 medium eggs, beaten

1 tsp vanilla paste or extract
  (optional)

For the coconut syrup

1 tsp cornflour

200ml water

200ml coconut milk

100g caster sugar

METHOD

To make the yeast dough

- Sift the flour into a bowl. Add the instant yeast, sugar and salt.
- Whisk together the warm water, milk, coconut milk, melted butter, beaten eggs and vanilla paste. Stir into the dry ingredients and mix well to form a dough.
- Turn the dough out onto a floured work surface and knead for about 10 minutes, adding more flour as necessary until smooth, elastic and no longer sticky.
- Place the dough into a bowl, cover with cling film or a damp cloth and leave to prove for around 45 minutes to 1 hour until the dough has doubled in size.
- Turn the dough out onto a lightly floured work surface and gently knock back to remove the air.
- Roll the dough out into a rectangle around 50cm x 25cm, roll tightly along the long edge and cut into 2.5cm thick slices.
- Divide the dough into 20 even-sized pieces and roll into small rolls.
- Lightly butter a 35cm x 25cm baking tin and arrange the buns, (cut side down if using the first method) and almost touching, in the tin. Cover with a damp tea towel and set aside at room temperature for about 45 minutes until risen.

To make the coconut syrup

- Mix the cornflour with a little of the water to a paste.
- Place the coconut milk, water and sugar in a saucepan, bring to a boil, reduce the heat, whisk in the cornflour and simmer, stirring continuously, for a couple of minutes.

To cook the buns

- Preheat the oven to 240°C.
- Once the buns have risen, pour over two thirds of the coconut syrup and place in the preheated oven. Turn the temperature down to 180°C immediately and bake for 20 minutes.
- Evenly pour over the remaining coconut syrup and return to the oven for a further 10 to 15 minutes until the buns are golden and slightly darkened at the edges and glazed on top.
- Leave the buns to cool in the tin for 30 minutes before turning them out to cool upside down on a wire rack. Keep the buns together and tear apart just before serving.

MALAYSIA

Words by
SQUADRON LEADER JONATHAN ROOKE

GLOSTER JAVELINS, MARCH 1965, WHICH WERE DEPLOYED ACROSS MALAYSIA

MALAYSIA IS AN important regional ally and a signatory to the Five Powers Defence Arrangements (FPDA), an agreement signed in 1971 alongside New Zealand, Australia, Singapore and the UK. As part of Britain's commitment to the FPDA, Royal Air Force aircraft and personnel are frequent visitors to Royal Malaysian Air Force (RMAF) stations across the peninsula.

RMAF Butterworth, on the island of Penang, was formally RAF Butterworth, built in response to Japanese aggression. In 1941, its Brewster Buffalos put up a brave fight against the better-equipped Japanese Navy Air Service A6M Zeros but to no avail, and Malaysia was occupied.

After the Second World War and prior to independence in 1957, the RAF maintained active airfields across Malaysia. In 1953, RAF Sunderland flying boats

of 205 Squadron supported the local population of Tawau through the delivery of food and medical supplies following a huge fire that damaged the town. A 205 Squadron Sunderland and its crew were making a routine flight in 1955 when the mighty flying boat had to make a forced landing. Local people supported the RAF personnel in helping beach the Sunderland and build a sandbag dam to protect her during repairs. Later, in 1964, during the Indonesia–Malaysia confrontation, RAF Gloster Javelins of 64 Squadron were deployed to RAF Tawau under Operation Claret.

In more recent times, the RMAF has become the first non-European operator of the Airbus A400M Atlas transport aircraft, also flown by the RAF's 70, 206 and 24 Squadrons based at RAF Brize Norton. In October 2016, 1(F) Squadron Typhoons arrived at RMAF Station Butterworth for Exercise Bersama Lima 16. The Typhoons were supported by 10 Squadron Voyager tankers and completed multiple air-to-air refuelling brackets en route from RAF Lossiemouth via several staging posts.

As well as demonstrating the global reach of the Typhoon, the exercise allowed RAF air and ground crews to operate alongside Royal Australian Air Force F/A18 Hornets and test their mettle against the Malaysian Su-30MKM Flanker aircraft. Following several weeks of exercises, the Typhoons continued on to South Korea and Japan as part of Exercise Eastern Adventure, before returning home to a hero's welcome.

Kari Ikan
Malaysian Bream Curry

Malaysian cuisine is highly complex as a result of its Malay, Chinese and Indian influences. This recipe uses gilt head bream but any firm-fleshed white fish, squid or prawns works well, with the tamarind giving a sweet-sour taste. Kari Ikan is often made with vegetables such as okra and aubergines. As an alternative to rice, it can be served with roti canai, a fried flatbread similar to Indian paratha.

INGREDIENTS

Serves 4

For the spice paste

1 tbsp coriander seeds

2 tsp fennel seeds

2 tsp cumin seeds

1 tsp shrimp paste

5cm piece of galangal (or ginger), finely chopped or grated

3 cloves garlic, coarsely chopped

1 large banana shallot, coarsely chopped

2 large red chillies, coarsely chopped

Green bird eye chillies (seeds removed), coarsely chopped

1 tsp turmeric

1 lime, juiced

For the curry

2 tbsp peanut oil (or sunflower oil)

4 kaffir lime leaves

125ml fish stock (or water)

1 tbsp tamarind paste

2 lemongrass stems, bruised and halved lengthways

300ml coconut milk

1½ tsp palm sugar (or soft light brown sugar)

600g gilt head sea bream, skinned, filleted and cut into 2 or 3 pieces each

salt and pepper

To serve

boiled rice or roti canai

malaysian lime pickle

METHOD

To make the spice paste

- Dry-fry the coriander, fennel and cumin seeds over a moderate heat until fragrant and the seeds have started to pop. Grind the spices to a powder in a spice grinder or pestle and mortar.
- Blend the shrimp paste, galangal, garlic, shallots, chillies, turmeric and ground spices in a small hand-held blender with half of the lime juice to form a smooth paste.

To cook

- Heat the oil in a wok over a moderate heat. Add the spice paste and cook, stirring constantly, for a couple of minutes.
- Add the lime leaves, fish stock or water, tamarind paste and the lemongrass to the spice paste. Bring to a boil, reduce the heat and simmer for a couple of minutes.
- Stir in the coconut milk and continue to simmer for 5 minutes until the sauce has reduced slightly.
- Stir in the palm sugar and season with salt and pepper. Add the fish fillets, simmer gently for 5 minutes until the fish has just cooked through and stir in the remaining lime juice taking care not to break the fish fillet pieces.

To serve

- Serve with steamed rice or roti and lime pickle.

NEW ZEALAND

Words by
MARTIN SIMPSON

NEW ZEALAND'S DISTANCE from Europe made it an ideal location to play a significant part in the Empire Air Training Scheme throughout the Second World War. New Zealand was the home for many wartime aircrew who learned the basics of flight before going on to serve for Royal Air Force, Royal New Zealand Air Force or Royal Australian Air Force squadrons.

The country was the destination for a secretive mission launched in October 1944 from RAF Shawbury. An unarmed Lancaster, named *Aries*, set off to be the first British aircraft to circumnavigate the earth. The objective was to establish a practical liaison between the Empire Air Navigation School (EANS) and training and operational units of the RAAF and the RNZAF. Another task was to test navigation techniques and equipment in preparation for Tiger Force, the RAF's planned bombing campaign against Japan. *Aries* arrived into

Auckland in November 1944 and visited a number of bases before continuing on to RAF Shawbury, where the junior rank mess is, to this day, named in honour of this unsung Lancaster and her crew.

In 1953, the RAF participated in what was probably the last "Great Air Race". Starting from London, five Canberras of the RAF and RAAF raced to Christchurch. The RAF's Canberra PR3, captained by Flight Lieutenant Monty Burton with navigator Flight Lieutenant Gannon, was the first to reach Christchurch. It covered the 11,796 miles in a flying time of 22 hours and 28 minutes, equating to an average speed of 494.5mph, a world record at the time. The winning aircraft, WE139, is preserved at the RAF Museum in Hendon.

In 1959, as part of the RAF's desire to demonstrate its long reach, the famous 617 Squadron deployed to New Zealand equipped with the Vulcan. The trip ended badly when one of 617's aircraft was damaged, leading to a crash landing at RNZAF Ohakea. The five crew members walked away, but Vulcan XH498 was badly damaged eventually returned home.

RAF Nimrods frequently competed against RNZAF and RAAF P3 Orions, as well as Canadian CP140 Auroras during Exercise Fincastle, a challenging anti-submarine competition. In 2005, the competition was held at RNZAF Whenuapai, when a crew from CXX Squadron, flying Nimrod XV226, won both the Fincastle and Lockheed Martin Maintenance trophies.

Hokey Pokey Ice Cream

This Kiwi favourite is a vanilla ice cream combined with pieces of honeycomb or cinder toffee. This recipe uses a sabayon base mixed with whipped cream and beaten egg whites and, although not traditional, a butterscotch sauce that goes very well, warm or cold, poured over the ice cream.

INGREDIENTS
Makes 2 litres
For the honeycomb
4 tbsp caster sugar
2 tbsp golden syrup
1 tsp bicarbonate of soda

For the ice cream
4 eggs, separated
200g caster sugar
1 tsp vanilla extract
500ml whipping cream

METHOD
To make the honeycomb
- Line a baking tray with a silicone baking sheet or baking parchment.
- Place the sugar and golden syrup in a deep saucepan, place over a low heat and stir until the sugar has dissolved.
- Once the sugar has dissolved, continue to heat until the mix starts to simmer. Leave the sugar and syrup mix simmering on the heat, without stirring, for around 3 minutes until the colour darkens slightly.
- Remove from the heat, add the bicarbonate of soda and stir until the mixture froths up. Tip immediately onto the lined baking tray and leave at room temperature to set completely.
- Once cooled, break the honeycomb into small rough-shaped pieces

For the butterscotch sauce (optional)
vanilla pod or 1 tsp vanilla extract
100g butter
100g light brown sugar
300ml double cream

and shake in a colander over a sheet of greaseproof paper to separate the fine crumbs. Keep the fine crumbs to sprinkle on top of the ice cream when serving and store in an airtight container.

To make the ice cream
• Whisk the egg yolks, sugar and vanilla extract together in a bowl, place over a saucepan of simmering water and whisk until the mixture forms thick ribbons when trailed over the surface; this is known as a sabayon.
• Set the sabayon aside to cool, meanwhile whip the cream until it forms soft peaks and beat the egg whites until they form stiff peaks.
• Fold the sabayon into the whipped cream, then fold in the egg whites.
• Transfer the mix to a container and place in the freezer for an hour until it starts to firm up.

To finish the ice cream
• Fold the pieces of honeycomb into the soft ice cream, transfer to a 2-litre container and freeze until firm.

To make the butterscotch sauce
• If using a vanilla pod, halve the pod lengthways and scrape out the seeds from both halves.
• Place the vanilla seeds and pod (or extract) into a heavy based saucepan with the butter, sugar and 250ml of the cream.
• Place the saucepan over a moderate heat and, stirring frequently to ensure the butter has melted and the sugar has completely dissolved, bring to a gentle boil.
• Continue to cook the sauce at a gentle boil for around 10 minutes until the sauce has thickened and noticeably darkened in colour.
• Strain the butterscotch sauce into a container through a sieve and set aside at room temperature, stirring occasionally, for about 20 minutes.
• Once cool, stir in the remaining cream for a thick but pourable sauce.
• Cover and store in the refrigerator until required.

To serve
• Take the ice cream out of the freezer and leave at room temperature for about 10 minutes to soften slightly.
• Scoop the ice cream into bowls, pour over the butterscotch sauce and scatter over some of the reserved crushed honeycomb.

MALDIVES

Words by
FLIGHT LIEUTENANT CRISPIN CHAPPLE

AN ARCHIPELAGO OF 26 islands southwest of India, the Maldives is known as a luxury holiday destination and a haven for wildlife, but perhaps not as a location for RAF operations. However, this is exactly what the island of Gan – the southern-most island of the Maldives' Addu Atoll in the Indian Ocean – was for nearly 20 years.

Prior to the arrival of the RAF, in 1941, the Royal Navy constructed airstrips, calling the area "Port T", to service the Fleet Air Arm. The RAF quickly saw its value, and the following year brought in Sunderland and Catalina aircraft for servicing from RAF China Bay in nearby Ceylon.

In 1957, the RAF took control of what soon became RAF Gan, constructing a runway to use as a staging post to its Far East Air Force (FEAF). All manner of aircraft passed over its clear-blue waters, including most of the "V bomber" force: Valiants, Victors and Vulcans; VC-10s from Brize Norton; and Britannias and Comets from RAF Lyneham. It was also used by other air forces, and at its height some 900 Maldivians and 100 Pakistanis were employed by the RAF in the daily running of the base.

Daily life was like nothing else; the sun shone for 10 months of the year, and the other two saw torrential monsoon weather. The temperature, however, presented a new perspective on puddles, with the suggestion being that one's feet were "nearly parboiled" when stepping in one!

RAF staff have memories of drinking lemonade under the low-roofed buildings alongside a "turquoise belt surrounding bright yellow golden sands", drinking coconut water from the shell, and eating tunafish curries al fresco. RAF personnel describe it as idyllic, particularly enjoying the colours – from bright fancy dress to flamboyant batik shirts, from tropical fish to frangipani blossom.

Normal activities enjoyed back in Britain required a degree of alteration for the region. Cricket, for example, became "monsoon-style brush cricket", with a sweeping-up brush substituting for the bat and a floating stage for the green. There was even a mountaineering society; amusing given that the highest point on the island was only 20 ft tall!

By the end of 1971, with the UK winding down its commitments east of Suez, the RAF FEAF was disbanded. This left RAF Gan with little remit, although it only finally closed on 1 April 1976 when the island was handed back to the Maldivian government. Further intermediate basing continued with the use of the US base at Diego Garcia, in the British Indian Overseas Territories. After the departure, RAF Gan fell into disrepair until funds allowed it to be developed as Gan International Airport.

THE LAST RAF BELFAST FLIGHT LEAVES RAF GAN, MALDIVES, APRIL 1976

Mas Riha
Maldivian Fish Curry

The staples of Maldivian cuisine are coconut, fish (particularly tuna), curries, rice and unleavened breads such as chapati, roti, naan and a Maldivian flatbread called roshi. Mas Riha is one of the most important dishes of the islands and comprises all of these Maldivian staples. The spice paste is the key to this simple dish; the ratio of chillies can be altered depending on taste.

INGREDIENTS

Serves 4

For the curry paste

3 tbsp coconut oil or 45g butter

1 medium onion, finely sliced

4 curry leaves

4 cardamom pods, crushed with
  the flat of a knife blade

½ tsp fennel seeds

3 red chillies (medium hot),
  deseeded and finely chopped

2 green bird's eye chillies, finely
  chopped

3 cloves of garlic, finely chopped
  or crushed

1cm piece of ginger, finely
  chopped or grated

1 tbsp tomato purée

2 tsp ground coriander

1 tsp ground turmeric

½ tsp ground cumin

½ tsp sea salt

½ tsp ground black pepper

For the curry

1 cinnamon stick

400ml coconut milk

100ml cold water

600g tuna or swordfish, cut into
  large chunks

125g coconut cream

To serve

4 tbsp coconut cream

roshi, chapati or boiled rice

To make the curry paste

- Heat the coconut oil or butter in a frying pan or saucepan over a moderate heat, add the onions and cook, stirring occasionally, for 10 minutes until softened and lightly browned.
- Add the curry leaves, cardamom pods and fennel seeds; cook, stirring continuously, for a couple of minutes until fragrant.
- Add the chillies, garlic, ginger, tomato purée, ground spices, salt and pepper; continue to cook for a further 2 minutes.
- Transfer the mix to a blender with a couple of tablespoons of cold water and blend to a thick paste.

To make the curry

- Place the curry paste into a saucepan over a high heat with the cinnamon stick, coconut milk and cold water. Bring to a boil, reduce the heat, and simmer for 15 minutes.
- Add the tuna, cover with a lid and continue to simmer gently for 10 minutes, until just cooked through. Stir in the coconut cream and a little boiling water to thin the sauce if necessary, bring back to a simmer and season with a little salt if required.

To serve

- Ladle the curry into bowls and drizzle with a little coconut cream to finish. Serve with roshi, chapati or rice.

EGYPT

Words by
WING COMMANDER BEN SHARP

THE ROYAL AIR FORCE'S role in Egypt was interwoven with the history of British interests in the Eastern Mediterranean and, in particular, with the protection of the Suez Canal: a vital shipping gateway from Britain to her Empire. After the opening of the canal in 1869, Egypt became a British protectorate in 1882 and Turkey's entry into the First World War in late 1914 led to the further deployment of British forces to defend Suez. This deployment included a Royal Flying Corps detachment, whose observation aircraft proved critical to detecting the Turkish invasion plans. By 1918, and the RAF's formation, the mission had grown to aerial bombardment and ground support, with the conceptual seeds sown for the air policing role that the RAF's founder Hugh Trenchard envisaged for his new force.

"In July 1956, Nasser announced that the Suez Canal Company was to be nationalised, threatening control of this shipping route"

The 1920s saw the RAF firmly establish itself in Egypt. To provide training and familiarisation for pilots being sent to the region, 4 Flying Training School was established at Abu Suier: an airfield strategically close to the canal that would prove essential during the Second World War and that later ended up as the last RAF base to be handed over to the Egyptians.

Also formed in Egypt was the first RAF Armoured Car Company (ACC). To support the speed and reach of the air policing force, flexible ground support under RAF control was required to protect air stations, landing grounds and other vulnerable points. In January 1922, 50 airmen formed No. 1 ACC at RAF Heliopolis near Cairo, where they reassembled the vehicles shipped from the UK, learnt how to drive them, became familiar with living in the desert and were then deployed to Palestine. The six ACCs served with distinction across the region before becoming part of the RAF Regiment in 1946, after notable service in Egypt defending against the 1941 Axis advance and taking the fight to the enemy during the Western Desert campaign.

The end of the war saw tensions between Britain and Egypt rise, leading to the withdrawal of British forces to the

Canal Zone. Following the move of the regional HQ to Cyprus, the British withdrew from Egypt in April 1956 with the canal seemingly safe in the hands of a commercial company, under Anglo–French control.

President Nasser of Egypt had other plans. In July 1956, he announced that the company was to be nationalised, effectively ripping up a 68-year-old treaty and threatening control of this international shipping route. Rapid negotiations, backed up by the threat of military force, failed to dissuade Nasser and so, on 31 October, Operation Musketeer began.

The RAF's new Valiants and Canberras saw their first operational service in reconnaissance and then bombing roles, with Venoms (and the Royal Navy's Sea Venoms) employed to attack Egyptian airfields. By 3 November the Egyptian Air Force has been effectively eliminated, clearing the way for an airborne assault force to be dropped from Valetta and Hastings aircraft. Ground forces went on to clear much of the canal before a ceasefire came into effect at midnight on 6 November. The political fallout from the intervention was contentious, but RAF action had been seen to be swift, courageous and effective.

Ful Medames
Egyptian Stewed Beans

Medames literally means "buried", suggesting that the name derives from a primitive cooking method in which the beans were placed in a sealed pot and buried in the ground to cook slowly overnight. Ful Medames dates back to the pharaohs and is regarded as Egypt's national dish, typically eaten for breakfast with grilled flatbread. It should be cooked with small dried fava beans, but dried pinto beans serve as a good substitute.

INGREDIENTS

Serves 4

For the roast garlic

4 cloves of garlic, whole and
  unpeeled

1 tsp olive oil

For the beans

1 tbsp olive oil

½ medium red onion, finely diced

METHOD

To prepare and pre-cook the beans

• Soak the beans overnight in cold water.

• Drain and thoroughly rinse the soaked beans, place in a saucepan, cover with cold water, place over a high heat and boil rapidly for 10 minutes.

• Reduce the heat to low, cover the saucepan with a lid and simmer the beans for 1 hour, topping up with boiling water as necessary to keep the beans submerged in the water, until the beans are tender, once cooked drain the beans in a colander.

1 tsp cumin seeds

200g dried pinto beans, soaked
  and pre-cooked

1 lemon, halved

salt and pepper

For the tahini sauce (optional)

4 cloves of garlic, finely chopped
  or crushed

4 tbsp tahini

4 tbsp cold water

1 lemon, juiced

salt

To serve

(with a selection of any

of the below)

extra virgin olive oil

grilled flat or pitta beads

diced tomato

diced cucumber

sliced shallots, spring onions or
  red onion

sliced hard boiled eggs

chopped parsley

sliced red chilli or dried red
  chilli flakes

natural yoghurt

lemon wedges

To roast the garlic

• Preheat the oven to 200°C.

• Toss the garlic cloves with the olive oil and a pinch of salt, place in
  a small ovenproof dish, cover with foil and roast in the oven for 15 to
  20 minutes until golden brown and very soft.

• When cool enough to handle, squeeze the garlic flesh out of the skins
  onto a chopping board and mash with a fork. Set aside until required.

To finish the beans

• Heat the olive oil in a saucepan, add the red onions and cook for
  5 to 7 minutes, stirring frequently, until they have started to soften
  and have lightly browned. Add the cumin seeds and cook for a
  further minute until the cumin seeds have released their fragrance.

• Add the beans to the pan with 125ml cold water and the roast garlic
  paste; stir well.

• Bring to a simmer, turn the heat to low, cover with a lid and cook
  the beans for 10 minutes.

• Using a potato masher, coarsely mash around half of the beans in
  the pan to create a thick sauce.

• Squeeze in the lemon juice, season with salt and pepper; stir well.

To make the tahini sauce

• Place the crushed garlic, tahini paste, water and half of the lemon
  juice in a blender with a little salt and blend to a creamy consistency –
  a small hand-held blender is ideal for this small quantity. Alternatively
  the ingredients can be whisked together in a bowl to a smooth sauce.

• Taste the tahini sauce and, if required, whisk in a little more lemon
  juice and salt to taste. Store in a sealed container in the fridge
  until required.

To serve

• Transfer the ful medames to bowls, drizzle over a little extra virgin
  olive oil and serve with the tahini sauce (if using), grilled flat or pitta
  breads and a selection of toppings.

YEMEN

Words by
FLIGHT LIEUTENANT CRISPIN CHAPPLE

THE ROYAL AIR FORCE first became established in Yemen as early as 1917, with the creation of RAF Khormaksar in Aden. It was enlarged in 1945 to meet the British requirement to spread influence deeper into the Arabian peninsula. The Tempest Mk4 was used to great effect here, against the all-too-frequent local revolts.

In 1958, a state of emergency was declared as anti-government Yemeni forces occupied nearby Jebel Jehaf, attacking commercial routes, and RAF squadrons were required to operate in support of the British Army. The drawback from RAF Deverosair in Egypt to Khormaksar gave greater air power to the RAF and led to the construction of several small landing strips, used to resupply the front line. Fighters improved too, with the introduction of the Venom Mk9 fighter/bomber.

In the 1960s, Khormaksar became the busiest RAF base outside of Britain, attracting ground attacks by rebels. It was at this time that Egypt became embroiled in the conflict, organising a coup alongside dissidents in 1962 to overthrow the British-sided Yemeni imam, which led to a new Egyptian-backed republican leadership.

The British were now fighting alongside recently demoted dissidents and French mercenaries against the Egyptian-backed Yemeni government in what became known as the Aden Emergency. This brought a further influx of aircraft including Whirlwinds, Shackletons and Hunters, and the construction of a second base in Beihan.

To the British back home, this life in Yemen would often be sold as a romantic sojourn; a break from the monotony of Britain, with beaches and sunshine. A 1965 documentary entitled "Routine Adventure in Aden" painted an idyllic picture of RAF crewmen hanging their boots out of the window of an airborne Whirlwind. The injured from the front line were also saved the long tortuous road route, instead travelling by Whirlwind helicopter – only 30 minutes back to base and the "crisp clean sheets in an air-conditioned ward".

The difference between these forward-operating bases and the main base in Aden was noted with an almost wry or diffident shrug. "In Khormaksar, off-duty sentries are allowed time off for a quick beer and a game of cards," reads one account. "On the front it was like a canvas council estate."

Shackleton aircraft recces were continuous, looking for movement in the hills. Artillery runs now took 30 minutes to an hour instead of days over land to the front line. With air mobility, one artillery piece previously moved by road would now become 10 by air, which was a massive bonus to troops. "The land soaks up troops as quickly as it soaks up water," said one British military figure.

It wasn't only mobility that grew over this period. Hunters, flying at 600mph, were always prepared for the fight. With their cannons and bombs (and even a camera in the nose cone "to prevent mere bragging"), they offered much-needed assistance to the frontline regiment, keeping rebels at bay. One quick attack from a Hunter could save months of tracking and sniping.

However, the conflict never improved. The Americans attempted to intervene to bring peaceful resolution under President Kennedy, but still it continued. The final straw was the use of chemical weapons by the Egyptian air force. Prime Minister Harold Wilson announced that a complete withdrawal must be complete by 1968.

RAF Khormaksar played a vital role in this withdrawal, with all British families from Aden evacuated over the summer of 1967. The station closed in November 1967, but the legacy of mistrust between Britain and Yemen continues to this day.

Malikia
Yemeni Bananas with Honey

Also known as masoub or masoob, malikia is a great way to use up over-ripe and mushy bananas. Popular throughout the Middle East, it is traditionally made with ground flatbreads, but other stale bread (from brioche to wholemeal), can also be used. To give the pudding a little more texture, add lightly toasted and coarsely chopped nuts (walnuts, pecans or almonds) to the banana and pitta mix. For a slightly boozy version, the dried fruits can be steeped in warmed rum or brandy.

INGREDIENTS
Serves 4

For the malikia
4 ripe or over-ripe bananas
4 pitta breads
a little cold milk

For the toppings
75g mixed dried fruit (raisins, sultanas, golden raisins, cranberries)
50g flaked almonds
125ml whipping cream
½ tsp ground cinnamon
100g natural yoghurt
4 tbsp runny honey

METHOD

To prepare the malikia
• Peel the banana and mash to a pulp.
• Tear the pitta breads into pieces, place in a food processor and blend to coarse breadcrumbs.
• Mix the mashed banana and pitta breadcrumbs together in a bowl, add a little milk if the mixture is too thick (it should just be mouldable).

To prepare the toppings
• Place the dried fruit in a heatproof bowl, pour over enough boiling water (or warmed rum/brandy if preferred) to barely cover and leave aside for 30 minutes to plump up. Drain then dry on kitchen paper.
• Heat the grill, scatter the flaked almonds in a single layer on a metal tray, place under the grill and toast the almonds until lightly browned (take care when toasting the almonds as they can quickly burn). Leave the almonds on the tray at room temperature to cool completely before serving; they can then be transferred to an airtight container to store if not using immediately.
• Lightly whip the cream to soft peaks with the cinnamon then whisk in the yoghurt.

To serve
• Spoon the banana mix into portion-sized containers, press gently then turn out onto plates. Alternatively, mound the mix in the centre of the plates and smooth the surface into neat shapes.
• Spoon over the cream and yoghurt mix. Scatter over the toasted almonds and dried fruit then drizzle with honey.

MOROCCO

Words by
WING COMMANDER BEN SHARP

THROUGHOUT ITS 100 years the Royal Air Force has had a proud tradition of providing swift and supportive responses to humanitarian disasters around the world. Shortly before midnight on 29 February 1960, the deadliest earthquake in Morocco's history destroyed the major city of Agadir. It was initially reported that 1,000 people had been killed but the death toll eventually reached 12,000. Such was the devastation, the Moroccan government eventually ordered the complete evacuation of Agadir to prevent the further spread of disease among the survivors.

An international relief effort swung into action. Shackleton transport aircraft were dispatched from 224 Squadron at RAF Gibraltar, with *The Times* reporting that they carried "tents, blankets, medical supplies, emergency rations, metal construction strips, chemicals and a gift of clothing from the Gibraltar residents". 224 Squadron's operational record noted that "all crews of the squadron participated", with 24 sorties carried out between 2 and 11 March. A Valiant reconnaissance aircraft of 543 Squadron flew an eight-hour mission from RAF St Mawgan, obtaining photos to show the extent of damage to Agadir – a sortie subsequently praised in the House of Commons.

Corporal Curly Knowlton was a ground crew tradesman on 242 Operational Conversion Unit at RAF Dishforth, a unit that trained aircrew to fly a variety of transport aircraft, including the Blackburn Beverley. Late on the afternoon of

Friday 4 March, after most personnel had left for the weekend, Curly and the other duty personnel were summoned to the sick quarters and jabbed with all manner of vaccines. With their passports in hand the following day, their Beverley took off and, having collected a consignment of quicklime from Switzerland, landed in Agadir at noon on 7 March.

"When we got to Agadir, the smell was dreadful," said Curly. "Although we arrived only a few days after the earthquake, the heat had caused horrendous decay. It seemed only the schools and other government buildings were still standing; everything else had fallen down."

The captain of the aircraft, Squadron Leader Groocock, was keen that they should help and agreed to evacuate as many children as they could fit into the Beverley – 81 in total. "We had no seats in the freight bay because we'd transported the quicklime", said Curly. "So, after the crew filled the few seats in the tail-boom, we knitted together some white lashing tape to form nets. We then threaded the children, who were sat on the floor, in among these nets to make them secure while the aircraft took off." The children were flown to Rabat, in northern Morocco, where an American relief force had erected a tented camp.

All of the units involved performed with distinction, providing much needed help to the government and people of Morocco in their time of critical need.

> ## *"The deadliest earthquake in Morocco's history destroyed the major city of Agadir. The death toll eventually reached 12,000"*

Lamb Tagine

A tagine is a North African dish named after the special clay cooking pot in which the fragrant spicy stew is cooked. The pot consists of a cooking base and a conical lid which is designed to return all of the condensed vapour to the dish. Tagine recipes vary greatly although generally they use cheap cuts of meat, braised slowly until very tender, with spices, dried fruits, nuts and preserved lemons.

INGREDIENTS

Serves 4

For the marinade

½ tsp cayenne pepper

2 tsp turmeric

1½ tbsp ground cumin

1½ tbsp paprika

2 tsp ground cinnamon

¼ tsp ground black pepper

600g lamb shoulder or mutton, cut into large chunks

For the tagine

4 tbsp sunflower oil or corn oil

2 large onions, finely diced

4 garlic cloves, finely chopped

2.5cm piece of ginger finely chopped or grated (or 2 tsp ground ginger)

2 tbsp tomato purée

1 cinnamon stick

500ml chicken stock

1 tin (400g) of chopped tomatoes

100g dried apricots, cut into quarters or shredded

50g sultanas

2 tbsp runny honey

½ orange, zest only (thinly peeled)

½ tsp saffron strands (optional)

1 preserved lemon (rind only), coarsely chopped (optional)

salt and pepper

2 tbsp coriander, coarsely chopped

2 tbsp parsley, coarsely chopped

To serve

1 lemon, cut into wedges

couscous

METHOD

To marinade

- Mix together the cayenne, turmeric, cumin, paprika, ground cinnamon and black pepper. Place the lamb in a bowl and add half of the spice mix. Toss to coat the lamb evenly in the spices.
- Cover with cling film and leave the lamb to marinate overnight.

To cook the tagine

- Preheat the oven to 180°C.
- Heat the oil in a casserole dish or large saucepan over a high heat, when hot add the lamb (in two batches if necessary to avoid overcrowding the pan) and sear stirring frequently until well browned all over, remove from the pan with a slotted spoon to a bowl.
- Keep the oil hot in the casserole and add the onions; cook, stirring frequently, until lightly browned all over, add the garlic and ginger and continue to cook for a further couple of minutes.
- Return the lamb to the casserole dish and stir in the tomato purée, remaining spice mix and cinnamon stick. Add the stock, tomatoes, dried apricots, sultanas, honey, orange zest and saffron. Bring to a boil, simmer for around 10 minutes until reduced slightly, skim off any impurities that have risen to the surface and season.
- Cover the saucepan with a lid, place in the oven and braise for 1½ to 2 hours (alternatively the tagine can be covered and simmered over a low heat on the stove top), stirring occasionally to keep the lamb covered with the sauce and to prevent sticking. If the sauce becomes too thick add a little boiling water and stir in.

To finish

- Stir in the diced preserved lemon around half an hour before the tagine is cooked.
- Remove the tagine from the oven, skim, check the seasoning and stir in half of the chopped coriander and parsley.

To serve

- Ladle the tagine into bowls, garnish with the remaining chopped herbs and serve with lemon wedges and couscous.

BRUNEI

Words by
SQUADRON LEADER GORDON PARRY

IN 1962, BRUNEI was a British Protectorate ruled by a Sultan, the autocratic ruler of a country that enjoyed considerable wealth from oil but which also had great poverty among its population. Brunei was bordered by the two British Crown Colonies of Sabah and Sarawak, and Britain was committed to protecting all three territories. Unfortunately, certain elements in these territories were opposed to the British-supported concept of the formation of Malaysia. There was an anti-colonialist, militant movement in Brunei, complete with a military wing, and there were rumours of a Brunei Liberation Army. With poverty, political dissatisfaction and militant groups in place, the ingredients for a fight were set.

On 7 December 1962, the Commander-in-Chief in Singapore learned that there could be an attack in Brunei the next day. The Far East Air Force (FEAF) already had a rapid reinforcement plan, codenamed Plan ALE, and preparations started. Unfortunately, that evening most of the officers of the 1st Battalion/2nd Gurkha Riffles were watching "The Longest Day" at the cinema and the Commanding Officer of the 1st Battalion Queen's Own Highlanders was at a mess guest night at the headquarters. The Intelligence Officer went to the map store and, with the storeman away for the weekend, he shot the lock off the door only to find that there were no maps of Brunei. The FEAF would not be ready to fly until 1600hrs, but that was not a problem: until the school run had been completed at 1300hrs, there would be no transport to move the Gurkhas!

The next day saw the start of what would become a four-year confrontation. Essentially amateurs, the poorly trained rebels were armed with shotguns, knives, swords, machetes, axes and spears. Attacks on government areas and the ruler's palace were repelled, but softer targets such as police stations and oil fields fell. By mid afternoon, most of the country was in the hands of the rebels.

Troops in Singapore were sent to Brunei by aircraft of the Far East Air Force and by a shiny Britannia from Transport Command, which happened to be at Singapore's Changi Airport and was commandeered for the task. Britain had the best counter-insurgency and counter-terrorism forces in the world, so it was never going to be an equal fight.

A Joint Force Headquarters was set up at a girls' school in Brunei, but met with initial resistance from all three services. The RAF was encamped at Labuan Airport on an island north-east of Brunei, the Army was in air-conditioned offices in Brunei and the Royal Navy was just not interested.

Priority was given to simultaneously recapturing the Seria oilfield and the nearby airfield at Anduki. The first Twin Pioneer aircraft landed near Seria on a rough, grassy and extremely soft spot. Braking hard, the Commanding Officer of the squadron stopped his aircraft just 10 yards from a roadside ditch, which was conveniently signposted "Halt Major Road Ahead". Seeing the risk to his other aircraft, he ordered them to land in the opposite direction, even though the other four aircraft had to brush their wings through tree branches as they landed. Although one aircraft became stuck in the soft ground, all the troops deplaned and retook the Panaga police station successfully.

The RAF continues to use Brunei to this day in support to the British Army.

Ayam Penyet
Smashed Spicy Fried Chicken

Ayam Penyet is Indonesian in origin but has been adopted throughout Brunei. The chicken is cooked in an aromatic broth before being "smashed" (or flattened to soften the texture), fried and served with rice, salad and a spicy chilli sambal. The stock from cooking the chicken can be used for soup or noodle dishes, but it is worth cooking the rice in the spicy chicken broth to give the dish some punch.

INGREDIENTS

Serves 4

For the chilli sambal

1 small red onion, finely diced

8 mixed red and green chillies, roughly chopped including seeds

2 cloves of garlic, finely chopped or crushed

1 tsp shrimp paste

1 tbsp vegetable oil

1 tomato, diced

1 lime, juiced

2 tsp soft brown sugar

2 tbsp basil, shredded

salt

For the dry spice mix

1½ tbsp coriander seeds

1 tbsp cumin seeds

1 tbsp fennel seeds

1 tbsp salt

1 tbsp turmeric

1 tsp ground black pepper

To boil the chicken

5 cloves of garlic, finely chopped

2.5cm piece of ginger, finely chopped or grated (or 1 tbsp paste)

2.5cm piece of galangal, finely chopped or grated (or 1 tbsp paste)

3 shallots, finely diced

METHOD

To make the sambal

- Place the onions, chillies, garlic and shrimp paste in a small hand-held blender with a tablespoon of cold water and blend to a coarse paste.
- Heat the oil in a frying pan over a moderate heat, add the paste and fry, stirring continuously, for about 10 minutes until the oil starts to separate from the paste and much of the liquid has evaporated.
- Stir in the diced tomato, lime juice, sugar and a pinch of salt and continue to cook for a further 2 minutes until the tomatoes have released their juice. Stir in the shredded basil and transfer to a clean bowl and allow to cool.

To make the dry spice mix

- Heat the coriander, cumin and fennel seeds in a frying pan over a moderate heat until fragrant and starting to pop. Cool then coarsely grind in a pestle and mortar.
- Mix the ground spices with the salt, turmeric and black pepper.

To prepare the chicken

- Place three quarters of the ground spices into a saucepan with the garlic, ginger, galangal, shallots, lemongrass and bay leaves. Place the chicken pieces on top then cover completely with boiling water.
- Bring to a boil then simmer over a medium heat for 20 minutes until the chicken is cooked through. Remove the chicken and strain the liquid into a clean saucepan. Rest the chicken for 10 to 15 minutes.
- Place the chicken between two double sheets of cling film, place the flat of a cleaver or large knife blade on top of one piece of chicken and, taking care to avoid the cutting edge, push down firmly with the palm of your hand (you don't want to completely break up the chicken pieces, just flatten). Continue to "smash" the remaining pieces of chicken, ladle over a little of the reserved stock and set to rest for a further 10 to 15 minutes before frying.

3 stalks of lemongrass, bruised

3 bay leaves

4 chicken legs, halved or 1 whole
  chicken, cut into 8 pieces (skin on)

For the rice

50g butter

300g long grain rice, soaked
  for 30 minutes in cold water
  and drained

1 cinnamon stick

2 star anise

6 cardamom pods

To fry the chicken

100g plain flour

vegetable oil for frying

To cook the rice

- Measure out 600ml of the reserved cooking liquid from the chicken
  (make up with water if there isn't enough), pour into a saucepan and
  bring to a simmer.
- Heat the butter in a saucepan over a moderate heat and, when
  foaming, add the rice and cook, stirring continuously for a couple of
  minutes until the rice is fragrant and thoroughly coated in the butter.
- Stir in the cinnamon stick, star anise and cardamom pods and
  continue to cook for a minute. Pour over the simmering stock, stir
  well and season with salt if required. Cover with a lid and simmer
  very gently over a low heat for 15 to 20 minutes until tender.

To fry the chicken

- Mix the flour with the remaining dry spice mix; toss the chicken into
  the seasoned flour to lightly coat.
- Pour oil to a depth of around 2.5cm into a large pan and place on a
  medium to high heat. Fry the chicken pieces until golden brown and
  thoroughly reheated through to the middle (alternatively deep fry at
  180°C). Drain well on absorbent kitchen paper.

To serve

- Serve two pieces of fried chicken per portion with a simple salad of
  lettuce leaves, cucumber, spring onions and tomatoes dressed with
  a little lime juice, some of the rice and a lime wedge. Serve a bowl
  of the chilli sambal separately.

BORNEO

Words by
SQUADRON LEADER GORDON PARRY

A SCOTTISH AVIATION PIONEER TAKES OFF FROM SARAWAK, BORNEO

BY THE 1960s, an undeclared war was underway on the island of Borneo due to Indonesia's policy of confrontation with the newly formed nation of Malaysia. The RAF was sent to support Malaysian ground operations in May 1963.

215 Squadron, flying the Argosy, was tasked to support the ground operations in Borneo. The climate, tropical storms, cumulus clouds and terrain in Borneo combined to make low flying a hairy occupation. The drop zones were small and often surrounded by high ground. The mornings in Borneo began with mist in the valleys, which made the first sorties of the day particularly hazardous. There was no possibility of letting down into the drop zones without being able to see the terrain. Once the mist had dispersed, there was a period of reasonably stable conditions but, after midday, the cumulus clouds began to develop and extreme turbulence made accurate flying very difficult.

The increase in the air temperature reduced the performance of the Argosy's engines, making the climb out from the drop zone a nail-biting experience. The aircraft's Rolls-Royce Dart engines were reliable but, if the throttle was opened suddenly, the surge of fuel could cause the turbine to overheat. This meant that it took time to accelerate the engine, and the propeller did not immediately respond to a request for power. Crews were always relieved to get rid of the first couple of one-ton containers, as the aircraft was then lighter and more responsive. The Argosy would often work with the cavernous Blackburn Beverley to airdrop bulky equipment. On one occasion, a bulldozer was needed to carve out an airstrip. The Argosy dropped the blade and small parts, while the Beverley dropped the main body of the vehicle.

209 Squadron, detached from Singapore to Labuan, flew Single and Twin Pioneer aircraft into jungle airstrips. The planes were good at short take-offs and landings, as they had been designed for the Royal Mail by Scottish Aviation to carry post into small rural airstrips in Scotland. But, in the tropical rains of Borneo, the rivetting on a Pioneer leaked like a sieve.

The main function of the squadron at Labuan was to fly the army to remote jungle airstrips. However, the Twin Pioneer was also tasked with psychological warfare operations. Large loudspeakers, driven by powerful amplifiers, were fitted to the aircraft. Taped messages, played loudly, would urge tribes in the interior of Sabah to listen to the forthcoming network radio broadcasts that would accompany the pending local elections. This propaganda technique had been used in Malay in the 1950s, and equipment fitted to the Twin Pioneers appeared to be of that vintage.

Sarawak Laksa
Bornean Chicken, Prawn & Noodle Curry

In Malaysia, laksa is usually a coconut milk-based curry soup, while asam laksa is a sour soup made with tamarind. Sarawak laksa, from the Malaysian province of Sarawak on Borneo, combines the two. This recipe makes twice the amount of paste needed for this recipe: freeze half for later use.

INGREDIENTS

Serves 4

For the laksa spice paste
(makes around 350g)

1 tsp fennel seeds

2 tsp cumin seeds

2 tbsp coriander seeds

2 cardamom pods, seeds removed

1 star anise, broken into small pieces

2 cloves

1 tsp ground nutmeg

½ tsp ground white pepper

2 tsp salt

2 tbsp granulated sugar

5 shallots, finely chopped

1 clove of garlic, finely chopped

1 tsp galangal paste

2 tsp tamarind paste

2 red chillies, finely chopped

1 stalk of lemongrass (white part
  only), finely chopped

2 tsp dried chilli flakes

12g candlenuts (or macadamia
  nuts), chopped

2 tbsp sesame seeds, toasted

35g peanuts, chopped

75ml peanut oil or vegetable oil

For the stock

1 whole chicken

350g whole prawns or langoustines
  with their shells on (or 200g raw
  prawn tails)

METHOD

To make the laksa paste

- Heat a frying pan or skillet over a moderate heat, add the fennel, cumin, coriander and cardamom seeds with the star anise and cloves. Toast, shaking the pan frequently, until the spices are fragrant and tip the spices into a mortar.
- Grind the spices in the mortar with a pestle to a coarse powder.
- Place the ground spices into a blender with 3 tbsp of cold water and the remaining spice paste ingredients, except the oil, then blend to a smooth paste; add a little more water if necessary.
- Heat the oil in a frying pan or wok over a low to moderate heat, add the paste, stir well and cook, stirring frequently, to ensure the paste doesn't stick or burn, for 10 to 15 minutes until the oil has separated from the paste.

To make the stock

- Remove the legs from the chicken (reserve for another use). Cut the chicken crown (the two breasts on the bone) from the lower part of the carcass (the back) and peel the skin off the breasts.
- Place the chicken crown with the rest of the carcass bones in a large saucepan, cover with about 2 litres of cold water and bring to a boil over a high heat then turn the heat down to a gentle simmer.
- Skim off the impurities from the top and simmer for about 30 minutes, continuing to skim as the impurities rise to the surface, until cooked through and tender.
- Transfer the chicken to a plate, allow to cool and keep the stock simmering.
- Add the whole shell on prawns and poach for 5 minutes until just cooked through. Remove from the stock and set aside to cool while keeping the stock simmering (omit this step if using raw prawn tails).
- When cool enough to handle, remove the chicken breasts from the crown and shred the meat; roughly chop the bones and add to the simmering stock.

175g laksa spice paste (see recipe
 on page 245)
250g coconut milk

For the omelette
2 eggs
1 tsp light soy sauce
1 tbsp vegetable oil

For the laksa
200g bee hoon (rice vermicelli),
pre-cooked or blanched
100g beansprouts

For the garnish
25g coriander, picked
2 red chillies, finely sliced
1 lime, cut into quarters
sambal oelek (optional)

- Remove the prawn tails from the shells, add the shells and heads to the stock (if whole shell-on prawns are unavailable, one or two tablespoons of fish sauce or a little shrimp paste can be added at this stage to boost the flavour) together with the laksa paste and simmer gently for 1¼ hours, skimming regularly to prevent the stock from becoming cloudy. Taste the stock after it has been simmering for 1 hour and, if it needs a little more flavour, a chicken stock cube or jelly pot can be added; continue to simmer for 15 minutes.
- Strain the stock through a fine sieve (there should be about 1 litre remaining), stir in the coconut milk, bring back to a simmer, and season with salt and pepper.

To make the omelette
- Beat the eggs with the soy sauce.
- Heat the oil in a non-stick frying pan over a moderate heat.
- Add the eggs, stir gently until the eggs start to set, turn the heat to low and cook until the eggs are just set. Turn the omelette out onto a chopping board.
- Once cool, shred the omelette into thin strips.

To assemble the laksa
- Soak the bee hoon noodles in boiling water for a minute, until hot, and drain.
- Blanch the beansprouts in boiling water for a few seconds, until just wilted, and drain.
- Reheat the chicken and prawns (if using raw prawn tails poach them for 4 to 5 minutes until just cooked through at this stage) in a little of the stock. Strain the stock back into the pan once the chicken and prawns are hot.
- Place the noodles, beansprouts, shredded omelette, chicken and prawns tails in bowls and ladle over the hot broth.
- Garnish with the picked coriander, sliced chillies and lime wedges.
- Optionally serve with sambal oelek, a ground raw chilli paste, on the side to stir into the laksa to taste.

SINGAPORE

Words by
MARTIN SIMPSON

FOLLOWING THE SECOND World War, the Royal Air Force maintained a significant presence in Singapore operating from a number of stations across this small island state. The headquarter element for the Far Eastern Air Force was based at RAF Changi, which was disbanded at the end of October 1971 and now serves as the site of the huge Changi International Airport.

Despite the drawing down of a permanent RAF presence, however, RAF squadrons continue to deploy through Singapore, either on exercise or in support of humanitarian missions in the region. In November 2013, for instance, a C17 Globemaster III of 99 Squadron routed via Singapore in order to deliver urgently needed heavy machinery to the Philippines in the aftermath of Typhoon Haiyan.

In the post-war era, the variety and spice of the aircraft operating from Singapore's RAF stations was almost as exciting as the local cuisine. Squadrons that operated from Singapore's airfields were deploying some of the most iconic aircraft ever to be flown by the RAF, from Spitfires and Mosquitos through to Lightnings, Javelins and Hunters, as well as Vulcans and Valiants. Lesser known types such as the Hornet and Brigand operated from the island in support of operations against Malayan communists. Early helicopters such as the Dragonfly and Belvedere were based at RAF Seletar, where RAF air and ground crews were learning the art of support helicopter operations in the oppressive tropical heat of the Far East.

Between 1948 and 1960, the region was embroiled in the Malayan Emergency, a guerrilla war fought between Commonwealth forces and the communist-backed Malayan National Liberation Army. Spitfires of 60 Sqadron flew the first offensive missions against terrorists using cannon and rockets to destroy a camp as part of Operation Firedog in June 1948.

Six years later, launching from Singapore, Spitfires made their final operational sorties for the RAF, flying photo reconnaissance missions over Malaysia. In addition to the legendary Spitfire, the airfields of Singapore bid operational farewells to other classic aircraft types such as the De Havilland Mosquito, Short Sunderland flying-boat and Bristol Beaufighter. Avro Lincolns, a direct descendent of the mighty Lancaster bomber, of the RAF and Royal Australian Air Force (RAAF) were deployed to RAF Tengah and conducted bombing sorties

> "*The variety and spice of the aircraft operating from Singapore was almost as exciting as the local cuisine*"

against terrorist targets on the Malayan peninsular during the emergency.

Between 1963 and 1966 Indonesia and Malaysia fought an undeclared war, euphemistically referred to as a "confrontation" by Indonesia's foreign minister, which involved forces from the UK and Australia. Both fixed-wing and rotary-wing aircraft of the RAF played a key role in deterring Indonesian aggression during this period. Javelins of 60 and 64 Squadrons provided air defence in their only combat role during their service.

LOADING A CASUALTY OF THE MALAYAN EMERGENCY INTO A WESTLAND DRAGONFLY

In 1964, a Javelin from RAF Tengah was credited with the downing of an Indonesian C130 Hercules that manoeuvred into the Straits of Malacca in an attempt to avoid the interceptor. Vulcans and Victors deployed to Singapore and maintained a presence in the region throughout the confrontation. Following the release of declassified Ministry of Defence documents in 2000, it has been disclosed that up to 48 Red Beard tactical nuclear weapons were secretly stored at a highly secure weapons storage facility at RAF Tengah in Singapore during the confrontation.

Hainanese Chicken Rice
Poached Chicken with Fragrant Rice

Although this dish is ubiquitous throughout Singapore, and is often regarded as the national dish, it is actually an import brought to the country by Chinese immigrants from Hainan Island. This recipe doesn't have many ingredients, but the flavour comes from the ginger and the spring onion-infused stock made by the poaching chicken. Some of the stock is then used to cook the rice. The remainder served as a broth to accompany the meal, along with the refreshing cucumber and a kick from the intense chilli sauce.

INGREDIENTS
Serves 4

For the chicken

1 whole free-range chicken (1.5kg)

75g ginger, thickly sliced

8 spring onions, cut into 2.5cm lengths

For the rice

750ml chicken stock, reserved from cooking the chicken

50g butter

4 cloves of garlic, finely chopped or crushed

2.5cm piece of ginger, grated (including the skin)

400g jasmine or long grain rice

½ tsp sesame oil

salt and pepper

For the chilli sauce

6 red chillies, coarsely chopped

2 birds eye chillies, coarsely chopped

2.5cm piece of ginger, grated

3 cloves of garlic, finely chopped

1 tbsp sesame oil

1 tsp white wine or rice vinegar

½ tsp salt

2 tsp sugar

METHOD
To cook the chicken

- Place some of the ginger and spring onions inside the cavity of the chicken and place in a casserole dish or large saucepan with the rest of the ginger and spring onions. Pour in enough cold water to completely cover the chicken by about 2.5cm.
- Place over a high heat, bring to a boil, skim off any impurities as they rise to the surface and turn the heat to low. Simmer for about 35 to 40 minutes until the chicken is thoroughly cooked through (to check if the chicken is thoroughly cooked through insert a small sharp knife into the thickest part of the thigh; the juices should run clear).
- Remove the chicken from the stock and set aside to rest. Measure out 750ml of the stock for the rice and return the rest to the saucepan (reserve about 2 tbsp for the chilli sauce).

To cook the rice

- Rinse the rice under cold water, drain then cover with clean cold water, soak for 10 minutes and drain.
- Bring the measured stock to a simmer in a saucepan.
- Melt the butter in a saucepan or casserole dish over a medium heat and, when foaming, add the garlic and ginger and cook, stirring frequently, for around 5 minutes until fragrant and just starting to turn a light golden brown colour.
- Add the rice, stir well and fry for a couple of minutes, stirring continuously, until the rice is well coated in the butter and has a slightly nutty smell (it shouldn't take on any colour).
- Stir in the sesame oil, add the simmering stock, stir well and bring to a boil. Season with salt and pepper and turn the heat to low.
- Cover the surface with a lightly buttered piece of baking parchment, cover the pan or casserole dish with a lid and cook for 20 minutes.

½ lime, juiced (1 tbsp)

2 tbsp chicken stock (reserved
from poaching)

To serve

chilli sauce

soy dipping sauce (equal quantities
of light and dark soy sauce mixed
with a little sesame oil)

4 spring onions, thinly sliced on
an angle

2 red or green chillies, finely sliced
(optional)

coriander leaves

1 cucumber, peeled, halved
lengthways and sliced

• Remove from the heat and let the rice rest, covered with the lid,
at room temperature for 5 minutes before stirring with a fork to
separate the grains.

To make the chilli sauce

• Place all of the ingredients in a small hand-held food processor
and blend to a smooth paste adding a little cold water if the
sauce is too thick.

To serve

• Bring the remaining stock to a simmer and season with salt.
• Carve the chicken breasts from the bone (ensuring you keep the
skin on the breasts) and cut each into four thick slices. Remove the
legs and cut into thighs and drumsticks.
• Place the chicken pieces into the simmering broth and allow to
warm through (the chicken should just be warm not hot).
• Remove the chicken, strain the stock, bring back to a simmer and
pour into four small bowls.
• Arrange the chicken on serving plates, two slices of breast per plate
with a piece of leg (alternatively serve all of the chicken on a large
serving platter), with the rice, drizzle a little of the soy dipping sauce
over the chicken and garnish with a few of the sliced spring onions,
chillies and coriander leaves.
• Garnish the bowls of broth (stock) with the remaining sliced spring
onions and coriander leaves and serve alongside the chicken and rice
with the chilli sauce, sliced cucumber and remaining dipping sauce.

MADAGASCAR

Words by
SQUADRON LEADER CHRIS POWELL

FOLLOWING THE UNILATERAL Declaration of Independence by Rhodesia (now Zimbabwe) in November 1965, UN sanctions were imposed in the hope that Ian Smith's government would change its stance on minority rule. The port of Beira, in Mozambique, through which it was believed Rhodesia was receiving oil, was blockaded. A Royal Navy task force patrolled the Strait of Mozambique with the RAF providing air surveillance from Madagascar, known then as the Malagasy Republic.

In March 1966, three Shackletons, known affectionately and secretly as X, Y and Z, were dispatched to Majunga in Madagascar, with support personnel from the Aden-based 37 Squadron. Despite some initial teething problems, the Shackletons were soon flying daily 12-hour missions, patrolling the shipping lanes of the Strait of Mozambique. Radar was used to acquire shipping contacts, which the aircraft would then overfly to investigate. Suspicious ships were identified and reported to the Royal Navy for interception and boarding for inspection.

Many French families had remained in Madagascar following its independence from France in 1960. Junior Technician David McCandless was one of the few RAF personnel to speak any French, and would help communicate between the RAF and the French-speaking locals, particularly at the weekly evening dances at "Le Village", attended by both RAF men and French girls from the town. At one dance, a friend requested McCandless use his French to ask "the most beautiful girl in the room" for a dance on his behalf. McCandless decided to ask the girl for a dance himself.

The girl's name was Christiane and a whirlwind romance ensued. Before long the couple were engaged, but the chain of command did not approve, returning him to Aden to "cool down". It was only a sympathetic flight commander pilot who sent McCandless back to Madagascar on a Shackleton training mission, under the guise of completing a "tool audit". On arrival in Majunga, he was met by the Engineering Officer, who handed him an envelope. "The audit is complete," he said. "Now go and get married!"

The couple were married two days later in Majunga Cathedral, with the reception in the Grand Hotel. Two days later, McCandless returned to Aden. Christiane remained in Madagascar for a year before she was able to be flown to the UK to be reunited with him.

The RAF remained in Madagascar until 1972 when the Malagasy Republic asked the RAF to remove the Shackleton detachment at Majunga. David and Christiane remain happily married today, and returned to Madagascar in 2008 for their 42nd wedding anniversary.

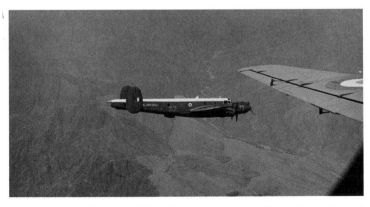

A SHACKLETON MARITIME PATROL AIRCRAFT OVER MADAGASCAR

Romazava
Malagasy Beef Stew with Greens

This national dish of Madagascar has many variations; this version just uses beef but it often contains a mix of chicken, pork or seafood. If you are making a chicken version of this follow the recipe and method as below but use about half the quantity of stock (use chicken stock) and simmer for about 25 to 30 minutes. The name derives from two words: "Ro" meaning soup and "Mazava" meaning clear. It should thus be thin and watery, with a large amount of green leafy vegetables. It may be necessary to allow the first batch of greens to wilt into the soup before the next batch is added.

INGREDIENTS
Serves 4–6

For the stew

1 tbsp sunflower oil

800g diced beef (chuck or shank)

1 medium onion, coarsely chopped

1 green pepper, coarsely chopped

1 red pepper, coarsely chopped

4 cloves of garlic, finely chopped
  or crushed

2 mild red chillies, halved
  lengthways and finely sliced

2.5cm piece of ginger, finely
  chopped or grated

400g tomatoes, coarsely chopped
  (or a 400g tin of chopped plum
  tomatoes)

500ml beef stock

400g spinach, coarsely chopped
  (frozen spinach also works well)

200g curly kale leaves (stalks
  removed), coarsely chopped

dash of tabasco (optional)

25g parsley, coarsely chopped

salt and pepper

To serve

100g watercress

boiled, steamed or braised rice

METHOD
To cook the stew

- Heat the oil in a large saucepan or casserole dish over a high heat, season the diced beef with salt and pepper, add to the casserole dish and sear until well browned on all surfaces.
- Turn the heat to medium and add the onions and peppers; cook, stirring frequently, for 5 minutes until they have started to soften.
- Add the garlic, chillies and ginger; continue to cook for a further 2 minutes.
- Stir in the chopped tomatoes and beef stock. Bring to a boil, turn the heat to low and season lightly with salt and pepper.
- Cover with a lid and simmer very gently for 1½ hours, topping up with a little boiling water if the sauce becomes too dry, until the beef is tender.
- Add the greens (in batches if necessary), continue to simmer, covered, for a further 10 to 15 minutes until tender, add a dash of tabasco for a little extra kick, stir in the chopped parsley and season with salt and pepper.

To serve

- Serve in large bowls or plates with lots of boiled, steamed or braised rice.

THE COLD WAR
1964–1989

AN EVOLVING ROLE

Words by
NICK FELLOWS

THE CUBAN MISSILE Crisis did much to help thaw Cold War relations, as both the USA and the USSR had seen that their game of brinkmanship had nearly ended in nuclear war. Not only was a "hotline" set up between the White House in Washington and the Kremlin in Moscow; but, for the rest of the Cold War, the superpowers avoided direct confrontation.

However, both used their proxies to fight for them to preserve or increase their influence, as was seen in Vietnam and the Middle East. Britain was not directly involved in either of these conflicts, but played a key role throughout the Cold War, both in Europe and also in former areas of the Empire. This was a period of withdrawal from the Far East, Middle East and Near East, all of which had dedicated branches of the RAF that were disbanded, leaving just the one overseas command, RAF Germany.

During this period Britain concentrated its military forces within NATO as it became clear that security depended heavily on this alliance, and the UK's three armed forces worked ever more closely together. In the area of sea communications around Britain's shores, patrols were carried out initially by Shackletons and later Nimrods. In Germany, new RAF bases were established west of the Rhine and a new joint headquarters was established with the British Army at Rheindalen. The RAF's role in Germany was to defend the air space of the northern half of the Federal Republic of Germany, and to provide air mobility to the British Army of the Rhine, reconnaissance, and the capability for either conventional or nuclear attack.

At home, one of the major concerns of the RAF was the patrol of Britain's neighbouring shores, the Atlantic and the North Sea due to the expanding "blue water" Soviet navy and the development of nuclear submarines. The maritime patrol and attack squadrons used in this role were deployed not only around the British Isles, but also in Gibraltar and Malta. In addition, in the event of war there was always the possibility of heavy air attacks by the Warsaw Pact across Denmark and the North Sea. During peacetime, the Soviet Union used long-range reconnaissance aircraft to test the northern reaches of the UK's air-space, and it became vital that these were turned away to limit their intelligence-gathering activities. There was also a growing and serious threat from Soviet bombers that could launch air-to-ground missiles against the UK from long distances, and it became crucial in the 1980s that the RAF increase its frontline fighter strength so that it had the capability to destroy the bombers before these missiles could be launched.

Throughout this period, however, the RAF was still involved in a number of events outside the continent. The first was in the south of the Arabian Peninsula where Britain attempted to bring stability by trying to persuade the numerous sheikdoms to form a federation in 1962. The RAF's role was to protect this federation and Aden (later Yemen) from outside attack and internal civil disorder. In 1964, armed tribesman in the Radafan mountains, supported by Yemeni forces, began an armed revolt. The RAF provided close support for ground troops as attacks were launched against rebel strongholds in the mountains and helicopters were used to move troops

A HAWKER SIDDELEY HARRIER IS PREPARED ON BOARD HMS HERMES DURING THE FALKLANDS CONFLICT, 1982

quickly in the inhospitable mountains. Such was the successful co-operation between ground forces and the RAF that Hunters were able to attack targets within 25 yards of friendly positions, an incredibly narrow margin for error.

Despite much initial success, the Aden Emergency caused by the Radafan rebels continued and then gathered momentum.

By 1967, the RAF was called upon to evacuate service families and British troops from Aden, which had been the major British and RAF base in the Middle East. The evacuation lasted from May to November 1967 and was the largest airlift since the Berlin Airlift. By November, 6,000 troops and 400 tons of equipment had been removed from RAF Khormaksar, bringing to an end the British connection with Aden, which had been established in 1839 by the East India Company and served the RAF since the First World War as a landing strip for aircraft being used against Turkish forces.

In Rhodesia the role of the RAF was to support the Commonwealth force that monitored the ceasefire between Rhodesian forces and those of the Patriotic Front before elections took place in May 1965. Initially, the RAF's role was to fly in the Commonwealth force and sustain it but, due to changing circumstances, this became a more complicated task, particularly as the ceasefire became increasingly precarious. The monitoring teams had to be flown to all parts of the country, where they and the Patriotic Front had to be supplied with food and other equipment by air, as other forms of transport were unsafe. The operation lasted four months, but the RAF again showed its flexibility to simply get on with the job.

Another feature of the RAF's operations, which continued beyond this period, was the support it provided during emergencies and humanitarian crises. At home this often meant deploying its Search and Rescue (SAR) forces, Mountain Rescue Teams and Marine Craft Units, rescuing people from mountains or rocks and off coasts when they had got into difficulties. The RAF was also called upon to support humanitarian operations much further afield, flying food, shelter and medical equipment into areas hit by natural disasters, including the aftermath of a 1961 hurricane in British Honduras (Belize), a 1970 cyclone in East Pakistan, a 1972 earthquake in Nicaragua, and 1973 famines in both Nepal and Mali.

Throughout this period, despite the lack of a major conflict, the RAF was continually involved in operations somewhere around the world, demonstrating the flexibility and mobility that air power offers, particularly through the use of rotary and fixed-wing air transport forces. In 1982, much of this changed as Argentine forces, in pursuit of a long-held territorial claim, occupied the Falkland Islands and South Georgia. The RAF would play a significant role in the task force that was assembled to retake the territories following the failure of diplomatic efforts. Forces were operating 8,000 miles from home against a numerically superior force. Ascension Island, located approximately halfway between Britain and the Falklands, would act as the hub of activity and soon became one of the busiest air strips in the world.

The vast distances that had to be covered meant that air-to-air refuelling would be crucial. It was this that allowed Victors to provide support for the Vulcan bomber to attack Port Stanley runway and also made possible the support that Sea Harriers could provide for HMS *Fearless*. The RAF also played a vital role in carrying men and supplies to Ascension, from which Hercules transport planes were able to drop supplies to the ships of the task force, often

"Without the Harriers, the task force would have had to face considerable Argentine forces without fixed-wing air support"

in terrible conditions. Land drops involved non-stop 8,000-mile flights and took about 25 hours. Some 40 drops were made between 29 May and 15 June.

Nimrods provided maritime surveillance as the task force moved towards the Falklands and such was their success that no Argentine submarine or warship attacked the force. Vulcans attacked the narrow air strip in Port Stanley and this gave the Argentineans warning that the RAF had the potential to hit targets elsewhere and led them to move their Mirage fighters further north, preventing them from escorting Sky Hawk attacks against British forces in San Carlos Waters. The attacks also helped to demoralise Argentine forces, with Mirage fighters being taken away from the combat zone to protect Buenos Aires from a possible attack.

However, it was probably the performance of the Harrier and Sea Harrier that caught the public imagination. They were able to operate from ships in the air defence, anti-shipping and offensive air-support role, something no other plane could do. The Sea Harriers were able to inflict considerable damage on the Argentine Sky Hawks, Mirage and Super Etendards. Then, with reinforcements from the Harriers, they provided offensive air support from the two aircraft carriers to the troops during the landings and advance across the island.

Without the Harriers, the task force would have had to face considerable Argentine forces without fixed-wing

air support and the consequences would have been severe. While the exploits of the air crews caught the imagination and the headlines, it was the impressive support achievements at such short notice that was the real enabler. Many of the aircraft needed modifications while the engineering and logistical support on the ground was exceptional. As a result, the Argentine force that had invaded on 2 April had been defeated by 14 June. Once again, the RAF had shown that air power was an essential part of any successful military operation.

Despite the collapse of the Soviet Union and the end of the Cold War, the RAF has certainly not been in less demand. Instead, its role has evolved. In particular, it has played a vital part in power projection without having to commit ground or naval forces. It has allowed political effects to be achieved rapidly, but also allowed force to be withdrawn once an objective has been achieved. This role became even clearer in the 1990s and beyond as Britain sought to project its power over large distances if, and when, required.

IRAN

Words by
FLIGHT LIEUTENANT (RETIRED) ART LESTER

IN 1955, BRITAIN signed the Baghdad Pact treaty with Turkey, Iraq, Iran and Pakistan in an attempt to prevent Soviet influence spreading to the Middle East. When Iraq left, the signatories then became the Central Treaty Organisation, or CENTRO; a military pact based on the model of NATO.

The efforts of CENTRO were effectively undermined by Egypt's refusal to sign, as its leader Nasser wished to receive weapons and support from the Soviet Union for other purposes. Although the treaty never became fully effective in its intent, and the Middle East was dragged further into the Cold War, it did last until the Shah left Iran and fled into exile in 1979, providing some very rare and unusual training opportunities. These included Operation Midlink in 1970, when Hawker Hunters of 8 Squadron made simulated ground-attack runs against targets in southern Iran, which were defended by Northrop F5s of the Imperial Iranian Air Force.

In 1956, the world reached a flashpoint with a series of complex events leading to the Suez Crisis. The UK's response was wide and ranging and, as well as providing air transport and insertion for UK paratroopers in the Canal Zone Area, there were several other small detachments, including 34 Squadron of the RAF Regiment being forward-based to Iran from Cyprus to provide assurances and screening cover.

The RAF had units based in Persia during both world wars and, although not a major theatre of conflict, the Anglo–Russian invasion of Iran was critical in ensuring Soviet access to Iranian oilfields and therefore their continuing capability on the Eastern Front.

On 23 May 1973, an RAF Vulcan B2 bomber of 9 Squadron, based in Cyprus, was damaged on landing at Shiraz airfield. A failure of the left undercarriage meant that the aircraft landed on a foam carpet and skidded into a gully that was not shown on the airfield charts, damaging the remaining undercarriage. An Iranian observer was on board at the time.

This example of the challenges that face air operations and the risk of compounding errors will be familiar to many aviators. Similarly, they will not be surprised at how quickly safe circumstances can turn into a poor or dangerous situation when you're operating away from home. Such challenges continue to be factors in air operations and the RAF is now leading in air safety best practices to endeavour to mitigate such issues.

The RAF helped to pioneer air transit routes through Persia in the inter-war years, especially in 1923. The ability to link East and West through a land corridor, and not through a hostile Soviet Union or over the Indian Ocean, provided the only real safe passage for long-distance aircraft at the time, when navigation capability and engine reliability meant that unscheduled or emergency stops were still fairly common on long-distance flights.

> "*The Anglo–Russian invasion of Persia was critical in ensuring Soviet access to Iranian oil fields*"

Joojeh Kabab
Persian Grilled Saffron Chicken

Joojeh (or Jujeh) kabab is a popular fixture on Persian restaurant menus. It's simple to prepare but a crucial factor is the lengthy marinating in onions, yoghurt and lemon juice, which tenderises the chicken. The onions are usually sliced or minced, but here they are blanched to eliminate any bitterness. The saffron gives the kababs their signature flavour and, along with the turmeric, a vibrant yellow colour. They can be served with rice and grilled vegetables, or wrapped in lavash, a naan-like bread flavoured with sesame or poppy seeds.

INGREDIENTS

Serves 4

For the joojeh kabab

a pinch of saffron strands

1 medium onion, peeled and
  quartered

125g Greek yoghurt

2 tbsp olive oil

2 lemons, juiced

½ tsp ground turmeric

½ tsp mild chilli powder

1 tsp salt

½ tsp freshly ground black pepper

800g chicken breast cut into
  4cm pieces

For the dressing

100g natural yoghurt

4 tbsp harissa paste

2 mint leaves, shredded

a pinch of cracked black pepper

To serve

2 lavash (see recipe on page 263)

2 large handfuls of rocket

extra virgin olive oil

salt and pepper

1 lemon, cut into 8 wedges

METHOD

To prepare the marinade

• Grind the saffron strands to a powder in a pestle and mortar (or with the back of a spoon on a chopping board), place in a small bowl or cup, pour over 2 tbsp of boiling water and leave to infuse for 10 minutes.

• Place the onions in a saucepan, cover with boiling water and simmer for about 7 to 8 minutes until tender. Drain, allow to cool and place in a food processor with the saffron water, yoghurt, olive oil, lemon juice, turmeric, chilli powder, salt and pepper; blend to a smooth consistency.

To marinate the chicken

• Place the chicken pieces in a bowl, pour over the marinade, mix well to thoroughly coat the chicken, cover and place in the fridge to marinate for around 6 hours or overnight.

To cook the chicken

• Thread the marinated chicken pieces onto four metal skewers and cook on a barbecue, on a griddle pan or under a hot grill, brushing frequently with the leftover marinade, until well coloured and cooked through.

To make the dressing

• Mix the natural yoghurt, harissa, shredded mint and black pepper together.

To serve

• Serve the joojeh kabab in the **lavash** with the rocket leaves (tossed with a little extra virgin olive oil, salt and pepper), dressing and lemon wedges. Alternatively, the grilled chicken can be served with rice, salad and/or grilled tomatoes and the lemon wedges.

Lavash
Middle Eastern Flatbread

INGREDIENTS

Serves 4

For the lavash

400g plain flour, sifted

1 sachet (7g) instant yeast

2 tsp caster sugar

½ tsp salt

150ml warm water

100g natural yoghurt

1 tbsp sesame seeds, lightly
 toasted

METHOD

To make the lavash

- Mix the flour, yeast, sugar and salt together in a bowl, make a well in the middle and add 125ml of the warmed water and the yoghurt. Gradually mix with your fingers, adding more water as necessary, to form a smooth kneadable dough.
- Turn the dough out onto a lightly floured work surface and knead well for around 10 minutes until the dough is smooth and free from stickiness.
- Transfer the dough to a lightly oiled bowl, cover with a cloth or cling film and prove in a warm place for about an hour until it has doubled in size.
- When the dough has nearly proved, preheat the oven to its highest setting, place a baking sheet in the oven and preheat the grill.
- Gently knock the dough back with your fingertips to remove any air, knead briefly, divide into four equal pieces and roll the pieces into balls. Cover the balls with a tea towel.
- Cook the lavash either individually or in pairs. Roll the balls out into rounds about 25cm in diameter on a lightly floured work surface, brush with a little water, sprinkle over the toasted sesame seeds (lightly press with the palm of your hand to help them stick), place on the preheated tray and cook in the hot oven for 3 to 4 minutes. Once they have puffed up, pierce the bottom with the tip of a small knife, cover with a tea towel, gently press to flatten, brush with a little olive oil and place the tray under the grill for a few seconds to brown the surface. Alternatively, the lavash can be cooked in a skillet over a medium to high heat until speckled brown on both sides.
- Pile the lavash on top of each other as they are cooked, keeping them wrapped in a tea towel (this keeps them from drying up and becoming crisp – they should stay soft enough to wrap around the kabab).

HONG KONG

Words by
WING COMMANDER MARC HOLLAND

HONG KONG HAS long been a key staging post for the Royal Air Force, allowing aircraft to transit the Far East's vast expanses of ocean. In 1935, the RAF established a permanent base at Kai Tak airfield – one that was initially run by the Royal Navy Fleet Air Arm – but had to abandon it when the Japanese entered the Second World War.

After the war, Kai Tak was home to Sunderland flying boats, then air defence fighters in the 1950s. It hosted numerous RAF squadrons that had been detached there for short exercises or operations. After the ambitious construction of an artificial runway that jutted out into the harbour, the 1960s and 1970s saw RAF Kai Tak become a main hub for the RAF's new long-range transport fleet of C130 Hercules, Belfasts, Britannias and VC10s.

Most of the RAF presence was transitory but a few units made Hong Kong their home, such as 28 Squadron, which flew Vampires, Venoms and Hunters from Hong Kong before converting to search and rescue helicopters, flying the Whirlwind and Wessex. The squadron mounted more than 1,000 rescue sorties in Hong Kong on top of its routine missions to support the local police and military. On 15 June 1981, the evacuation of a pregnant casualty ended with the crewman and on-board nurse delivering a baby girl mid-flight!

The RAF Marine Craft Service was also based in Hong Kong. These boats were operated by airmen and protected the security of the coastal airport, as well as helping those in trouble on the water. By the end of the 1960s, it was disbanded as the RAF began to draw down its motor-launch capability.

By the end of the 1970s, most RAF personnel had moved to RAF Sek Kong in the centre of Hong Kong to make room for Kai Tak's expanding international airport and high-rise buildings. Kai Tak quickly earned a reputation as one of the hardest approaches in the world. In poor weather, pilots had to fly, in cloud, towards the city and high ground to get "visual" beneath. Close to the ground, they had to bank aggressively and follow a giant checker-board that marked a safe passage to the airport through the high-rise buildings.

In 1997, 28 Squadron was the last RAF unit to leave Hong Kong as the territory was handed back to China. The following year, Kai Tak airport was closed to make way for a modern airfield with a safer approach lane, bringing this iconic RAF base to an end.

A WESTLAND WESSEX OVER KOWLOON, HONG KONG

Wonton Noodle Soup
Chinese Dumpling Soup

The quality of the broth is crucial to this soup which should, ideally, be made with pork trotters to give it a gelatinous quality. Traditionally, the broth base is made with Jinhua ham, which can be substituted with chopped gammon or back bacon. Kombu (dried seaweed) is optional but imparts robust umami notes. Dried shrimp is available in speciality Chinese shops but can be substituted with shrimp paste, which will infuse into the stock then settle with the sediment as it chills. Refrigerate the stock overnight and it will become gelatinous, enabling you to scoop the set fat off the surface and decant the broth. Noodles are not essential – the broth can be enjoyed with just the wontons.

INGREDIENTS
Serves 4

For the broth

200g chopped or minced pork

1 litre chicken stock (chopped-up roast chicken carcass, boiled in 1½ litres of water with chopped onion, carrot and celery; or a good quality ready-made)

8 spring onions, cut into 2½cm batons (separated into green and white parts)

5cm piece of ginger, peeled and sliced

100g back bacon or gammon, roughly chopped

1 piece of kombu, 9cm square (optional)

25g dried shrimp (or 2 tsp shrimp paste)

For the wonton dough
(or use 24 ready-made wonton wrappers)

1 egg, beaten

125ml cold water

250g plain flour (plus extra for dusting)

¾ tsp salt

METHOD
To make the broth

- Place the pork in a saucepan with the chicken stock, chopped green parts of the spring onions, sliced ginger, bacon and kombu (if using). Bring to a boil, reduce the heat and simmer for 30 minutes.
- Add the dried shrimp or shrimp paste and continue to simmer for a further 20 minutes.
- Strain the broth through a fine sieve into a clean container, cool, then cover and chill in the fridge (preferably overnight in order for the fat to set).
- Once chilled, spoon off the set fat from the top and decant the broth into a clean container leaving the sediment in the bottom of the container. This will ensure a nice clear broth.

To make the wonton dough

- Mix the egg with half of the water.
- Sift the flour into a bowl, mix in the salt, make a well in the centre and add the egg and water mix.
- Mix the flour into the liquid, adding more water as required to form a stiff dough.
- Knead the dough on a lightly floured work surface for around 5 minutes until smooth and workable.
- Wrap the dough in cling film and rest in the fridge for 30 minutes.
- Divide the dough into four equal pieces. Roll the dough out on a lightly floured surface as thin as possible (a pasta machine can be used for this) and cut into 24 9cm x 9cm squares. Lightly dust the squares with flour and cover each layer with cling film to prevent them from drying out.

For the wonton filling

250g raw prawns, coarsely
  chopped
250g pork shoulder, minced or
  coarsely diced
2.5cm piece of ginger, grated
½ tsp salt
¼ tsp white pepper
2 tsp caster sugar
1 tsp light soy sauce
2 tsp sesame oil
2 tsp chives, finely chopped

To finish

150g egg noodles
4 Chinese or white savoy cabbage
  leaves, thickly shredded
reserved white spring onion
  batons

To make the wonton filling

• Place the chopped prawns, minced pork, grated ginger, salt, pepper, sugar, soy sauce, sesame oil and chopped chives in a large bowl and mix well. At this stage, it is best to poach, steam or shallow fry a small patty of the filling to taste, adding a little more seasoning if necessary.

To make the wontons

• Place a wonton wrapper square in the palm of your hand or on a work surface, place about three-quarters of a tablespoon of the filling in the centre (you can divide the filling into 24 small portions in advance to speed up the filling process), moisten the edge with your finger dipped in a little cold water and one by one fold the edges up to the top pleating as you go to form a small sealed pouch; give the top a twist to help the seal. Repeat with the remaining wonton wrappers keeping them covered with a damp tea towel or cling film to prevent them from drying out.

To cook the wontons and serve

• Soak the noodles in cold water for 30 minutes to soften.
• Pour the broth into a saucepan and bring to a simmer with the cabbage and cook for 5 minutes until the cabbage is just tender. Add the spring onion whites for the last 2 minutes of simmering.
• Meanwhile bring a large pan of water to a rapid boil, add the wontons, simmer for about 5 minutes until cooked through (the wontons can be cooked directly in the simmering broth but any residue flour on the dough will make the broth cloudy), remove from the water with a slotted spoon or similar and keep warm. Alternatively, the wontons can be cooked in a bamboo steamer.
• Return the water to a boil, drain the soaking noodles then add them to the boiling water, cook for a couple of minutes, until just tender, and drain again.
• Divide the noodles between the bowls, place six wontons on top of each mound of noodles and ladle over the broth.

UNITED ARAB EMIRATES

Words by
FLIGHT LIEUTENANT (RETIRED) ART LESTER

THE ROYAL AIR Force's involvement in the United Arab Emirates was at its peak in the decade leading up to December 1971, when the main station at RAF Sharjah was formally closed. It was particularly useful to have an airfield capable of handling the largest long-distance flights in this corner of the Arabian Peninsula, so Sharjah – one of the region's six "Trucial States" that formed the UAE in 1971 – became a hub for regional and inter-regional transport. It was one of the RAF's busiest stations, and its proximity to the Jeb-e-Jib air weapons range made it a second home for RAF Hawker Hunter Jets and Canberra aircraft.

The RAF station at Khormaksar, near the city of Aden in modern-day Yemen, closed in 1967, so RAF Sharjah became home to a pair of Shackleton MR3s, which provided valuable air-sea operational awareness in the Persian Gulf and Straits of Hormuz. The weather was hot, humid and tiring, but interesting people were always passing through. Indeed, the air officer commanding the Near East Air Force would sometimes transit through the station in his official transport – a Canberra B2 bomber!

The leisure facilities in the 1960s were rudimentary, and airmen had to make do with a trip to one of the local beaches, or play football or hockey. Occasionally, a "desert safari" would take interested servicemen to remote spots in the interior sands by Bedford three-ton truck, sometimes meeting locals or visiting ruined desert forts.

For several years, RAF Sharjah was home to 8 and 208 Squadrons. These had previously been based at other locations including Cyprus, Yemen and Kenya, and were now providing training and protection to the wider Middle East. They were equipped with Hunters, and had a remit to patrol a vast area, from Kenya through Yemen to Bahrain.

Sharjah, along with Aden, Bahrain and Masirah, played an important role in the Buraimi and Jebel Akdar conflicts between 1952 and 1959. Complex tribal politics in Oman had led to the RAF being asked to provide air support against rebels. Shackleton bombers and Venom fighter-bombers were used to conduct reconnaissance, attack rebel positions and provide air support to the Sultan's forces. Transport aircraft were used to resupply fighters and aid negotiations.

Most servicemen were housed in basic, prefabricated Twyneham huts, and the occasional intense downpour brought relief from the heat. A "fort" or more substantial building was used for the operations and air-traffic facilities. Humour was important in such conditions: one officer's mess had a door labelled "TV room", which would lead unsuspecting visitors into a four-foot drop onto the desert floor!

As the town of Sharjah expanded, the original airfield was subsumed into the city, the main runway becoming King Abul Aziz Street. A new, larger, airport was built further to the south in 1977. In recent years, the UAE has regularly hosted the annual Advanced Training and Leadership Course (ATLC), where air forces from around the world are invited to meet and practice operational planning and tactics. These exercises, similar to training serials in the US and Europe, help to prepare aircrew and support staff for the full remit of air operations. They help to bring a greater sense of cohesion to the region and strengthen decades-old ties between Western and Middle Eastern governments and their air forces.

Luqaimat
Fried Sweet Dumplings

The Arabic equivalent of doughnuts, these tasty little deep-fried dumplings are crispy on the outside, soft and airy on the inside and coated in a sweet syrup flavoured with lemon, vanilla and spices. During Ramadan, luqaimat are a favourite snack for Emiratis at Iftar – the feast that is taken after the sun sets and observant Muslims break their fast.

INGREDIENTS

Serves 4–6

For the batter

125g plain flour

15g cornflour

1 tsp instant yeast

¼ tsp caster sugar

a pinch of salt

30g natural yoghurt

200ml tepid water

For the syrup

200g caster sugar

1 cinnamon stick, broken into
  pieces

1 tbsp cardamom pods, crushed
  with the flat of a knife

a pinch of saffron strands

1 vanilla pod, split lengthways and
  seeds scraped out

½ lemon, juice and zest pared
  into strips

200ml water

To deep fry and serve

sunflower or vegetable oil

1 tbsp sesame seeds (optional)

METHOD

To make the batter

• Mix the flour, cornflour, yeast, sugar, salt and yoghurt together
  in a bowl.
• Mix in half of the water then gradually add enough of the remaining
  warm water to form a thick lump-free batter; it should be a dropping
  consistency (traditionally this is done with the fingers to ensure a
  smooth texture). Cover with cling film and set aside in a warm place
  to prove, until doubled in size, for a couple of hours.

To make the syrup

• Place the sugar into a saucepan with the cinnamon stick, cardamom
  pods, saffron, vanilla pod, vanilla seeds, lemon juice and zest. Stir
  in the water, place over a medium heat and bring to a boil, stirring
  continuously until the sugar has dissolved.
• Reduce the heat and simmer without stirring for 5 minutes. Remove
  from the heat and set aside at room temperature to infuse.

To cook the luqaimat

• Heat the oil in a large saucepan, wok or deep fryer to 180°C.
• Cook the luqaimat in batches by scooping up about half a
  tablespoon of the batter with your fingers and dropping it into the
  hot oil by pushing it off your fingers with your thumb (alternatively
  use a tablespoon and push it off with another spoon) and fry,
  stirring continuously, with a large slotted spoon, until puffed up,
  golden brown and crispy on the outside (fry in batches to ensure
  the luqaimat cook evenly and to avoid overcrowding the pan).
  Transfer to absorbent kitchen paper to drain.

To serve

• Strain the syrup into a large bowl, add the warm fried luqaimat
  and sesame seeds, if using. Stir to thoroughly coat with the syrup
  and serve immediately.

AUSTRALIA

Words by
MARTIN SIMPSON

THE VALIANT CREW THAT DROPPED BRITAIN'S FIRST H-BOMB, 1957

THE VAST EXPANSE of Australia has been home to a large number of Royal Air Force personnel and aircraft throughout its history. As the Allies recovered from their defeats across Southeast Asia, Spitfires from 54 Squadron arrived in 1942 to support the defence of Darwin from Japanese air attack. From early 1945, the British Pacific Fleet operated from Sydney Harbour and its Fleet Air Arm Seafires, Corsairs, Avengers and latterly Fireflies could be seen along the Australian East Coast.

In the 1950s, RAF units in Australia played their part in the testing of the UK's nuclear deterrent. In October 1956, Maralinga in South Australia was the location for Operation Buffalo, the first air-dropped British fission weapon, known as Blue Danube. The weapon was released from a 49 Squadron Valiant, and Canberra's 542 Squadron performed survey duties. A year later, another 49 Squadron Valiant bomber dropped Britain's first hydrogen bomb, Yellow Sun, near Christmas Island in the Pacific. The aircraft involved, XD818, is now preserved at the Royal Air Force Museum Cosford.

The Valiant's V-bomber stablemates were also a feature in Australian skies during the early 1960s as part of the Blue Steel stand-off missile trials. Victors and Vulcans were used to transport Blue Steel test rounds to Royal Australian Air Force (RAAF) Edinburgh in South Australia during Operation Blue Ranger.

Four Lightnings of 74 Squadron operated from RAAF Darwin in June 1969 to participate in an air defence exercise with RAAF Mirages. The aircraft, based in Singapore, set the record for the longest non-stop flight by a Lightning on the 2,000-mile transit to Northern Australia.

The RAF's presence in Australia has also enabled it to provide humanitarian aid. In December 1974, Cyclone Tracy devastated the city of Darwin within a few hours. An RAF Hercules, XV199, flew to Darwin with a cargo of diesel and transported evacuees to RAAF Richmond. A Nimrod on detachment to Singapore was also deployed to Darwin and served in its alternate role of troop transport to evacuate British civilians from the disaster zone.

In March 2015, an RAF C17 Globemaster III departed from RAF Brize Norton carrying vital shelter and relief supplies to help people whose lives had been devastated by Cyclone Pam on the island of Vanuatu. The C17 operated out of RAAF Amberley, in Queensland, where it joined a huge international relief effort.

Passion Fruit Pavlova

by SOPHIE WRIGHT

FOOD WRITER, PRESENTER AND CO-OWNER OF SOPHIE WRIGHT CATERING

Its provenance is disputed between Australia and New Zealand, but this dessert was named after the Russian ballet dancer Anna Pavlova after her famed tours of the antipodes in the 1920s. Meringues are usually just made with whipped egg whites and sugar (in France) or hot sugar syrup (in Italy), but pavlova contains vinegar and cornflour, giving it its crisp shell and marshmallow-like interior.

INGREDIENTS

Serves 8

For the meringue bases

8 medium egg whites (room
   temperature)
large pinch of cream of tartar
400g caster sugar
2 tsp cornflour
2 tsp malt vinegar
2 tsp vanilla essence

For the filling and topping

850ml double cream
100g icing sugar, sieved
1 lemon, finely grated zest
6 passion fruit, juice and seeds
400g raspberries, washed
200ml mango coulis
25g mint leaves, picked

METHOD

To make the meringue base

- Preheat the oven to 150°C.
- Place the egg whites and cream of tartar into a mixing bowl and whisk until light and foamy.
- Add half the sugar and whisk well on a medium speed, then add the rest of the sugar, whisking until very glossy. Remove the bowl from the machine (if using one) and fold in the cornflour, vinegar and vanilla, mix well.
- Draw two circles using a 25cm dinner plate on greaseproof paper. Place the paper onto two flat baking trays.
- Fill the centre of the circles with equal quantities of meringue mix. Keep the sides nice and high while creating an indentation in the centre.
- Place the trays in the oven and immediately turn the oven down to 120°C and cook for 1 hour. You will find the meringue will expand quite a lot, slightly colour and may crack, this is normal.
- After the hour check that the pavlova is cooked, it should be firm to the touch, yet if squeezed lightly will crack. This will ensure a soft marshmallowy inside, essential for a good pavlova.
- Leave to cool completely in the oven with the door ajar. Then peel off the greaseproof paper and place one pavlova layer onto a cake stand.

To fill and top the pavlova

- Whip the double cream and add the icing sugar and lemon zest.
- Pile half onto the first pavlova, add the pulp from 3 passion fruits, half the raspberries and half of the mango coulis. Add the top pavlova and repeat the process, this time finishing with the mint leaves as well. Allow the filling and topping to ooze over the edges a little for effect.
- Dust with icing sugar and serve in slices.

NORTHERN IRELAND

Words by
NICK SMART

"The province was to play a critical role against German U-boats in the Battle of the Atlantic"

THE HISTORY OF the Royal Air Force in Northern Ireland dates back to the time of the formation of the RAF itself in 1917, when the airfield at Aldergrove was selected as a testing base for V1500 bombers. As the service began to expand in the 1920s, so too did its Northern Ireland base. The Auxiliary and Reserve Squadrons were formed, one of which, 502 Squadron, was formed at the base in 1925 and equipped with Vickers Vimys and later Vickers Virginia heavy bombers. By 1939, as war was declared, Aldergrove had expanded further to include Ansons and a diverse range of other aircraft.

By the summer of 1942, RAF Aldergrove had returned to its previous role as a training base, but operations resumed in 1943 when 86 and 120 Squadrons returned with Liberators and 220 Squadron with Flying Fortresses. 59 Squadron entered the fray on 20 May 1943. This was a period of great expansion in the province, which was to play a critical role against German U-boats in the Battle of the Atlantic.

In the early days of the squadron, stoves were supplied by the galley room but the practice proved time-consuming so metal boxes were placed on aircraft before take-off. These usually contained sandwiches, hard-boiled eggs, nuts, raisins, chocolate and gum. This arrangement occasionally caused difficulties. For instance, on 10 June 1943, Wing Commander Bartlett of 59 Squadron and crew flew a 16-hour sortie with no food rations at all, due to an oversight by canteen staff. The hungry airmen were less than satisfied with the Horlicks tablets from their emergency supplies!

Operation Banner brought a changing role for Aldergrove from the late 1960s as it became a base for anti-terrorist operations during the Troubles. 72 Squadron took up residence with the Wessex, and later, in the 1990s, the Puma – a type which was also operated from Aldergrove by 230 Squadron. RAF Aldergrove's illustrious history includes visits from Air Force One, Lockheed C-5 Galaxys carrying Marine One helicopters, C-17 Globemasters and many others.

In 2009, the RAF's association with Aldergrove appeared to have ended when 230 Squadron relocated to England. However, the Army Air Corps retained a presence and, with half of the site serving as Belfast International Airport, the future of Aldergrove is secure. Happily, in 2013 the oldest reserve squadron in the RAF, 502, returned to renew the association.

A WESTLAND WESSEX HELICOPTER OF 72 SQUADRON IN NORTHERN IRELAND DURING OPERATION BANNER

Irish Stew

The ingredients of an Irish stew can be a fraught issue. Some recipes include root vegetables such as carrots, parsnips, swede and turnips; others contain cabbage and bacon, and many include pearl barley. One thing they all have in common is lamb (or mutton), onions and potatoes, and some purists will insist that, apart from stock or water, these should be the only ingredients. This version has been kept simple to focus on the flavours and textures of the few ingredients. Instead of pearl barley to thicken the stew, it uses two types of potatoes; the floury potatoes break down to give body, while the waxy potatoes are added towards the end of cooking for flavour and texture.

INGREDIENTS

Serves 4

8 lamb neck chops (about 175g each)

1.25 litres cold water

1 lamb stock cube

50g plain flour for dusting

1 tbsp rapeseed oil (or vegetable oil)

1kg carrots, peeled and cut into large pieces

4 medium onions, peeled, halved and cut into thick slices

2 sprigs of thyme

500g floury potatoes (e.g. King Edward or Maris Piper), peeled and cut into small pieces

500g waxy potatoes (e.g. Jersey Royals or Charlotte), peeled and cut into large pieces

salt and pepper

To serve

2 tbsp parsley, coarsely chopped

a few small thyme tips (optional)

soda bread

METHOD

To make the stew

- Trim the excess fat and sinew from the chops (the chops can be cut into large pieces at this stage if preferred). Place the trimmings in a saucepan over a moderate heat and cook, stirring occasionally, to render the fat (it should yield about a tablespoon of rendered fat). If there's no excess fat on the chops use 2 tbsp of oil when it comes to heating the oil with the lamb dripping.
- Transfer the browned trimmings to a saucepan with a slotted spoon (reserving the lamb dripping), add the cold water and bring to a simmer, skimming off the fat as it rises to the surface. When simmering, dissolve in the lamb stock cube and simmer for 45 minutes.
- Season the flour generously with salt and freshly ground black pepper.
- Heat the oil and lamb dripping in a casserole dish or heavy-based saucepan over a high heat.
- Coat the lamb with the seasoned flour, tap off the excess and sear on both sides in the hot oil until well browned. Transfer the chops to a plate and set to one side.
- Turn the heat to medium and add the carrots and onions, cook, stirring frequently, for 5 minutes until the onions are translucent.
- Return the chops to the casserole with the thyme sprigs strain over the hot stock, cover with a lid, turn the heat to low and simmer gently for 1 hour, occasionally skimming off the fat and any impurities as they rise to the surface.
- Season with salt and pepper, add the floury potatoes, replace the lid and simmer for 15 minutes until the potatoes start to break up.
- Add the waxy potatoes, top the stew up with a little boiling water if necessary and continue to cook for a further 15 to 20 minutes until the waxy potatoes are just cooked through.

To serve

- Spoon the hot stew into bowls, scatter over the chopped parsley, garnish with a couple of thyme tips and serve with warm soda bread.

EAST INDIA

Words by
FLIGHT LIEUTENANT TOM MARSHALL

THE TERM "EAST INDIA" can cover any part of the area stretching around the Bay of Bengal, from Madras (now Chennai) on the south-east Indian coast, up and around Bangladesh, across to Burma (or Myanmar) and down to Singapore. This was the area covered in the Second World War by the exotically named Far East Air Force.

After the fall of Singapore in 1942, the RAF HQ was moved from Singapore's RAF Changi to India and renamed Air Headquarters Bengal to fight the Burma campaign. A wide variety of aircraft provided close air support to the 14th Army during the battles of Kohima and Imphal; strafing and bombing the besieged Japanese troops, often at very low level.

After the defeat of the Japanese in Assam, the monsoon season intervened before many counterattacks could take place. Following an enforced period of reduced operations, the RAF once again supported the army in re-establishing control of the area, leading to the HQ being re-designated HQ RAF Bengal and Burma.

On 2 September 1945, the Japanese formally surrendered, signalling the end of the Second World War. Many RAF members were civilian conscripts; willing to do their duty but understandably eager to return home once the war had finished, and the demobilisation of troops from India proved incredibly slow and frustrating.

One eyewitness, David Van Vlymen, recalls the following extraordinary event.

"In January 1946, some five months after VJ-Day, the airmen of RAF Bamrauli – near Allahabad in Uttar Pradesh, India – were preparing for their morning parade. The Station Warrant Officer watched the Indian pipe band begin to form up. Outside the huts, 2,000 British airmen began to assemble, and then moved off towards the parade ground. The airmen looked smart and well-disciplined as their marching columns converged on the parade square. Then the unthinkable happened. As each contingent arrived at the periphery of the parade ground they veered away, marching determinedly towards the huge camp cinema. The RAF station had gone on strike!"

This "mutiny" spread across the whole subcontinent until assurances were made for a speedier demobilisation, and the first strike in the history of the RAF ended in January 1946. Interestingly, hardly anyone was punished for these protests, as few "regular" RAF personnel were involved. The RAF Police tried to infiltrate the ranks to discover the ring-leaders but – as the RAF Police normally wore trousers instead of shorts – they were easily spotted due to their pale knees among the heavily tanned airmen!

Following Indian independence in 1947, the RAF withdrew from the region. That was until November 1970, when a cyclone devastated the coastal area of East Pakistan. As part of Operation Burlap, the VC10s of 10 Squadron flew medical

and other supplies to Dhaka in what was to become Bangladesh. From there they were distributed by the Hercules of 48 Squadron. The following year, further heavy rains brought yet more flooding to East Pakistan. Some 400,000lb of supplies were brought in by VC10s of 10 Squadron, Belfasts of 53 Squadron and Hercules of 24, 30, 36, 47 and 48 Squadrons. These also brought in medical supplies to prevent a cholera epidemic.

Civil war between West and East Pakistan eventually involved India from November 1971. Dhaka was surrounded by Indian forces by 12 December, leaving only the air as an escape route for British civilians. The RAF Hercules of 70 Squadron evacuated 409 Britons before Indian AF Hunters destroyed the runway; 925 evacuees were also airlifted from West Pakistan.

The RAF is no longer present in this corner of the old empire, but relations with the countries of the region remain strong, due to a shared history and a shared ethos in both war and peace.

Nandu Varuval
Tamilian–Style Masala Fried Crab

by CYRUS TODIWALA OBE DL
CAFÉ SPICE NAMASTÉ

Crab is popular across the coastal belt of India, as well as the interior of the country where, near several rivers, land crabs flourish. Hundreds of crab recipes abound along both the western and eastern coasts of India; this is a Tamilian-style recipe that hails from the area around the city of Madras, now Chennai. It includes two methods for killing the crabs: boiling in water and, for those loath to do so, placing them in the freezer so they are numbed to any pain and can be used raw.

INGREDIENTS

Serves 4

For the nandu varuval

2 large whole crabs

1 tbsp ground turmeric

2 tbsp vegetable oil

2 medium onions, finely chopped

5cm piece of ginger, peeled

4-5 large cloves of garlic, peeled and pulped to a paste along with the ginger

2-3 medium tomatoes, finely chopped or pulped in a blender

salt (to taste)

1 tbsp chilli powder

1½ tsp ground coriander

20-25 fresh curry leaves, shredded (use dried if not available but the flavour will differ)

3 tbsp coriander (stalks and leaves), coarsely chopped

To serve

boiled white rice or chapati

METHOD

To prepare the crab

- If boiling the crabs, clean them well and rinse under cold running water, place in a deep vessel (dead or alive) and pour over enough lightly salted boiling water to just cover them.
- Cook for 2 to 3 minutes, drain the water and set the crabs to one side. When slightly cooled, clean and cut into the desired sized pieces. Remove the feathery gills, crack the claws with the back of a large knife and toss in the ground turmeric.
- If using the freezer method, just cut the crabs into pieces, clean and wash them, and toss them with the turmeric, making sure you coat the exposed meat as much as possible.
- Check the quantity you have and select the cooking pan accordingly.
- Heat the oil and sauté the onions until slightly browned or pale golden in colour. Add the ginger and garlic paste; fry for a minute or so until the garlic changes colour.
- As soon as the garlic has changed colour, add the tomatoes, salt, chilli powder and ground coriander. You can add a few spoons of the water in which you cooked the crab (or, if cooking from raw, a couple of tablespoons of boiling water) to the masala to prevent the ground spices from sticking.
- Continue to sauté the mixture until the oil begins to separate from the masala and most of the moisture has evaporated.
- Add the cut crab, shredded curry leaves and chopped coriander (add some finely chopped green chillies if you like).
- Toss everything together for around 5 minutes if using boiled crab or for around 10 to 15 minutes if cooking from raw, until all the crab pieces are nicely coated with the masala and, in the case of raw crab, cooked.
- Take off the heat and check the seasoning.

To serve

- It is best to eat this dish with your fingers.
- Clean out and eat as much crab meat as you can, and then use the remaining juice to serve with white rice or chapati.

NEPAL

Words by
WARRANT OFFICER SIMON FELLOWS

NEPAL, LANDLOCKED BETWEEN China and India, is a mountainous region that's home to eight of the world's highest peaks, including Everest. Its population predominantly live in the southern hills and lowlands, the largest city being Kathmandu. It is home to the Ghurkhas, who have been an integral part of the British Army for more than 200 years.

In the early 1970s, after a number of very poor harvests and torrential rains, the Nepalese requested emergency assistance from Britain. Prime Minister Edward Heath authorised the Royal Air Force to initiate the largest airlift since Berlin in 1948 and, subsequently, 24 Squadron Hercules transport aircraft were deployed – along with supporting personnel – under the name Operation Khana Cascade. The advanced party from the RAF's 46 Group, based at RAF Lyneham, arrived in Nepal on 15 February 1973, via refuel stops in Cyprus and Masirah in the Persian Gulf.

Two airfields were initially used for the relief task: RAF Bhairawa in the west, near the Indian border, and RAF Bretenga in the east, with a plan to deliver 1,850 tons in 60 days. The first flight took off from Bhairawa on 2 March and was the first of more than 150 relief drops. Each Hercules carried approximately 10 tons of food, grain and maize per sortie, triple-wrapped on pallets and "free-dropped" without parachute, via the ramp at the rear of the aircraft.

Although crews normally train and fly at 250ft for daylight drops, in Nepal these were carried out at much lower levels, through very difficult terrain. It was arduous work for all concerned, with aircraft heavily tasked on flying duties or in maintenance in difficult environmental conditions. Fuel was housed in large rubber bladders and piped into the aircraft using heavy hoses. At night the Hercules were loaded by army air dispatch teams, thus enabling flying to continue at first light.

The detachment base at Bhairawa held 144 personnel supporting the operation, with field kitchens, messes, a post office and recreational areas all providing some normality. The Task Force Commander, Group Captain Cedric Symonds, would also visit to monitor moral, although sometimes necessitating impromptu inspections of the area that was known as "Canvas City", much to the ground crew's chagrin.

On 21 March 1973 another crucial airstrip at South Kemp was finally dry enough to accept the weight of the Hercules, enabling even more supplies to be provided. By 30 March the last airdrop was mounted, bringing Operation Khana Cascade to an end. During the whole of the operation, 1,756 tons of grain was dropped, from 153 sorties; 129 from Bhairawa alone.

In the aftermath, the then Under-Secretary of State in Heath's government, Anthony Royle, stated how successful Operation Khana Cascade had been.

"The operation has gone very well indeed," he said in an address to Parliament. "I am glad to take this opportunity to pay tribute to the RAF and army personnel involved for their hard work and efficiency and to express appreciation for the effective support arrangements made by the Nepalese authorities. I am confident that this British effort will greatly strengthen the bonds of friendship between Nepal and the United Kingdom."

Aircraft XV202, one of the three C-130K Hercules used, can now be seen at the RAF Museum, RAF Cosford.

Nepali Momos
Nepalese Steamed Dumplings

Momos are bite-sized meat dumplings, steamed or boiled, wrapped in a simple flour dough, and popular throughout Nepal and Tibet. There are fish and vegetarian varieties, but traditionally the filling can be pork, chicken, lamb, turkey, water buffalo, yak or goat, mixed with a fatty pork mince to prevent dryness. This recipe includes a tomato achar, a popular pickle to accompany the momos.

INGREDIENTS
Makes around 40

For the golbheda ko achar
(tomato achar)

400g baby plum or cherry tomatoes

1 tbsp mustard oil (or vegetable oil)

1 tsp cumin seeds

2 tsp mustard seeds

½ medium red onion, finely diced

4 cloves of garlic, finely chopped

1.25cm piece of ginger, finely grated

2 red chillies, finely chopped

½ tsp timur (ground Szechuan
  pepper) or cayenne pepper

METHOD
To make the golbheda ko achar

- Preheat the oven to 220°C.
- Toss the tomatoes in a little oil, place on a baking sheet and roast for 20 minutes until charred. Allow to cool slightly then remove and pinch off the charred skin. Reserve the roasting juices.
- Heat the oil in a frying pan, add the cumin and mustard seeds and fry for about a minute until they start to pop. Add the onion and continue to cook, stirring frequently, until it starts to soften. Add the garlic, ginger, chillies, timur (or cayenne pepper), turmeric, ground coriander and ground fenugreek. Cook for a couple of minutes.
- Transfer the mix to a blender with the roast tomatoes. Add the juices from the roasting tray, the coriander and the lime juice, and blend to a smooth purée. Season with salt and set aside to cool completely.

½ tsp turmeric

½ tsp ground coriander

¼ tsp ground fenugreek

2 tbsp coriander, coarsely chopped

1 lime, juiced

salt

For the momo wrappers
(or use 40 ready-made wonton wrappers)

250g plain flour (plus extra for
 dusting)

½ tsp salt

1 tbsp vegetable oil

125ml water (room temperature)

For the spice mix

1½ tsp garam masala

1 tsp soft brown sugar

½ tsp ground coriander

¼ tsp ground fenugreek

¼ tsp ground cumin

¼ tsp ground turmeric

a pinch of ground nutmeg

For the filling

250g minced pork

250g minced chicken, turkey,
 lamb or beef

½ medium red onion, finely chopped

2 spring onions, finely chopped

2 mild/medium hot red chillies,
 deseeded and finely chopped

1 hot green chilli, deseeded and
 finely chopped

2.5cm piece of ginger, finely grated

3 cloves of garlic, finely chopped

25g coriander, coarsely chopped

2 tbsp vegetable oil

salt and pepper

To make the momo wrappers

- Sift the flour into a large bowl, mix in the salt, add the oil and gradually add the water, mixing with your hands or a wooden spoon, until the dough just starts to form a mass.
- Turn the dough out onto a floured surface and knead for about 5 minutes until it is smooth and elastic, adding a little more flour or water if the dough is too wet or dry.
- Return the dough to the mixing bowl, cover with a tea towel and leave at room temperature for 30 minutes to rest.

To prepare the spice mix

- Mix all of the spice ingredients together.

To prepare the filling

- Mix all of the ingredients in a bowl with the spice mix, season with salt and pepper and fry a small patty in a little oil to check the seasoning. Add a little more salt and pepper to mix as necessary.
- Cover the bowl with cling film, place in the fridge for an hour.

To make the momos

- Divide the dough into 40 equal sized pieces (about 10g each), roll into small balls, flatten with the palm of your hand and roll out as thin as possible with a rolling pin to about 8.5cm in diameter (they can be neatened with a suitable sized pastry cutter)
- Place a wonton wrapper in the palm of your hand or on a work surface, place a heaped teaspoon of the filling in the centre, moisten the edge with your finger dipped in a little cold water and, one by one, fold in half and seal the edges creating small pleats on one side as you go creating a crescent shape. Repeat with the remaining wonton wrappers keeping them covered with a damp tea towel or cling film to prevent them from drying out.

To cook the momos

- To steam: oil the steamer rack to prevent the momos from sticking, bring the water to a rapid simmer and steam the momos for 10 minutes until the filling is cooked through. Alternatively the momos can be cooked in lightly salted simmering water for 10 minutes.

To serve

- Transfer the momos to a serving plate and serve with a bowl of the tomato achar to either spoon over or to dip the momos.

CYPRUS

Words by
SQUADRON LEADER HELEN TRAIN

ON 1 JULY 1955, 30 RAF personnel established themselves on the flat, dry scrubland of a windswept peninsula. The location, RAF Akrotiri in Cyprus, was to become the most important RAF station outside the UK and a key staging post for operations in the Middle East. Few RAF personnel have not spent some time at Akrotiri during their tenure.

By the end of August 1956, a massive influx of personnel meant that RAF Akrotiri was home to 260 officers and 2,864 other ranks. This included around 1,430 personnel on the daily sick-parade, mainly the result of the over-crowding and insanitary conditions, as construction lagged behind the demand for accommodation. Eventually, roads were made and hangars and permanent buildings constructed.

The idyllic lifestyle at this successful base came to an abrupt halt when the Turkish government sent troops to the island to protect Turkish Cypriots, following a military coup. Fighting began on the island on 15 July 1974, changing the lives of the military families based in Cyprus.

At this time, 15,000 people associated with the military were living in Limassol. Most had good relations with their Greek Cypriot and Turkish Cypriot neighbours. Initially, Nicosia was declared out of bounds but, as the coup spread, Limassol, Larnaca and Famagusta were also placed on the prohibited list, and the order was given to evacuate British families from Limassol on 20 July 1974. This process was hugely assisted by the British Forces Broadcasting Service (BFBS), which was providing regular bulletins to families; all service men were recalled to work to assist.

At a British nursery school in Limassol, men were being killed outside while the wife of an officer managed to keep 70 children under the age of five safe by persuading them to stay on the school floor. Later, with RAF Police assistance, she personally delivered every one of her charges safely home to their parents.

Once the evacuated families arrived at RAF Akrotiri, they were formed up in orderly queues. Each household from RAF Akrotiri was then requested to collect and accommodate three or four families from this stage and compensatory rations were dispatched onto the front lawns twice a day. This continued until these families could be evacuated back to the UK, with just a single suitcase in their possession.

The events of 1974 served to reinforce the strengths of the military families. Group Captain K J Parfit, Station Commander RAF Episkopi, recalls: "I shall always remember with pride the cheerful, zealous and selfless way in which serving personnel, civilians, wives and dependants alike combined their prodigious efforts to overcome every besetting contingency throughout this final phase in the station's history."

PAY PARADE AT RAF AKROTIRI IN CYPRUS, 1960

Grilled Halloumi & Watermelon Salad

This recipe is based on a classic Cypriot combination. Halloumi and watermelon are often served for breakfast but it is also great as a starter, snack or light lunch. Although simple, this recipe has a careful balance of temperature, texture and flavour combinations – salty olives, hot halloumi, cold and sweet watermelon, with a hint of sour from the balsamic vinegar.

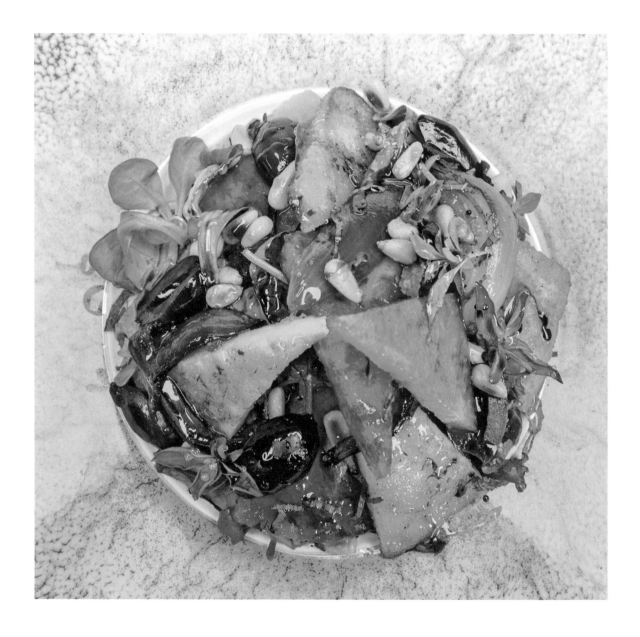

INGREDIENTS

Serves 4

For the roast onions

1 tsp olive oil

1 small red onion, peeled and
 cut into 8 wedges

salt and pepper

For the salad

2 tsp olive oil

250g halloumi cheese,
 cut into 4 thick slices

¼ watermelon, seeds removed and
 cut into 4cm long pieces (chilled)

3 tbsp extra virgin olive oil

1 tbsp mint leaves, shredded

100g salad leaves

50g kalamata olives, pitted and
 halved

4 tsp runny honey

4 tsp balsamic vinegar

2 tbsp pine nuts, toasted

fresh oregano leaves, picked

mint tips, picked

METHOD

To roast the onions

• Preheat the oven to 180°C.

• Toss the onion wedges in the olive oil and season lightly with salt
 and freshly ground black pepper.

• Place the onions on a baking tray and roast in the oven for about
 15 to 20 minutes until well browned and soft; set aside at room
 temperature to cool.

To prepare the salad

• Rub the sliced halloumi with the olive oil and cook on a griddle pan
 or barbecue until hot through to the middle, cut each slice into four
 even-sized pieces and keep hot. Alternatively, coat the halloumi slices
 in seasoned flour and shallow fry in a little olive oil (the flour can
 be plain and seasoned with salt and freshly ground black pepper
 or flavoured with spices such as chilli powder/flakes, paprika and
 cinnamon or chopped herbs such as oregano, mint, basil and parsley).

• While the halloumi is grilling, toss the watermelon in a bowl with half
 of the extra virgin olive oil and half of the shredded mint.

To serve

• Dress the salad leaves on a serving dish or individual plates, arrange
 the chilled watermelon, hot halloumi and roast onions on top of the
 salad leaves.

• Scatter over the olives, drizzle with honey (for an added sweetness
 if preferred), balsamic vinegar and the remaining extra virgin olive oil.

• Scatter over the toasted pine nuts and garnish with sprigs of oregano
 and mint tips.

BELIZE

Words by
FLIGHT LIEUTENANT TOM MARSHALL

LYING ON THE Caribbean coast, Belize is the only country in Central America whose official language is English, and is a proud part of the Commonwealth. Until 1973, it was known as British Honduras, gaining full independence from the UK in September 1981. Due to a long-standing land dispute, its neighbour Guatemala did not recognise Belize as an independent nation until 1991.

Prior to independence, RAF Transport Command helped provide humanitarian relief following Hurricane Hattie in 1961, which almost destroyed the then capital Belize City. But it was in the following decade that the Royal Air Force – and in particular its Harrier and Puma forces – got to know the country intimately.

In 1975, with Guatemala in the grip of a bloody civil war, there was a real fear that Guatemalan forces might invade Belize, or at the very least widen their Caribbean coastline. To bolster the resident British Army garrison, a detachment of six Hawker Siddeley Harrier GR.1As from 1 Squadron RAF Wittering was sent to the international airport at Ladyville in November 1975. This was a precursor to the modern air-power concept of the RAF being an Expeditionary Air Force; small and agile yet having a big impact. The show of force by the Harriers, deployed from various semi-permanent hides, helped keep the peace for over 20 years.

As a posting, RAF Belize quickly became a bit of a gem, particularly for the Harrier pilots. This was due primarily to the lack of restrictions placed on them with regards flying, but also because of the challenging nature of the missions they faced.

However, not all missions were politically motivated. In the late 1970s, the RAF decided to send a public relations team to the country to film the Harriers operating in this exotic location. It was decided to shoot a bit of film over the Caye Chapel's runway, which was little more than a powdered coral strip with a hardened surface. Unfortunately, the pilot came to a hover over the runway too low and the jet efflux ate through the surface, releasing the powdered coral underneath, which was immediately sucked up by the engine and jammed the reaction controls, forcing it into an unrecoverable heavy landing. This then left an RAF jet stranded on a coral atoll, miles from anywhere, with a bemused film crew having witnessed the whole event.

From an official perspective, however, the Harriers of 1417 Flight were instrumental in securing diplomatic assurances for the future of Belize, after taking part in air shows at La Aurora International Airport, Guatemala City, for the 68th and 70th anniversaries of the Guatemalan Air Force in 1990 and 1991, respectively.

Belize remained a training area for the British military through until 2011, when the last of its forces left Ladyville Barracks, leaving behind only those retired Harrier pilots who had bought hotels in this Caribbean paradise.

A HARRIER JUMP JET IN THE BELIZE JUNGLE, 1975

Fry Jacks
Belizean Breakfast Fritters

In Belize, these fritters are usually eaten for breakfast with refried beans, eggs, bacon and sausage. But are also great eaten on their own, as in the recipe below, with fresh berries, dusted with sugar and drizzled with honey.

INGREDIENTS
Serves 4–8
For the fry jacks
250g plain flour
2 tsp baking powder
½ tsp salt
10g baking fat
200ml cold water
vegetable oil for frying

To serve
icing sugar to dust
jam, golden syrup, maple syrup
  or honey
fresh berries

METHOD
To make the dough
• Sift the flour, baking powder and salt into a large mixing bowl.
• Add the baking fat and rub into the flour.
• Gradually add enough of the water to make a smooth dough and knead for a minute until smooth.
• Divide the dough into eight equal-sized pieces, roll into balls, set aside covered with a tea towel for 20 minutes.

To cook the fry jacks
• Roll each ball of dough into a circle about 15cm in diameter.
• Cut each circle into halves or quarters and cut a slit in each piece.
• Pour vegetable oil to a depth of around 8cm into a large pan and heat to 180°C (alternatively the jacks can be deep fried).
• Fry the jacks on each side until golden brown and puffed up and drain on kitchen paper.

To serve
• Either serve the fry jacks as part of your cooked breakfast or stacked on a plate dusted with icing sugar and served with jam, golden syrup, maple syrup or honey and fresh berries.

FALKLAND ISLANDS

Words by
SQUADRON LEADER NAT WINSOR

SEAPLANES HAD ALREADY landed in Stanley Harbour when, in 1952, the Falkland Islands Company commissioned Aquila Airways to fly from Britain to the South Atlantic. Aquila used a Hudson Royal Mail flying boat from its base in Southampton to make the journey over a seven-day period, requiring six stops en route. Later, from February 1971, the Argentine military airline LADE (Líneas Aéreas del Estado) operated seaplanes on a bi-weekly basis, and in 1973 an airstrip was co-funded by the UK and Argentina and built at Hookers Point. Sir Vivian Fuchs, an English explorer who completed the first overland crossing of Antarctica, subsequently opened Port Stanley Airport there in 1979.

However, the first time that the Royal Air Force really became involved in the Falkland Islands was during the 1982 conflict, when a British task force was deployed in defence of the islands. The RAF elements included: 10 Harrier GR3s, transported on the container ships *Atlantic Conveyor* and *Atlantic Causeway*; eight Chinook HC1s, transported on the *Atlantic Conveyor* and MV *Contender Bezant*; and RAF Regiment gunners, operating short-range air defence missiles. The GR3s subsequently operated alongside RN Sea Harriers on HMS *Hermes*. Ascension Island saw three Phantom FGR 2 arrive for air defence and a substantial number of Nimrod, Victor, Vulcan and C130 aircraft, which flew countless hours in support of Operation Corporate.

While preparing to unload, *Atlantic Conveyor* was struck by two Exocet missiles fired from a pair of Super Etendards from the 2nd Argentine Attack Squadron, Rio Gallegos. The six Harriers had already disembarked to HMS *Hermes*, but three of the four Chinooks were still onboard and were lost. The other one, known as Bravo November, serial No. ZA7183, was fortunately airborne so survived. Later in the conflict, Bravo November struck a lake en route to San Carlos, having delivered three 105mm guns and 8,300 rounds of ammunition to Mount Kent, but again survived to tell the tale. It now has its own Wikipedia page,

having seen action in every major conflict involving the RAF since.

Seven Vulcan bombing missions were planned against the runway at Port Stanley Airport, departing from Ascension Island under Operation Blackbuck. These missions were extremely complex and planning was ably assisted by a £4.95 pocket calculator bought in Swaffham Market. The bombers carried either a load of 1,000 lb bombs or AGM-45A Shrike anti-radar missiles and flew 6,800 nautical miles over 16 hours; the longest-ranged bombing raid in history, surpassed only by the USAF in the 1991 Gulf War.

After the conflict, once Port Stanley runway was re-opened, four RAF Phantom FGR.2s were based there in order to provide a measure of defence and warning, lest the Argentine forces should attempt another invasion. In 1985, RAF Mount Pleasant was created outside of Stanley in order to house the permanent military presence on the islands. Tornado F3s arrived in 1992, and Typhoons in 2009. Transport support originally came from C-130K Hercules, VC-10 and Tristar tankers, however, there are now C-130J Hercules and A-330 Voyager aircraft.

The RAF Regiment continued to operate Rapier air defence missiles until 2005, when the role was handed over to the Royal Artillery.

Last, but certainly not least, is the sterling search-and-rescue service provided from the end of the Falklands conflict until March 2016 by RAF Sea King helicopters. During their watch they responded to over 1,300 separate callouts, giving much needed assistance to nearly 2,000 people.

THE FLIGHT DECK OF HMS HERMES IN THE SOUTH ATLANTIC, 1982

Grilled Trout
with Lemon & Herbs

Due to the large farming community and unpredictable weather, the cuisine of the Falklands is quite robust, comprising roast meat and stews. The local soil is acidic and infertile so, although some vegetables and salads are grown locally in nurseries, most are imported. The estuaries, inlets and several rivers of the islands are full of beautiful sea (brown) trout, available between September and April. This recipe showcases the delicate flavour of the trout infused with aromatic herbs, served with herby butter dressing. Try it with steamed vegetables and new potatoes.

INGREDIENTS

Serves 4

For the trout

4 whole trout, cleaned and scaled

1 lemon, cut into 6 thin slices and
  halved

12 sprigs of parsley

12 sprigs of dill

12 sprigs of tarragon

12 sprigs of thyme

4 bay leaves

½ small red onion, thinly sliced

3 tbsp olive oil

salt and pepper

For the herb butter

75g butter

1 tbsp parsley, coarsely chopped

1 tbsp tarragon, coarsely chopped

1 tbsp dill, coarsely chopped

½ lemon

To serve

½ lemon, cut into wedges

steamed vegetables, e.g. purple
  sprouting broccoli, chantenay
  carrots, fine green beans and
  fennel

METHOD

To stuff the trout

• Trim the fins from the trout, season the inside with salt and pepper. Stuff each fish with three half slices of lemon, 3 sprigs each of the herbs, a bay leaf and a quarter of the sliced red onion.

To cook the trout

• Heat a griddle pan over a medium heat and rub the trout on both sides with olive oil.

• Cook the fish for 5 to 6 minutes on each side until cooked through; trout is very delicate so it is important that, during cooking, it is not moved or lifted until it is ready to be turned over.

• While the trout is cooking, heat the butter over a moderate heat until foaming. Remove from the heat and stir in the chopped herbs and squeeze in the lemon juice.

To serve

• Season the cooked trout with a little sea salt and freshly ground black pepper to taste. Place on warmed plates and pour over the herb butter. Serve with the lemon wedges and steamed vegetables.

CHILE

Words by
FLIGHT LIEUTENANT TOM MARSHALL

CHILE HAS NEVER officially been an ally of the UK, but the Royal Air Force has enjoyed an almost covert relationship with the important and diverse country. During the Second World War, Chile tried to remain neutral despite pressure from other countries in the region to support the Axis powers. However, for one lady at least, this situation was unacceptable and she travelled halfway around the world to join the RAF's Air Transport Auxiliary (ATA).

The ATA was responsible for ferrying every variety of RAF aircraft around the UK, relieving the burden on the front-line pilots and solving an extremely important logistical issue for the RAF. It was largely made up of pilots who were either too old or had been too badly injured to fly for the front-line commands. It was also revolutionary in that it both trained and employed women as pilots.

Margot Duhalde qualified in Chile as a pilot in 1938 before joining the ATA. She made 1,360 flights delivering Halifax, Liberator, Wellington, Mosquito, Mustang, Spitfire, Hurricane and Swordfish aircraft. She was awarded the French Legion d'Honneur before returning to Chile to work as an instructor. However, upon first arriving in Britain, she spoke no English, and was grounded until she had learned. The techies tasked to teach her nicknamed her "Chile", but it soon became apparent that the plan was flawed as she knew no English beyond the swear words the engineers thought it funny to teach her.

Following the war, the RAF maintained good relations with Chile, with various squadrons visiting over the years. Then, in the spring of 1982, the world's focus was drawn to the small collection of sparsely populated islands in the South Atlantic called the Falklands. Publically, Chile adopted a position of "strict neutrality"; a policy dictated by its need to defer to Latin American solidarity with Argentina. However, due in no small part to its own long-running dispute with Argentina over the sovereignty of the Beagle Channel, Chile helped the UK in a covert manner. Shortly after the start of the conflict, a Wing Commander Sidney Edwards was received by the Chief of the Chilean Air Staff, General Fernando Aubel. Edwards brought a personal message from the Chief of the Air Staff of the RAF and requested an urgent interview.

The exact nature of Edwards's work can be read in detail in official files and his own book *My Secret Falklands War,* but, in short, the RAF suddenly gained access to bases, long-range radar and intelligence, all within a short distance of the conflict.

At the Chilean airport on the island of San Felix, the RAF stationed several aircraft, disguised in Chilean colours. However, the Wing Commander purposefully never met the country's dictator; General Pinochet. This allowed Pinochet complete deniability, despite being an ally of the then British Prime Minister, Margaret Thatcher.

When an SAS mission in an RAF Sea King helicopter went wrong, Edwards quickly held a press conference claiming it was a routine flight and nothing to do with the conflict. A Chilean journalist did not believe him and continued to investigate the matter until he was kidnapped by Pinochet's officials. He survived, but this was a stark reminder of the type of administration Edwards was dealing with.

Following the end of the conflict, the MoD sold three Canberra aircraft to the Chilean Air Force, which it flew out of RAF Wyton later that year. Since then, official RAF involvement with the country has been mostly limited to skiing and gliding expeditions, taking advantage of the magnificent Chilean natural landscape and, of course, food.

Empanada de Pino de Horno
Chilean Baked Beef Pastry

Portuguese in origin, empanadas are prevalent throughout Latin America, Europe and Southwest USA in a plethora of diverse-shaped pastries. Chile has three main types: cheese, seafood, and beef (or "Pino"), the last being the nation's favourite. Its dough is similar to a hot-water pastry, and it is usually baked and occasionally deep fried. To retain its texture, the beef should not be minced but chilled, cut into thin slices and then cut into a fine dice. The filling can be made and chilled just before stuffing the empanadas, but it benefits from being made a day before and chilling overnight.

INGREDIENTS

Makes 12

For the pebre (Chilean chilli salsa)

50g coriander (including stalks),
  coarsely chopped

6 spring onions, halved lengthways
  and finely sliced

4 cloves of garlic, finely chopped
  or crushed

2–4 hot red chillies, finely diced

1 large tomato, peeled, deseeded
  and cut into small dice

1 tsp dried red chilli flake

2 tbsp red wine vinegar

1 tbsp olive oil

1 lime, juiced

salt and pepper

For the filling

400g beef topside, cut into very
  small dice

1½ tsp ground cumin

1½ tsp paprika

1½ tsp cumin seeds

1½ tbsp vegetable or sunflower oil

2 medium onions, finely diced

2 tsp plain flour

100ml beef stock

20g raisins, soaked in a little
  boiling water

2 tsp dried oregano

1–2 red chillies, finely chopped
  (optional)

salt and pepper

12 black olives, pitted and
  halved

3 hardboiled eggs, cut into
  4 crossways slices each

METHOD

To make the pebre

- Mix the chopped coriander, spring onions, garlic, chillies, tomatoes and dried chilli flakes together in a non-metallic bowl.
- Stir in the vinegar, olive oil and lime juice, and season with salt and pepper.
- Pour over 125ml of hot (not boiling) water, stir and set aside to cool at room temperature. Once cool, cover the bowl and leave for a couple of hours in the fridge to allow the flavours to deepen and develop.

To make the filling

- Mix the beef with the ground cumin and paprika in a bowl, cover and marinate in the fridge for 30 minutes.
- Heat a large frying pan or sauteuse over a moderate heat, add the cumin seeds and toast until they are fragrant and start to pop. Add the oil and onions; reduce the heat to a low setting and cook, stirring frequently, for 10 to 15 minutes until softened but not coloured.
- Increase the heat, add the marinated beef, season lightly with salt and cook, stirring continuously, until the beef is lightly browned.
- Stir in the flour, cook for a minute, pour in the stock, drained raisins, oregano and chillies (if using). Bring to a simmer and stir until the sauce is smooth. Season with salt and pepper.
- Set the filling aside to cool completely and refrigerate until required.

To make the pastry

- Pour the milk and water into a saucepan with the salt and heat until tepid. Whisk in the beaten egg and melted butter.
- Tip the flour onto the work surface, make a well in the centre and pour in three quarters of the liquid. Mix the liquid into the flour with your hands, adding more liquid as required.
- Knead the dough for about 5 minutes until it is smooth and elastic.

To make the empanadas

- Preheat the oven to 200°C.
- Divide the dough into 12 equal sized pieces, roll each into a ball and cover with a clean tea towel.
- Make the empanadas one at a time; roll the dough to a thickness

For the pastry

125ml milk

125ml water

1 tsp salt

1 egg, beaten

75g butter, melted

400g plain flour

1 large egg, beaten to glaze

of around 3mm into a 15cm-diameter circle.

- Place about two level tablespoons of the beef mix neatly on one half of the circle, push 2 olive halves into the beef mix and place a slice of boiled egg on top. Sprinkle the egg with a little salt and pepper.
- Fold the dough over the filling and, ensuring there is no trapped air inside, press the edges firmly together to seal.
- Crimp the edge of the empanada by folding small sections of the sealed edge over on itself or, for a traditional shape, fold the sealed edges over to form a rectangle (or for chilli empanadas into a traditional triangle shape). Chill for 30 minutes before baking (this will help to ensure the edges seal and prevent leaks)
- Brush with a little beaten egg, prick the top with a skewer or toothpick to allow the steam to escape during cooking, place on a baking sheet and cook in the preheated oven for 30 to 35 minutes until golden brown on top and piping hot inside.

To serve

- Let the empanadas sit for 5 minutes at room temperature then serve with the pebre.

ASCENSION ISLAND

Words by
SQUADRON LEADER NAT WINSOR

VOLCANOES RISE FROM the seabed along the mid-Atlantic ridge that separates Africa from South America. Some of these rise above sea-level to create islands and – along with the Azores, Cape Verde, St Helena and Tristan de Cunha – these include Ascension Island. While the first aircraft landing at Ascension was not made until 15 June 1942, the history of how there came to be a runway in the middle of the South Atlantic and why we were there at all is worth a mention.

The island was discovered by Portuguese explorer Joao de Nova in 1501 and rediscovered by Portuguese general Afonso de Albuquerque in 1503, who named it Ascension Island after the day he dropped anchor. However, neither registered a claim, and there was no indigenous population. From then until 1815 it was used as a mail drop by the UK and the Netherlands on Far East routings. In 1815, Napoleon Bonaparte was imprisoned on St Helena and 60 Royal Navy personnel were garrisoned on Ascension Island to prevent the French from building a liberating force. The Rear Admiral who delivered Napoleon, Sir George Cockburn, declared the island "HMS Ascension".

In 1899, the first telegraph cables from the UK to South Africa and South America were laid across the Atlantic seabed, and when, in October 1922, the British military moved off the island, the manager of the Eastern Telegraph Company became the head of the island. The military returned during the Second World War in the shape of the US who, under agreement with the UK government, built Wideawake Airfield to enable aircraft to be shuttled from Brazil to Africa in support of the North African Campaign.

The UK deployed a small RAF detachment, which led to the first landing in 1942 by an RAF Swordfish on anti-submarine recce from HMS *Archer*, delivering important information to the Admiralty. However, there were no more significant events during this period and after the war, both militaries left the island. The US returned in the 1950s to use the island as a base for its Eastern Test Range tracking missile firings, while NASA also tracked the Moon landings and Space Shuttle flights from there.

However, all changed in 1982 when Argentina invaded the Falkland Islands. Halfway between the UK and the Falklands, Ascension Island proved to be a vital staging post during the Falklands Conflict. As luck would have it, the United States Air Force-administered airfield had a long runway and ample parking for large aircraft and helicopters. Ships could also be refueled there, with over 12½ million gallons of fuel having been transferred to the UK task force before it set sail on 18 April.

The famous Operation Black Buck bombing raid on Port Stanley airfield, which included 11 Victor Tankers and two Vulcan Bombers, was launched to fly a total return distance of 6,800 nautical miles from Ascension Island to the Falkland Islands and back. Three Harrier GR3s were positioned on Ascension Island to provide air defence to counter any Argentinian long-range attack – these were later replaced by three F4 Phantoms. For a time, it was actually the busiest airfield in the world, logging even more aircraft movements than Chicago O'Hare International or London Heathrow.

Ascension Island has been described as "the hub of the greatest British logistic operation since 1945". It remains essential in the air resupply of the Falkland Islands by the RAF.

> *"Halfway between the UK and the Falklands, Ascension Island proved to be a vital staging post during the Falklands Conflict"*

Saint Helenian Fishcakes

As there is no indigenous or permanent population on Ascension Island, the food culture is dictated by its transient inhabitants. The majority of them come from the neighbouring island of Saint Helena, most famous as the location of Napoleon's exile from 1815 until his death in 1821. These fishcakes are made with fresh tuna, which is plentiful in both Saint Helena and Ascension Island, but can be made with tinned tuna, salmon or any white or smoked fish with firm flesh. These fishcakes are very versatile: they can be made as a starter, main course or in a soft bap as a snack.

INGREDIENTS

Serves 4

For the fishcakes

250g floury potatoes, peeled and
  cut into large even-sized pieces

25g butter

250g fresh tuna fillet or drained
  canned tuna pieces

4 tbsp sunflower oil

1 medium onion, finely diced

50g streaky bacon, finely diced

1 clove of garlic, finely chopped
  or crushed

2 medium red chillies, deseeded
  and finely diced

¼ tsp dried thyme

1 tbsp parsley, roughly chopped

salt and white pepper

flour to dust

**For the sweet chilli and
capsicum salsa**

1 red pepper, finely diced

½ medium red onion, finely diced

1 clove of garlic, finely chopped
  or crushed

1 tbsp coriander, coarsely chopped

75ml sweet chilli sauce

1 tbsp olive oil

½ lemon, juiced

salt and pepper

To serve

2 handfuls of mixed salad leaves

½ lemon, cut into 4 wedges

METHOD

To make the fishcakes

- Boil the potatoes in salted water until soft, drain well, mash and season with salt and a little white pepper.
- Mix the butter into the hot mashed potatoes and set aside to cool.
- If using fresh tuna, poach in a little lightly salted simmering water until cooked through, drain and set aside to cool.
- Heat 1 tsp of the oil in a frying pan over a moderate heat and cook the onions with a pinch of salt for 5 minutes until they have started to soften, add the bacon and continue to cook for a further 5 minutes. Add the garlic, chillies and thyme; cook for another couple of minutes until soft. Drain off any excess oil.
- Set the onion mix to one side to cool, meanwhile flake the tuna into large pieces.
- Add the onion mix to the mashed potatoes with the chopped parsley, mix well, taste the mix and season with salt and pepper.
- Carefully fold the flaked tuna pieces into the potato mix, taking care not to break the pieces up too much.
- Shape the fishcake mix into 8 slightly flattened balls and place in the fridge to chill well before use.

To make the salsa

- Mix the diced red pepper, red onion, garlic, chopped coriander, sweet chilli sauce, olive oil and lemon juice together in a bowl. Season to taste with salt and pepper.

To cook the fishcakes

- Season a little flour with salt and pepper.
- Coat the fish cakes with the flour. Dust off the excess and shallow fry in the remaining sunflower oil over a medium heat for around 4 to 5 minutes on either side until golden brown and heated through to the middle.

To serve

- Serve two fishcakes per portion with a little mixed leaf salad, a lemon wedge and the sweet chilli and capsicum salsa.

A BOEING CHINOOK HELICOPTER TRANSFERS A DAIMLER FERRET FROM BEIRUT TO THE SUPPORT SHIP RFA RELIANT, 1984

LEBANON

Words by
AIR COMMODORE MARK GILLIGAN
& FLIGHT LIEUTENANT CHRISTOPHER COOPMAN

AS THE UK'S military sought to recover from its efforts in the Falklands Conflict of 1982, the British government's attention was diverted to the Middle East. Lebanon was on the point of civil war. Its government's forces had been fighting a collection of militias and had asked for United Nations support to maintain the peace.

The Americans, French, Italians and British all responded to a request for peacekeeping forces, with The Queen's Dragoon Guards of the British Army sent to Beirut in January 1983. Initially, life for the soldiers was relatively safe, to the extent that they were able to ski and sunbathe on their "down days". Indeed, when the British Embassy was inadvertently hit by a rocket, the offending militia commander personally contacted the ambassador to apologise for the stray ordinance – and promptly moved the fight half a mile down the road!

Things were to change in September 1983, when an eruption of violence in Beirut left the UK soldiers feeling isolated. With no safe land route back to the Mediterranean, they needed to be re-supplied by other means. The UK Cabinet directed the RAF to provide support through both the delivery of supplies and to show that bomber aircraft could support British troops in any fight.

Both of these tasks were conducted by squadrons that were only too pleased to switch the UK's autumnal weather for Cypriot sun. As an overt demonstration to the militias of the UK's ability to respond quickly to any attack on its soldiers, an exhibition of the might of the RAF was conducted on 9 and 11 September, with six Buccaneers of 12 Squadron flying so low above the rooftops of Beirut that the crews were using road maps to navigate their way around the city.

Between 70 and 100 soldiers were also able to receive supplies on a routine basis by helicopter flight, with 7 Squadron Chinooks flying in and out of the city on a daily basis while regularly contending with small arms fire, despite their limited protection.

Such flights were invaluable for the troops on the ground, with the return flights offering an opportunity for rest and recuperation in Cyprus. On one occasion, an inbound flight brought the comedian Jim Davidson along with its cargo. His effect on morale has not been recorded.

The situation in the Lebanese civil war continued to deteriorate and, in October 1983, 299 American and French peacekeepers were killed by a suicide bombing of their Beirut headquarters. In February 1984, the UK government took the decision to evacuate all British citizens, military personnel and their equipment. Royal Navy and RAF helicopters flew throughout the day, eventually uplifting 115 troops and 518 civilians to ships stationed off the coast before their onward transit to Cyprus.

In the years since, the RAF has conducted similar missions in Lebanon and the Middle East. In 2006, helicopters evacuated British civilians from Beirut to Royal Navy ships stationed in the same positions off the Lebanese coast that their predecessors had occupied in 1983. The RAF has also continued to fly Jim Davidson into many war zones and he has survived them all!

Fattoush
Lebanese Salad

Fattoush is a quintessentially Lebanese dish packed with fresh salad and herb flavours, crunchy toasted flatbread, lemon and sumac. Pomegranate seeds give the salad a wonderful sweet note that cuts through the salad's citrusy sourness. It can be eaten as a starter, as part of a tapas or with grilled meat.

INGREDIENTS

Serves 4

For the croutons

4 pitta bread (preferably a day or two old), cut into large dice or torn into pieces

For the tahini yoghurt dressing

200g natural yoghurt

2 tbsp tahini

½ lemon, juice and finely grated zest

2 tbsp fresh dill, coarsely chopped

For the salad

300g cherry (or cherry plum) tomatoes, halved

1 cucumber, halved, deseeded and coarsely diced

1 red pepper, coarsely diced

1 green pepper, coarsely diced

8 spring onions, cut into 2cm lengths

3 baby gem (or 1 romaine) lettuce, torn or coarsely chopped

150g radishes, cut into wedges

1 tbsp flat leaf parsley, coarsely chopped

½ tbsp fresh mint leaves, shredded

1½ tbsp sumac

3 tbsp extra virgin olive oil

½ lemon

salt and pepper

½ pomegranate, seeds removed

METHOD

To make the croutons

• Preheat the oven to 200°C.

• Place the pitta pieces onto a baking sheet and bake in the oven for 10 to 15 minutes until crisp; set aside to cool.

To make the tahini yoghurt dressing

• Mix the natural yoghurt, tahini, lemon juice, lemon zest and dill together. Add a little cold water to thin a little and season lightly with salt and pepper.

To prepare the salad

• Combine the prepared cherry tomatoes, cucumber, peppers, spring onions, lettuce, radishes, parsley and mint in a bowl. Sprinkle over 1 tbsp of the sumac, add the extra virgin olive oil and squeeze over the lemon juice. Season well with salt and cracked (or freshly ground) black pepper.

• Toss the salad well to coat with the sumac, olive oil, lemon and seasoning.

To serve

• Arrange the fattoush on a serving dish or plate, sprinkle with the remaining sumac, scatter over the pitta croutons and pomegranate seeds. Drizzle over a little of the tahini yoghurt dressing and serve the remainder separately in a small bowl or sauce boat.

THE MODERN AGE
1990–2018

A NEW FOCUS

Words by
NICK FELLOWS

A TORNADO ABOUT TO DEPART GIOIA DEL COLLE ON ANOTHER SORTIE OVER LIBYA, OPERATION ELLAMY, 2011

THE COLLAPSE OF Soviet power in Eastern Europe in the autumn and winter of 1989–90 changed the political map of the world. No longer was the Soviet bloc Britain's most easily identifiable enemy. Instead, a new international order emerged in which the RAF would be called upon to act in a variety of ways, through expeditionary wars and humanitarian relief operations.

The Iraqi invasion of oil-rich Kuwait in August 1990 was in part a response to the economic problems faced by Iraq after a costly and bitter eight-year war against Iran. The Kuwaitis had angered Saddam Hussein by extracting large amounts of oil from the region close to their borders and also refusing to write off Iraqi debts from the Iran–Iraq war. Threats to Kuwait from Iraq were not new: the RAF had actually sent a small land force to deter Iraqi action in 1961. However, on this occasion, Iraq invaded and Kuwait City was soon taken.

The United Nations demanded Iraq's withdrawal and, when this did not happen, it authorised a military response. Britain was part of a 17-nation coalition that was built up, primarily based in Saudi Arabia. RAF aircraft were sent, as part of the international force, to Dhahran in Saudi Arabia from Cyprus, followed by a squadron of Jaguars to Oman. At the same time, air reconnaissance was carried out in the Persian Gulf and the Gulf of Oman, while tanker aircraft were also provided to support both the RAF and other air forces of the coalition. The RAF was also prominent in the airlift of equipment, moving some 31,000 tonnes of freight and, by March 1991, transporting some 25,000 people to the Gulf.

While the UN attempted to persuade Iraq to withdraw from Kuwait by peaceful means, the coalition continued to build up its forces. With Saudi air-space secured, a missile shield in place and UN approval, the coalition launched Operation Desert Storm on 17 January, 1991. Air support was provided for coalition forces on the ground. Troops, supplies and weapons were ferried to the front and, within 100 hours of ground combat, the coalition was able to call a halt to the fighting as the Iraqi army withdrew. Given the low-level flying missions involved, the losses only amounted to six Tornado GR1s and five aircrew.

However, this did not bring an end to activity in the region. Encouraged by the success of coalition forces, the Kurds of northern Iraq attempted to overthrow Saddam Hussein, prompting a massive retaliatory campaign from Hussein, who attacked Kurdish areas with chemical weapons. The UN created a safe zone and enforced a no-fly zone, with Britain one of 13 volunteer nations. RAF forces, based at Incirclik in Turkey, helped to oversee the safe zone once it had been established by ground forces. Meanwhile, in the south, Iraqi forces started to single out Marsh Arabs for reprisals. Other groups, including some Shi'a Muslims, attempted to overthrow the Iraqi regime, believing that the coalition would help them. As in the north, they were brutally repressed and again the UN imposed a no-fly zone.

Involvement in the region continued, largely as a result of UN Resolution 687, which attempted to force Hussein to hand over his weapons of mass destruction (WMD). His refusal to co-operate with the UN Special Commission in November 1998 brought the RAF back into the area, with forces deployed to Kuwait. As the situation deteriorated, the coalition resorted to military force and attacked targets around Baghdad, Tikrit and Basra. Yet the problem of WMDs remained unresolved and the UN Security Council passed a resolution in November 2002 declaring that Iraq was in breach of previous resolutions. Based on UN authority, Britain joined a US-led coalition that was willing to use force to ensure compliance; an approach that was initiated on 20 March 2003.

Precision attacks against military targets were launched and support was provided to ground forces, while air attacks took place against Iraq's elite Republican Guard. Meanwhile, reconnaissance and refuelling work ensured that coalition forces were kept in the air, and helicopters ferried troops and equipment. On 1 May 2003, President Bush declared the war was over but coalition troops remained as the country descended into chaos. Reconstruction was slow, but by 2008 the daily death toll was decreasing and the final US troops were able to leave Iraq in 2011.

It was the collapse of communism in Europe that brought the RAF into its next zone of conflict. With the break up of Yugoslavia, age-old ethnic tensions erupted in the region. Croatia and Slovenia broke away from the Yugoslav Federation in 1991 and the Croat and Muslim population of Bosnia-Herzegovina supported a referendum calling for an independent republic. However, the Serb population of Bosnia refused to break away and, in 1992,

a bitter civil war broke out, leading to ethnic cleansing.

Initially, the RAF was involved in humanitarian flights bringing in food and medical aid to the capital Sarajevo, operating at first from Zagreb in Croatia and then Ancona in Italy. However, when the Serbian President Slobodan Milosevic increased attacks on Muslims in Bosnia to remove them from areas claimed by Serbia, the UN intervened to order a general economic blockade of Serbia-Montenegro and to enforce a no-fly zone.

British aircraft were soon sent to Italy to help enforce the no-fly zone, with tanker aircraft in Sicily and then helicopters deployed to Split in Croatia. The UN's initial actions were ineffective and, although safe havens were created for fleeing Muslims, the UN could do little to prevent attacks and NATO was asked to intervene, with the RAF using Jaguars based in Italy. The subsequent infamous seizure by the Serbs of the safe area of Srebenica and the mortar attack on Sarajevo's market place in August 1995 prompted NATO to act. The RAF bombed Serb targets, the first time that air power had been used offensively in Europe since 1945. This time the aim was not to defeat an enemy, but to contain aggression, save lives and force Serbia to accept the UN peace framework. The agreement was then enforced by a NATO force and the RAF helped implement the no-fly zone.

However, this did not bring an end to the problems in the Balkans. In Kosovo, where ethnic Albanians were in the majority, the Serbian president encouraged ethnic Serbs to settle and Albanians to leave. An ethnic Albanian guerrilla movement developed, but Serbia was determined to crush this and sent in the army and police special units. Stories of brutality soon emerged and NATO, determined to prevent the situation from escalating, threatened air strikes, alongside diplomatic efforts.

Despite a ceasefire, violence continued and Serbia refused to sign a peace agreement. Once again NATO launched air attacks, with the RAF again flying from a range of bases in Italy. This time, however, the air strikes had little impact on Serbia, which continued its policy of ethnic cleansing. More RAF aircraft were sent

to Italy and attacks on Serb forces increased. At the same time, tents, blankets and medical supplies were also flown in to Tirana in Albania and Skopje in Macedonia by RAF Hercules transport planes to try and ease the humanitarian problem. Despite this, Serbia did not capitulate and NATO increased the number of planes and missions again, with the RAF sending aircraft from RAF Bruggen to Corsica to enable an increase in operations. Finally, through a joint EU/Russian approach, Serbia agreed to proposals to end the conflict and attacks were reduced.

This period also witnessed further British involvement in Central America. Just as the country's commitment to Belize was coming to a close, Guatemala, which borders Belize, was becoming ever more threatening and an RAF presence was maintained in Belize until the threat ended.

THE RED ARROWS
OVER CHINA, 2016

It was events in New York on 11 September 2001 that ultimately brought the RAF into further expeditionary action. The terrorist attack had been orchestrated by Osama Bin Laden and prompted the US President, George W Bush, to issue a demand to the Taliban leadership to hand over Bin Laden to American authorities. When this failed, the US quickly assembled a coalition of forces, including anti-Taliban forces in Afghanistan, to overthrow the Afghan government. The Prime Minister, Tony Blair, offered Britain's full support.

The RAF undertook reconnaissance action and air-to-air refuelling in Afghanistan as part of Operation Enduring Freedom. Overwhelming air power and cruise missiles soon destroyed Al Qaida's bases and training camps and, following a land campaign, the government soon fell. However, the problem was maintaining and extending control across the whole region. RAF involvement now took on a new role, with Harriers and then Tornados based at Kandahar to support US forces and helicopters supporting ground troops. Members of the RAF Regiment also provided a vital ground defence capacity. In addition, a base was established at Camp Bastion, near Lashkar Gar in Helmand province, which became the UK's fifth-largest airfield, with the capability of 600 aircraft and helicopter movements per day. However, overthrowing the Taliban government proved much easier than establishing a stable alternative. Britain finally withdrew from Afghanistan in 2014.

Humanitarian disasters require a quick response and it is therefore not surprising that the RAF's air power has played an increasing role in delivering essential supplies to victims of disasters, from Kenya in 1961 to Ethiopia in 1984. Far from being dominated by combat missions, the 1990s and 2000s saw the RAF take part in many humanitarian interventions. In 1994, it was involved in delivering aid in Rwanda after the genocide and civil war; and the following year saw humanitarian missions in Angola. From 1996, the RAF played its part in many missions to monitor the humanitarian crisis in Zaire. It was also used to evacuate British nationals from Yemen, Albania, Central Africa, Eritrea and Sierra Leone.

When natural disasters struck, the RAF was also involved. It flew missions to Chile in 1991 after mud slides; to Turkey in 1992 following the earthquake; to the Caribbean in 1992 after hurricanes; to Somalia in 1993 to cope with a horrific famine; to Mozambique in 2002 in the aftermath of floods; to Montserrat in 1995 after volcanic eruptions; and to Cyprus in 1995 and 1998 following forest fires. Closer to home, the RAF helped in the event of floods in the Netherlands in 1995 and even in the UK in 1998.

However, there have been occasions when humanitarian missions have developed into something more dangerous, as happened in Sierra Leone in 2002. Following bitter fighting in the country, the UN was to oversee disarmament, but many of its personnel were captured, including some British forces. The RAF took part not only in the evacuation of British citizens, but also in actions deep in the jungle to successfully free the hostages.

BAHRAIN

Words by
FLIGHT LIEUTENANT (RETIRED) ART LESTER

THE HEADQUARTERS BUILDING, RAF BAHRAIN

THE ROYAL AIR FORCE has been involved in Bahrain extensively over its 100 year life. Initially, in 1924, Bahrain was used as a forward deployment base for aircraft operating from Iraq and on to locations further east. In the 1930s, an agreement was signed with the monarch and RAF Bahrain – later RAF Muharraq – was established. The base, often referred to by the name of the nearby capital, Manama, was in active RAF service until the country declared independence in 1971. It is now the main international airport with a subsection for military ops.

Bahrain's strategic importance was first recognised nearly 70 years ago. That, combined with the locals' desire for stability and security, has meant that the island nation is still a very important regional base for "hub-and-spoke" regional air operations in the Middle East.

In the Second World War, Bahrain assisted in the purchase of 10 Spitfires for the war effort through the Fighter Fund, six of which bore the name "Bahrain". In 2014, the RAF Museum, along with long-time RAF industrial partner BAE Systems and the Bahrain-based Gulf Air

Academy, brought an original Spitfire back to Bahrain for the international air show. Such an iconic link was surely a star attraction!

The islands were also used by RAF aircraft in response to the Kuwait crisis in 1961. It was not the first or last time the RAF has swiftly reacted to violent annexations in the region. The airfield was used by RAF Tornado bombers and VC10 refuelling aircraft during the 1990–91 Gulf War and by the RAF refuelling aircraft that supported the subsequent no-fly zones in Iraq. 32 (The Royal) Squadron, normally based at Northolt, also have a strong history of operating from the kingdom.

The Muharraq base has also played host to a number of specialist units and HQs, including HQ Air Forces Gulf and HQ RAF Persian Gulf. Several communications units and search-and-rescue units have operated form the island. Bahrain is also a home from home for visiting naval units.

The efforts required to generate strategic air power from a relatively small island should not be underestimated. An often limited aircraft handling space and the need to share facilities with multi-national partners are key factors. However, being able to get on with strangers in unfamiliar, cramped conditions is just one of the skills the RAF develops.

The surrounding nations all have a strong traditional of tribal rivalry and political interplay, meaning that Bahrain's neighbours will always take an interest in RAF operations from Bahrain.

Machboos Rubyan
Spiced Prawns with Rice

Bahrain has long been an important trading port and its cuisine has been influenced by African, Indian, Persian, European, Asian and Arabic cultures. This popular Bahraini staple is a rice dish most commonly made with either chicken or lamb, but this version of machboos pays homage to the popularity of seafood in Bahrain. Basmati rice gives a more fragrant and stickier dish, while long-grain rice giving a slightly lighter dish with more emphasis on the spice flavours.

INGREDIENTS

Serves 4

For the spice marinade

2 tsp baharat spice mix (see recipe
  on page 133)

2 tsp ground turmeric

1 tsp ground cumin

1 tsp salt

600g raw king prawns, shelled

For the rice

50g butter

2 medium onions, finely diced

2 cloves of garlic, finely chopped

1 bird's eye chilli, finely chopped

2.5cm piece of ginger, finely
  chopped or grated

1 cinnamon stick

6 cardamom pods, crushed with
  the flat of a knife

1 bay leaf

1 lime, halve and finely grate the zest

300g tomatoes, coarsely chopped

500ml chicken stock

350g basmati or long-grain
  rice, soaked in cold water for 15
  minutes, rinsed and drained

sea salt

For the prawns

2 tbsp olive oil

2 tbsp parsley, coarsely chopped

To finish

2 tbsp rosewater (optional)

METHOD

To prepare the prawns

• Mix the baharat, turmeric, cumin and salt together.

• Place the prawns in a bowl, add half of the spice mix, toss to thoroughly coat and place in the fridge to marinate until required.

To cook the rice

• Heat a casserole dish over a medium heat with the butter.

• When the butter is foaming, add the diced onions and cook, stirring frequently, for about 10 minutes until softened and lightly caramelised, add the garlic, chilli, ginger and remaining spice mix; continue to cook for a further couple of minutes.

• Add the cinnamon stick, cardamom pods, bay leaf, lime zest, diced tomatoes and stock. Mix well, season lightly with salt, bring to a simmer, turn the heat to low and simmer for 20 minutes (at this stage the cinnamon stick, bay leaf and cardamom pods can be picked out if preferred).

• Stir in the soaked rice, stir well, bring back to a simmer, season lightly with sea salt if required (remember there is salt in the spice blend), cover with a lid and cook for a further 15 minutes or until the rice is cooked.

To cook the prawns

• Heat the oil in a frying pan or wok over a high heat and quickly stir-fry the prawns until just cooked through. Add to the rice and fold in.

• Stir in three quarters of the parsley, squeeze in the lime juice from the two reserved lime halves, mix well and check the seasoning.

To serve

• Pile the machboos onto a warmed serving dish, drizzle over the rosewater (if using) and garnish with the remaining chopped parsley.

VEGETARIAN ALTERNATIVE

PANEER MACHBOOS

• Substitute the prawns with 400g of paneer cut into 1.5cm-thick slices; coat in the spice mix marinade as in the stage above.

• Cook the rice as above substituting the chicken stock for vegetable stock.

• Pan-fry the paneer slices, drain on absorbent kitchen paper and cut into 1.5cm dice.

• Fold the diced paneer into the rice and serve as above.

ROMANIA

Words by
FLIGHT SERGEANT MICK BLACKALL

ROMANIA HAS BEEN in the public eye all too often for the wrong reasons. Harrowing pictures of abandoned children in the orphanages were beamed around the world in the 1990s, prompting much international concern.

Tony Williams, a former RAF Warrant Officer stationed at RAF Laarbruch in Germany, became involved with aid runs to the north of the country in 1993 and made more than 40 trips there. "Myself and a group of colleagues were asked to accompany an aid run to Romania as they needed engineering support," he says. "When we first went we were overawed. The kids were crammed into rooms that just had wall-to-wall beds – no other furniture. They had only the clothes they were stood up in and, for more than 200 of them, there were six showers, six sinks and three toilets."

Tony was part of a small team of RAF personnel who created the RAF Laarbruch Romanian Organisation. Staff from RAF Wittering visited the country, taking medical supplies, food and expertise. Tony himself visited Baia Mare twice a year from 1991, and was shocked by what he saw. Its name means "the big mine" and the town's lead mines and sulphur-processing plants meant that lung diseases were prevalent. One visit focused on the local TB hospital, where the RAF team donated an operating table, cardiac monitor and a full anaesthetic suite, along with beds, mattresses, wheelchairs and disposable rubber gloves. At home, Senior Aircraftsman Kelvin Green painted Harrier Jets, but in Baia Mare he put his expertise to use decorating the unit.

Romanian Tina Horotan was the Chief Nurse at the hospital during the early visits. "When Tony first rang to tell me what he was bringing, I couldn't believe it," she says. "They improved the medical department, the children's ward and the surgical ward. It meant we were able to start a 'rooming-in system' so mothers could stay in hospital as their children were treated."

Another project aimed to find homes for orphans once they reached the age of 18. A furnished flat in the town of Baia Mare was provided for three girls and, with their help, a hostel was refurbished to provide a home for other girls who, otherwise, would have been forced to live on the streets.

The organisation's missions also spread wider. Flight Sergeant John Young described the opening of a new clinic in nearby Cehu Silvanie as the group's finest achievement. This was a small town with no medical centre until the organisation brought and converted a small flat. Now, two doctors could serve more than 3,000 patients. "When you come here," says John, "the first thing you see is how lots of things we discard in the UK could make a real difference in Romania."

Tony was also contacted by the mayor of Timisoara, 600 miles away, asking if the group could spare anything for townsfolk who had lost everything. It emphasised how widely regarded the help of the RAF Wittering staff was. "It's nice to put something back," says Tony. "I get a real kick out of helping people."

> *"When you come here you notice how lots of things we discard in the UK could make a real difference in Romania"*

Mititei
Skinless Romanian Sausages

The story goes that an inn in mid-19th century Bucharest ran out of its famed sausages one night. Desperate not to let his patrons down, the chef rolled some minced meat into sausage shapes and grilled them. These lightly spiced, garlicky skinless sausages soon became famous. The process of using baking soda in meat recipes is common in Balkan countries. It tenderises the meat, minimises shrinkage and keeps small pieces of meat juicy during the cooking process. Mititei – literally "little ones" – are traditionally eaten with mustard or sour cream, chips and pickled vegetables.

INGREDIENTS

Serves 4

For the mititei

250g minced beef

250g minced pork

5 cloves of garlic, finely chopped
  or crushed

2 tsp paprika

1½ tsp salt

1½ tsp fresh thyme leaves, coarsely
  chopped

1 tsp caraway seeds

1 tsp dried oregano (or marjoram)

½ tsp freshly ground black pepper

½ tsp dried chilli flakes

2 tbsp soda water

1 tsp bicarbonate of soda

For the cooking liquid

2 tbsp olive oil

150ml beef stock

To serve

4 tbsp sour cream

2 tsp mustard (dijon or German
  style according to taste)

4 tomatoes, thinly sliced

½ small red onion, finely diced or
  2 thinly sliced spring onions

1 tbsp extra virgin olive oil

salt and pepper

paprika to dust

baked, chipped or boiled potatoes
  (or rice if preferred)

METHOD

To make the mititei

- In a large mixing bowl, mix all of the mititei ingredients (except the soda water and bicarbonate of soda) together until thoroughly combined.
- Dissolve the bicarbonate of soda in the soda water and mix into the meat mixture.
- Knead the mixture in the bowl for 5 minutes, wetting your hands occasionally to keep the mixture moist.
- Cover the bowl with cling film and refrigerate for 6 hours (or overnight). This marinating process will help the sausages to remain juicy and tender when cooked.
- Divide the mix into 12 even-sized pieces and, working with wet hands, roll each piece into a ball then form each ball into a thin sausage shape (around 9cm long).

To cook

- Heat the oil in a large frying pan over a medium heat and cook the mititei for around 15 minutes, turning frequently, until well browned and cooked through (alternatively brown the mititei all over in the oil and finish cooking in the oven at 180°C for 10 minutes or until thoroughly cooked through). Once seared, baste frequently with a little beef stock to prevent them from becoming dry during the remaining cooking time.

To serve

- Mix the sour cream and mustard together.
- Arrange the sliced tomatoes, overlapping, on individual plates (or on a serving plate) season with salt and freshly ground black pepper, scatter over the red (or spring) onions and drizzle over a little extra virgin olive oil.
- Arrange three mititei on each plate, dust lightly with a little paprika and serve with the mustard sour cream and potatoes (chips, jacket or boiled) or rice.

KUWAIT

Words by
**AIR COMMODORE MARK GILLIGAN
& SQUADRON LEADER KATHERINE INGRAM**

BRITAIN'S KEY ROLE in Kuwaiti history dates back to the Uqair Conference in 1922, when Sir Percy Cox, the British Ambassador to Baghdad, partitioned the Ottoman province of Basra to form Kuwait. The threat of Ottoman invasion prompted Amir Mubarak Al-Sabah to cede foreign and defence responsibility to Britain until 1961, when Kuwait gained its independence.

In June 1961, Iraq's Prime Minister General Kassim claimed that Kuwait was an integral part of his country, drawing Britain into a potential crisis through its obligation to maintain Kuwaiti independence. Operation Vantage, a British plan to militarily reinforce Kuwait, was enacted with alacrity. Moves for a defensive force were ordered within four days of Kassim's statement and, by 9 July, RAF Hunters, Beverleys, Valettas and Twin Pioneers, along with 5,000 troops, had been deployed within Kuwait, supported by HMS

Victorious's Sea Vixens, reconnaissance Canberras in Bahrain and Canberra bombers in Sharjah and Cyprus. No Iraqi invasion was initiated. Tension eased and forces were gradually pulled out, although a permanent presence was maintained in Bahrain thereafter.

History repeats itself and, three decades later, another Iraqi premier, Saddam Hussein, asserted the same historical territorial claim and, on 2 August 1990, his army invaded Kuwait. In response, a helicopter gunship – part of a huge UN coalition – crossed the border in the early hours of 16 January 1991, marking the first of 100,000 sorties of the 43-day air campaign of the 1991 Gulf War. Following the aerial bombardment, a ground assault, starting on 23 February 1991, liberated Kuwait in four days. Under Operation Granby, the RAF flew over 6,000 sorties in support of the multi-national force. Buccaneer, Jaguar, and ground attack, air defence and reconnaissance variants of Tornado all took part in the air war, delivering over 3,000 tonnes of ordinance in attacking airfields and suppressing enemy air defences. The Support Helicopter Force, Nimrod Maritime Reconnaissance, Tanker Force and Air Transport Force were also heavily involved.

In 2003, Iraq was again deemed in breach of resolutions over Kuwait, and the Second Gulf War played out from 20 March of that year. The RAF flew over 2,500 sorties on Operation Telic from Kuwait's Ali Al Salem Airbase, including around 1,350 offensive strikes. As in all wars, air operations were supported by the unheralded. 51 Squadron RAF Regiment, Tactical Supply Wing, 5131 Bomb Disposal Squadron and 3 RAF Force Protection Wing HQ, among others, all played their part. Due to the combined efforts of the many, on 9 April 2003, Baghdad was overrun and Saddam Hussein's statue toppled.

While decades apart from each other, Operations Vantage, Granby and Telic all demonstrated the flexibility of air power, achieved by well-trained ground and aircrews.

A HERCULES LANDS IN KUWAIT AFTER LIBERATION, 1991

Shaurabat Adas
Kuwaiti Lentil Soup

This hearty soup, full of spices, lentils and vegetables, is a great warming lunch or supper on a cold winter's night. Variations of spiced lentil soups are common throughout the Persian Gulf and are often flavoured with a spice blend prevalent throughout the area known as baharat.

INGREDIENTS
Serves 4

For the spice mix

2 tsp baharat (see recipe on page 133)

¾ tsp ground coriander

½ tsp ground turmeric

For the soup

3 tbsp olive oil

1 medium onion, finely diced

1 medium carrot, finely diced

1 stick of celery, finely diced

3 cloves of garlic, finely chopped
  or crushed

1 lime, finely grated zest and juice

250g red lentils, soaked in cold water
  for 30 minutes, rinsed and drained

4 medium tomatoes, coarsely
  chopped

1 tbsp tomato purée

1½ litres chicken or vegetable stock

1 bay leaf

200g potato, peeled and coarsely
  diced

salt

To serve

olive oil

2 tbsp flat leaf parsley, coarsely
  chopped

lemon or lime wedges

grilled flatbread

4 tbsp natural yoghurt (optional)

METHOD
To make the spice mix

• Mix all of the spices together and store in an airtight container until required.

To make the soup

• Heat the oil in a saucepan over a moderate heat, add the onions, carrots and celery; cook, stirring frequently, for around 5 minutes until starting to soften.

• Stir in the garlic, spice mix and lime zest; continue to cook for a further couple of minutes then mix in the lentils, chopped tomatoes, tomato purée, stock, bay leaf and potatoes.

• Bring to a boil, skim, season with a little salt and simmer for 30 to 40 minutes until the potatoes are tender and the lentils are soft.

• Pick out the bay leaf and stir in the lime juice; season with a little more salt if required.

• Transfer between a third and half of the soup to a blender or food processor and blend until smooth, add back to the saucepan and bring back to a simmer. Alternatively, for a chunkier soup, this step can be omitted.

To serve

• Ladle into warmed bowls, drizzle over a little extra virgin olive oil, garnish with the chopped parsley and serve with the lemon or lime wedges and warm grilled flatbreads. For a slightly sharp finish, a swirl of natural yogurt can be spooned over the soup before serving.

TURKEY

Words by
WING COMMANDER TEO BRADLEY

FOLLOWING THE FIRST Iraq War of 1990–91, Incirlik Air Base in southern Turkey hosted Combined Task Force Provide Comfort, which oversaw Operation Provide Comfort. This operation aimed to deliver humanitarian relief to millions of Kurdish refugees in northern Iraq, protect them in a UN secure area and ultimately repatriate them to Iraq. Thirteen nations contributed to land and air elements, with the British contribution including RAF helicopters and Royal Marines, supported by air-transport assets. This force, together with elements from the other 12 nations, established a safe haven in September 1991.

Once the ground forces were withdrawn from the safe haven, an air task force assumed responsibility for enforcing a no-fly zone over the area of Iraq north of the 36th parallel. The coalition effort was re-named Operation Northern Watch in 1997, with the British contribution, designated Operation Warden, consisting of Tornado GR1s, Jaguars, Harriers and Tanker support. As part of this operation, RAF Hercules and Chinook detachments operating from Incirlik, delivered tons of food, clothing and medical supplies. Between 1992 and 1997. VC10s from 101 Squadron established a detachment here, flying over 1,200 sorties before the detachment moved to Muharraq in Bahrain for operations over southern Iraq.

Incirlik Air Base also played an important bridge role by providing support in the relief operation that was initiated following the Kashmir earthquake on 8 October 2005. It was ostensibly used as a co-ordination point for the aid that was brought in by road from United Nations High Commission for Refugees (UNHCR) warehouses in İskenderun, Turkey. The relief effort was then able to use the air base as a forward-operating base for the onward journey to Pakistan.

C-130-J Hercules of 24 and 30 Squadrons based at RAF Lyneham – accompanied by members of the RAF's UK Mobile Air Movements Squadron, RAF Engineers, Police and the Tactical Air-Land Coordination Element (TALCE) – conducted the airlifts, flying urgently needed supplies to Islamabad, Pakistan on 19 October 2005 under Operation Maturin. Alongside four other air forces, the UK assisted in the delivery of 860 tonnes of aid comprising 104,000 blankets, 10,000 tents and 2,400 stoves.

"The relief operation confirmed once again the ability of British forces to step up to the mark and do a fantastic job in the harshest of environments," said Defence

> *"Incirlik Air Base played an important bridge role in the relief operation started after the 2005 Kashmir earthquake"*

THREE RAF JAGUAR
RECONNAISSANCE
PLANES DURING A SORTIE
SUPPORTING OPERATION
NORTHERN WATCH, 1997

Secretary John Reid at the time. "I am tremendously proud of the work of our armed forces."

In more recent years, the RAF has participated in the Turkish Air Force's flagship exercise Anatolian Eagle, which is now in its 16th year. It usually takes place at Konya Air Base (south of Ankara) with the aim being to train fighter pilots for the first few days of a modern conflict. It provides the RAF with the opportunity to further enhance interoperability with its allies and ensures that it maintains the highest levels of readiness for operations. Typhoons of 11 Squadron from RAF Coningsby participated in 2014 (with a composite squadron alongside 3 Squadron) and in 2015 with eight aircraft and over 150 personnel.

Köfte
Turkish Meatballs on Flatbread

by GRAHAM HOWARTH

EX-FLIGHT SERGEANT AND HEAD CHEF AT CHEQUERS ESTATE

Although synonymous with Turkey, köfte (the word derives from the Persian verb "to grind") are popular throughout the Middle-East, Southern-Europe, North Africa and India. These delicious meatballs were first experienced on holiday in Turkey. I loved them so much that I asked the chef to share his recipe with me. Fortunately he agreed!

INGREDIENTS

Serves 4–6

For the meatballs

1 tbsp olive oil

1 large onion, diced

2 cloves of garlic, chopped

500g minced beef

200g pork mince

a handful of fresh breadcrumbs

2 tsp ground cumin

1 tsp smoked paprika

1 tsp garlic granules

a good bunch each of fresh
  coriander and flat leaf parsley,
  chopped

salt and pepper

For the tomato sauce

1 tbsp olive oil

1 large onion, chopped

3 cloves of garlic, chopped

1 tbsp tomato purée

2 tins (2x400g) tinned chopped
  tomatoes

250ml white wine

a pinch of sugar

a good bunch of flat leaf parsley,
  coarsely chopped

To finish and serve

2 large flatbreads

a good handful of grated mature
  cheddar

500g thick natural yoghurt

village salad (tomatoes, cucumber,
  green peppers, red onion,
  Kalamata olives and feta with a
  dressing of olive oil, lemon juice,
  red wine vinegar and oregano)

METHOD

To make the meatballs

• Fry off the onion and garlic in the oil until softened and allow to cool.

• In a large bowl place the meats, the cooled onion and garlic, followed by the rest of the ingredients, give them a good mix with your hands.

• Fry a small amount of mixture off to test for seasoning and taste before you mould the rest, adjust the seasoning as necessary.

• Mould the mixture into short fat oval shapes, place on a clean tray and refrigerate.

To make the tomato sauce

• Sauté the onion and garlic in the olive oil until softened and starting to colour, add the tomato purée and cook out a little, add the tinned tomatoes, white wine and sugar. Simmer gently for about 1 hour or longer if possible.

• Transfer the sauce to a blender, add the parsley and season with salt and pepper. Give the mixture a good blitz in the blender until smooth, again check the seasoning.

To finish

• If you feel inclined, you can make flatbread, although a good supermarket bought one will do just fine.

• Place the flatbread on a hot griddle pan rubbed with olive oil, char it a little and turn over, Cut the bread into 2.5cm rough chunks

• Preheat the oven to 200°C.

• Heat up your griddle pan again and sear the meatballs until charred on both sides, finish them off in the hot oven for 15 minutes or until cooked through.

• To finish, place the flatbread chunks in an ovenproof serving dish, sit the meatballs on top, pour over the tomato sauce, and cover with grated cheese, Blast again in the hot oven for 5 to 10 minutes until everything is piping hot.

To serve

• Serve with thick natural yoghurt over the top, and a fresh village salad.

SAUDI ARABIA

Words by
FLIGHT LIEUTENANT (RETIRED) ART LESTER

THE ROYAL AIR FORCE was fundamental in the creation of Saudi Arabia's own air force in the 1920s. Not only did it provide a model for the structure, but it also trained and equipped the Saudis' fledgling force. That initial connection has been reinforced many times and the UK continues to play a very important role in the equipping, training and maintenance of many air forces across the Gulf region.

However, it is for the Gulf War and Operation Desert Storm that many will remember these links with Saudi Arabia. Entrants to Cranwell and Halton are frequently reminded that flexibility is the key to air power, and this was ably demonstrated in the UK's reaction to Saddam Hussein's invasion of Kuwait on 2 August 1990.

The first wave of UK aircraft arrived in Saudi Arabia within 48 hours. More were deployed to Saudi airfields at Tabuk and Dhahran, and to Muharraq in Bahrain. The numbers steadily grew during high-pressure negotiations during the winter of 1990 until the defensive posture could be transformed into an attacking one.

Then, after all diplomatic efforts had been extensively explored and following Iraqi Scud attacks against Saudi Arabia and Israel, came the coalition bombardment of key Iraqi targets on 17 January 1991. Thirty-eight days of strategic aerial bombardment were conducted before air power continued to support the land offensive that started on 24 February. Four days later, Kuwait was liberated and air power continued to be used until the final Iraqi agreement to a formal ceasefire on 11 April 1991. These operations led directly to the continued manning of overwatch operations under Operation Warden, and to Operation Southern Watch for years to come.

The tempo of operations in the Gulf War of 1991 was almost entirely dictated by the coalition's ability to gain and maintain air superiority over the Iraqis. This ability to transform almost instantly from a Cold War footing to defensive air operations in a protective role and then again to a campaign of strategic and operational attacks is one of the best examples of flexibility in the history of any air force in the world.

Key to this success were the extremely low-level bombing runs, coming in under Iraqi radar systems to attack airfields and other key infrastructure. These raids came at a price. During the campaign, the RAF lost eight Tornado aircraft and one Jaguar aircraft. The initial high-risk sorties were absolutely vital to the effort, effectively opening up the Iraqi air defences so that bombing could later switch to medium-level runs and concentrate on more strategic targets. No other country in the coalition had the capability to conduct the ultra-low level attack profiles that were vital to the initial attack phases. This relied on high-pressure skills that the RAF had learnt on training courses and exercises in the UK and abroad over the previous decade.

A particularly impressive part of the RAF's response was the sheer number of aircraft types that were involved in the campaign. Tornado fighters and bomber variants, Jaguars, Buccaneers, Nimrod, Hercules, VC10, Tristar, Victor, Chinook and Puma were all involved in operations. The RAF Regiment deployed Rapier short-range air defence missile systems and much-needed expertise in chemical weapons defence. In total, over 2,000 sorties were flown.

Samak Quwarmah
Saudi Arabian Fish Curry

by PAUL GAYLER MBE
CHEF AND DIRECTOR/OWNER AT FEEDBACK CONSULTANCY

This "quwarmah" is a tomato-based sauce, rather than the creamy, almond and coconut sauces of an Indian korma. It uses a traditional eight-spice mix called kabsa, one usually used to flavour the popular Saudi chicken-and-rice dish, Al Kabsa. Loomi are sun-dried limes, also known as black limes, which can be substituted with lemon zest, but this won't give the slightly smoky sour taste.

INGREDIENTS

Serves 4

For the al kabsa spice mix

3 cardamom pods

1 tsp coriander seeds

½ tsp cumin seeds

6 black peppercorns

3 whole cloves

1cm piece of cinnamon stick,
  crumbled into small pieces

1 dried bay leaf

a pinch of ground nutmeg

For the samak quwarmah

800g fish fillets

2 tbsp olive oil

2 medium onions, finely diced

2 cloves of garlic, finely chopped
  or crushed

2.5cm piece of ginger, finely
  chopped or grated

½ tsp red chilli powder

½ tsp paprika

1 tsp ground turmeric

¼ cinnamon stick

½ tin (200g) of chopped tomatoes

2 loomi dried limes or thinly pared
  zest of ½ lemon

sea salt

To serve

steamed rice

1 lemon, cut into wedges

METHOD

To make the al kabsa spice mix

• Crush the cardamom pods with the flat of a knife, remove the seeds and discard the pods.

• Heat a frying pan over a moderate heat, add the spices (except the nutmeg) and dry-fry, stirring constantly, for a couple of minutes until fragrant. Transfer to a plate and set aside to cool.

• Once cool, grind the spices with a pestle and mortar or spice grinder to a coarse powder and mix in the ground nutmeg.

To make the samak quwarmah

• Cut the fish into largish pieces, lightly season with sea salt.

• Cover and leave to one side.

• Heat the oil in a heavy-based shallow frying pan or skillet, add the onion, fry until soft.

• Add the garlic, ginger, chilli powder, paprika, turmeric, cinnamon stick and kabsa spices; cook together for 2 to 3 minutes.

• Add the tomatoes, loomi (pricked with a cocktail stick), or lemon zest and 200ml water.

• Bring to the boil, reduce the heat and simmer gently for 10 to 15 minutes.

• Lay the fish fillet pieces on top of the sauce in the pan, cover with a lid, simmer gently for 10 to 12 minutes or until the fish is cooked.

To serve

• Place the fish onto a bed of steamed rice on individual plates.

• Remove the loomi or lemon zest and cinnamon stick from the sauce, season with a little sea salt if required and spoon over the fish.

• Garnish with the lemon wedges and serve.

BOSNIA & HERZEGOVINA

Words by
WING COMMANDER TEO BRADLEY

"TODAY IN THE Balkans, we don't have war but we don't have real peace," said US peace envoy Richard Holbrooke in February 1995. "NATO must not underestimate the hatred, mistrust and enmity on all three sides."

The federation of Yugoslavia crumbled in 1991 when Croatia and Slovenia declared their independence. The Serb population in Bosnia refused to secede and, between 1992 and 1993, Bosnia-Herzegovina descended into a bitter civil war. The UN provided food and medicine to besieged towns and cities, including the capital, Sarajevo.

The Sarajevo airlift from July 1992 to February 1996 became the longest-running airlift in history. The RAF contributed under Operation Cheshire, with Hercules operating from Croatia and Italy delivering 26,577 tonnes of supplies in 1,977 sorties. This symbolised the commitment of the international community to Sarajevo's survival.

With Bosnian Serbs increasing their attacks on the Muslim population, the UN established a no-fly zone. In April 1993, the RAF deployed six Tornado F3s to Italy as part of Operation Deny Flight; by February 1996, they had flown nearly 3,000 sorties. A Sentry E3-D and two VC10 tankers also supported the operation, while RAF Chinooks and Pumas were deployed to Split in Croatia. Nimrod and Canberra aircraft patrolled over Serbia and the Adriatic.

In May 1993, Bosnian Serbs rejected a UN Peace Plan and stepped up their actions against Bosnia-Herzegovina. The UN then created shelter areas for Muslims but were unable to prevent Serb attacks. NATO was asked to intervene and strike attack aircraft were deployed under Operation Deliberate Force.

The following two years saw a number of failed ceasefires climaxing in several hundred UN peacekeepers being taken hostage, the massacre of 4,000 Muslim men at Srebenica and the mortaring of Sarajevo's market place. Between August and September 1995, Harriers flew 144 operational sorties, dropping 48 laser-guided bombs and 32 1,000lb bombs. The RAF also used Tornado F3s, Tristars and E3D Sentrys. Altogether, the RAF flew 326 sorties – 9.3 per cent of all the operational missions against Serb targets.

A ceasefire was agreed in October 1995, followed by US-sponsored talks and the Dayton Peace Accord. This agreed the partition of Bosnia-Herzegovina between the Bosnian Serbs and the Muslim/Croat Federation, and was enforced by a NATO Implementation Force of 60,000 troops. The air element, Operation Decisive Edge, was supported by six RAF Harrier GR7s.

In December 1996, Operation Decisive Edge became Deliberate Guard, with Jaguars replacing the Harrier GR7s. The RAF Regiment Field Force, deployed in 1992, became part of the British Army roulement until early 1998. It provided security for the divisional HQ and inspected weapon storage sites, monitored Bosnian Serb military activities and supervised elections. By April 1998, the situation in Bosnia-Herzegovina was sufficiently stable to allow a reduction of forces in the region.

> *"The Sarajevo airlift from July 1992 to February 1996 became the longest-running airlift in history"*

Zeljanica
Feta & Spinach Filo Pie

One of the most popular dishes in the Balkan region, zeljanica is made with layers of filo (also known as phyllo) pastry, spinach, feta and ricotta cheese. It is one of the best known varieties of Bosnian "pita", a thin dough filled with vegetable, meat or cheese. This recipe includes a vinaigrette sauce.

INGREDIENTS

Serves 8

For the pie

400g spinach

2 tbsp salt

3 large eggs

200ml sour cream

400g feta cheese, crumbled
  into small pieces

400g ricotta cheese

200g Greek yoghurt

METHOD

To make the pie

- Wash and coarsely chop the spinach, place in a colander, sprinkle with the salt, toss well and leave to drain for 20 to 30 minutes.
- Place the spinach in a tea towel and twist to extract all of the salty bitter juice.
- Whisk the eggs in a large mixing bowl then add the sour cream, crumbled feta, ricotta, yoghurt, grated cheddar, ground cinnamon and nutmeg. Mix well then beat in the chopped spinach and season lightly with freshly ground black pepper.
- Brush a baking dish with a little olive oil, line with a sheet of filo pastry,

100g cheddar cheese, grated

1 tsp ground cinnamon

¼ tsp ground nutmeg

freshly ground black pepper

350g filo pastry

olive oil, to brush the filo layers

For the glaze

4 tbsp sour cream

2 tbsp milk

For the lemon vinaigrette

2 lemons

2 tsp dijon mustard

100ml extra virgin olive oil

100ml groundnut oil

salt and pepper

1 tbsp flat leaf parsley, finely
  chopped

To serve

tossed salad

lemon vinaigrette

brush with a little olive oil and repeat until there are six layers of
filo pastry.
- Add a third of the filling in an even layer and top with another six
  layers of pastry (brushing with oil between each sheet).
- Repeat the previous stage two more times, brush the top with a
  little olive oil, trim off the excess pastry and score the top into eight
  even-sized portions.

To cook the pie
- Preheat the oven to 180°C.
- Cook the pie in the oven for 45 minutes until the pastry on top is
  browned and crisp.
- Mix the sour cream and milk together to make the glaze, remove
  the zeljanica from the oven, pour over the glaze, brush over to ensure
  an even glaze, and return to the oven for a further 15 minutes.

To make the vinaigrette
- Finely grate the zest of the lemons, blanch in a little boiling water for
  1 minute. Drain through a very fine sieve, refresh under cold-running
  water and drain thoroughly.
- Squeeze the juice from the lemons, whisk with the mustard, season
  and whisk in the oils until emulsified.
- Add the lemon zest and finely chopped parsley.

To serve
- Let the zeljanica stand for about 15 to 20 minutes, cut through the
  scores on the pastry and serve warm with tossed salad dressed with
  lemon vinaigrette

CROATIA

Words by

WING COMMANDER TEO BRADLEY

THE ONLY ISLAND In the Adriatic that withstood Hitler's onslaught during the Second World War was the small, vine-covered land-mass of Vis. Vis was the hideout of Josep Tito, Yugoslavia's Partisan leader and later the country's communist president. The stationing of a small British combined force from 1943 transformed it into one of the most important outposts of the war, one that provided a base for attacks on Nazi-dominated Yugoslavia. While the initial British commitment, ordered by Winston Churchill, to assist the Yugoslav Partisans on the mainland was modest, it quickly expanded, with the Royal Navy sending motor torpedo boats to attack German supply ships and the Royal Air Force launching air raids. Hundreds of sorties were flown by the RAF's 351 and 352 Squadrons (operating

> ## *"As Yugoslavia descended into bitter civil war, the UN Protection Force was granted authority to deliver humanitarian assistance"*

Hurricanes and Spitfires) from what was to become the Allies' unsinkable aircraft carrier in attacks against the south-eastern flank of the retreating Axis powers.

Almost 50 years later, the RAF returned to Croatia through the creation of the UN Protection Force (UNPROFOR) that was in Croatia and Bosnia between 1992 and 1995 as Yugoslavia descended into bitter civil war. UNPROFOR was granted extended authority to deliver humanitarian assistance and provide protection for so-called "safe areas" within the Former Republic of Yugoslavia. NATO air forces (which included UK personnel) were also mandated to provide support for the delivery of the peacekeepers' mandate on the ground.

The United Nations organised a relief effort to provide food and medicine to besieged towns and cities, including the Bosnian capital, Sarajevo. The Sarajevo airlift began in July 1992 and became the longest-running airlift in history, ending in January 1996. The RAF's contribution, under the name Operation Cheshire, was Hercules aircraft from 47 Squadron operating initially from Zagreb in Croatia. 47 Squadron's Special Forces Flight maintained a single aircraft on detachment at Zagreb's Pleaso Airport and later at Ancona-Falconara

A HERCULES TRANSPORT AIRCRAFT TAKING SUPPLIES TO SARAJEVO AS PART OF OPERATION CHESHIRE, 1995

Airport, on Italy's Adriatic coast, for just over three years, flying daily relief flights into Sarajevo. 47 Squadron was allocated this task because its aircraft were equipped to defeat the heat-seeking missiles that ringed Sarajevo's airport. It was also a regular occurrence for the aircrew to have to fire chaff to break "radar lock" of radar-guided anti-aircraft guns.

By the end of Operation Cheshire, the RAF had delivered 26,577 tonnes of supplies in 1,977 sorties. The airlift came to symbolise the commitment of the international community to the survival of Sarajevo and its people. The mission was not without its hazards and there were more than 260 security incidents, with an RAF Hercules hit by enemy ground-fire and an Italian air force aircraft shot down in September 1992.

By April 1993, the RAF had deployed fighters to the region to support Operation Deny Flight, an aerial monitoring task to enforce compliance with UN Security Council Resolution 816 (which attempted to stop Serbian incursions into Bosnian airspace). Alongside these efforts, in August 1995, five RAF Chinook HC2s and six Puma HC1s deployed to Split, to provide airlift support to the elements of 24 Airmobile Brigade already deployed there.

Ajngemahtec
Zagreb Chicken, Vegetable & Dumpling Soup

This recipe is a refined version of a soup that is traditional made with chicken offal. These days, it is often made with jointed chicken legs, but this can make the broth quite greasy, so this recipe uses diced thigh meat instead. Ideally, the broth should be made with fresh homemade chicken stock.

INGREDIENTS
Serves 4
For the stock
1 roast chicken carcass, chopped
  into even-sized pieces
2 litres cold water
1 medium onion, roughly chopped
1 medium carrot, roughly chopped
½ medium leek, roughly chopped
50g white button mushrooms,
  thickly sliced
1 clove of garlic, crushed with the
  flat of a knife
1 large tomato, roughly chopped
1 bay leaf
15g parsley stalks (reserve the
  leaves for the soup)
15g tarragon
6 black peppercorns

For the dumplings
1 medium egg
60g semolina
¼ tsp salt

For the soup
6 skinless chicken thighs
2 medium carrots, finely diced
2 sticks of celery, finely diced
1 medium parsnip, finely diced
75g garden peas
parsley leaves, finely chopped
salt and pepper

METHOD
To make the stock
- Place the chicken bones in a large saucepan, cover with the cold water and, over a moderate heat, bring to a boil, reduce the heat and simmer for 10 minutes skimming off any impurities that rise to the surface.
- Add the rest of the stock ingredients.
- Reduce heat to a simmer and cook for 1½ hours skimming regularly.
- Once cooked, carefully strain the stock, ladling from the top through a fine sieve, discarding the bones and vegetables as you go; ladling rather than pouring will prevent the stock from becoming cloudy – you should be left with about 1 litre of stock (if not top up with a little water).
- Cool the stock then chill in the fridge (preferably overnight) and remove any fat that has solidified on the surface.

To make the dumplings
- Whisk the eggs with the salt then beat in the semolina until thoroughly mixed. Place a piece of cling film over the surface to prevent a skin from forming and set aside to rest and allow the semolina to absorb the egg.

To make the soup
- Bring the stock to a simmer, season, add the chicken thighs with the diced carrot, celery and parsnip. Poach for about 10 minutes until the chicken is cooked through. Remove the chicken thighs and cool slightly, continue to simmer the soup until the vegetables are soft. When cool enough to handle, cut the chicken thighs into small even-sized pieces.
- Add the peas to the soup and simmer for 5 minutes, or until tender, add the chicken pieces back to the soup and bring to a gentle simmer.
- Skim off any fat that has risen to the surface and drop small balls of the dumpling mix into the simmering soup and simmer for 5 minutes.
- Stir in the chopped parsley for the final minute of cooking,

To serve
- Ladle into warmed serving bowls and serve with warm crusty bread.

SIERRA LEONE

Words by
SQUADRON LEADER CHRIS POWELL

A BATTLEFIELD AMBULANCE UNLOADED FROM AN RAF C17, SIERRA LEONE, 2014

THE ROYAL AIR FORCE'S involvement in Sierra Leone dates back to 1941, when three Sunderland flying boats were based at the capital, Freetown, for a two-year period to conduct anti-submarine missions over the South Atlantic during the Second World War.

The RAF only returned to the country in 1998. After a prolonged civil war, rebel forces had made rapid gains, and two C-130K Hercules of 47 Squadron were called in to evacuate British personnel from Freetown. Two years later, a further British intervention saw RAF Harriers operating from an aircraft carrier moored off the west coast, and four Chinooks, which made the astonishing 3,500-mile transit in 30 hours – the longest ever self-ferry by RAF helicopters. Later, in 2000, Chinooks and Hercules were involved in the rescue of six soldiers of the Royal Irish Regiment, who had been held hostage by the notorious West Side Boys gangsters, a splinter group of the Armed Forces Revolutionary Council.

The most recent RAF involvement was in response to the outbreak of the Ebola virus in West Africa. The virus first appeared in 1976, simultaneously in Nzara, Sudan and Yambuku in the Democratic Republic of Congo. Previous

outbreaks had soon been bought under control, but the outbreak of December 2013 in Guinea reached epidemic proportions, creating an unprecedented humanitarian crisis across the region.

William Pooley was a British volunteer nurse who worked in the Sierra Leonean capital, Freetown, before volunteering at a makeshift clinic in Kenema, where other nurses had either died from Ebola or were too scared to work. In August 2014, he contracted the virus. 99 Squadron was tasked to return him to RAF Northolt.

Squadron Leader Andy Crichton was the C17 captain for the task. Although 99 Squadron had flown many injured patients back from Afghanistan, this was the first time an Ebola-infected patient would be flown in the Air Transport Isolator (ATI) – a "bubble" designed to minimise the risk of contamination. The medical team departed the aircraft in full protective equipment to transfer Pooley into the "bubble" at a safe distance. This was a carefully rehearsed, slow and deliberate process to reduce any risk of infection. After treatment in London, Pooley made a full recovery.

Over the coming months, 99 Squadron's C17s would become regular visitors to Freetown's Lungi airport, bringing in aid and supplies for the 750 British military personnel deployed to the country to establish treatment centres and an Ebola Training Academy. By October 2015, after claiming more than 11,000 lives, the Ebola outbreak was finally brought under control.

Spinach Plasas
Beef & Spinach Stew

This stew from Sierra Leone is, in many ways, similar to a large number of dishes from the west coast of Africa. This one is lightly spiced and thickened with pounded groundnuts or, as in this case, peanut butter. This variation, however, is quite distinctive in that, in addition to the meat, it is finished with hot smoked (or sometimes dried) fish and brown shrimps.

INGREDIENTS

Serves 4

For the stew

400g diced stewing beef

4 tbsp red palm or vegetable oil

2 medium onion, cut into large
dice

2 cloves of garlic, finely chopped

1 tsp cayenne pepper

750ml beef stock

2 bay leaves

2 red peppers, de-seed and cut
into large dice

125g smooth peanut butter

100g spinach, washed

100g smoked fish e.g. smoked
mackerel or trout, flaked into
large pieces

100g cooked brown shrimps or
small prawns

salt and pepper

To serve

boiled or steamed rice

3 tbsp parsley, coarsely chopped

METHOD

To make the stew

• Season the beef with salt and freshly ground black pepper.

• Heat 2 tbsp of the oil in a casserole dish over a high heat, add the beef and sear all over until well coloured. Transfer the beef to a bowl and set aside.

• Return the casserole to a medium heat with the remaining oil. Add the onions and cook, stirring frequently, for 5 minutes until softened and translucent. Stir in the garlic and cayenne pepper; continue to cook for a further 2 minutes, stirring continuously.

• Stir in the beef (together with any juices that have accumulated in the bowl), beef stock and bay leaves, reduce the heat, cover with a lid and simmer, stirring occasionally, for 1½ hours until the beef is tender.

• Stir in the peppers and peanut butter, bring back to a simmer, adjust the consistency with a little boiling water if necessary, and continue to cook, stirring occasionally for a further 15 minutes.

• Stir in the spinach, flaked smoked fish, prawns or shrimps and about two thirds of the chopped parsley. Bring back to a simmer and cook for about 5 minutes until the fish is warmed through and the spinach has wilted into the sauce, season with salt and freshly ground black pepper.

To serve

• Spoon rice into the bottom of serving bowls, ladle the stew over the top and garnish with the remaining chopped parsley.

ITALY

Words by
WING COMMANDER TEO BRADLEY

IN RECENT DECADES, the Royal Air Force's association with Italy has centred on the use of Italian bases to prosecute United Nations and NATO missions in the former Yugoslavia and Libya. In 1999, Operation Allied Force was planned "to degrade and damage the military and security structure that President Milosevic has used to depopulate and destroy the Albanian majority in Kosovo," according to US Secretary of Defense, William S Cohen.

As part of this operation, Harrier GR7s from 1(F) Squadron deployed to Gioia del Colle (GDC) air base in southern Italy and two Tristar air-to-air refuelling (AAR) tankers deployed to Ancona. The GR7s operated from GDC throughout the operation, flying over 800 missions against Serb targets in Kosovo and southern Yugoslavia. By the end of the operation in June 1999, the Harrier detachment had grown to 16 aircraft and was bolstered by Tornado GR1s from 14, 9 and 31 Squadrons. In all, a total of 1,618 sorties were flown by UK aircraft.

More than a decade later, the RAF reacquainted itself with the Mediterranean during Operation Ellamy in Libya. This was preceded by Operation Deference, with RAF operations beginning in February 2011 when a non-combatant evacuation of "Entitled Persons" (EP) from Libya was ordered. Two Sentry E3Ds were deployed from RAF Waddington on 26 February and the first was on station within 17 hours of the request from Permanent Joint Headquarters. RAF Lyneham forward-

deployed three C-130 Hercules to Valetta Airport, Malta on 22 and 23 February since the task had belatedly changed from evacuating EPs from Benghazi to recovering them from desert strips in central Libya. On 26 and 27 February, more than 400 EPs from more than 30 different nations were evacuated by the RAF to Malta.

Operation Ellamy itself was conducted from 19 March to 31 October 2011. UN Security Council Resolution 1,973 was passed on 17 March, authorising "all necessary measures, short of the deployment of a foreign occupation force, to protect civilians and civilian populated areas from attack". That same day, the Typhoon Force was given warning of deployment and a day later, Tornado GR4s were prepared to strike targets from the UK. On 20 March, 10 Typhoons deployed from RAF Coningsby to GDC and, by lunchtime the next day, two Typhoons were flying combat air patrols in support of the no-fly zone. On the same day, the first of four Tornado GR4s deployed from RAF Marham to GDC via missions in Libya.

Combat aircraft were supported by E-3D Sentry, Nimrod R1, Sentinel and VC10 AAR, which were forward-deployed to RAF Akrotiri. As the campaign progressed, AAR aircraft and E-3Ds were moved to Trapani in Sicily, and Sentinel was moved to GDC. On average, 953 RAF personnel were forward-deployed at any one time; working from Poggio, GDC, Trapani and Akrotiri, with almost 2,000 passengers and more than 890,000kg of freight being moved by air.

AN RAF PILOT BOARDS HIS TYPHOON FIGHTER AT GIOIA DEL COLLE DURING OPERATION ELLAMY, 2011

Maple & Lavender Semi-Freddo

by CHRIS & JAMES TANNER
CHEF-PATRONS AT THE KENTISH HARE

In Italy, a "semi-freddo" is a half-frozen mousse, one that is often made using the same method as a frozen mousse. These are generally frozen then left to thaw slightly in the refrigerator until semi-freddo. This delightful dessert combines a sweet hit from the maple syrup followed by the delicate lavender flavour – a stunning combination.

INGREDIENTS

Serves 6–8

For the semi-freddo

50g lavender flowers

100ml water

115g granulated sugar

3 egg whites

350ml whipping cream

100g maple syrup

To serve

maple syrup

icing sugar (optional)

METHOD

To make the semi-freddo

- Line a 450g loaf tin with cling film. Allow the edges to hang over the sides of the tin as this will ensure the semi-freddo can be easily removed later.
- Preheat the oven to 160°C, lay the lavender flowers on a baking sheet and place in the oven for about 5 minutes; this will dry out the lavender and give a much more perfumed aroma to the ice cream.
- Place the water, sugar and lavender flowers in a small, heavy-based pan and heat gently, stirring all the time, until the sugar has dissolved. Bring to the boil and cook, without stirring, for at least 2 minutes, then add the maple syrup and cook for a further 5 minutes. Remove from the heat and strain carefully to remove the lavender.
- In a large, clean bowl, whisk the egg whites until stiff and dry, then slowly pour in the syrup in a thin stream, whisking all the time, until the mixture is thick and fluffy; continue to whisk until the mixture is cold.
- Whisk the cream until it holds its shape then fold it into the mixture until it is well blended. Pour into the prepared loaf tin, cover and freeze for at least 5 hours until firm.

To serve

- Remove the cover and stand the tin in hot water for a few seconds to loosen the sides. Using a hot knife, cut into slices and drizzle with a little maple syrup. Finish with a dusting of icing sugar, if you wish.

MACEDONIA

Words by
WING COMMANDER TEO BRADLEY

THE RAF'S MODERN-ERA involvement with Macedonia resulted from the repercussions of the break-up of Yugoslavia in the 1990s. When it declared independence on 8 September 1991, Macedonia was the only ex-Yugoslav republic that managed to secede non-violently from the federation. Because of this, Macedonia was considered one of the bright spots in the former Yugoslavia. However, in 1999, Serbian forces invaded Kosovo with the intention of annexing territory, bringing war to Macedonia's doorstep.

NATO's Operation Allied Force was sanctioned in 1999 as a systematic air bombing campaign against Serbian forces in Kosovo and infrastructure targets in Serbia itself, aiming to force the withdrawal of Serbian troops from the province. The success of this air campaign, combined with intense international diplomatic pressure, forced the Serbian leadership to withdraw Serb forces from Kosovo without a NATO ground assault. NATO forces did, however, enter the Kosovo region in June 1999 when eight Chinooks from 27 Squadron (based at Camp Piper, Macedonia) and six Pumas from 33 Squadron (based at Pristina, Kosovo) played a starring role in the NATO insertion operation into Kosovo.

They carried troops of the British Army's 5 Airborne Brigade to seize key high ground along the Kacanik gorge, along which NATO troops had to drive to enter the province from Macedonia. Elsewhere, 34 Squadron RAF Regiment personnel were responsible for the physical security of Puma Helicopters in a forward operating base near the Kosovan border. Operation Agricola was the UK's contribution to NATO's Kosovo Enforcement Force and marked the largest support helicopter deployment since Operation Granby in the first Gulf War.

The turmoil in Kosovo eventually overspilled into Macedonia as the country opened its borders to 360,000 displaced Albanian refugees. At the same time, insurgents from the Kosovo Liberation Army began crossing the border and entrenching themselves in Albanian-populated municipalities of Macedonia. This period of instability almost broke out into full-scale war between the Macedonian government and the ethnically Albanian guerrillas of the National Liberation Army (NLA), in 2001. In the chaos, the NLA tried to leverage political and geographic gain for ethnic Albanians in Macedonia.

Following a number of serious incidents, NATO declared another peacekeeeping

THE RAF'S BOEING
CHINOOK HELICOPTERS
ARRIVE IN MACEDONIA, 1999

mission (Operation Amber Fox) to disarm the rebels, followed by Operation Allied Harmony. One high-profile mission of 99 Squadron from RAF Brize Norton (flying C-17 Globemasters) was the deployment of Lynx helicopters and support equipment to Macedonia in 2001 to aid Operation Bessemer.

While many RAF aircraft were involved in the wider air campaign over Kosovo (as an example, two Canberra reconnaissance aircraft flew from Gioia del Colle Air Base in Italy to conduct NATO verification missions), the RAF "footprint" in Macedonia was limited and concentrated on the Support Helicopter Force supporting British Army deployments. In March 2003, NATO's peacekeeping mission in Macedonia finally came to an end and was formally handed over to the European Union.

Tavče Gravče
Macedonian Baked Beans

This recipe is considered the national dish of Macedonia and, although traditionally made with dried beans, canned beans can be used. To make the dish more substantial, leftover cooked meat can be added. For a brunch version, add some cooked chopped bacon, sausage or black pudding and, once transferred to the baking dish, make a hole in the centre and crack in an egg before baking.

INGREDIENTS

Serves 4

For the beans

375g dried cannellini beans

1 large onion, coarsely diced

1 red pepper, de-seeded, one half coarsely diced and the other half thinly sliced

1 yellow pepper, de-seeded, one half coarsely diced and the other half thinly sliced

1 green chilli, shredded

cooked meat (optional, e.g. diced roast meat, bacon, ham or sausage)

100ml olive oil

1 large red onion, halved and thinly sliced

2 cloves of garlic, finely chopped or crushed

1 medium tomato, coarsely chopped

1 tbsp smoked paprika

2 tsp chilli powder

1½ tsp plain flour

2 tbsp mint, shredded

2 tbsp parsley, coarsely chopped

salt and pepper

To serve

crusty bread

METHOD

To prepare the beans

- Wash the beans under cold running water, place in a bowl, cover with plenty of cold water and leave overnight to soak.

To cook the beans

- Drain and thoroughly rinse the soaked beans, tip into a saucepan, cover with cold water, place over a high heat and boil for 10 minutes.
- Drain the beans, cover with cold water and bring to a boil over a high heat. Reduce the heat to low, cover the saucepan with a lid and simmer the beans for 45 minutes, topping up with boiling water as necessary to keep the beans submerged in the water.
- Add the chopped onions, diced peppers (do not add the sliced peppers at this stage) and chillies (add any cooked meat at this stage if using). Simmer for around 20 minutes until the beans are soft, but not breaking up, and much of the water has been absorbed then season well with salt and black pepper.
- Once the beans, onions and peppers have been simmering for 10 minutes, heat the olive oil in a frying pan or saucepan over a moderate heat, add the red onion and sliced peppers; cook, stirring frequently, for 5 minutes until the onions are translucent and just softened.
- Add the chopped garlic, diced tomato, paprika and chilli powder; cook, stirring continuously for 2 minutes, sprinkle over the flour and cook, stirring continuously, for a further 2 minutes.
- Add the contents of the frying pan to the beans, stir in the shredded mint and half of the chopped parsley. Check the seasoning, adding a little more salt and black pepper if required, and simmer for 2 minutes. The sauce should be quite thick at this stage but if it's too thick add a little boiling water.

To bake the beans

- Preheat the oven to 200°C.
- Transfer to either individual ovenproof dishes (ideally earthenware) or one large dish.
- Bake in the preheated oven for 25 to 30 minutes until a crust has formed on top. Allow to sit at room temperature for 10 minutes before serving.

To serve

- Garnish with the remaining parsley and serve with crusty bread.

SERBIA

Words by
FLIGHT SERGEANT MICK BLACKALL

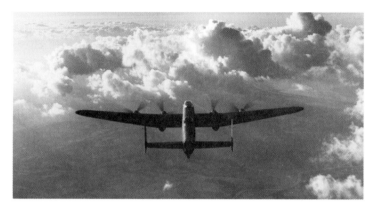

AN AVRO LANCASTER BOMBER IN FLIGHT, 1943

DURING THE SECOND World War, the Kingdom of Yugoslavia – which included modern-day Serbia – was occupied by the Axis Powers and was under the control of German military administration. Between 1941 and 1945 the whole area was heavily bombed by the Royal Air Force and the US Air Force.

Fast forward to March 1999 and, under Operation Allied Force, the RAF took part in 73 continuous days of NATO bombing to force Serbia to withdraw from Kosovo, which they finally did on 10 June. The operation involved Harrier GR7 and Tornado ground-attack jets as well as an army of support aircraft. In December 2002, battle honours were awarded to 1, 7, 8, 9, 14, 23, 31, 51, 101 and 216 Squadrons.

History shares with us a personal tale of a Serbian teenager who later became an RAF hero in the Second World War. For Nebosja "Neb" Kujundzic, to leave his home town of Belgrade as a teenager and move to Leeds to study engineering must have been an extraordinary life event.

Neb spoke excellent English; he was a talented musician and a popular student on the Leeds University campus. When war broke out in 1939, he was unable to return to his native Yugoslavia and, in 1941, he was in one of the first groups of students to be trained for the newly formed Leeds University Squadron. After further training in Florida, he served at RAF Lindholme, completing many bombing missions over enemy territory, before being posted to 103 Squadron, Bomber Command at Elsham Wolds, Lincolnshire, as an RAF Lancaster pilot.

On the morning of 4 March 1943, Flying Officer Kujundzic and crew boarded Lancaster W4333 PM-B for a day-time training flight from Elsham Wolds. During this routine flight somewhere over Cambridgeshire, one of the Lancaster's engines burst into flames. Neb would have known that the plane was destined to crash and gave the order for his crew to bail out. As his crew parachuted to safety, 24-year-old Neb stayed at the controls as his plane crashed, close to the village of Yaxley, four miles south of Peterborough. He did not survive the crash.

Nebojsa Kujundzic had steered the doomed bomber away from houses in Yaxley, and villagers praised the pilot's skill and bravery. A road in Yaxley – Lancaster Way – was named to mark his bravery, and he was buried with full honours at Eastfield Cemetery in Peterborough. He continues to be remembered by the villagers of Yaxley and, in 2003, representatives from the Serbia and Montenegro Embassy in London, the Serb community in Britain, the RAF Elsham Wolds Association and the Peterborough Aircrew Association took part in a commemoration of the 60th anniversary of this event at his graveside.

Karađorđeva Šnicla
Karadjordje Steak

This classic Serbian dish is named after Prince Karađorđe, founder of modern Serbia and the leader of the first Serbian uprising against the Ottoman Empire. Traditionally made with veal, it is often made with pork, chicken or beef and was created by the renowned Serbian chef Milovan Mića Stojanović. Kajmak is a thick and creamy fresh, or unripened, cheese product made by simmering full fat unpasteurised milk very slowly for a couple of hours before skimming the cream off the top.

INGREDIENTS
Serves 4
For the kajmak
100g cream cheese
50g butter, room temperature
¼ tsp sea salt

For the pork
4 pork leg (or loin) steaks,
   flattened out to 6mm thick
2 large eggs, beaten
75g plain flour
150g breadcrumbs
salt and pepper
vegetable oil for frying

To serve
1 lemon, cut into wedges
tartare sauce
baked potato wedges or chips

METHOD
To make the kajmak
• Beat the cream cheese and butter together until smooth (take care not to over mix as the cream cheese may split), add the salt and mix in.
• Store in the fridge if making in advance and bring to room temperature before using.

To prepare the pork
• Place each pork steak on the worktop, lightly season the top with pepper, divide the kajmak between the steaks, spread evenly and roll each up to a neat tube.
• Secure each of the rolls with a toothpick, trim the ends square and place in the freezer for 30 to 40 minutes to firm up before crumbing.

To breadcrumb the pork
• Remove the toothpicks from the steaks.
• Season the flour with salt and freshly ground pepper, dust the rolled steaks in the flour and tap off the excess.
• Dip each in the beaten egg until coated all over then roll in the breadcrumbs until thoroughly coated, dip back in the egg then give the steaks a second coat of breadcrumbs.

To cook
• Heat the oil in a deep fryer or deep-sided pan to 180°C and deep-fry the steaks until golden brown, crisp and thoroughly cooked through. Drain on kitchen paper.

To serve
• Serve the fried steaks with lemon wedges, tartare sauce, baked potato wedges or chips.

MOZAMBIQUE

Words by
SQUADRON LEADER CHRIS POWELL

DURING OCTOBER AND November of 1999, Mozambique suffered exceptionally heavy rainfall. More followed in January 2000, with some areas of the country experiencing a year's worth of rainfall in less than two weeks. As a result, the rivers Incomati, Umbuluzi and Limpopo exceeded their banks. The country was now experiencing its most severe flooding in nearly 50 years.

Worse was to follow; the full force of Cyclone Eline hit the coast of Mozambique on 22 February, with wind speeds reaching up to 160mph. The floods claimed the lives of nearly 500 people and drove 360,000 from their homes. The government of Mozambique appealed to the world for assistance. Operation Barwood was the UK's response.

Four Puma helicopters and personnel from 33 Squadron, RAF Benson, were put on standby to deploy. On Wednesday 1 March 2000, they were informed they would definitely not be going until at least Saturday. The following day, they were somewhat surprised to be told they were leaving in three hours. F S Strawson was a crewman instructor on the Operational Conversion Unit and was not part of the potential deployment. He was enjoying the sight of his colleagues frantically packing and preparing their kit when he was given the unexpected news that he was now deploying with them!

33 Squadron deployed to Hoedspruit, South Africa, by Tristar, flown by 216 Squadron. Due to a misunderstanding, the South Africans were not informed the RAF were deploying and initially barred access. This was soon resolved and four Pumas followed in a chartered Antonov, which were unloaded and rapidly reassembled and prepared for operations. The helicopters and the detachment personnel then flew into Maputo, the capital city. It was the first presence of the British armed forces in Mozambique.

On a daily basis, the Pumas departed Maputo and flew into Palmeira, which was a field location and the main base for the World Food Programme. 33 Squadron worked alongside the South African Oryx helicopters, a Puma derivative. Palmeira soon became very busy and a "Beachmaster" was required to coordinate the movement of supplies and the helicopters in and out of the field.

The task for 33 Squadron was distributing aid. Pots, pans, shelters and food were flown out to remote and isolated villages. One task involved taking urgent medical equipment to a faraway village, which was at the absolute limit of the Puma's flying range. Given the urgent nature of the tasking, one aircraft flew out with another following, carrying sufficient supplies of fuel for both aircraft to fly back.

The detachment worked flat out. The tasking was unrelenting with the Pumas flying constantly from first-light to last-light for 14 straight days. A standard crew for a Puma is two pilots and a crewman; however, due to the intensive and complex nature of these operations, a second crewman operated on all flights.

The last aid distribution flights were flown on the 19 March 2000. In two weeks, the Pumas delivered 425 tonnes of aid and supplies to the country and airlifted 563 people to safety. Defence Secretary Geoff Hoon said: "The achievements of our young men and women in helping in the region is testament to the high degree of training, dedication and commitment of our armed forces personnel."

Frango à Cafreal
Grilled Piri Piri Chicken

The culture and cuisine of Portugal was brought to Mozambique by Portuguese settlers and colonists in the late 15th and early 16th centuries, who introduced new crops, flavours and cooking techniques to the country. Among these new crops were lemons and chillies – the two main ingredients of piri piri sauce or marinade. These are rubbed into chicken, or other meat or fish, and cooked – in typical African fashion – over charcoal.

INGREDIENTS

Serves 4

1 medium chicken or 4 chicken legs

For the piri piri sauce

1 tsp dried chilli flakes

2 lemons, juiced

2 tbsp white wine vinegar

4 tbsp olive oil

2 cloves of garlic, finely chopped
 or crushed

1 tbsp paprika

½ tsp salt

2 red chillies, finely chopped

2 birds eye chillies, finely chopped

2 tsp dijon mustard

For the marinade

2 cloves of garlic, finely chopped
 or crushed

1cm piece of ginger, grated

90ml piri piri sauce (approx. half
 of the above recipe)

250ml coconut milk

salt and pepper

To serve

2 tbsp coriander, coarsely chopped

1 lemon, cut into wedges

boiled or steamed rice

remaining piri piri sauce

METHOD

To make the piri piri sauce
(24 hours in advance)

• Place the dried chilli flakes in an eggcup. Pour over 2 tsp of boiling water and leave to stand for 20 minutes.

• Place all of the ingredients, including the liquid with the dried chillies, into a bowl and mix until well blended. Place in a container, cover and store in the fridge for at least 12 hours to infuse.

To prepare the chicken

• Remove the legs from the chicken and cut each through the joint into thighs and drumsticks. Remove the backbone from the chicken by cutting either side, cut in half through the breast bone then cut each breast in half.

• With a sharp knife, score each piece of chicken two or three times, this will help the marinade penetrate the chicken and cook evenly.

To marinate the chicken
(at least 8 hours in advance)

• Mix the chopped garlic, grated ginger, piri piri sauce (about half of the prepared sauce), coconut milk and seasoning together in a bowl.

• Place the chicken pieces in a bowl, pour over three quarters of the marinade and toss to coat thoroughly, cover and allow to marinate for at least 8 hours, or overnight, in the fridge.

To cook the chicken

• Remove the chicken pieces from the marinade.

• Preheat the oven to 200°C.

• Line a baking tray with aluminium foil, place a wire rack on top and arrange the chicken pieces on the rack, skin side down.

• Bake the chicken in the oven for 10 minutes, remove from the oven, turn each piece over, brush with a little of the reserved marinade then return to the oven for a further 10 to 15 minutes until the chicken is well browned and thoroughly cooked through.

• Give the chicken pieces a final brush with the marinade and glaze for a few minutes under a hot grill until the skin is slightly charred.

To serve

• Transfer the piri piri chicken to a serving dish, garnish with the chopped coriander and serve with the lemon wedges, rice and the remaining piri piri sauce.

CÔTE D'IVOIRE

Words by
SQUADRON LEADER MAL CRAIG

THE FORMER FRENCH colony of the Ivory Coast – or Côte d'Ivoire, as it is known today – may not have featured frequently in the annals of RAF history since the withdrawal of Coastal Command Forces conducting anti-submarine patrols during the Second World War. But, in light of a volatile civil war in a divided county, the Ministry of Defence began to develop plans for an evacuation of British and French civilians from this troubled land.

Troops were placed on standby and a Royal Navy ship was diverted to the area, but it was the flexibility and speed of response that only the RAF's aircraft can provide that would prove critical to what would become known as Operation Phyllis. Three C130 Hercules Tactical Air transport aircraft from RAF Lyneham in Wiltshire were prepared and pre-positioned in Ghana in order to rescue those civilians and consular staff trapped in Ivory Coast.

At the request of Gordon Wetherell, the British High Commissioner in Accra, the small fleet of Hercules aircraft began their descent into war-torn Ivory Coast in the early hours of 12 November 2004. Through the muggy, tropical, night-time air, they began ferrying 220 UK nationals and other evacuees to safety. By 11am the next day, the British High Commissioner declared that the rescue had been completed.

It was a remarkably efficient operation. The last aircraft that lifted into the African skies from Abidjan, the capital city of the Ivory Coast, reached its destination less than 50 hours after leaving its Wiltshire base.

On 11 November 2004, in anticipation of the imminent mission, the Defence Secretary Geoff Hoon addressed the House of Commons. His statement showed confidence in UK forces – and the RAF in particular – to achieve success in the face of adversity. "The UK places the utmost priority on protecting its citizens, whether at home or abroad," said Hoon. "In light of the deteriorating security situation in Côte d'Ivoire, a military reconnaissance team deployed earlier this week to assess the requirement to evacuate UK nationals. I wish to inform the house that, following this, the Foreign and Commonwealth Office has requested British forces to undertake an evacuation of UK nationals and others over the next few days. Some 400 people are entitled to our protection.

"Our ability to react quickly to the situation in Côte d'Ivoire is testament to the flexibility and capability of Britain's armed forces, and to the professionalism of British servicemen and women."

"In light of a volatile civil war, the MoD began to develop plans for an evacuation of British and French civilians"

Mango & Passion Fruit Fool

Desserts don't feature heavily in Ivorian cuisine, so it might be considered an anomaly that, with its French heritage, Côte d'Ivoire's most popular dessert, the mango fool, is based on a traditional English pudding. This embellishes the traditional recipe to include passion fruit, a common fruit indigenous to the country. It gives a perfect tangy contrast to the creamy mango fool. The mangoes for the fool should be ripe and soft when squeezed with minimal green colour on the skin.

INGREDIENTS

Serves 4

For the passion fruit coulis

9 passion fruits

1 orange

50g caster sugar

2 tbsp cold water

For the fool

3 ripe mangoes, peeled and
 coarsely chopped (or 650g frozen
 mango pieces)

50ml Cointreau or Grand Marnier
 (optional; 50ml is one miniature
 bottle)

500ml double cream

To garnish

1 mango, peeled and diced

2 tbsp desiccated coconut, lightly
 toasted

4 sprigs of mint

METHOD

To make the coulis

• Cut the passion fruit in half. Scoop out the seeds and pulp into a saucepan, squeeze the juice from the oranges and add to the passion fruit with the sugar and cold water.

• Place the saucepan over a low heat and gently bring to a boil, reduce the heat and simmer for 5 minutes.

• Push the contents through a fine sieve, ensuring as much of the pulp is forced through, into a clean container (the coulis should have a syrupy consistency and should just coat the back of a spoon); it will thicken slightly when chilled. Cool the coulis at room temperature then cover the bowl and place in the fridge to chill.

To make the fool

• Place the coarsely chopped mango flesh, Cointreau or Grand Marnier (if using) and cream in a blender. Blend on high speed until the mango has puréed and the cream has thickened; it should have a lightly whipped cream consistency.

• Spoon a third of the passion fruit coulis into the bottom of your chosen glasses or bowls, pipe or spoon half of the mango fool over the top followed by another third of the passion fruit coulis then the remaining mango fool. Place in the fridge to firm up.

To serve

• Remove the glasses from the fridge, top with the finely diced mango, pour over the remaining passion fruit coulis and garnish with the toasted coconut and a sprig of mint.

INDONESIA

Words by
SQUADRON LEADER CHRIS POWELL

DURING LATE 1941 and early 1942, Japanese forces made rapid advances throughout the Far East, resulting in all RAF units being driven back to Singapore. With airfields under Japanese fire it became imperative to disperse some aircraft. Bombers were moved to Sumatra, where airfields were being developed as refuelling grounds for reinforcements inbound from India.

225 (Bomber) Group, consisting of Blenheims and Hudsons, was formed on 16 January 1942 and sent to Palembang. The main airfield had two hard runways and was known as P1. Another airfield, known as P2, was a huge natural field with good cover for aircraft. It was not visible from the road and its construction had been kept secret from the Japanese. Similar clearings in the area made it incredibly difficult to spot from the air. Even though, at one time, more than 100 aircraft were based there, Japanese reconnaissance aircraft never located it.

"Anti-British feeling escalated, culminating in the burning of the British Embassy, and the looting of the homes of British nationals"

To avoid Japanese fighter patrols, bombing missions were conducted at night and flown over long ranges, which necessitated refuelling at landing grounds in northern Sumatra. The long flights imposed great strain on the crews, especially during monsoon season. With no radio aids for navigation, bomber crews needed night-flying skills and massive endurance.

In February 1942, fighters, including 48 Hurricanes from HMS *Eagle*, were deployed to P1, and the Japanese increased attacks in response. On 14 February, P1 was attacked by Japanese paratroopers. The airfield defences held off the initial attack and the returning aircraft were diverted to P2. However, a large Japanese convoy consisting of an invasion force had been detected entering Palembang River.

Aircraft from P2 attacked, inflicting heavy casualties and ultimately brought the landing to a standstill, making the Japanese pay a heavy price for their failure to discover P2. Further paratrooper landings took place the following day and all flyable aircraft and personnel were evacuated from Sumatra to Java. However, the Japanese had suffered heavy casualties and initially were unable to continue their advance.

In 1963, the Federation of Malaysia was formed from Malaya, Singapore, and the British Protectorates of North Borneo and Sarawak. Indonesia viewed this as a major diplomatic defeat. Strong anti-British feeling escalated rapidly, culminating in the burning and sacking of the British Embassy, and the looting of the homes of British nationals. One woman was hidden under the bed of her Indonesian neighbour to save her from a mob that was burning her house down. On 19 September 1963, British, Australian and New Zealand personnel evacuated 400 people from Jakarta to Singapore, using three Argosies and one Hastings transport aircraft.

In recent years, the RAF has responded to natural disasters in Indonesia. Following the tsunami in 2004, which left 140,000 people dead and millions homeless, RAF C17 and Tristar aircraft flew repeated missions to the region, including 11 into Banda Aceh in Sumatra to deliver vital aid. In 2009, further C17 sorties delivered aid equipment and search-and-rescue specialists after Sumatra suffered a massive earthquake. The equipment included thermal cameras and lifting gear to detect survivors trapped under collapsed buildings.

THE RAF CONTRIBUTES TO THE BANDA ACEH RELIEF EFFORT, FOLLOWING THE DEVASTATING 2004 TSUNAMI

Rendang Daging
Dry Beef & Coconut Curry

Although widely found across Far Eastern countries, rendang originates from Indonesia. Unlike other highly spiced curries, rendang is cooked very slowly until there is no liquid left, leaving the meat coated with the spices and coconut, and caramelised in the remaining oil.

INGREDIENTS

Serves 4

For the spice paste

3 stalks of lemongrass

200g shallots, peeled and chopped

1 tsp salt

1 tsp ground coriander

½ tsp turmeric

a pinch of ground cloves

2.5cm piece of ginger, peeled and
finely chopped

4 cloves of garlic, crushed

1–2 tbsp dried chilli flakes

For the rendang

1 stalk of lemongrass

60g desiccated coconut

100ml sunflower oil or vegetable oil

800g diced beef (chuck or shin)

1 small cinnamon stick

3 whole star anise

4 green cardamom pods, crushed

2.5cm piece of galangal, peeled
and cut into thin slices

400ml coconut milk

1 tbsp red wine vinegar

4 dried kaffir lime leaves, crumbled

1 tbsp palm sugar

To serve

steamed or boiled rice

2 red chillies finely sliced

1 lime, zest pared and shredded

METHOD

To make the spice paste

- Remove the tough outer leaves of the lemongrass stalks, coarsely chop the white parts (bottom two thirds) and discard the woody top third.
- Place the chopped shallots, salt, ground coriander, turmeric, ground cloves, ginger, garlic, chilli flakes and chopped lemongrass in a food processor with 2–3 tbsp of cold water and blend to a paste.

To make the rendang

- Cut the lemongrass stalk in half and bruise to release the flavour.
- Toast the desiccated coconut in a dry frying pan until lightly coloured.
- Heat the oil in a large casserole or saucepan, add the spice paste and stir-fry for 2 to 3 minutes until aromatic.
- Add the diced beef and cook, stirring continuously, for a few minutes until the beef is lightly coloured
- Add the cinnamon stick, star anise, cardamom pods, galangal, coconut milk, vinegar, kaffir lime leaves, palm sugar, pounded lemongrass stalk and toasted coconut. Bring to a simmer and cook on medium heat, stirring frequently, for 10 minutes.
- Lower the heat, cover with a lid and simmer for 3½ to 4 hours until the meat is very tender and the sauce is well reduced (stir in a little water if the sauce becomes too dry during cooking).
- Remove the lid, increase the heat and continue to simmer, stirring frequently until there is very little sauce left and the beef starts to caramelise in the oil.
- Season with salt and add more sugar and vinegar if required to balance the sweet and sour flavour.
- Pick out the lemongrass stalk, cinnamon stick and star anise if preferred.

To serve

- Serve with steamed rice and garnish with sliced chillies and shredded lime zest.

LIBYA

Words by
WING COMMANDER BEN SHARP

LIBYA CAME TO the centre of the world's attention in 2011 when civil war broke out in the country. In late February of that year, the Royal Air Force, along with the Royal Navy, was tasked under Operation Deference to evacuate British "Entitled Persons": a challenging task as many worked at oil installations spread across a country that is more than three times the size of France.

Hercules C-130s, watched over by Sentry E3-Ds and refuelled by VC-10s, reached deep into Libya and withdrew more than 400 people. One month later, a United Nations Security Council Resolution authorised "all necessary measures... to protect civilians and civilian populated areas from attack". Within two days, the RAF response began under Operation Ellamy. Typhoons deployed to Italy to enforce a no-fly zone over Libya; a role that later evolving into the aircraft's first use in ground attack.

Tornado GR4s conducted the longest bombing raids ever flown by the RAF from the UK, supported by VC-10s and Tristar tankers; all also deployed forward to Italy within a week. The RAF's surveillance aircraft Sentry E3-D, Sentinel R1 and Nimrod R1 all played key roles, the latter retiring immediately after its return home.

Over Libya in 2011, the RAF employed with remarkable effect the four air power roles: air mobility; control of the air; attack; and intelligence and situational awareness. This was also the case 71 years previously when, in 1940, Air HQ Middle East recognised the need to keep logistics lines open, fend off air raids, attack enemy land and maritime forces, and maintain a sound awareness of Axis actions. Libya was at the heart of the action as the Allies sought to contain and defeat Italian (and later German) forces that threatened the region.

The RAF was ordered to "maintain close cooperation with the General Officer commanding the Army in the Western Desert" and, over the next three years, the tide of the war ebbed and flowed as land losses and gains were realised. At its peak, the Western Desert Air Force comprised over 30 Allied squadrons, with aircraft types including Spitfires, Warhawks, Hurricanes, Beaufighters and Mustangs; this in addition to the bombers and fighters under the command of other HQs in the region. Living conditions were challenging: small tents were the typical sleeping accommodation, erected over slit trenches to provide extra headroom and additional shelter from air attack. As the war progressed and personnel moved further forward into Libya, they found themselves living in sandholes at abandoned bases littered with mines, eating tinned rations of bully beef or stew, and receiving strict rations of water. In January 1943, Tripoli was captured, unlocking the future campaigns in Tunisia and Sicily.

The RAF learned much in Libya in the Second World War, particularly how to make a whole air force mobile in response to rapidly changing land and maritime situations. These lessons were to prove invaluable 70 years later in 2011.

Cuscus bil-Bosla
Libyan Lamb with Couscous

Cuscus bil-Bosla is Libya's national dish, a lamb stew in a tomato-flavoured sauce cooked with kammon hoot (a hot chilli paste), chickpeas and potatoes accompanied by couscous. The dish is traditionally served in a big bowl with the lamb and sauce poured over the couscous, set in the centre of the table for communal eating.

INGREDIENTS

Serves 4

For the kammon hoot

(makes more than is required

for this dish)

4 tsp dried hot chilli flakes

1½ tsp cumin seeds

½ tsp coriander seeds

½ tsp caraway seeds

½ tsp dried mint

2 cloves of garlic, finely chopped

METHOD

To make the kammon hoot

- Place the dried chilli flakes in a small cup, cover with 3 tbsp of boiling water and leave to rehydrate for 20 minutes.
- Dry fry the cumin, coriander and caraway seeds over a moderate heat until fragrant. Transfer to a mortar and grind with a pestle to a coarse powder (alternatively use a spice grinder).
- Once the chillies have soaked place in a small hand-held processor with the soaking water, ground spices, dried mint and chopped garlic. Blend to a thick paste, adding a little cold water as required. Alternatively, the paste can be made with the pestle and mortar.

For the lamb stew

3 tbsp olive oil

800g lamb, cut into large chunks

6 medium onions, one third finely
  diced and two thirds finely sliced

2 green chillies, finely sliced

2 tsp ground turmeric

2 tbsp tomato purée

1½ tsp kammon hoot (see recipe
  on page 357) or hot harissa paste

1 litre chicken stock

1 bay leaf

1 cinnamon stick

50g butter

400g potatoes, diced

1 tin (400g) of cooked chickpeas,
  drained

salt and pepper

To serve

200g couscous

½ orange, juice and finely grated
  zest

½ lime, juice and finely grated zest

2 tbsp mint, shredded

- Transfer the kammon hoot to a clean container, cover with a thin layer of olive or vegetable oil, cover and store in the fridge until required.

To cook the lamb stew
- Heat half of the olive oil in a casserole dish over a high heat, add the lamb and sear all over until well browned. Transfer the lamb to a bowl with a slotted spoon and return the casserole to a medium heat.
- Add the remaining 1½ tbsp of olive oil, add the diced onions and cook, stirring frequently, for 5 minutes until softened, add the chillies and continue to cook for a further minute.
- Stir in the ground turmeric, cook for a minute, stirring constantly, add the tomato purée and 1 tsp of the kammon hoot, mix well then stir in the chicken stock. Bring to a simmer, add the bay leaf, cinnamon stick and seared lamb (including any juices). Season, cover with a lid and turn the heat to low then simmer for 1½ hours.
- While the lamb is simmering, heat the butter in a saucepan until foaming over a moderate heat, add the sliced onions with a pinch of salt, turn the heat to low and cook, stirring occasionally, for 30 minutes until caramelised and sticky. Stir in the remaining ½ tsp of kammon hoot and set to one side until required.
- Stir the diced potatoes into the casserole and simmer for a further 10 minutes.
- Stir in three quarters of the caramelised onions and the chickpeas; continue to cook for 10 minutes or until the potatoes are tender and check the seasoning.

To cook the couscous and serve
- Cook the couscous as per the packet instructions.
- Place the orange and lime juice in a small saucepan with the zest of both, bring to a simmer and poach the zest in the juice for 1 minute then stir into the couscous with the remaining caramelised onions. Season with a little salt and pepper
- Place the couscous either in individual bowls or a large serving bowl.
- Ladle the lamb and sauce over the couscous and garnish with the shredded mint.

SUDAN

Words by
FLIGHT LIEUTENANT VICTORIA SISSON

SUDAN'S RELATIONSHIP WITH the Royal Air Force is illustrated by two stories, separated by almost a century. They highlight two very distinguished achievements, and two decorated pilots.

Before the RAF's inception, when it was still part of the army and known as the Royal Flying Corps, the British Governor General of the Sudan, Reginald Wingate, was very concerned that Sultan Ali Dinar of Darfur was being put under pressure by Germany to stir a rebellion. With his track record of being anti-British, the discomfort grew until, in July 1915, Ali Dinar declared jihad on the British in Sudan.

An expeditionary force of 2,000 men was sent, supported by four BE2c aircraft of C Flight 17 Squadron RFC. These were the first military aircraft in Darfur. In order to reach their destination, this force suffered an exasperatingly long deployment, culminating in 350 miles by air. This last element was aided by Sudanese troops, who would navigate for the pilots.

"I was not sure this was an awfully good idea," recounted Lieutenant John Slessor.

"Bashawish Badda had never before seen anything more mechanised than a camel in his life. I need not have worried. The old boy wormed himself into the front seat between the centre-section struts without turning a hair and took me straight to Hilla, following the rather indistinct tracks through featureless bush country."

From May onwards, the RFC was able to make daily reconnaissance flights. As well as tracking Ali Dinar's movements, it also dropped propaganda leaflets. On one flight, Lieutenant Slessor came across the patrol of Ali Dinar himself. "A rather disorganised rabble," said Lieutenant Slessor. "We had been specifically briefed about Ali Dinar – his large banner and his splendid white Bishareen camel. Sure enough, he was in the midst of the milling crowd of demoralised Dervishes. Much more by good luck than judgement, I made a remarkably good shot with my last bomb... but Ali Dinar got away with it."

Lieutenant Slessor would later be wounded by ground fire and sent back to the UK to recover. He went on to receive the Military Cross for his actions in Sudan. He would later lead Coastal Command during the Battle of the Atlantic in 1943, and became Chief of the Air Staff from 1950–52, finally retiring as Marshall of the RAF.

Wind the clock forward to December 2013 and Sudan was facing troubles in the south as government troops and rebel factions fought for power. A C-17 from 99 Squadron, RAF Brize Norton, was tasked

> *"While we were aware of the dangers of the civil war below, I was more concerned for the safety of those on the ground"*

with evacuating 45 British nationals from Juba. However, it soon becomes clear that there were also a great number of other EU and Commonwealth citizens. The decision was made to evacuate all 182 people, many more than should have been possible on that particular flight. As the crew prepared for the additional passengers, it became apparent that a Boeing 737 had crashed and blocked the runway at Juba's airfield.

The captain, Flight Lieutenant Tim Eddy, recalls: "While we were aware of the dangers of the civil war below us, and the added complication of a 737 blocking the runway, I was more concerned for the safety of those on the ground. Our mission was to evacuate our people to safety and that's exactly what we intended to do."

Running low on fuel and using binoculars to judge the situation, Flight Lieutenant Eddy made a steep approach and braked as hard as he could to ensure the C-17 stopped ahead of the crashed aircraft. Keeping the engines running they were able to load all 182 passengers and evacuate them in quick time to Uganda.

Flight Lieutenant Eddy was subsequently awarded the Air Force Cross for his actions. "It is a great honour to have been presented with such a prestigious award," he said. "I feel, however, that it represents the exceptional tenacity and teamwork displayed by the entire crew. No one person can operate a C-17 and on that day it took us all working together to ensure success."

VICKERS VINCENT BOMBERS OF 47 SQUADRON IN SOUTH SUDAN, OCTOBER 1937

Gorraasa be Dama
Sudanese Pancakes with Beef

In Sudanese culture, dinner is traditionally a communal event, the food eaten with the diner's hands from large dishes. This recipe is typical of a dish enjoyed as part of a group meal. The gorraasa is a thin pancake and used to scoop up the lightly spiced tomato and onion-flavoured beef stew (dama). The dama can also be eaten wrapped up in the gorraasa pancake similar to a burrito.

INGREDIENTS

Serves 4

For the dama

16 green cardamom pods (or 1 tsp ground cardamom)

600g beef (chuck or shin), cut into large chunks

¼ tsp ground black pepper

1 tsp salt

2 tsp ground cinnamon

100ml sunflower oil

5 medium onions, coarsely chopped

4 cloves of garlic, finely chopped or crushed

6 medium tomatoes, coarsely chopped

75g tomato purée

1 green pepper, coarsely chopped

½ lemon

For the gorraasa

300g plain flour

½ tsp baking powder

1 tsp salt

500ml cold water

vegetable oil for frying

To serve

half a medium red onion, quartered and thinly sliced

100g cherry tomatoes, quartered

½ lemon, cut into wedges

METHOD

To make the dama

- Crush the cardamom pods with the flat of a large knife blade, remove the seeds and grind to a coarse powder in a pestle and mortar.
- Place the diced beef in a bowl, add the ground pepper, half a teaspoon of salt, ground cardamom and cinnamon. Toss to thoroughly coat the beef.
- Cover, place in the fridge and marinate for 2 hours.
- Heat 75ml of the oil in a casserole dish or saucepan over a moderate to high heat, add the onions and fry, stirring frequently for around 15 minutes until the onions have softened and caramelised, taking care not to burn the onions.
- Add 250ml of boiling water with half of the chopped garlic and half a teaspoon of salt to the onions; cover with a lid and simmer for 10 minutes.
- Transfer the onions, with all of the liquid, to a blender and blend until smooth.
- Iin the same dish that the onions were cooked in, heat the remaining oil over a high heat, add the marinated beef and sear all over.
- Reduce the heat to low, stir in the onion and garlic purée, chopped tomatoes and tomato purée. Take care at this point as, if the casserole is too hot, the onion purée will bubble and spit.
- There should be enough liquid to completely cover the beef; if there is not, add a little boiling water, stir well, cover with a lid and simmer for 1½ hours until the beef is tender and the sauce has thickened slightly.
- Remove the lid, increase the heat slightly, add the diced green peppers and continue to simmer, stirring occasionally, for 20 minutes until the sauce has reduced and thickened.

- While the peppers are cooking make the gorraasa (see below).
- Stir the remaining garlic into the dama. Simmer for a minute, check the seasoning, adding a little salt and freshly ground black pepper as required, squeeze in the lemon juice and remove from the heat.

To make the gorraasa
- Sift the flour, mix in the baking powder and salt then whisk in the cold water to make a smooth batter.
- Lightly oil a frying pan, place over a moderate heat and, when hot, ladle in a thin, even layer of the batter (spread it as thin as possible over the base of the pan).
- Cook for around a minute until the bottom of the gorraasa is lightly browned. Flip over and continue to cook for a further minute or until the bottom is speckled brown.
- Repeat with the remaining batter to make eight gorraasa, stacking them on top of each other on a wooden board or plate, while keeping them covered with a tea towel; this will keep them soft until ready to eat.

To serve
- Transfer the dama to a serving bowl and serve with the gorraasa, red onions, cherry tomatoes and lemon wedges.

ALBANIA

Words by
FLIGHT SERGEANT MICK BLACKALL

FROM THE END of the Second World War, up to Albania joining NATO in 2009, the British military – and in particular the Royal Air Force – has been involved in various tasks in Albania. These have fulfilled the whole spectrum of air power: from evacuating British nationals during periods of civil unrest, to deploying Tornados during the Kosovo War. The RAF now mostly undertakes exercises involving the UK's Response Force Task Group and Albanian forces. These represent a significant cooperation and military engagement between the two countries.

In early 2015, a heart-warming story emerged via the News24 network, originating in Albania's capital, Tirana. It involved the disappearance of Aeronautical

Engineer, Flight Sergeant John Thompson of 148 Squadron, whose Halifax bomber was shot down while resupplying resistance fighters in the country in October 1944. Due to the secrecy that shrouded this mission at the time, his family in Derbyshire was unable to ascertain his fate, a situation later exacerbated by Albania's communist rule, as it became one of Europe's most secretive and paranoid states.

The Halifax bomber had crashed some 60km south-east of Tirana, having clipped a ridge after being shot. Seven crew members were never heard from again. The plane's fate remained a mystery until 1960, when local villager Jaho Cala found a ring bearing the inscription "J & J" while chopping wood.

His son Xhemil Cala took the ring and passed on the details to reporters. "A bit further away were some parts, probably of a plane, but, under Enver Hoxha's dictatorship, we did not dare talk about it," said Xhemil. "My father carefully kept this ring and, before dying, he begged me to find its owner." Xhemil was faithful to his father's last wishes, which led him to contact the British embassy and start the process that led to the return of the ring.

"We knew he was serving somewhere in Libya or Italy but nothing more," said Thompson's nephew Alan Webster. "One day he came to us presenting his bride and he soon left again." The airman's wife Joyce, who remarried two years after he disappeared, died of cancer in 1993 aged 70. The couple had only been married six months when John went missing.

The wedding ring was finally returned to his family in 2015. "Today, my brother came home," said John Thompson's sister Dorothy Webster. Aged 93, she fought back tears at a ceremony held at Albania's defence ministry. In her hands she held a small box containing her brother's ring, a stone from the crash site and a piece of the plane's wreckage.

Qofte të Fërguara
Albanian Fried Meatballs

Albania's culinary culture is heavily influenced by Turkey, Greece and Italy, with flavours enhanced by fresh Mediterranean herbs. The main meal of the day is generally eaten at lunchtime and commonly consists of a meat dish served with a lightly dressed salad of local vegetables. This recipe pairs the lamb patties with roast cherry tomatoes to complement the qofte with a wonderful sweetness.

INGREDIENTS

Serves 4

For the qofte

90ml olive oil

1 medium onion, finely diced

2 cloves of garlic, crushed

1 slice of stale bread, crusts
  removed

500g minced lamb or beef

2 tbsp mint leaves, shredded

2 tsp dried oregano

½ tsp ground cinnamon

75g feta cheese, crumbled

salt and pepper

50g plain flour, to dust the qofte

For the yoghurt sauce

200g plain Greek yoghurt

½ lemon, juice only

1 tbsp mint leaves, shredded

1 tbsp clear honey

For the roast tomatoes

200g cherry tomatoes on the vine

2 tsp olive oil

For the salad

1 red cos lettuce, leaves separated
  and trimmed

1 courgette, thinly sliced on a
  mandolin (or vegetable peeler)

1 red pepper, quartered and thinly
  sliced

8 spring onions, cut into 3cm
  lengths

24 black olives

24 caper berries (or 2 tbsp of
  rinsed and drained salted capers)

2 tbsp extra virgin olive oil

½ lemon, juice only

METHOD

To make the qofte

- Heat 2 tbsp of the olive oil in a frying pan, add the diced onions and
  sauté with a pinch of salt for 5 minutes until softened. Add the crushed
  garlic and cook for a further minute. Remove from the heat and cool.
- Soak the bread in cold water, squeeze out all of the excess liquid and
  place in a bowl with the minced lamb or beef, cooled onions and garlic,
  shredded mint leaves, dried oregano, ground cinnamon, crumbled feta
  cheese and season with salt and pepper.
- Mix well until all of the ingredients are thoroughly combined, remove
  a small amount of the mixture, roll into a ball and flatten into a small
  patty. Fry this patty in a little olive oil until cooked and taste. Add more
  salt and pepper to the main mixture as required.
- Divide the mix into 12 equal-sized pieces, roll into balls and flatten
  slightly to form neat patties about 3cm thick. Place the patties onto
  a tray, cover with cling film and place in the fridge to rest for an hour.

To make the yoghurt sauce

- Mix the Greek yoghurt, lemon juice, shredded mint and honey together.

To cook the tomatoes

- Preheat the oven to 200°C
- Brush the tomatoes with a little olive oil and season with salt
  and pepper.
- Roast in the oven for 10 minutes until the skins just start to split open.

To cook the qofte

- Lightly season the flour with salt and pepper, coat the qofte in the
  seasoned flour and dust off the excess.
- Heat the remaining 4 tbsp olive oil in a frying pan and shallow fry
  the qofte in batches until cooked through to the middle.

To serve

- Arrange the lettuce leaves, courgette strips, peppers, spring onions,
  olives and caper berries (or capers) on the plates. Season lightly
  with salt and pepper, squeeze over the lemon juice and drizzle with
  olive oil.
- Serve three qofte per portion and one truss of roast cherry tomatoes
  onto the plates dressed with the salad and spoon over a little of the
  yoghurt dressing.

VIETNAM

Words by
SQUADRON LEADER GORDON PARRY

THE VIETNAM WAR saw America fighting against the communist regime of North Vietnam, with the aim of halting the Soviet Union's influence in Southeast Asia. The United States spent close to 25 years attempting to destroy communism's hold in the region, fighting communist forces in Vietnam, Laos and Cambodia, against both the conventional forces of the North Vietnamese Army and the communist and nationalist guerrilla allies that were known at the Viet Cong (VC), or National Liberation Front (NLF).

So, where was the USA's best friend, the UK, in all this, and what did the Royal Air Force do? Very little, as it happened. Harold Wilson became Prime Minister in 1964, and his Labour government had significant differences of opinion with President Johnson on foreign policy, repositioning the Anglo–American relationship as a "close" relationship rather than a "special" one. Johnson took a dislike to Wilson, once referring to him as "a little creep".

Wilson's government was focusing on home issues, including the growing social services and the NHS, and wanted a peaceful solution to the Vietnam war. "We must not join with nor in any way encourage an anti-communist crusade in Asia," he said. "A settlement in Asia is imperilled by the lunatic fringe in the American Senate who want some holy crusade against communism." A furious Johnson replied: "I won't tell you how to run Malaysia; you don't tell me how to run Vietnam." On top of this, the Malay conflict had become unpopular with the British people and there was little appetite to fight in Vietnam.

Nevertheless, the RAF did play some small roles in Vietnam. Flying from bases in Thailand, the RAF flew missions throughout Southeast Asia, including sorties into Vietnam, Laos and Cambodia. 34 Squadron's Beverleys reportedly flew directly into Nui Dat. However, what is known is that Beverleys from the Far East Air Force Transport Command, based at Seletar in Singapore, were deployed on humanitarian missions, delivering relief aid, medical supplies, rice and other food. Manifests show that these flights from RAF Seletar went directly into Vietnam, to such locations as Can Tho, Ban Me Thuot (now known as Buôn Ma Thuột), An Lôc and nearby Lôc Ninh. Operating directly into Vietnam, many qualified for the South Vietnam General Service Medal.

Even during the war, Vietnam proved to be an invaluable refuel stop for RAF aircraft routing through to Hong Kong and Brunei. It was used so much, in fact, that an RAF Liaison Officer was based in Saigon to ease their passage.

Since the end of the war, the RAF had very little to do with Vietnam as long-range aircraft no longer needed their refuel stops. That was the case until in 2016, when the Red Arrows decided to visit China. Their Hawk aircraft lacked any air-to-air refuelling capability and had a range of around 600 nautical miles. Suddenly, in order to route from Malaysia to China, Vietnam once again became a valuable ally and watering hole, with the team spending the night at Da Nang as their last stop before the air-show at Zhuhai. The Red Arrows were not alone: they were accompanied by an ever-present C-130J, the long-standing workhorse of the RAF, now based at RAF Brize Norton, carrying essentials tools and spares to keep the tour on the road.

UNLOADING A HERCULES MILITARY TRANSPORT AIRCRAFT OF 48 SQUADRON, SAIGON, 1968

Pho bò
Vietnamese Beef Pho Noodle Soup

The national dish of Vietnam, pho is a broth made with flat rice noodles, vegetables, herbs and meat, poultry or seafood. This recipe is quite adaptable; other meat such as chicken or pork can be substituted or even tofu or meat-free "chicken style" pieces for a vegetarian alternative. Other vegetables such as pak choi, baby corn, mushrooms, broccoli or sugar snap peas can also be added.

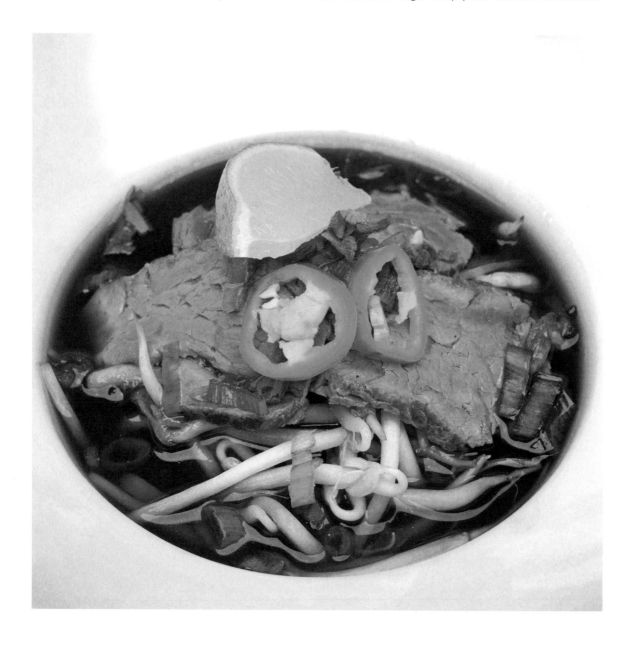

INGREDIENTS

Serves 4

For the broth

3 star anise

6 whole cloves

1 cinnamon stick

1 tsp fennel seeds

2 medium onions, peeled and
thickly sliced

2.5cm piece of ginger, thinly sliced

½ tsp black peppercorns

2 litres good quality beef stock

2 sticks of celery, coarsely chopped

1 medium carrot, peeled and
coarsely chopped

2 spring onions, thinly sliced
(green and white parts separated)

2 tbsp fish sauce (nuoc mam or
nam pla)

**For the beef, vegetables and
noodles**

200g fillet steak

1 tbsp sunflower oil or vegetable oil

150g beansprouts, washed and
drained

200g rice noodles (banh pho)

10g fresh coriander, picked

1 tbsp mint leaves, shredded

2 red chillies (or 4 bird's eye
chillies), thinly sliced

To serve

1 lime, cut into wedges

METHOD

To make the broth

• Heat a small frying pan or skillet over a moderate heat, add the star anise, cloves, cinnamon stick and fennel seeds. Lightly toast the spices, shaking the pan constantly, until lightly browned and fragrant. Tip the toasted spices into a bowl and return the pan to the heat.

• Place the sliced onions and ginger into the pan in a single layer and cook on both sides until lightly charred. Alternatively, the onions and ginger can be charred under a grill or over an open gas flame.

• Add the charred onions and ginger, toasted spices, peppercorns, stock, celery and carrots to a saucepan, bring to a boil, reduce the heat and simmer for 45 minutes.

• Strain the broth through a fine sieve or muslin into a clean saucepan, add the sliced white spring onions (reserve the green parts for the garnish) and fish sauce. Taste the broth at this stage, add a little more fish sauce if preferred, season with a little salt if required, bring to a gentle simmer and cook for 10 minutes.

To assemble

• Heat a frying pan over a high heat, rub the beef fillet with a little sunflower or vegetable oil, season with salt and pepper. Sear the beef fillet all over until well browned but uncooked in the middle.

• Rest the beef for 10 minutes and cut into very thin slices.

• Blanch the beansprouts for 1 minute in boiling water then drain.

• Cook the rice noodles until just tender and drain.

• Divide the noodles between individual bowls and arrange the sliced beef on top. Scatter over a few of the coriander leaves, shredded mint and sliced chillies.

• Place half of the bean sprouts on top of the beef, pour over the boiling broth and scatter over the spring onion greens.

To serve

• Serve the pho bo with the remaining bean sprouts, fresh herbs, sliced chillies and lime wedges on the side.

WALES

Words by
FLIGHT SERGEANT ROBIN KIRKPATRICK

THE ROYAL AIR FORCE has had a long association with Wales, from the large number of Welsh people who have served and continue to serve in the RAF, to the large number of RAF stations that have grounded the service on Welsh soil. At one time or another, Wales has been home to at least 32 RAF stations.

The most important of these is now RAF Valley, on the island of Anglesey. It opened on 13 February 1941 as part of No. 9 Group, Fighter Command and, for the first few weeks of its existence, was called RAF Rhosneigr. It was also home to Czech and Australian squadrons during the Second World War and was initially used to launch patrols over the Irish Sea, after which it became a staging post for the military build up to D-Day. The station is currently home to the Advanced Fast Jet Training School, training tomorrow's Typhoon, F-22 Raptor and F-35 Lightning II pilots.

Move down the country and you'll pass many former RAF stations. These include RAF Llanbeder, situated next to the beautiful Shell Island, home to the RAF target drones used for gunnery practice by RAF fighter pilots. Or RAF Towyn – watched over by Craig yr Aderyn (Bird Rock) – which became a joint unit for adventure training, with the mountains at its back and the sea to its front.

RAF Aberporth was home to 595 Squadron and No. 1 Anti-Aircraft Cooperation Unit, training ground troops in the art of anti-aircraft artillery. It used a variety of aircraft, from a Tiger Moth to Spitfires and Hurricanes. During the Cold War, it became a testing unit for the Bloodhound anti-aircraft missiles. With the launch site only 1km from the local beach, the sound and sight of a missile going supersonic before it even cleared the launch rail and then reaching Mach 3 just seconds later must have been amazing to witness.

RAF St Athan in the Vale of Glamorgan was home to No. 4 School of Technical Training and No. 14 Radio school. It trained more than 42,000 personnel in its time, in everything from radio mechanics through to major aircraft servicing. At one time, it was also home to Mechanical Training, teaching air force personnel to drive all the different types of RAF

vehicles on its narrow winding lanes. The easy-to-pronounce name was fortunate for visitors: it is rumoured that the nearby town of Eglwys Brewis was not chosen as the name of the base as English service personnel couldn't pronounce it!

Walking in and around the Welsh countryside, you will often see low-flying aircraft, this being one of the UK's main low-level training areas, used by both training and operational aircraft ranging from the small and agile Hawk trainers and Tornado GR4s to the mighty C-130J Hercules and A400M Atlas, all preparing and training for whatever may come next.

It isn't all technical training and flying, however. Wales has been and continues to be a place to participate in a plethora of Adventurous Training (AT). From hill walking and mountaineering, to canoeing and caving, the RAF training in Wales pushes service personnel into challenging environments, extending them physically and mentally to be the best they can be, but also to identify their own personal strengths and weaknesses. The RAF's motto, "Per Ardua Ad Astra", literally means "through adversity to the stars". The struggle might not always be where we think it is. Without training and preparation, we will never be able to fully meet it.

RAF HOLYHEAD IN WALES
WITH TWO 63FT PINNACES
MOORED TO ITS JETTY

Picau ar y Maen
Welsh Cakes

Welsh cakes are basically griddled discs of rich sweetened pastry with dried fruit. Although usually made with currants, other dried fruits such as raisins, sultanas, dried figs, mixed dried fruit or dried cranberries can be substituted. They are traditionally eaten plain-dusted with sugar, but are delicious buttered with jam or with whipped cream and seasonal berries in the summer and autumn.

INGREDIENTS

Makes 8

For the cakes

250g self-raising flour

½ tsp mixed spice

125g salted butter, diced (plus
  extra for greasing)

75g caster sugar

75g currants (or raisins or sultanas)

1 medium egg, beaten

cold milk as required

To finish

caster sugar

To serve

butter, jam, cream (can be
sweetened and flavoured with
vanilla) or fresh berries as preferred

METHOD

To make the cakes

• Sieve the flour and mixed spice into a large bowl and rub in the
  butter until it resembles coarse breadcrumbs.
• Add the sugar and currants then mix in the beaten egg and mix to
  form a smooth dough, adding a splash of milk if the dough is too dry.
  Take care not to overwork the dough as you want the cakes to be
  quite crumbly (overworking the dough will make the texture tight
  and the cakes will become tough). Wrap the dough in cling film and
  rest in the fridge for 30 minutes.
• Lightly flour the work surface, roll out the dough to about 1cm thick
  and, using a 5cm or 6cm cutter, cut out rounds of the dough (re-roll
  and cut the trimmings to get as many cakes as possible).

To cook

• Heat a large non-stick frying pan or skillet over a medium heat,
  very lightly grease with a little butter and cook the Welsh cakes
  for 3 to 4 minutes on either side until golden brown.
• Transfer the cakes to a cooling rack and sprinkle generously with
  caster sugar.

To serve

• Eat either just warm or at room temperature with butter and jam or
  with whipped crème Chantilly (whipped cream flavoured with vanilla
  extract or paste, sweetened with a little icing sugar) and fresh berries
  such as strawberries, raspberries, blueberries, blackberries etc.

THE NEXT 100 YEARS?

Words by
WING COMMANDER CHRIS HUNTER

THE HISTORY OF the Royal Air Force over its first 100 years is a truly remarkable record of achievement. This was a period in which the service grew and developed its own distinct traditions and ethos, drawn originally from the experiences of its older siblings, which now bind together highly talented and motivated personnel to fight for the nation under the most demanding and unforgiving conditions in the air, on the ground, and at sea. As the custodian of the nation's air power, the RAF has overseen its development, from a useful adjunct to land and maritime operations in 1918 to now being the common denominator of all military operations, providing Britain with a decisive military edge.

In recent years, it would be a challenge, if not impossible, to identify a military operation in which the RAF was not a key contributor, working in concert with its sister services. As former Prime Minister David Cameron said: "the Royal Air Force is not just important to our nation's security, it is completely and utterly essential."

So, what of the next 100 years? Predicting the future is a notoriously problematic activity. If, as Stephen Hawking said, "one can't predict the weather more than a few days in advance", then trying to anticipate the challenges the RAF may face in any future conflict is unlikely to be a fruitful activity. However, there are three predictions that we can make with a fair degree of confidence.

Firstly, that the superb individual and collective professionalism, commitment, skill, self-discipline and judgement of all of the RAF's personnel will continue to form the bedrock of the service. Their excellence in the practical delivery of air power cannot and will not change – it is what defines the RAF. Also, as a meritocracy, the force will continue to draw on the talent of a diverse range of personnel from the length and breadth of the country, be they regulars, reserves, civil servants or industry contractors.

Secondly, that the RAF's air power roles are likely to endure. The force will still need to defend Britain from threats in the air and ensure that we can fight where we need to (air control). It will still need to understand our country's adversaries (intelligence and situational awareness) and be able to attack them if necessary. And it will also still need to move the plethora of military equipment and personnel associated with any conflict (air mobility).

Thirdly, in order to provide our country with realistic military options, the RAF will need to be able to deliver such capabilities worldwide and quickly.

The challenges facing the RAF in the future will be no less testing than those of the past 100 years. Air power is in consistently high demand and will no doubt continue to be so for the foreseeable future. However, at the forefront of RAF thinking must be providing the government and our country with viable military options, with the ability to fight and win the essential criteria on which we must be judged.

THE RAF100 APPEAL

ALL ROYALTIES FROM the sale of this book will go to the RAF100 Appeal, a joint venture between the Royal Air Force and four major RAF charities – the RAF Benevolent Fund, the RAF Museum, the RAF Charitable Trust and the RAF Association. The aim of the appeal is to raise money for the RAF family and to create a lasting legacy as it celebrates its centenary.

THE RAF BENEVOLENT FUND

Founded in 1919, the RAF Benevolent Fund is the RAF's leading welfare charity, providing financial, practical and emotional support to serving and former members of the RAF, as well as their partners and dependants. It helps members of the RAF family deal with a wide range of issues: from childcare, relationship difficulties, injury and disability to financial hardship and debt, illness and bereavement.

THE RAF MUSEUM

The RAF Museum welcomes visitors from around the world to its two public sites: one in Colindale, north London, the other in Cosford, Shropshire. Both sites, commemorate how the RAF has shaped our nation and society, and influenced how we live our lives today through its impact on world events, society and technology. The Museum inspires a broad range of people by sharing the story of the RAF and ensuring that it endures for future generations. It helps people to understand the RAF's impact on the world; makes the story of the RAF and its collections relevant and stimulating; and preserves, honours and shares the stories of RAF service personnel.

THE RAF CHARITABLE TRUST

The RAF Charitable Trust is the youngest member of the RAF's family of charities. Since it was established in 2005, trustees have approved more than £4million worth of grants which have been used to promote the RAF, support its people and encourage youngsters to become both inspired and excited by aviation and the related STEM (science, technology, engineering and maths) subjects in the curriculum. From junior engineering challenges to a wide range of flying opportunities, the RAFCT is funding projects, expeditions and scholarships that have a positive influence on the lives of RAF personnel and encouraging the development of young people.

THE RAF ASSOCIATION

When one of the RAF family needs a friend, they turn to the RAF Association who can be there on the doorstep, in person, to help sort out the problem and share the load. When times are tough, nothing beats friendly, face-to-face support from someone who really cares. Injury, bereavement, illness, loneliness, financial difficulties – if things go wrong, the charity's network of warm-hearted, practical and highly trained people flies into action. Members, volunteers and employees work together to make sure everyone who needs it gets the one-to-one support they deserve. In 2016, the RAF Association carried out 13,800 home visits across the UK, helped tell thousands of bedtime stories to children whose parents were away on operations, and gave respite breaks to 2,500 RAF veterans, widows and family at its Wings Breaks hotels.

SPECIAL THANKS

WE STARTED FOUR years ago with a mere handful of people. Over time this number grew to well over 50: writers, chefs, photographers, marketing and a gamut of keen contributors, all of whom you can thank for the book you hold right now.

First and foremost, we need to express our huge gratitude to our Head Chef Stu Harmer, whose dedication to researching and creating recipes for each country was nothing short of exceptional. We also extend our thanks to his keen sous chefs, WOs Paul Phillips and Paul Miles. Hand in hand with Stu we must pass on our great thanks to ISS for their unwavering belief in our project, and for their generosity and support throughout – Allan Vaughan and Craig Smith, we thank you wholeheartedly.

Once cooked, we had to capture the dishes to the highest standard, and for that we have the team from JADTEU (the Joint Air Delivery Test and Evaluation Unit) to thank. Their exposure to this project proved a welcome break from the day job, so they snapped up the chance to be involved, and were always positive and forward-thinking in composing their shots, with Sgt Nige Green leading a team that comprised Cpl Andrew Ferguson, Cpl Dave Parnham, SAC Matt Aherne, SAC Kat Jacques, SAC Ben Lees, SAC Connor Payne and SAC Dave Turnbull.

Next are our 30 or so enthusiastic, and largely amateur, writers, researchers and contributors, who provided the history pages. Air Cdre Mark Gilligan; Wg Cdrs Teo Bradley, Ben Sharp, Marc "Dutch" Holland and Chris

Hunter; Sqn Ldrs Jonathan Rooke, Rob Swinney (Retd), Helen Train, Katherine Ingram, Si Moore, Mal Craig, Chris Powell, Nat Winsor, and Gordon Parry; Flt Lts Jamie Wilyman, Emma Stringer, Art Lester (Retd), Chloe Bridge, Christopher Coopman, Victoria Sisson, Simon Stafford, Tom Marshall and Paul Crocker; WO Simon Fellows; FS Mick Blackall and Robin "KP" Kirkpatrick; Steve Broadhead and the whole of 290 Squadron (Weston-super-Mare) ATC, Martin Simpson, Nick Smart, Steve Broadhead, Victoria Edwards, Alison Stafford, Peter Devitt, Ed Sharman, Andrew Renwick and Nick Fellows; we thank you all for your patience and hard work. We'd also like to thanks Sebastian Cox of the Historical Branch and Chris Hobson at the Shrivenham Defence College library for setting us on the right track; and finally to Andrew Bennett and David and Christine McCandless for their personal stories.

For strategy, marketing and coordination our thanks go to Sqn Ldr Vic Hodgson, whose work will really increase now the book is published! Alongside newcomers Flt Lts Andy Stanney and Samantha Broderick, we thank you in advance for your support over the life of this book, as well as Jim Pullen, our website designer. Additionally, his team undertook the task of canvassing and bringing in our guest chefs, and we thank Trudy Baddely and Sergeant Jodie Dunleavy for their work here. Cpls Tom Maddock and Lizzie Driver have kept us true, ably organising and coordinating meetings, and maintaining online resources; and we must also thank MEng (Retd) Dave Dodd and Sheena Whyatt for their cooking, tasting and feedback on some of our recipes, as well as Flt Lt (Retd) Leigh Shaughnessy for her early marketing work.

Over the course of the project we've made some fantastic new friends and a word must go to our charitable colleagues and their representatives. Sqn Ldr Joanne Roe and Zerrin Lovett at the RAF100 Programme Team Organisation; Mike Neville at the RAF Benevolent Fund, without whom we may not have forged the relationships we have, Simon Footer and Fiona Yates also at the RAFBF, and Ed Sharman, now at Help For Heroes, who was really the first and foremost enthusiast we roped in at the RAFBF.

Thank you! At the RAF Museum, we must say a massive thank you to Derek O'Brien for all his hard work liaising between all involved; to Frances Galvan for opening the museum door for us to become involved, and Karen Whitting and Maggie Appleton for their work towards final contracts.

And, of course, thanks to our newest friends at publisher St James's House, for their belief and hard work in producing and publishing this book; Richard Freed for allowing us in the door and listening, Anna Danby, Stephen Mitchell, John Lewis and Ben Duffy, we thank you. Thanks also to John Clarkson of JohnClarksonDesign for providing the initial cover image inspiration.

There are several other people whose support over the years we must credit: the Gateway House staff for allowing us to use their facilities every month for cookery; RAF Brize Norton Station Commander Gp Capt Tim Jones and his predecessor Gp Capt Simon Edwards for letting us run free around Brize Norton, and particularly Air Cdr Stephen Lushington, our first project Station Commander; his strapline suggested at our first meeting nearly made it all the way!

Last, but definitely not least, we must thank our families for all of their support. Our very patient wives, Helen and Katie, who listened as we ranted; absorbed and tempered our enthusiasm; tasted numerous recipes; allowed us the freedom to disappear into the world of the project at a whim; and were there when no one else would listen – we thank you wholeheartedly for your unwavering support.

— Jon and Crispin

INDEX

St James's House

298 Regents Park Road

London N3 2SZ

T: 020 8371 4000

E: publishing@stjamess.org

W: www.stjamess.org

Chief Executive

Richard Freed

richard.freed@stjamess.org

Managing Director

Stephen van der Merwe

stephen.vdm@stjamess.org

Sales Director

Richard Golbourne

r.golbourne@stjamess.org

Communications Director

Ben Duffy

ben.duffy@stjamess.org

Head of Creative

Anna Danby

anna.danby@stjamess.org

Head of Editorial

Stephen Mitchell

stephen.mitchell@stjamess.org

Deputy Editor

John Lewis

Food Stylist

Elayna Rudolphy

Cover Photographer

Rob Streeter

Photography

A. Bennett Collection, Cristian Barnett, Issy Croker, Getty Images, Jay Rowden, Chris Terry, UK MOD Crown Copyright, Veronica Stewart Photography

Tom Kerridge's recipe is an extract taken from *Tom's Table* published by Absolute Press, 2015

2017 Regal Press Limited.
All rights reserved.

Printed in Italy by Graphicom on 120g Tauro. This paper has been independently certified according to the standards of the Forest Stewardship Council® (FSC)®.

ISBN: 978-1-906670-48-1